THE AGE OF JIHAD

THE AGE OF JIHAD

Islamic State and the Great War
for the Middle East

Patrick Cockburn

VERSO
London • New York

This edition published by Verso 2016
© Patrick Cockburn 2016
First published as *Chaos and Caliphate*
© O/R Books, New York, NY 2016

1 3 5 7 9 10 8 6 4 2

Verso
UK: 6 Meard Street, London W1F 0EG
US: 20 Jay Street, Suite 1010, Brooklyn, NY 11201
versobooks.com

Verso is the imprint of New Left Books

ISBN-13: 978-1-78478-449-2
ISBN-13: 978-1-78663-166-4 (EXPORT)
ISBN-13: 978-1-78478-450-8 (US EBK)
ISBN-13: 978-1-78478-448-5 (UK EBK)

British Library Cataloguing in Publication Data
A catalogue record for this book is available from the British Library

Library of Congress Cataloging-in-Publication Data
A catalog record for this book is available from the Library of Congress

Printed and bound by CPI Group (UK) Ltd, Croydon, CR0 4YY

Contents

Introduction

Things fall apart; the centre cannot hold;
Mere anarchy is loosed upon the world,
The blood-dimmed tide is loosed, and everywhere
The ceremony of innocence is drowned.
The best lack all conviction, while the worst
Are full of passionate intensity.
                                                —W. B. Yeats

A rmed conflicts ranging between full-scale wars and a general break-down of security are engulfing the Middle East and North Africa. Other parts of the planet are more peaceful than 50 years ago, but chaos and conflict are spreading in a great swath of Islamic countries between north-west Pakistan and north-east Nigeria. Central governments have collapsed, are weak, face powerful insurgencies or are fighting for their lives. In the central core of this region civil wars are tearing apart Iraq, Syria and Yemen with a ferocity that probably means none of them will come together again as unitary states. The war in Afghanistan continues without winners and in Libya central government has disintegrated since 2011, as it did 20 years earlier in Somalia, a country that remains in a state of armed anarchy. At either end of this vast region of instability the Turkish–Kurd civil war has resumed in the mountains of south-east Turkey and Boko Haram suicide bombers slaughter people in Nigeria, Chad and Cameroon.

It is between the Iranian border and the Mediterranean that these conflicts are at their most intense and have the greatest impact on the rest of the world. This region has never been truly stable in the hundred years since the fall of the Ottoman Empire: it has seen foreign invasions and occupations, the Arab–Israeli wars, military coups d'état, insurgencies, conflicts between Sunni and Shia and between Kurds and Arabs and Turks. It is here, more than anywhere else, that political, national and religious tectonic plates meet and grind together with devastating effect. For this region's inhabitants life has never been so dangerous and uncertain, with 9.5 million people displaced in Syria and 3.2 million in Iraq.

The roots of these conflicts are longstanding, but eruptions have become more frequent and destructive since 2001. We have entered a period of civil wars in which Sunni fundamentalist jihadis play a leading role. It was 9/11, the crashing of planes into the World Trade Centre, that was the starting pistol for a series of calamitous events which destroyed the old status quo. The attack provoked—as it was probably intended to do—US military intervention in Afghanistan and Iraq, actions which transformed the political, sectarian and ethnic landscape of the region and released forces, the power of which went beyond anything imagined at the time. Who would have guessed at the end of 2001, just as the Taliban was being overthrown with such apparent ease in Afghanistan, that within 13 years another fanatical Sunni fundamentalist movement, the Islamic State of Iraq and the Levant (variously known as ISIS, ISIL and Daesh), would be establishing its own caliphate in western Iraq and eastern Syria? The Taliban regime evaporated quickly when it came under sustained attack by the US and its allies, but the Caliphate has proved far more resilient to international opposition. A year after it was founded in 2014 it was still there and still winning victories, notably the capture of Ramadi in Iraq and Palmyra in Syria in May 2015. As other states in the region disintegrate, ISIS alone has been able to create a new state, monstrous though it may be, capable of conscripting soldiers, taxing its people and defending its borders.

The start of the war in Afghanistan was the prelude to a more general crisis. There were already many fault lines in the Arab and Islamic worlds, but the US-led invasion of Iraq in 2003 was the earthquake whose aftershocks we still feel. It energised and expanded existing conflicts and confrontations such as those between Shia, Sunni and Kurds; Saudi Arabia and Iran; countries opposed to US policy and those favouring it. In addition, there are other trends in the region which are long-term and attract less attention, but which involve profound changes in the balance of power within and between countries. The vast wealth of the oil states in the Gulf— Saudi Arabia, UAE, Qatar and Kuwait—has turned into political power. It is these Sunni absolute monarchies which today hold the leadership of the Arab world, a position that 40 years ago was largely in the hands of secular-nationalist states like Egypt, Syria, Iraq, Algeria, Libya and Yemen. A related and important ideological shift took place over the same period as mainstream Sunni Islam became increasingly dominated by Wahhabism, the variant of Islam espoused by Saudi Arabia. Saudi wealth has spread the influence of this intolerant and regressive strain, which denounces other Islamic sects like Shi'ism as heretical and which treats women as being under the permanent subjection of men. Nowhere else in the world but Saudi Arabia and the Caliphate are women forbidden to drive a car.

A different but significant change in the political terrain was the collapse of the Soviet Union in 1991. This opened the door for full-scale Western military intervention, previously deterred by fear of the other superpower's reaction. One of the more rational explanations given by Saddam Hussein for his invasion of Kuwait in 1990 was that the Soviet Union was about to cease to be the counter-balance to the US, the absence of which would in future constrain the freedom of action of states like Iraq. As with many of Saddam's calculations about foreign affairs, he got this one disastrously wrong, and the Soviet Union gave him no protection against an overwhelming US-led counter-attack that defeated his army in Kuwait. But his perception was correct that the era was ending when regional leaders could balance to their own advantage between the two superpowers.

The invasion and occupation of Iraq by the US is at the heart of this book because it destroyed Iraq as a united country and nobody has been able to put it back together again. It opened up a period when Iraq's three great communities—Shia, Sunni and Kurds—are in a permanent state of confrontation, a situation that has had a deeply destabilising impact on all of Iraq's neighbours. The natural response of any Iraqi community under pressure from a domestic foe is not to compromise but to look for foreign allies. Internal Iraqi crises swiftly become internationalised. Given that there are 22 Arab countries with a combined population of 366 million, and about 50 Islamic ones with a population of 1.6 billion, this has had serious implications for a quarter of the world's population. In addition, there is the impact of the Iraq war on the US and Britain, whose governments had believed they would fight a short victorious war but ended up being mired in a long, draining and unsuccessful one. They may not have suffered an outright military defeat, but the very public nature of their failure meant that it became more difficult for either country to make credible threats of military force. The fact that for the moment American public opinion does not support US ground troops being sent to the Middle East is an important feature of the war now raging in Iraq and Syria.

The explosive pressures building up after 2003 only fully detonated in 2011, in what was misleadingly labelled 'the Arab Spring'. It is a term containing a large nugget of truth, which is why it became the shorthand for a series of complicated events, but the word 'Spring' over-stresses the progressive and benign nature of what was happening. It is true that in 2011 there were millions of people in Tunis, Benghazi, Cairo, Sanaa, Damascus, Bahrain and beyond who wanted to see an end to the rule of police states run by corrupt and brutal elites and to replace them with honest, accountable, law-bound governments. But these moderate sounding demands, including free elections and an end to discrimination, meant a real revolution in a country like Bahrain where the Shia majority would inevitably take over from the Sunni minority that had monopolised power for centuries. In Syria the exact opposite was the case: civil and political liberty would mean the Sunni Arabs, 60 per cent of the population, would replace the Alawites, the heterodox Shia sect that has dominated the ruling circles of the regime since the 1960s.

Some well-informed people may object that analysing the situation by using crude sectarian categories is an over-simplification. And so it is, but sectarian and ethnic struggles play a central though not exclusive role in the crises in Iraq, Syria, Turkey, Afghanistan and Yemen.

———

This era of civil wars is the main theme of the diaries and writings I produced between 2001 and 2015, and which appear in this book. I want to look at events from two angles: one is contemporary description; the other is retrospective explanation and analysis from the perspective of today. Both have their advantages. Eyewitness reporting undiluted by knowledge of later events should have a vividness lacking in accounts written later and a credibility in explaining why people acted as they did. But a retrospective account, written a dozen or more years after the start of the Afghan and Iraq wars and four years since the uprisings of 2011, also has benefits. Common features in these conflicts jump out and make it possible to draw general conclusions about the origin and course of distinct but interrelated events. I have always found it a weakness in discussions of these wars and conflicts that people who are expert about Syria do not have much first-hand knowledge of Iraq and may know little or nothing about Turkey, though developments in any one of these countries cannot be fully grasped without an understanding of the others. I remember attending a conference on Syria just before ISIS captured Mosul in June 2014 and vainly trying to persuade the assembled Syrian experts that the most important development in the region—which was bound to affect the war in Syria—was ISIS's growing strength in Iraq. My fellow specialists were politely impatient during my interventions and swiftly returned to discussing exclusively Syrian matters. On the other hand, generalising usefully about anything in history without full command of the details is dangerous because it is too easy to be tempted into over-simple parallels. I remember how, when I was a correspondent in Moscow in the 1980s, my heart would sink whenever visitors would glibly compare the complex situation in the Soviet Union with some country such as South Africa which they knew well, remarking on similarities that did not really exist. This is why I have put many of my ideas about these very diverse and complicated events in a lengthy 'Afterword' at the end of this book, following the presentation of the evidence for my conclusions.

Much of my working life during the past 14 years has been spent covering wars in four countries: Afghanistan, Iraq, Syria and Libya. This adds up to more than four wars because at some moments there was more than one conflict going on in the same country at the same time. For instance, in 2004 the US Army was fighting two very different wars in Iraq, one against a Sunni insurgency in which al-Qa'ida in Iraq played a leading role, and another against the Shia Mehdi Army militia of Muqtada al-Sadr. Likewise, in 2015 ISIS was fighting separate wars against the Syrian Army in the centre of Syria and the Syrian Kurds in the north-east, who were aided by the US. In addition to covering these full-scale wars, I was visiting Bahrain, where protests were savagely repressed in 2011. That same year I was in Iran until I was ordered out of the country. Yemen has been teetering on the edge of war ever since I first went there in 1978, but it was only in 2014–15 that it finally collapsed into all-out armed conflict.

I have deliberately left out my writings on Egypt because the country is not at war, though there is brutal state repression and growing guerrilla violence. At the height of the demonstrations in Cairo in 2011 the Egyptian protests were a bright and encouraging example to the rest of the Arab world. Slogans first heard in Tahrir Square were echoed in Bahrain, Sanaa and Damascus. But the protesters never seized state power and two years later Egyptians were under the power of an even more repressive police state than they had experienced under President Hosni Mubarak. The political trajectory is different from the rest of the region.

It is worth emphasising that the governments, peoples and communities I am writing about are fighting civil wars, because failure to understand this has produced many misleading analyses and disappointed expectations. These are not black-and-white situations, good guys against bad, vile tyrant against a risen people like a scene out of *Les Misérables*. It is astonishing and depressing to see Western governments, presumably advised by well-informed diplomats and intelligence services, repeatedly committing their countries to wars without recognising this basic fact. I recall attending US press conferences in the Green Zone in Baghdad in 2003 at which the official spokesman invariably blamed sporadic guerrilla attacks against US forces on discredited 'remnants' of the old regime unwilling to join 'the new Iraq'. At first I thought this was just a bit of crude propaganda, but I came to recognise that the spokesmen believed it was true and did not realise that the US and its allies were slipping into armed conflict against the entire 6 million Sunni Arab community in Iraq. The same thing happened in July 2015 when US and European officials cavalierly supported Turkish air strikes and military action against the 'terrorists' of the Kurdistan Workers' Party (PKK), without appreciating that they were applauding an assault by the Turkish state on its 18 million Kurdish citizens.

A problem with propaganda is that nobody believes it as much as those who propound it: the demonisation of Saddam Hussein, Muammar Gaddafi and Bashar al-Assad and the lauding of their opponents as selfless freedom fighters, whatever its immediate political utility, created a distorted and misleading picture of the problems of Iraq, Libya and Syria. Governments are prone to indulge in wishful thinking and see those opposing them as belonging to a small unrepresentative gang (though this does not prevent these same politicians and officials then acting as if the precise opposite is true and inflicting collective punishments on much larger groups, thus acting as recruiting sergeants for whatever insurgency they are trying to suppress).

The diaries and reports that follow have not been updated, though they are edited down from their original impressive bulk. It seems to me important to present them here, first of all because people forget quite soon what really happened in recent history. Public awareness of recent news may be high, as it is often well covered by the media, but developments over the previous half dozen years are hazy. There is frequently an unfortunate 'knowledge gap' about the very period in which current events were gestated. Thus in the UK there is an almost obsessive interest in what happened in 2002 and 2003 when the country controversially went to war in Iraq, but limited knowledge of the disastrous British occupation of Basra between 2003 and 2006, or of what happened in Iraq generally in later years. As American forces withdrew after 2008, interest in the US about what was going on in Iraq petered out. It became yesterday's crisis. Television and newspapers closed down news bureaux in Baghdad and covered the story only scantily, right up to the moment ISIS captured Mosul in June 2014 and the country fell apart. People are mystified and ill-informed about why this happened because so much of importance took place in the crucial but neglected time zone between the immediate and distant past.

There is a further need for eyewitness history written before we knew the names of the winners and losers in any given crisis. A historian once remarked that 'it is important to remember that what is now in the past was once in the future.' This is one way of saying that many options seemed open that in retrospect appear closed. Because one course of action was taken, the decision to act in that way acquires a false sense of inevitability and, of course, those who took it—particularly if it turns out to have been calamitously wrong-headed and mistaken—have every incentive to pretend that nothing else could have been done. In the US the grisly phrases 'Monday morning quarterbacking' and '20:20 hindsight' are used to accuse critics of making judgements from a position of knowledge not available to the original decision-maker, while in reality much of what went wrong in a given situation was predictable—and often had been predicted—from facts visible at the time. For instance, I believed in 2003, before the overthrow of Saddam Hussein, that the US and its allies might get away with invading Iraq and overthrowing its leader. By that time most Iraqis—Sunni as well as Shia and Kurds—had decided that Saddam had destroyed their country and they wanted to be rid of him. But I was convinced that if coalition forces tried to occupy Iraq long term they would face ferocious and irrepressible resistance from inside and outside the country's borders. This was not difficult to foresee and I certainly was not the only person saying it even before US tanks entered Baghdad. I wrote about it with some confidence at the time because it was what well-informed Iraqis were telling me. It was baffling that political leaders in Washington and London managed to so cut themselves off from what Iraqis—who are an intensely political people—were saying, when it would have been in their own self-interest to listen. There have always been plenty of Iraqis willing to tell truth to power, though balanced by an equal number who make it a rule to tell foreigners exactly what they want to hear. During the occupation the truthful informants were not intellectuals watching events obscurely from the sidelines, but active politicians and ministers who met senior Western officials almost every day.

The same thing happened between 2011 and 2013 when influential Iraqis like the foreign minister Hoshyar Zebari, former minister and historian Ali Allawi, politician Ahmed Chalabi and the veteran Kurdish MP Dr Mahmoud Othman were saying to me that if the war in Syria continued it would reignite the civil war in Iraq. By 2013 I was being told by some of the same people that the 350,000-strong Iraqi Army would not fight and would flee the battlefield. The Western powers seemed to have convinced themselves, in the face of compelling evidence, that Assad was going to fall and the crisis in Syria would not destabilise Iraq. I used to wonder if the Iraqis I spoke to said the same things to me as to foreign leaders, who were endlessly visiting Baghdad after 2003 but seemed to go away as ill-informed as when they arrived. I decided eventually that many of these visitors must have privately guessed how bad things were. Why else were they flying by helicopter the short distance from Baghdad airport to the Green Zone wearing a helmet and a flak jacket, and not travelling by road? In Afghanistan, diplomats from Kabul would visit Afghan Army positions and listen to accounts of its latest triumphs while averting their eyes from the black Taliban flag flying from a high point in a village a few hundred yards down the road. Presumably they were determined not to be the bearers of bad news to their home governments.

———

War reporting is easy to do but very difficult to do really well. There is great demand for a reporter's output during the fighting because it is melodramatic and appeals to readers and viewers. This is what I used to label in my own mind as 'twixt shot and shell' reporting and there is nothing wrong with it. The first newspapers were published during the Dutch Wars with Spain, the Thirty Years War and the English Civil War at the beginning of the

17th century. People rightly want to know the latest news about momentous and interesting events such as wars, natural calamities and crime. But single-minded preoccupation with combat may be deceptive, because such exciting events are not necessarily typical; neither do they always tell one who is winning or losing the war. I covered the overthrow of the Taliban in 2001 and the beginning of 2002, which was largely reported as a military victory by the anti-Taliban Northern Alliance supported by US air strikes. Television viewers would have seen impressive pictures of exploding bombs and lines of dejected prisoners. But I followed the Taliban from Kabul to Kandahar and their villages outside the city and saw their forces retreating and breaking up but without really being defeated. There was little serious fighting, but a lot of giving up and going home by Taliban fighters who had been told to do so by their commanders and knew that they were bound to lose the war anyway. At one moment, south of Ghazni, I accidentally drove through the Taliban front line, which had disintegrated. I nervously had to tell my driver to turn the car around and get back as quickly as possible without attracting attention to Northern Alliance positions. I kept thinking that I must have unaccountably missed the real fighting, but finally decided that there had not been much of it. This was important because if the Taliban had not been truly beaten it meant they could make a comeback in the years to come, as indeed they did with spectacular success.

There is a risk here of saying 'I told you so' too vociferously, which does no good to the writer or reader. There is also an implied criticism of other reporters as shallow fellows who were caught up in the drama of war and failed to take the longer view. In practical terms, the journalist who spends so much time explaining the whys and wherefores of a conflict and neglects to cover the actual fighting will not hold his or her job for very long. War reporters are occasionally belittled in two wholly opposite ways as either 'hotel journalists', cowering in their rooms while covering the action second hand, or 'war junkies', tragic figures addicted to the excitement of armed conflict. The first accusation is easily disposed of since those reporters averse to being caught up in a conflict in which they might be killed— not an unreasonable attitude—take the elementary precaution of staying out of dangerous places like Baghdad, Kabul, Beirut, Damascus, Tripoli and the like. As for the allegation that some reporters are 'war junkies', an intense interest in any professional speciality risks giving the impression that one is nursing an unhealthy obsession. But in fact few correspondents are so enamoured with combat that they believe nothing else matters. A surprising aspect of wars since 2001 is that the journalists have often spent a much longer period of time in these countries than Western diplomats or officials. When ISIS captured Mosul in 2014 the political section of the British embassy in Baghdad had just three junior diplomats on short-term deployment.

Of course there may be a certain *déformation professionnelle* involved in the reporting of wars. When doing so in Afghanistan, Syria, Libya or Iraq, it is difficult not to convince oneself of the significance of whatever skirmish one is describing. This failing is almost impossible to avoid, because everybody is prone to exaggerate the importance of an event in which others are being killed. There is also a natural identification with those soldiers and militiamen, however thuggish and unsavoury, who are being shot at or shelled alongside oneself. Some, but not all, correspondents romanticise rebels who may be heroic defenders of their own communities but are quick to loot and kill when they advance beyond their home ground. All these factors combined in the early days of the uprisings in Libya and Syria to make rebel gunmen sound less sectarian and brutal than they really were. It was only in the first half of 2015 that there was a general admission that, ruthless though the Syrian government might be in barrel-bombing civilian areas, the armed opposition was by then almost entirely dominated by ISIS and Jabhat al-Nusra, the al-Qa'ida affiliate. Sympathetic reporting of rebel-held areas in Iraq, Syria and Libya largely died away because they had become too dangerous for any local or foreign journalist to visit without risking kidnapping or decapitation. As for government-held areas in Iraq and Syria, in the past the Baathist governments in both countries had always made a sort of fetish of their own brutality as a sign of loyalty and determination and regardless of civilian casualties. The Syrian government used the same gangster methods of assassination, bombings and indiscriminate shelling to rule Lebanon during its long occupation as it used against its own civilian population after 2011.

Reporting wars has become much more dangerous now than it was half a century ago. The first armed conflict I wrote about was in Belfast in the early 1970s, when I used to joke that newly formed paramilitary groups appointed a press officer even before they bought a gun. In the first years of the Lebanese Civil War after 1975, the different militias used to hand journalists formal letters telling their checkpoints to allow free passage. There were so many militias that I was afraid of mixing up the letters, which looked rather alike, and used to keep those from left wing groups tucked into my left sock and those from right wing groups into the right one. This relationship broke down from 1984 as Shia fundamentalist groups began to see journalists as targets for abduction for ransom or as political bargaining chips. Iraq at the height of the sectarian warfare of 2006–07 was dangerous, though not as dangerous as it has since become. I used to have a second car tailing mine in Baghdad to see if I was being followed and would make sure the staff in my hotel were well-paid so they could tip me off if anybody was taking too great an interest in my activities. Friends and colleagues who have been killed, such as David Blundy in El Salvador in 1989 and Marie Colvin in Syria in 2012, were very experienced journalists. Once I had imagined that it would be young and over-enthusiastic freelancers trying to make their name who would be killed. In the event, it turns out to have been the veterans who lost their lives more frequently, not because they made any great mistakes, but because they went to the well too often, and got away with it so many times that they took one risk too many.

There is a peculiarity about these present wars that makes them difficult to report because the military activity is not all-out armed conflict. It is a sort of quasi-guerrilla warfare with strong political content, in which the most striking features are the religious fanaticism, cruelty and military expertise of ISIS and other al-Qa'ida type groups that differ little from it in ideology and behaviour, like Jabhat al-Nusra and Ahrar al-Sham. But it is important not to focus only on their attention-grabbing atrocities, but the striking weakness of their enemies, whether they are in Washington or Baghdad. The military prowess of ISIS is less surprising than the speed with which the Iraqi Army disintegrated in 2014 when attacked by far smaller forces. Perhaps this should not have come as the shock that it did: in 2013 I had spent some months in Iraq on the tenth anniversary of the US invasion and decided that the government and army were saturated by corruption and wholly dysfunctional. The following year I had written extensively and begun a book on the growing strength of the extreme Sunni jihadis. Even so, I never conceived that ISIS was going to capture Mosul and most of northern and western Iraq. I had forgotten a golden rule when predicting the future in Iraq, which is to forecast the worst possible outcome, which may take longer to happen than one had expected, but when it does occur will be far worse than one's direst imaginings. Similarly pessimistic calculations made about Syria, Yemen and Libya in recent years would likewise have accurately forecast their present grim situation.

It is easy to be a professional pessimist over Iraq and much of the rest of the region, but I have tried to avoid this, sometimes in the face of the evidence. I have liked Iraqis since I first went to their country in 1977 and have always had close Iraqi friends. During that first visit it all looked very different as the country enjoyed one of its rare moments of peace. The Kurdish rebellion had temporarily ended following the 1975 Algiers Agreement, when Saddam Hussein did a deal with the Shah of Iran who, with the backing of the US, betrayed his former Kurdish allies. The country had a standard of living that was about the same as Greece, as oil revenues soared, and there were good administrative, education and health systems. Saddam was vice chairman of the Revolutionary Command Council and had not achieved complete power. Still unknown were his capacity for extreme violence against his own people and his proneness to titanic miscalculations that would lead him to fight wars against Iran and the US that Iraq could not possibly win. I had just been in Iran in 1980 when there were the first rumours that Saddam might invade, something I discounted at the time on the grounds that he would not do anything so foolish. I was wrong, but 10 years later, as Iraqi tanks were massing north of the Kuwait border, I had learned my lesson and believed that no act of megalomaniac folly was beyond him. I knew a few of his senior advisers who were certainly aware of the likely consequences of attacking Iran or invading Kuwait, but I doubt if they ever expressed their misgivings. A Russian diplomat, who knew Iraq's ruling circles well, once told me that the only safe course for a senior member of the regime was 'to be 10 per cent tougher than the boss'. In other words, if Saddam said he was going to invade Kuwait, even his best-informed lieutenants might urge him to push on to Saudi Arabia. This tradition of Iraqi leaders grotesquely misinformed about their military and political strength did not end with the fall of Saddam. Prime Minister Nouri al-Maliki, who presided over one of the biggest military debacles in history in 2014, continued to have himself pictured staring intently at a large map and addressing his generals like Napoleon before the battle of Austerlitz. His less autocratic successor, Haider al-Abadi, was grandstanding in the streets of recaptured Tikrit in 2015, telling the world that his army would soon push into ISIS-held Anbar province. A few weeks later ISIS over-ran Ramadi.

Journalists are sometimes patronisingly congratulated for providing 'the first draft of history', though often the first draft is better than the last draft.

There is credibility about eyewitness reporting before it has been through the blender of received wisdom and academic interpretation. Journalists are often over-modest about what they know, and their editors are even more so—ever nervous when their man or woman in the field is saying different things from some pundit they have just seen on television or read in an op-ed column. In the US such 'talking heads', who have the great advantage to TV stations of providing their services for free, are often the despair of journalists in the front line. One night in Baghdad in 1998, as American missiles exploded in central Baghdad and pieces of shrapnel from anti-aircraft fire rained down, I remember watching a journalist friend crawl outside to use a satellite phone. On his return I asked him why he had done such a dangerous thing and he explained wryly that his office in New York had told him to call some expert on Iraq in a think tank in Washington to get their assessment of the US air strikes. My newspaper, *The Independent*, never put me under any such constraints or questioned my judgement in any of these wars and conflicts. I used to sympathise with American colleagues in 2003 and again in 2008 who knew very well that the war in Iraq was not won, but were being confidently contradicted by their home offices. I recall in 2008 a correspondent for one US television network gloomily telling me he had not been on air for 60 days despite the ongoing violence because 'New York is convinced that the war here is over.'

Of course, the war never ended in Iraq or any of the other countries covered in this book. This is one of the striking features of the present era: wars turn into bloody stalemates with no outright winners or losers, aside from the millions of civilians who are the victims. Political systems decay or are overthrown but nobody is strong enough to replace them. An Islamic cult motivates people so they are prepared to die for it in a way that is no longer true of nationalism or socialism. There is outrage at the atrocities and destructiveness of the Caliphate as its militants blow up the ancient buildings of Palmyra and cut off the head of the chief archaeologist. But as yet there is no sustained counter-attack to eliminate the Islamic State. The Syrian Kurdish victors of the four-and-a-half-month siege of Kobani—the first big battle lost by ISIS—were rewarded by the US reaching an agreement with Turkey in July 2015 that hurts the Syrian Kurds more than the jihadis. It is difficult to see any armed threat to the Caliphate that the Islamic militants cannot handle. When I was living in a disease-ridden and impoverished Afghan village north of Kabul covering the last days of the

Taliban, they seemed like an exotic but temporary throwback with their treatment of women as chattels and their hatred of other Islamic sects. Instead, against all the odds, they turned out to be the harbingers of an embattled and violent future.

PART I: AFGHAN PRELUDE

When 9/11 happened I was in Moscow where I was correspondent for The Independent. *It became obvious almost immediately that the US would seek to overthrow Taliban rule in Afghanistan where Osama bin Laden had his headquarters. There was little chance of getting into the country through applying to the Taliban for a visa so I flew to Dushanbe, the capital of Tajikistan, which shares a common border with Afghanistan along the Amur Darya River. The north-east corner of Afghanistan was the last stronghold of the Northern Alliance, the anti-Taliban grouping that the Taliban had driven back into the mountains in a series of ferocious campaigns. Its leader, Ahmad Shah Massoud, had been assassinated two days before 9/11 by two al-Qa'ida operatives who pretended to be journalists wanting to interview him, and who had then blown themselves up.*

Once in Dushanbe I discovered that it was going to be less easy than I had hoped to get to Northern Alliance territory because there was a Russian military detachment at the main crossing point over the Amur Darya who would not allow foreign journalists to cross. I began to make elaborate plans to travel up the Amur Darya and then to cross the river aided by smugglers after which I would travel through the Hindu Kush Mountains in order to reach the Panjshir valley north of Kabul.

Fortunately, I had been to the local Afghan embassy that was controlled by the Northern Alliance and had rather hopelessly added my name to a long list of journalists trying to get into Afghanistan. An embassy official said he would do what he could to help, though he sounded pessimistic. But after a few days he rang up and said that the Northern Alliance had an ancient Russian helicopter and the Tajikistan government had unexpectedly given permission for it to take a few journalists into Northern Alliance–controlled territory. I spent the next months in the impoverished village of Jabal Saraj a few miles from the Taliban front line north of Kabul.

The war in Afghanistan in 2001 was the first of the wars that followed 9/11 and had many similarities with the conflict in Iraq which started a year-and-a-half later. One surprising parallel is that Afghanistan and Iraq saw only limited fighting, though this was not obvious to the outside world as the media focuses almost exclusively on the melodrama of war. In reality, the Taliban fighters and Iraqi Army soldiers largely went home and had not suffered a decisive defeat on the battlefield. The US and its allies were less victorious than they imagined and could not afford to make the unforced errors they proceeded to make in the aftermath of their supposed military success. In Afghanistan the US and its local allies restored many of the much-hated warlords, whom the Taliban had displaced, and in Iraq they dissolved the army and penalised membership of the Baath Party to which many Iraqis belonged.

In the period between the two wars I spent several months in Washington and occasionally tried to explain what I thought the real situation was on the ground in Afghanistan and Iraq. I did not get a sympathetic hearing as American officials were in a peculiarly arrogant mood. They had been told that the Afghan war would be difficult and dangerous, but instead success appeared to have come swiftly and easily. What Iraqis and Afghans thought did not seem to matter in the face of overwhelming American might. When one distinguished American journalist outlined US plans for Iraq post-invasion, I replied mildly that ordinary Iraqis might not agree with this programme. 'Who cares what they think?' he asked. 'Who cares?' As it turned out, the US should have cared a great deal because, a year after its great victory, the US-led coalition controlled only islands of territory in Iraq.

Afghanistan was a prelude in other respects to the Iraq war and other post-9/11 conflicts. In all cases, the US and the Western powers lacked a reliable local partner, contrary to their claims, and though they might appear to have had many allies, this was deceptive. I remember Hoshyar Zebari, a Kurdish leader and later Iraqi foreign minister, saying to me early on after the US invasion that the most important feature of the situation was that 'there is not a single neighbour of Iraq which likes the US occupation.' Iran and Syria in particular had every incentive to destabilise a US-controlled Iraq because they feared that it might be a launching pad for action to overthrow their governments. Likewise in Afghanistan, Pakistan or more specifically the Pakistan Army was the sponsor of the Taliban before and after 2001. When the US balked at a confrontation with Pakistan as an old and powerful ally, it ensured that its war against the Taliban would become unwinnable.

This chapter is not a narrative history of the Afghan war of 2001 but a series

*of snapshots of events which help explain what really happened then. It is pecu-
liarly important to have been an eyewitness in Afghanistan at the time because
so much that was claimed by the triumphant opposition, reported by the international media and believed by the rest of the world was misleading. The views
of Afghan villagers at the time were much more revealing. In February 2002 I
went to a mud-brown village called Kalawal north of Kandahar. The farmers
had just planted opium poppies. They had been forced in 2000 by the Taliban
to uproot their previous poppy crop and plant cauliflowers instead. When the
farmers heard American bombs exploding in Kandahar they had decided that
the Taliban would fall, but that any succeeding government would be too weak
to stop the villagers cultivating opium poppies. I asked if I could meet local
Taliban and a few minutes later I was drinking tea with tough, confident men
who had gathered in the village guesthouse. Several had held medium-level
appointments in the Taliban administration such as district police chief. They
looked very undefeated and unlikely to accept being permanently excluded from
power. It occurred to me then that the Afghan war was not over.*

ONE

The Overthrow of the Taliban

Afghanistan, 2001

24 September 2001

Our ageing Russian-built helicopter flies into the Panjshir valley from the north, high over desolate, brown hills. We land at Changaram, a narrow point in the valley where lush, green fields and terraces cling to the sides of the mountains.

All along the narrow dirt road are signs of the fate of armies which have tried to fight their way into the Panjshir over the past quarter of a century. I stop counting the carcasses of burnt out and long-abandoned Soviet tanks after a few miles. In some places, old tank treads have been used to fill in potholes in the road. The top of another tank can be seen just below the surface of the river.

The Panjshir valley—perhaps the greatest natural fortress in the world— is one of the last strongholds of the Afghan opposition. It points like a bright green arrow at Kabul, which is controlled, like the other nine-tenths of the country, by the Taliban militia.

In the garden of his headquarters at Jabal Saraj, a dusty town 20 miles from the front line, Abdullah Abdullah, the foreign minister of the Northern Alliance, the main opposition grouping, is in a cheerful mood. He sits surrounded by flowers, and for some reason a small, yellow canary has been placed beside him. Abdullah, a suave, engaging man, has for years tried, with limited success until two weeks ago, to interest the rest of the world in his views. The Afghan opposition felt itself to be alone, even abandoned.

Suddenly world leaders from Washington to Tokyo are repeating every-thing they say about the Taliban.

Abdullah has one serious worry, however. It is extraordinary that the US appears to be relying on Pakistan and above all on Pakistan's intelligence service to go after the Taliban, he says, reasonably. This 'is the same deadly organisation which created the Taliban. It is now meant to be acting against them. But I assure you that Pakistani intelligence has people in it who are as fanatical as bin Laden or Mullah Omar.' Among the Afghan opposition, hatred of Pakistan for creating the Taliban is almost visceral.

The world may be waiting for the war to start but here it has been going on for 20 years. Northern Alliance forces have already launched an offen-sive far to the west, he says. They are trying to recapture Mazar-i-Sharif, a city held by the Taliban since they took it and conducted a particularly savage massacre against the Shia Muslim minority in 1997.

The Afghan opposition forces in the north are not large. They have about 15,000 well-trained men, many of them in the Panjshir, and another militia of 40,000, but they are now—finally—likely to receive as much money and as many arms as they want. Not that there is much of a shortage of weaponry in the Panjshir valley. A large number of old Soviet tanks sit in jerry-built military compounds beside the road. I watch a family being driven around in a tank from which the gun has been removed. Apparently it is being used as a taxi.

25 September 2001

After almost a quarter of a century of war, Afghanistan has become a land of donkeys and tanks. Most Afghans live in conditions of terrible poverty. On the main road between Kabul and the mouth of the Panjshir valley, we meet two men waiting with donkeys and broken down carts for passengers. In countries like Afghanistan I often look at people's shoes to see how poor they really are. In this case the two men, called Abdul Hamid and Abdul Haliq, are wearing the cheapest green plastic sandals. But there are only three of them. Abdul Haliq has lost one plastic sandal and is too poor to replace it.

They say they have little knowledge about what is happening in the outside world. They live with 150 other people in no-man's-land. 'When the Talibs open fire, we go away,' says Abdul Hamid. 'Our main problem is that we don't have enough water. We try to farm the land.' Yet there is interest in what is happening further afield. As we talk an elderly man with a dark blue turban arrives in a donkey cart, holding a primitive battery in a wooden box. He tells us: 'We have no electricity. I bought the battery because I wanted to listen to the radio so I can hear the news about Afghanistan.'

Afghans are less excited about President George Bush's policies of war against all those who support terrorism because most of them have been at war all their lives. Just possibly a war that destroys the Taliban will make life better for a man like Abdul Haliq, living in no-man's-land, with little water and only able to afford one green sandal. But it is easy to understand why, after the last quarter of a century in Afghanistan, he has his doubts about it.

7 October 2001

From a hilltop 40 miles north of Kabul, across a clear night sky illuminated by half a silver moon, I see flashes on the skyline as the Allied air strikes begin. Under a canopy of stars, plumes of fire are visible across the flat, heavily populated Shomali plain, which leads to the outskirts of Kabul. Distant thumping reverberates across the still air, signalling the long-awaited turn in the fortunes of the anti-Taliban forces dug in along a front line that snakes within 25 miles of the city.

As the horizon lights up with anti-aircraft fire, Taliban and opposition forces begin to blaze away at each other with artillery. At one moment, there is an explosion high above Kabul, which may be a missile directed at Allied planes overhead. At another, there are flashes of white light, almost certainly anti-aircraft fire.

From the rocky hilltop overlooking the village of Jabal Saraj there is a straight view south towards the Afghan capital. This has been one of the great battlefields during almost a quarter of a century of warfare in Afghanistan, and is likely to see fierce fighting in coming days as the Northern Alliance forces attempt to take the capital. Alliance reserves are already pouring towards the front.

Intercepted radio traffic between Taliban forces reveals that they have little idea as to what is going on, according to Northern Alliance commanders. Mass defections from the Taliban are expected now, but changing sides is not easy in present-day Afghanistan. One young Taliban deserter crossed enemy lines just hours before the bombs started to fall. Khan Jan, a 23-year-old with a turban and black beard, unwillingly conscripted into the Taliban army, says he waited until 4 a.m. to make his escape. 'By then the other soldiers were all sleeping,' he tells me. 'I did not feel any fear because I took a heavy machine gun, a Kalashnikov and a pistol.'

For a man who must have been close to death during the delicate and dangerous process of deserting the Taliban, Khan Jan seems perky and relaxed. 'I owned a small shop, just a booth, in Kunduz city in the north,' he explains. 'One day two Taliban came and said I should come with them. Then they put me with 70 other people in a helicopter and flew us to Sedarat camp in Kabul.' Khan Jan, like most of the others picked up in Kunduz, is a Tajik, while the Taliban are primarily Pashtun.

After the attacks on the World Trade Centre and the Pentagon, Khan Jan probably had a good idea that something unpleasant was about to happen to Taliban soldiers. 'Many soldiers said: "Now the Americans will attack us,"' he remembers. 'But then Mullah Omar said: "Don't worry about America."' The last point makes the Northern Alliance soldiers in the room laugh loudly.

13 October 2001

Conditions here in a small village in Afghanistan's Panjshir valley are atrocious. But after three weeks, we have settled into an odd sort of routine. I arrived as one of a small group, given lodgings in an official 'guest house' run by the opposition Northern Alliance. But with 200 foreign correspondents now crammed in to the village, the overcrowding is severe. We are billeted in the former home of the manager of a local cement factory.

Initially we had two lavatories between 15 people. Now we are down to one for 45. The Afghan definition of a lavatory is little more than a hole in the ground. Four of us share a room; we sleep on the floor with a cushion and a blanket. But if conditions are testing for us, the villagers live in circumstances of medieval poverty and hardship.

The village, with a population of about 2,000, has only a few tiny shops, one selling second-hand women's shoes from Europe and Pakistan. There are so few things to be bought and so many hundred-dollar bills in circulation, thanks to the international media influx, that the value of the dollar to the Afghani has halved locally in the past three weeks.

We have electricity only between 3 p.m. and 9 p.m. and the generator is unreliable. It gets dark at six and with winter not far off it is getting cold. The dust storms are frequent and blinding and play havoc with our equipment. I managed to buy a car battery to run my satellite phone for a few minutes every day so I can send my copy.

Dysentery is a constant hazard. You get it from the water or eating the vegetables. One of my colleagues was struck down the other day and I took him to the nearest hospital. Then I got the symptoms myself. I get up at 6 a.m. every morning to race to the washroom and toilet before everyone else.

You get a breakfast of tea, bread and jam and a hard boiled egg. For dinner there is rice. There is what passes for a restaurant in the village. It also serves as a hotel—after the meal people settle down on the low carpeted tables to sleep for the night. These days a lot of the customers are fighters carrying machine guns.

15 October 2001

American warplanes pound Kabul as the air war against the Taliban and Osama bin Laden enters its second week. But the soldiers who mill about in the villages behind the opposition front line north of Kabul have the air of men who are expecting great events and are a little bemused by the fact that so little is happening. The sense of a phony war is almost palpable.

It cannot last. The Northern Alliance promised it would launch a military offensive against the Taliban a few days after the American bombing started. Its commanders say they are waiting for the United States to hit front line Taliban positions. This is easier said than done. The Shomali plain, which has been divided between the Northern Alliance and the Taliban for five years, is heavily populated. American bombing would kill many of the civilians who are still living in their half-ruined villages.

The nature of the front in northern Afghanistan makes it difficult to use air power effectively. The very words 'front line' evoke images of the Western Front in the First World War, with opposing armies crouched in well-defended trenches protected by machine guns and barbed wire. In Afghanistan it is not like that. Armies are small. Front lines are usually a trip wire, held by few men, with forces for counter-attacks held further to the rear. 'Fighting here is partly like regular warfare using fixed positions and partly like guerrilla war,' says General Babajan, who commands the Northern Alliance forces at Bagram airport.

So far the biggest blow to the Taliban has been the loss of its control of the air. This is important as Taliban troops in the northern cities of Mazar-i-Sharif and Kunduz are now isolated, apart from a single road. The Taliban have no way across the Hindu Kush mountains which divide Afghanistan. The obvious strategy for the Northern Alliance is to try to

take all of Afghanistan north of the Hindu Kush. This is a land of minorities, all of which have suffered at the hands of the Taliban. To the north-east
are the Tajiks in the great mountain fortress of the Panjshir valley. Further
north are the Uzbeks, who were badly defeated in the civil wars of the
1990s. In central Afghanistan are the Hazara, a fifth of the country's population, distinguished physically from other Afghans by their Mongolian
appearance. They are Shia Muslims, which has prompted savage persecution by the fanatically Sunni Muslim Taliban, who regarded the Hazara
as heretics.

It is difficult to see how the Taliban can survive the cumulative military
pressures on them. They no longer have the support of Pakistan and Saudi
Arabia, which was so critical to their rise. Their many enemies at home
scent blood.

5 November 2001

We drive through the village of Jorm, a huddle of mud-brick houses surrounded by trees in an upland valley in northern Afghanistan. Suddenly
about 50 people run towards us in a bewildered panic. As they grow closer
we see that two of them are carrying children with faces covered in blood.
We stop and ask a man beside the road what has happened. He says a mine
exploded—one of the thousands of devices that litter this land after two
decades of war.

Villagers, almost all men, mill about in ineffective confusion. Even in
this emergency Afghan women do not leave their houses, apart from one
old woman who cradles a boy's head in her lap. She is wailing and rocking
to and fro, but she has not even wiped the blood off his face.

We find that three small boys are injured, not just the two we had originally seen. One of them, Barot Mohammed, aged 10, lies on the stony
ground, bleeding heavily from wounds in his right leg where pieces of flesh
have been torn away by the blast. His left hand is wrapped in a sodden
brown bandage, but whatever it covers looks too small to be a fist. The boys
are so drenched in blood that I cannot see how badly they are wounded.
One of them is half sitting up, clutching his stomach. None of the men,
some armed with submachine guns, seem to know what to do.

Through our driver, Daoud, whose knowledge of English is limited to
about 20 words, we ask where is the nearest hospital. They reply that it is
in Baharak, a market town about an hour's drive away, but they have no
car or truck. I am with two other correspondents, one from France and the

other from Spain, with whom I have driven in a sturdy Russian-made jeep through the mountains from the Panjshir valley north of Kabul. None of us knows much about first aid, or has any bandages, but it seems possible that unless the boys receive help soon they will bleed to death.

My two colleagues volunteer to stay behind in Jorm to make room for the children in the small jeep. We lift them in, wrapped in blankets. None of the three cry out or make any sound other than a whimper, either because they are in shock or because Afghan boys are expected to endure pain without complaint. Two older men also cram themselves into the jeep. One is the boy's uncle. He says the boys are brothers. Barot Mohammed is the oldest and the other two are called Rajab Mohammed, 7, whom I saw clasping his stomach, and Najmaddin, 5, who does not seem quite so badly hurt.

It is a horribly bumpy ride to Baharak. Daoud is a highly skilful driver and the dirt road, by Afghan standards, is not too bad. But even so the boys are jolted up and down as he nurses the jeep across deep gullies where streams cut across the road. Rajab's eyes, deep-set and very dark like those of most Afghans, keep closing and his head falling sideways, as if he is dying.

The hospital in Baharak, a typical dusty market town, represents the best hope of safety for the boys. There are no lights inside. I walk through several rooms shouting for a doctor. I see two women in the distance and explain about the mine explosion. They cluck sympathetically, but do nothing, presumably because they are not wearing veils. Finally a man appears who says he is an assistant doctor. In a cluttered room with two operating tables he begins to treat Najmaddin. Another doctor called Dr Suleiman arrives and a German nurse called Mathias, an energetic looking man with long brown hair, offers to come and help.

With three doctors and nurses treating the boys I am more hopeful. When I ask the assistant doctor how they are he says 'good, good' in an absent way. He and Mathias work on Barot's right arm, which has deep cuts in it. But when they gently remove the blood-sodden bandage on his left hand, only the little finger is left. Barot must have been holding the mine or shell in this hand when it exploded. It had ripped away four fingers, leaving white tips of bone sticking out of the flesh. 'I'm afraid we'll have to cut away the whole hand,' says Mathias, sadly shaking his head.

A little later Dr Suleiman reveals that Rajab has a puncture wound in the abdomen. He says both boys must go for surgery to a proper hospital two hours' drive away in the large town of Faizabad. As we leave, Dr Suleiman is saying he will look in the bazaar for somebody with a car.

23 November 2001

Few political movements have come so far so fast. A month ago, the Northern Alliance was clinging on by its fingertips in a few strongholds amid the crags of the Hindu Kush mountains. Today, thanks to the US air offensive, it is master of Kabul, seems about to take Kunduz, and is preparing to attend talks with other Afghan leaders to decide the future of the country in Bonn, Germany.

The aim of the talks is to set up an interim government uniting all factions and ethnic groups, but ultimately it is guns that will count. They are the symbol of the new Afghanistan just as they were of the old. Stalin's wartime jibe about the importance of the Vatican—'How many divisions has the Pope'—is wholly true of Afghan politics.

The problem facing the Northern Alliance is similar to that which faced the Taliban until a few days ago. Its base is too narrow for it to hold on to the power it has seized. In such a militarised society, stability is difficult to achieve because the threat of armed force is always just beneath the surface. This is exacerbated by deep ethnic divisions. The Pashtuns, on whom the Taliban rely, make up 42 per cent of the population. The Tajiks (25 per cent) and the Uzbeks (8 per cent) generally stand behind the Northern Alliance. Massacres, particularly around the northern city of Mazar-i-Sharif, have exacerbated ethnic hatreds over the past five years. Already the Hazara Shia Muslims, who make up 19 per cent of the population, are protesting at the Tajik takeover of Kabul.

Power in Afghanistan is fragmented and will remain so. Even villages behave like independent republics. A foreign peace-keeping force might help to reduce the friction between different parties, armies and ethnic groups. But, as the UN discovered in Somalia, failure to be seen as wholly neutral would have disastrous results.

1 December 2001

Confident, swaggering, but with an air of jovial menace, General Abdul Rashid Dostum, the burly Uzbek warlord who has just conquered much of northern Afghanistan, is explaining how his men have come to kill hundreds of Taliban captives during a prison uprising. It was reported that a hardcore group of Taliban fighters made a last desperate stand from a crumbling tower inside the ancient fortress of Qalai Janghi, whose blue-domed citadel long served as Dostum's headquarters. Two thousand reinforcements from Dostum's army poured in, and US jets streaked overhead, directed by 12 American and British advisers in the fort.

It is not clear what exactly happened in the prisoners' revolt. But, ironically, even if the general was not directly responsible for the massacre, his reputation for ruthlessness and the fear he inspired may well have encouraged the prisoners to revolt in the first place. On past record, troops fighting with the Taliban have little to expect from the man, whatever his promises to the Americans.

The slaughter has made Afghans nervous. It is not that many feel sympathy for the Taliban. But, as one observer in Kabul, quoting an old Afghan proverb, puts it: 'What you do to your enemies today, you will do to your friends tomorrow.'

General Dostum's friends and enemies have tended to switch places with bewildering rapidity, even by Afghan standards. Once the commander of a Communist armoured corps in northern Afghanistan he has, at one time or another, been allied to, and has betrayed, every other Afghan leader and political movement including the Taliban. In his defence it could be said that he generally only betrayed his friends before they betrayed him, and sometimes they were quicker than he was. Twice he was forced to flee Mazar-i-Sharif, his capital, which he has now recaptured. Once, in 1997, he was compelled to bribe his own soldiers to let him escape into Uzbekistan.

But it is not the treachery which is surprising. It is rather that Dostum, the son of poor Uzbek peasants, once a farmhand and a plumber, has been able to survive defeat so often. In 1992 it was his defection, at the head of his private army, from the Communist government, which doomed the regime and ensured his survival. Now, once again, the general is in a key position. Discussions of power-sharing between Afghan parties will be an exercise in fantasy if they disregard men like Dostum, who, however unsavoury, have real armed forces at their disposal.

It is easy enough to demonise the general. Ahmed Rashid, a Pakistani writer and journalist, once noticed, on visiting him in his headquarters in the Qalai Janghi fortress—the name means Fort of War—outside Mazar, that there were smears of blood and pieces of flesh in one corner of the courtyard. At first he thought a goat must have been killed. Guards explained that, an hour earlier, Dostum had ordered a soldier accused of stealing to be tied to the tracks of a tank that drove around until he was reduced to mincemeat.

But as ruler of a quasi-independent state, made up of seven Afghan provinces in the plains north of the Hindu Kush mountains, the general gained a reputation for effective administration. His private kingdom had a health and medical service. It was also, whatever bows Dostum made towards Islam, largely secular. Some 1,800 women attended university in Mazar at a time when they were banned from work and education by the Taliban in Kabul.

Three years ago Dostum was forced to flee into exile, for the second time, as the Taliban took over the territory he once ruled. But earlier this year he returned to a mountain stronghold south of Mazar, which the Taliban have never penetrated. As a member of the Northern Alliance, it did not look like a very hopeful venture—until 11 September. The US needed anti-Taliban allies on the ground in Afghanistan. Its initial efforts to pick and choose came to naught. Bombing alone could not destroy the Taliban. Somebody had to occupy the ground. The first to move, sometimes riding a white horse, was the general.

Dostum, along with other opposition leaders, advanced on Mazar in three columns, initially without co-ordination, and fell back in confusion. It was only a temporary setback. Just as Dostum's army had dissolved in the face of superior force three years before, so the Taliban now fell apart. He was able to recapture his old headquarters at Qalai Janghi where last weekend's fearful massacre took place.

6 December 2001

Abdul Ahmed, a warlord whose fiefdom is just outside Kabul on the road to Kandahar, is among those who will decide the fate of the power-sharing government agreed in Bonn. So far he is not impressed. Hamid Karzai, the Pashtun leader who will chair the interim government, is there 'because of pressure from the outside world, but he is not wanted by Afghans. He has done no fighting against the Taliban,' Ahmed says sourly.

Surrounded by his retainers in the village of Maidanshar, the warlord claims Karzai has exaggerated accounts of the assault he is leading against the Taliban in Kandahar. He says: 'Karzai told people he was an old man who had come to unify, not to fight. If he had really done any fighting, like the Northern Alliance, we might be in Kandahar by now. He is not a well-known person.'

It is impossible to check Ahmed's allegations, but the views of warlords matter because they control most of Afghanistan. The interim government will find it hard to operate without their assent. Although the Northern Alliance has captured Kabul, warlords are determined to assert their control over their own districts. Ahmed has just fought a small private war with Gholam Mohammed, another leader who recently switched sides from the Taliban with 2,000 men. 'It was really just about power,' one of his soldiers says. 'He wanted Gholam's heavy weapons.'

Ahmed is also dubious about international troops. He says: 'We will welcome the UN if they bring peace, but then many Afghans welcomed the Soviets when they first came.' Afghans are hopeful but wary about what has been agreed in Bonn. They remember that some of the factions agreeing to share power fought a civil war from 1992 to 1996 that killed 100,000 people in Kabul.

7 December 2001

The end could be foreseen from the moment the night sky over Kabul turned a bright yellow as the first American bombs and missiles landed near the airport two months ago. In few wars has the disparity of force between the two sides been so obvious.

'They could not take any more American bombing, so they had to surrender,' says a young Northern Alliance officer called Abdul Razeq as we drive down the road from Kabul towards Kandahar. He explains that his commander has just received a call from Hamid Karzai, the anti-Taliban Pashtun leader fighting just north of Kandahar, saying that the Taliban fighters are going to give up.

It has been the strangest war, decided mainly by defections. Afghans saw the first bombs come down and concluded that the United States and its local ally, the Northern Alliance, must win. Nobody here likes to bet on a loser. In a quarter of century of war in Afghanistan, sudden betrayals and switches of alliance, not battles, have decided the victor.

All this is obvious in Ghazni, the fortress city on the Kandahar road. Abdul Razeq had earlier explained that what we were doing was a little dangerous. He said that in Wardag, the first province we came to, the Taliban 'have joined our side, but only very recently and they still have the same commanders. Sit in the back of the car and don't get out.'

Ghazni, a bleak city dominated by the guns and tanks in its thousand-year-old citadel, has already led the way for Kandahar. In return for giving up power, the Taliban have received a de facto amnesty. 'I don't see any Taliban here,' says Qari Baba, the newly appointed governor of Ghazni province, which is surprising, since the courtyard in front of his office is crowded with tough-looking men in black turbans carrying submachine guns. 'Every one of them ex-Taliban,' Abdul Razeq says as we get back in the car.

The reasons for the Taliban defeat are obvious enough. There was the US bombing. There was the hatred felt towards them by the non-Pashtun minorities, who make up 60 per cent of Afghans. Of the remaining 40 per cent, half are women—whom they treated as a sub-species. And the Pashtun themselves were never united behind the regime.

The Northern Alliance was also weak and its military strength uncertain, but it played its cards with great skill. At a moment when the world was desperate for news from Afghanistan, it organised an airlift of journalists across the peaks of the Hindu Kush mountains from Tajikistan to the Panjshir valley. This put it on the political map of the world. Working with the Northern Alliance, which is partly armed and supported by Russia and Iran, was a little difficult for the US to swallow. But it needed a local ally, and the Alliance was the only game in town. Despite the offence caused to Pakistan, which is bitterly opposed to the Northern Alliance, America had to bomb the Taliban's front line trenches to aid the Alliance advance if the US was to win.

The Taliban were always thought likely to unravel in northern Afghanistan, where there are few Pashtun. But at some point a hard core of Taliban fanatics was expected to turn and fight. They never did. The surprise of the war has been how few genuine fanatics belonged to the group.

A problem of covering the war was that it was difficult to meet members of the Taliban. This is their own fault, since they banned the media at the start of the crisis. After the fall of Kabul, I did meet Mullah Khaksar, who had been the deputy interior minister. He said: 'They did not know what all the world knows, that the people hated them.' Yet when the Taliban had first taken Kabul in 1996, he had 'liked them because they provided security'—and he had not been alone.

The savage civil war between the different parties of the Northern Alliance, which preceded Taliban rule, has reduced most of Kabul to ruins. But the brutality of the Taliban and their obsession with controlling people's private lives meant that they had long outlived their welcome. Even those fond of innocent pleasures such as kite-flying were rewarded with a beating or even prison.

There is still something terrifying about the way in which the Taliban pursued their obsessions. In Bamiyan, a valley in central Afghanistan, they destroyed two colossal 1,500-year-old Buddhist statues, condemning them as un-Islamic, earlier this year. I thought one smaller statue in a distant glen might have survived. But when I got there a local farmer pointed to an empty stone niche in a cliff face, saying: 'There is nothing left. They destroyed it like they destroyed everything else.'

PART II: THE OCCUPATION OF IRAQ

When the US, Britain and their allies invaded Iraq in 2003 they started a revolution. They did not mean to do so since their aim was to get rid of Saddam Hussein and his regime and they did not perceive the radicalism of what they were doing. The invasion and occupation meant revolutionary change because it ended Sunni Arab rule, which had been continuous for hundreds of years under the Ottomans, the British and after independence. The Americans dissolved the army and the security services that were the prime instruments of Sunni control over the 80 per cent of the population who were Shia or Kurds.

American officials frequently saw themselves then and in coming years as a mediating force between competing Iraqi communities. But their military presence also destabilised the sectarian balance of power between communities which knew they did not have to reach compromises with other Iraqis if they could get the Americans (or in later years the Turks, Saudis, Iranians or Qataris) on their side. The occupying powers never took on board the fact that the identification of the new post-Saddam government with the Americans and a former imperial power like Britain delegitimised it from the beginning in the eyes of Iraqis.

Since not all the Americans and their allies who occupied Iraq were stupid, why did they make so many mistakes in those first two years? The most obvious cause was simple arrogance and the second was that the occupiers did not think it much mattered what Iraqis from any community thought or did. The White House had been told by many who claimed to know Iraq that the US Army was plunging into a quagmire, but the invasion had gone off astonishingly well with a swift victory and low American casualties. The Iraqi Army, including Saddam Hussein's vaunted Republican Guard, had barely fought. Abandoned tanks littered the roads. All Iraqis knew that Saddam was going to lose the war and saw no reason to die in a lost cause. Moreover, the majority of Iraqis, including Sunni, were pleased to see the old regime go, even if they did not welcome the occupation. The Baathists had brought nothing but misery and defeat, including 13 years of devastating economic sanctions which had tipped millions of Iraqis into poverty and malnutrition. The Americans, without thinking about it very much, believed that because Iraqis did not fight in 2003, it meant they could not fight. As their casualties mounted in the second half of 2003, American spokesmen kept explaining that it was only a tiny 'remnant' of the old regime that was fighting against the birth of a new Iraq.

The US occupation was weaker than it looked for another reason: it was opposed by all states neighbouring Iraq–Saudi Arabia, the Sunni monarchies of the Gulf, Jordan and Turkey because they were dismayed to see a Sunni state replaced by a Shia one likely to have close relations with Iran. Iran and Syria, for their part, were glad to see the end of Saddam Hussein, but they were frightened by the arrival of a large American army on their frontiers. They read vainglorious boasting by politicians and officials in Washington saying that regime change in Baghdad today could be repeated in Tehran and Damascus tomorrow. This sort of jingoism may have been rhetorical, but Syrian and Iranian leaders understandably preferred to fight the US in Iraq before it stabilised its rule there. Syria gave free passage to Sunni jihadis and Iran supported the anti-American Shia militias.

I was in Washington for a few months before the invasion, working briefly at the Centre for Security and International Studies. Contradicting the general mood of optimism, an American colleague said to me one day that he thought the invasion of Iraq was going to be as disastrous for the Americans in 2003 as the Suez Crisis had been for the British when they invaded Egypt in 1956. It was a step too far, my colleague argued, intended as a demonstration of political and military strength but would achieve the exact opposite. I thought this might be going too far, but I remembered what he said when I travelled to Iraq to cover the war. The Baghdad government had decided I was an inveterate enemy and would not give me a visa so I had to drive through Syria and then cross the Tigris River into the area held by the Kurds where I spent the war, moving south towards the capital as the Iraqi Army broke up.

For the Americans the Iraq War was a disaster, though not quite on the scale that Suez was for the British. The US was a great power in the Middle East in 2003, and it still was in 2015, although its authority was diminished. It had not been defeated in Iraq but it had very publicly failed to put in power a compliant pro-American state. It was evident that US public opinion would not support another American army being sent to the Middle East unless there was some other atrocity like 9/11. At the same time, President Obama has been able to use the US Air Force against ISIS in Iraq and Syria since 2014 without paying a political price at home. Perhaps a better analogy would be to compare the US war in Iraq with the Boer War, which the British Army actually won after great exertions, but in doing so exposed the limitations of British military strength.

Much has changed in Iraq over the last 12 years but much is the same. I saw Mosul and Kirkuk fall to the Kurds in 2003 and they are still embattled cities today. Fallujah was held by Sunni jihadis in 2004 and ISIS controls it today. Baghdad was a dangerous, dysfunctional place 10 years ago, short of water and electricity, and this is still true today. It turns out that the Shia were no more able to permanently subdue the Sunni than Saddam had been able to subdue the Shia and the Kurds. By 2005 the Americans were realising that they had wandered into another Vietnam, though all the while denying that any such thing had happened. I remember a member of a US bomb disposal team telling me how he had vainly requested a Pentagon handbook on Viet Cong booby traps and IEDs (Improvised Explosive Devices), only to be reprimanded and told that there were no similarities between Vietnam and Iraq so the book had been withdrawn.

As with Vietnam, the US wanted to get out of Iraq without admitting defeat. In this they largely succeeded. Claims of victory stemmed from the 'surge'—the increase in US troop numbers—combined with a split in the Sunni armed resistance brought on by al-Qa'ida in Iraq's premature attempt to monopolise power and murderous pressure on the Sunni from the Shia militias. But the promoters of the surge were over-optimistic about what they had achieved. Al-Qa'ida was weakened but not destroyed, as became all too apparent after the final US withdrawal in 2011 when the Syrian Sunni uprising offered new opportunities for extreme Sunni militants in Iraq. Many astute Iraqis could see what was going to happen—I recall a minister saying to me: 'If the war goes on in Syria, it will de-stabilise Iraq once again.' The blindness and over-confidence of the US and its allies then was just as great, and with similarly disastrous consequences, as it had been in 2003.

TWO

Iraq Under Sanctions

Iraq, 1990–2003

UN sanctions devastated Iraq in the 13 years between 1990 and 2003. Iraqis saw their social and economic standards fall from the same level as Greece to those of Mali. The World Health Organisation said that in 1996 'the vast majority of the country's population has been on a semi-starvation diet for years.' The UN estimated that between six and seven thousand Iraqi children were dying every month as a result of sanctions. Millions of Iraqis who had once held good jobs and lived in comfort were reduced to poverty and often to crime. The country's once high-grade education and health services collapsed as distinguished professors and doctors found that they were being paid the equivalent of $5 a month. A visiting foreign medical team 'witnessed a surgeon trying to operate with scissors that were too blunt to cut the patient's skin'. There were shortages of electricity and drinking water because power and water treatment plants were targeted in the bombing campaign of 1991 and only partially rebuilt. With no money to pay officials, the administrative system became hopelessly corrupted and has never recovered to this day. The US-led invasion of 2003 destroyed the Iraqi state and army, but sanctions had already shattered the country's society and economy.

This book is primarily about the armed conflicts that followed 9/11, but UN sanctions may have killed more Iraqis than any of the wars that followed. Begun in 1990 after Saddam Hussein's invasion of Kuwait, they imposed a tight economic siege on a whole country that was only slightly mitigated by the oil-for-food programme in 1996. Their supposed aim was to keep Saddam

Hussein weak by starving his regime of money or any goods that would allow him to rebuild his military machine. Given the speed with which the Iraqi Army had collapsed in 1991 it was always an absurd exaggeration to see it as much of a potential threat. Even so, inoffensive items like lead pencils were banned because the graphite might be used to manufacture nuclear weapons; chlorine to cleanse polluted water for drinking could not be imported because it might be turned into poison gas; ambulances were in short supply because they could be used for ferrying troops. None of these measures did anything to lessen Saddam Hussein's grip on power, but they did have a calamitous impact on the Iraqi people.

The disasters that followed the US invasion of 2003 have sparked much dispute about responsibility for what happened. But there is far too little realisation of the degree to which sanctions had already ruined Iraq, and created conditions in which Iraqis were very ready to take up arms or opt for religious extremism. This is not just retrospective wisdom. In 1998, Dennis Halliday, the UN Humanitarian Co-ordinator for Iraq, resigned in protest against UN sanctions and warned of their effect on younger Iraqis. He compared them to young Afghans brought up in refugee camps who became the foot soldiers of the violent and fanatical Taliban movement. 'What should be of concern is the possibility of more fundamentalist Islamic thinking developing,' said Halliday prophetically. 'It is not well understood as a spin-off of the sanctions regime. We are pushing people to take extreme positions.' Ignored at the time, the truth of his words are all too evident today now that the extreme Sunni sectarian Islamic State rules a third of Iraq, and Shia religious parties dominate the government in Baghdad.

I wrote frequently about UN sanctions and their disastrous effect in Iraq over the 13 years during which they were implemented. But nothing I or anybody else said or did about sanctions gained much of a hearing in the outside world, though Iraqis thought and talked about little else. The problem was that people are far more conscious of casualties of direct military action such as children killed or injured by air strikes. An economic blockade may cause more deaths by a factor of a hundred, but it does so silently and behind closed doors. Its first victims are the very young, the very old and the very sick. The numbers of children dying before their first birthday increased from one in thirty when sanctions were imposed to one in eight seven years later. Many Iraqis were simply not getting enough to eat. I wrote about how even the garbage collected from the streets of Baghdad told of a people near starvation. Before sanctions one third of garbage had been food scraps but now the scraps had disappeared.

Nobody was throwing away anything that could be eaten and even melon skins were being saved and devoured.

The following chapter contains glimpses from the era of sanctions as they affected all Iraqis—even those in Kurdistan outside Saddam Hussein's control who lived off defusing lethal mines and selling the contents. I remember being pursued across fields in Diyala province north-east of Baghdad by farmers who thought I was a foreign doctor and wanted me to look at ageing x-rays of their sick children. Many cruel and outrageous things were to happen in Iraq in the years after the invasion, but I still feel a surge of anger when I recall the sheer destructiveness of sanctions and the unnecessary suffering they inflicted on Iraqis without bringing the demise of Saddam's rule a day nearer. Throughout this period the world leaders responsible for this man-made disaster blamed it all on Saddam Hussein or denied it was happening. They never took any blame for creating the quagmire into which they were about to plunge.

20 October 1996

It is probably the most dangerous way to make a living in the world. 'I do it because I would prefer to die than see the rest of my family starve,' says Sabir Saleh, a middle-aged man who used to be a farmer but is now too poor to hire a tractor to plough his land. Every morning he goes out into the minefields laid around Penjwin, a Kurdish village in northern Iraq shattered by fighting in the Iran–Iraq War. Saleh looks for one mine in particular: the Italian-made Valmara, one of the most lethal anti-personnel mines in existence. It is not easy to spot, because its five khaki-coloured prongs look like dried grass. Pressure on any one of them causes the Valmara to jump to waist height and explode, spraying 1,200 ball bearings over a range of 100 yards.

'I defuse the mine with a piece of wire,' says Saleh. 'Then I unscrew the top of it and take out the aluminium around the explosives. When I have taken apart six mines I have enough aluminium to sell for 30 dinar [about 75 pence] to a shop in Penjwin.' After a day in the minefields he hopes to have recovered enough aluminium to feed his family of eight. 'I make enough money to buy food for them, but not enough to buy clothes or anything else,' he says. He was a farmer before being drafted into the Iraqi Army for six years to fight the Iranians. To plough his land he would need to hire a tractor for £2.50 an hour, money he does not have. So, in the last few years, he has defused 2,000 Valmaras.

The mountain slopes around Penjwin are infested by mines. More than anywhere in the world it is mines that shape the lives of local people. Bahktiar Ali, an 18-year-old orphan, says his mother was killed in February last year when she trod on a mine while looking for firewood. Now he earns money guiding people illegally into Iran through the minefields.

Everybody in Penjwin knows somebody who has been killed by mines, and many point to their own injuries, mostly sustained when looking for Valmaras. 'You can divide people in Penjwin into those who make their money from dismantling mines and selling the aluminium and those who don't,' says Abdullah Ahmed, a local man who works for the Mines Advisory Group (MAG), a British-based charity which clears minefields. Over 2,000 Kurds are known to have been killed by mines since 1991, but the real figure is probably 50 per cent higher.

Most Valmaras are buried underground with only the prongs, one of which is usually connected to a trip wire, visible. 'Defusing is very difficult,' says Selwar Hama Mustafa, who has now given up and works in a garage in Penjwin. 'You have to get a wire into a hole, and then sometimes you can't unscrew the top of the mine because it is rusty.' The Valmaras are usually surrounded by smaller anti-personnel mines. Abdullah Ali, his left leg ending in a stump, says: 'I was looking for aluminium. I didn't notice there was a little pressure mine under my foot.'

Even though the Iran–Iraq War ended in 1988, there is no danger of mines being in short supply. Polly Brennan of MAG says the Iraqi Army planted between 10 million and 20 million along the border with Iran, one for 'every man, woman, child, chicken and donkey.' Hunting for mines may be a dangerous and not very profitable occupation but, apart from taking goods and people across the Iranian border, there is no other way of making a living. Sabir Saleh has started taking his children into the minefields to learn how to defuse a Valmara, 'so they can earn a living, too.'

21 April 1998

The reason his doctors expect eight-month-old Hussein Ali Majhoul to die is that the oxygen bottle beside his bed is empty and there is no chance of getting a new one. A week ago, his mother Nada brought Hussein, brown eyes bright with fever, to the Ibn al-Khatib hospital for infectious diseases in the southern outskirts of Baghdad. Now he has almost ceased to breathe.

'He has meningitis,' says Dr Deraid Obousy, director of the hospital, gently pressing the side of Hussein's neck. 'He is already unconscious. It is in the hands of God. We don't have any more oxygen bottles in the hospital and we don't have any money to hire a truck to pick up a new one from the factory that refills them on the other side of Baghdad.'

Dr Obousy, 46, but looking older, is obviously depressed by the conditions around him. The reason he cannot send one of his hospital vehicles to pick up the oxygen bottle which might save Hussein Ali is that they have no wheels, or engines. They were long ago cannibalised to keep at least one going, and now stand rusting in the hospital forecourt, axles supported by rocks. This is just one consequence of the sanctions imposed on Iraq by the United Nations Security Council in 1990, after Iraq's invasion of Kuwait.

When I enter his office Dr Obousy is reading an old copy of the British Medical Journal, which has found its way to Baghdad despite sanctions. He says that in Britain, where he worked in hospitals for four years, 'a place like this would definitely be closed. They would say it is rubbish. It is getting into the hot season and we have no mosquito netting for the windows, or air conditioners, or even enough sheets for the beds.' All this is confirmed by a tour of the wards. The smell of disinfectant does not quite mask the stench of the lavatories. The patients are eating a meagre meal of rice and chickpea soup.

Hidden away south of the capital the al-Khatib hospital, and Ibn-Zuhr TB hospital beside it, deal with the infectious diseases which were a rarity in Iraq before the UN embargo. Eight years later, measles, typhoid, meningitis, diphtheria and even polio are common. The resurgence of these diseases has gone hand in hand with malnutrition. Dr Obousy says: 'We now often find children with thickening of the wrist, which means rickets or calcium deficiency, things we used to know about only from textbooks.' In Baghdad, Dr Nada al-Ward, a public health specialist at the World Health Organisation, confirms the medical consequences of semi-starvation: 'In 1989–90 the number of babies in Iraq who died before they were 12 months old was 36.5 out of 1,000. Currently the figure has more than tripled to 120 out of 1,000.'

A diplomat in Baghdad says of the embargo: 'It affects the 21.5 million ordinary Iraqis, but not the 500,000 members of the elite.' In the al-Khatib hospital the semi-starved parents and their dying children are the obvious victims of the sanctions. As eight-month-old Hussein Ali dies of meningitis, the Iraqi government is watching a march-past of 140,000 volunteer soldiers—as if to confirm how little its hold on power has been weakened by eight years of sanctions.

2 May 1998

In Baghdad, people say the only Iraqis doing well out of sanctions are black marketeers and the farmers. The success of the former is obvious enough. I drive west from Baghdad to Diyala province to see how the farmers are doing. Unlike most Iraqis they can feed themselves and take advantage of the high price of foodstuffs. Beside the Diyala river I sit in the garden of a successful farmer who agrees he has made money from selling oranges, though he complains the price of grapes has collapsed.

Then he produces x-ray plates. They are of the chest of his 24-year-old cousin Ahmed, who has a weak heart, taken in London 13 years ago. He has not been able to go back for a second operation because of the Iran–Iraq War, the Gulf War and then sanctions. I go to another, poorer farm and the same thing happens. The farmer produces an elderly x-ray of the skull of his five-year-old daughter Fatima. She cannot stand upright.

There is something infinitely touching about these old x-rays. They seem to symbolise the desperation of ordinary Iraqis over sanctions. The farmers should be better off than the townspeople, but almost all of them have at least one relative ill or dying because he or she cannot get proper medical help.

8 August 1998

Iraq is not the first country in the world to see its economy collapse and its people impoverished. But it is unique in one respect. The disaster to its people was caused directly by the action of the United Nations. In 1990, before the UN Security Council imposed sanctions, the main health problem for Iraqi children was obesity. In March this year a survey by UNICEF showed that 58 per cent of Iraqi children under five suffer from malnutrition.

The highly experienced and skilled heads of UN agencies in Baghdad, people who have spent their lives aiding developing countries, are in the bizarre position of overseeing the return of Iraq to a pre-industrial age. 'Acute malnutrition here is about the same as in Haiti,' says Dr Habib Rejeb, who heads the World Health Organisation in the Iraqi capital. 'Everything is breaking down. People have to drink polluted water … so they become too sick to benefit from food.'

Officials from the United States and Britain, the hawks on the Security Council over maintaining sanctions, say that hunger and disease are being dealt with by the oil-for-food plan agreed between the UN and Iraq in

1996. Iraq would be allowed to export some oil and the revenues, under UN control, would be largely spent on food and medicine. The plan is failing. In the bland words of the UNICEF report: 'The "oil-for-food" pro-gramme has not yet made a measurable difference to the young children of Iraq in terms of their nutritional status.' In other words, they are still dying.

Ali al Fawaz, at the Iraqi Ministry of Health, says an additional 50,000 Iraqi children under five died last year compared to 1990. Foreign-aid offi-cials say the true figures are impossible to know because many Iraqis no longer use hospitals. Philippe Heffink, the Belgian head of UNICEF in Iraq, says: 'Whether it is 45,000 or 65,000, the fact is that the number has increased substantially.'

The reason why more food and medicine, which started to arrive 18 months ago, has not reduced the number of Iraqis starving or dying is simple. The infrastructure is collapsing. Iraq lies on the flat Mesopotamian plain. Water and sewage have to be pumped. This requires electricity, but output has dropped from 10,000MW eight years ago to 4,000MW today.

What has thrown the infrastructural breakdown into stark relief is a freak heat wave this summer. At its best, Iraq is really a desert, split by the Tigris and Euphrates rivers, and has one of the most torrid climates in the world. At this time of year the temperature in Baghdad is normally about 45C (113F) in the shade. This summer it is four or five degrees hotter. People and animals need more water. Air conditioners are used more. The pressure on the power station is too great and there are electricity cuts, seven or eight hours a day in Baghdad and 20 hours in the country.

Denis Halliday, the UN's Humanitarian Co-ordinator for Iraq, resigned last month because of his frustration at what he sees as the UN's 'Band-Aid' approach to the crisis in Iraq. America and Britain argue that if the Iraqi people are suffering so badly, then it is the fault of Saddam Hussein and his government. If they came clean to the UN about Iraq's non-conventional weapons, then sanctions would be lifted. But the UN has always been ambivalent about the circumstances under which it would agree to lift sanctions. Sometimes it is said that they will stay until Saddam Hussein is removed, as well as disclosure on weaponry. Ordinary Iraqis say they have no influence over either decision and ask why they should be made to suffer.

None of the heads of the UN agencies in Baghdad I speak to show any doubt that the present system is a disaster. Ironically, before the Gulf War, it was doves in the West who wanted sanctions and the hawks who called for bombing. Iraq suffered both, and eight years later sanctions have turned out to be the crueller option, killing far more Iraqis than the bombs.

18 December 1998

By daylight they look like large black aerial torpedoes moving surprisingly slowly towards their target. By night they are invisible until they explode. They are the cruise missiles which have been falling on Baghdad for two days, sending fire into the air.

Already war in Iraq has its routine. The first warning of an attack is the howling of the air-raid sirens. The United States and Britain say they have wiped out Iraq's air defences, but some radar must still be operating because the sirens are usually right in predicting an attack.

The streets start emptying in the Iraqi capital soon after dark. This is a city where life is traditionally nocturnal. Shops and restaurants stay open late. No more. Even in districts like the mixed Christian-Muslim neighbourhood of Karada, which is known for its nightlife, most shops put up their metal gratings an early hour. There are still cars in the streets but they drive fast and ignore traffic lights.

Some minutes after the sirens sound come the first specks of anti-aircraft fire. Red balls of fire drift upwards slowly. Then the anti-aircraft shells burst into flecks of white light. There is little tracer fire, though occasionally you hear the rattle of a Kalashnikov machine gun, as if an Iraqi was firing into the air in frustration.

It is not like the V1s which hit London in 1944. There is no sound from the incoming rockets. The anti-aircraft fire weaves uncertainly across the sky, as if the gunners are unsure of their aim, and a ball of light expands on the horizon as the missile strikes. For a moment the tall buildings in Baghdad are illuminated by the flash. Then, depending on the distance from the explosion, there is the crash of the rocket's detonation. When the missile strike is close, you feel the warm gust of air from the blast.

This is a televisual war. The camera crews, gathered on the roof of the Iraqi Ministry of Information on the banks of the river Tigris, provide a graphic but somewhat deceptive view of what is happening. Their night vision equipment, amplifying ambient light, makes the explosions look even more spectacular than they really are.

Most of the missiles are falling on the outskirts of the city. But the centre is also being hit. One fell on the Military Industry Ministry near the Al-Rashid hotel. But the 'surgical strikes' are not as surgical as the Ministry of Defence in London, or the Pentagon in Washington, make them sound. One missile landed on a substantial house in a residential district; it is difficult to see what the bombers were aiming at. It seems likely that the rocket was off course, or had been shot down.

The attack is not as dangerous or devastating as the Gulf War. Then the allies destroyed the city's power station on the first flight, dropping metallic strands on the power lines to fuse the wires. The telecommunication towers disappeared entirely and the telephones ceased to work. Refineries were destroyed and there was no petrol in a country which has some of the biggest oil reserves in the world. None of this has happened this time.

But although the bombing is not as bad as 1990–91, Iraq is weaker than it was. Nothing angers ordinary Iraqis more than to hear that they are not suffering from real malnutrition because of international sanctions. Dr Al Bayauni, a scientist, says he has just heard Tony Blair claim Iraq is a food exporter. 'What do we export except a few dates?' he says with disgust.

20 January 2001

Iraqis tell a story illustrating the ruthlessness of their government. It seems the Americans, Russians, British and Iraqis held a competition to capture rabbits in a forest. The Americans won. They offered money and visas and were overwhelmed by enthusiastic rabbits rushing out to give themselves up. The Russians came second. They bombarded the forest with heavy artillery and, in a few hours, the surviving rabbits surrendered. The British approach took longer. Through cunning diplomacy they managed to divide the rabbit forces into two factions, one of which handed the other to the British.

The Iraqi team went into the forest and failed to re-emerge. Hours passed. The other teams became worried, and started searching for the Iraqis. Eventually they heard the sound of blows. In a clearing they found the Iraqi team, who had captured a deer and tied it to a tree. The Iraqis were beating it, shouting fiercely: 'Go on, admit it! Confess you are a rabbit.'

To write stories about atrocities in Saddam Hussein's Iraq has always been easy. He became president in 1979 after a bloodbath at the top of the ruling party. In 1988–89 some 182,000 Kurds disappeared. Ali Hassan al-Majid, a cousin of Saddam's, oversaw their disappearance. When a Kurdish delegation asked him what had happened to them, he shouted angrily: 'What is this exaggerated figure of 182,000? It couldn't have been more than a hundred thousand!'

The regime takes a certain macho pride in its brutality. Its cameramen have shot film of firing squads in action. The government tackled a crime wave by cutting off the hands of alleged offenders and showing the severed limbs on television. Defectors from Iraqi security forces have disclosed horrific details of torture and mass executions in the prisons.

I used to write extensively about the atrocities, but in the late 1990s I began to have misgivings about their impact. The problem is that they give a distorted view of what is happening in Iraq. The country is obviously run by a very nasty regime, but since the crushing of the rebellions at the end of the Gulf War in 1991, exactly 10 years ago, UN sanctions have killed far more ordinary Iraqis than Saddam Hussein.

Sanctions against Iraq have never been fully understood by the outside world. They are far more rigorous than those imposed on South Africa, Serbia or any other country. They are more an exaggerated version of the old Soviet system of central planning. Under the oil-for-food programme all Iraqi government contracts are processed by the UN in New York. Most are examined by a special UN committee, dominated by the US and Britain, which decides if any item has a military use.

The result of this prolonged economic siege of the Iraqi people has been devastating. Iraq's economy has been destroyed. This comes through even in the lumbering bureaucratic prose of the latest UN report, which speaks of 'pauperisation and growing food insecurity'. Because of the central control of New York, the Iraqi government cannot perform day-to-day maintenance. So the oil industry, electric power system and water supply are collapsing. Some 90 per cent of raw sewage goes into the rivers from which people drink.

Kofi Annan, the UN secretary-general, has admitted that the sanctions regime has led to 'the worsening of a humanitarian crisis'. Only Peter Hain, the British foreign office minister with responsibility for Iraq, has the gall to claim that the Iraqi government has lots of money and wonders: 'Why do we still see pictures of malnourished and sick children?'

THREE

Regime Change

Iraq, 2003

8 April 2003

Even Saddam Hussein, arch-survivor though he is, must see that the end of his regime is near as American columns easily penetrate the heart of Baghdad after a war in which the US and Britain have so far lost no more than 121 dead. But in his victory, President Bush has created the very situation that his father avoided at the end of the 1991 Gulf War, when he refused to press on to Baghdad and allowed Saddam to crush in blood the great Kurdish and Shia uprisings. His son could just get away with it if he plays his cards very carefully. The Iraqis are exhausted by almost a quarter of a century of wars and deprivation. There is an almost palpable desire for a normal life.

But the omens are not very good. The first great difference between the 1991 and the 2003 wars is that the international context is completely altered. In the first war there was a genuine international alliance. In the second, after US and British failure at the UN, there is a lack of legitimacy. Regional powers such as Turkey, Syria and Iran all feel threatened by what has happened. While a large American land army remains in Iraq there is not much they can do about it, but in the longer term they will seek to make sure, by backing one Iraqi faction or another, that they have a say in the future of the country.

Everything depends on what kind of government the US tries to impose on Iraq. The declared aim of the war by the US and Britain was that Saddam posed a threat to the region and the world because of his secret arsenal of weapons of mass destruction. The low level of allied casualties and the lack of any evidence so far that Saddam possesses such weapons makes the supposed threat from the Iraqi leader look ever more mythical.

This puts a particular onus on the US to justify the war by making sure that the Iraqis have a better life after it. The best course for the Americans would be to turn over the running of Iraq to a transitional United Nations authority until a democratic government is elected. But since one of the purposes of the neo-conservatives in Washington in launching the war was to downgrade the functions of the UN to a purely humanitarian agency, this is unlikely to happen.

A problem is that there is no Iraqi opposition ready to take over that would not be seen as carpetbaggers by the majority of Iraqis. Indeed, many carpet bags have been packed in the last few months. 'I keep getting excited telephone calls in the middle of the night from Iraqis abroad saying the Americans have asked to see them,' one opposition leader tells me. 'They all think they are going to be minister of this or that and almost all are going to be disappointed.' Opposition to Saddam within Iraq in the last 30 years has been almost impossible because of the savagery of the repression. As a result, the only parts of the opposition not wholly dependent on foreign powers are the Kurdish parties that rule a de facto independent state in northern Iraq. But they have their own Kurdish agenda.

The US may not have a lot of time. If it could immediately raise the living standards of Iraqis by ensuring that an interim administration has cash to spend, then this might defuse hostility for the moment. But it is not clear that an administration as ideological as the present one in Washington will be able to address Iraqi needs. According to CNN, US troops were at one moment trying to charge thirsty villagers in southern Iraq for bottles of water.

The US has quarrelled with so many allies in order to carry out its invasion of Iraq that it has to try to make a success of its occupation. But it has done little political planning. It has created a host of enemies with every reason to make sure that the US does not have a happy time here. The entry of US tanks into Baghdad may be the high point of American involvement in this complex and dangerous country.

14 April 2003

A machine gun chatters just outside the gate of the biggest hospital in Mosul just as Dr Ayad Ramadani, the hospital director, is blaming the Kurds for the orgy of looting and violence which has engulfed Iraq's northern capital. 'The Kurdish militias were looting the city,' he explains. 'Today the main protection is from civilians organised by the mosques.' This is not quite fair on the Kurds, since Arabs have also been doing their share of looting in Mosul over the past few days, ransacking everything from the Central Bank to the university. But there is no doubt that the Arabs, who make up three-quarters of Mosul's population, are blaming the Kurds for devastating their city.

The downfall of Saddam Hussein has exacerbated, to a degree never seen before, the ethnic and religious tensions between Kurds, Sunni Arabs and Shia Arabs, the three great communities to which almost all Iraqis belong. But, deep though differences were between them in the past, there is little history of communal violence in the country on the scale of Protestants and Roman Catholics in Belfast or Muslims and Christians in Beirut. This may now be changing. Much of the looting in Baghdad is by impoverished Shia from great slums like Saddam City attacking the homes of wealthier Sunni, who have traditionally made up the establishment.

The United States has a lot to answer for in allowing the violence to continue for so long. In Baghdad, American troops have been notoriously inactive while shops and homes are being looted. Mobs of looters were able to take over Mosul because almost no American soldiers were present. The reason for their absence was that the US had rushed 2,000 men, most of its slender force in the north, to take over the Kirkuk oilfields. Only a few hundred soldiers were available for Mosul. The chants of anti-war protesters about how the conflict is all about control of Iraqi oil do not seem as over-stated today as they did a month ago.

The failure of the US Army to stop the looting is only the latest manifestation of a theme evident in American policy before and during the war. Although the conflict is justified as a fight to liberate the Iraqi people, their involvement has been discouraged and their existence ignored. According to one Iraqi who met George Bush just before the war, the president was intrigued to learn, apparently for the first time, that Iraq is inhabited by two sorts of Muslims, Sunni and Shia, with deep differences between them.

Some of the ethnic and religious conflicts emerging should not come as a surprise. Soon after the British captured Baghdad in 1917, the civil commissioner, Captain Arnold Wilson, wrote a plaintive note to London, arguing that the new state being created out of three former Turkish provinces could only be 'the antithesis of democratic government'. This was because the Shia majority rejected domination by the Sunni minority, but 'no form of government has been envisaged which does not involve Sunni domination.' The Kurds in the north, Wilson prophetically pointed out, 'will never accept Arab rule'.

It is important not to project these arguments too far into the future. Iraqi nationalism did develop after British occupation. Iraqi Shia, the majority in the Iraqi Army, did fight against Shia Iran during the Iran–Iraq War. Kurdish leaders today do recognise that, surrounded by hostile powers, full independence for Kurdistan is not feasible. Real autonomy within Iraq, and a share of power in Baghdad, is the better option.

Iraqi liberals often argue that the extent of communal differences in Iraq has been exaggerated and that the violence experienced by Shia, Sunni and Kurd has come from the government in Baghdad. They point out that neither the Sunni nor the Shia communities are monolithic and, in any case, Saddam Hussein stoked communal differences to his advantage. Some truth is evident in this, but even Iraqi opposition politicians who argue this optimistic view to me soon start talking about Shia, Sunni and Kurd as if they are immutable categories.

Saddam Hussein's state was always deeply sectarian. On the day Kirkuk fell I talked to 10 Iraqi Army deserters, all private soldiers, who had been defending a large village. Nine of them were Shia from the south of Iraq and one was a Turkoman. Although they came from different units, not one of the soldiers had met a Sunni Muslim who was a private soldier or a Shia who was an officer.

The history of the past 30 years has exacerbated ethnic differences. For instance, Kurds in the northern three provinces, which have had de facto independence for 12 years, seldom now speak Arabic. Six weeks ago I was speaking to about a hundred Peshmerga, as Kurdish soldiers are known. (This started off as a private interview with their commanders, but in true democratic spirit their men gathered round to shout agreement or disagreement.) When I asked how many spoke Arabic as well as Kurdish only three put up their hands.

In 1991 the Shia and Kurds rose against President Saddam but the Sunni heartland did not. In the following years, Shia religious leaders within Iraq were systematically assassinated and their followers persecuted. I used to think that Sunni or Christian friends in Baghdad were exaggerating when they expressed terror at what would happen if the Shia of Saddam City or the south ever revolted, but it turns out that they were right.

What gives these differences such a terrible edge is the economic misery of most of the Iraqi population. Many of the looters in Kirkuk and Mosul triumphantly take home almost valueless stolen goods like broken pieces of corrugated iron or shabby old chairs. In Kurdistan, often presented as doing better than the rest of Iraq, 60 per cent of the population would be destitute without the food rations provided by the United Nations' Oil-for-Food Programme.

With so many Iraqis living on the edge of starvation, it is hardly surprising that they have taken the chance over the past week to loot anything they can get their hands on. For the last 12 years in Baghdad you would see men standing all day in open-air markets trying to sell a few cracked earthenware plates or some old clothes. They were the true victims of UN sanctions while Saddam Hussein could pay for gold fittings to the bathroom in his presidential palace.

For all the crimes of Saddam Hussein, the greatest reality in the lives of most Iraqis for over a decade has been this economic devastation. The terrible poverty fuels the fury of the mobs of looters raging through Iraqi cities. It is exacerbating religious and ethnic tensions which otherwise might lie dormant. Unless the Iraqi poor feel their lives are improving, the US and Britain—now responsible for Iraq—may soon find that they too have become a target for their rage.

28 April 2003

At an American military checkpoint on the road north of Kirkuk, two US soldiers are holding up placards, each of which has a message written in Kurdish. One says: 'Drivers must get into one lane,' the other: 'Carrying weapons is forbidden.'

The problem is that the soldiers, being unable to read Kurdish, have mixed up the placards so one is angrily waving his sign—forbidding weapons—in front of a car which has tried to jump the queue, while a hundred yards down the road a harassed-looking officer is asking drivers in English, which they do not speak, if they are armed and he is only receiving benign smiles and thumbs-up signs in return.

It is easy enough to mock ordinary American soldiers being baffled in trying to establish their authority in one of the most complicated societies in the world. But it is still extraordinary that the US should have spent so long planning a military campaign with so little thought about the likely political consequences inside Iraq.

The looting of cities should not have come as a great surprise. It is an Iraqi tradition in times of war. In the First World War the British and Turkish armies, fighting each other in the provinces which became Iraq, complained of the speed with which looters ransacked battlefields, sometimes pausing to slit the throats of the wounded, long before the shooting had stopped.

During the great Shia and Kurdish uprisings of 1991, government offices and museums were systematically sacked, as they were in 2003. Driving around northern Iraq over the past few weeks I always became nervous if I could not see looters in battered pick-ups—because only something very dangerous could have deterred them.

The failure to stop the looting has damaged American prospects for restoring even temporary stability. So too has the slowness in restoring electricity, water and petrol supplies. The US only convened a meeting of the Iraqi official in charge of public utilities in Baghdad yesterday. In Berlin in 1945 Soviet generals had called together German officials in charge of electricity, water and sewage six days before the city's fall.

The US could claim to be the victim of some horribly bad advice from Iraqi expatriates. Take the account of Professor Kanaan Makiya, a veteran opponent of Saddam Hussein, for example. Describing his meeting with George Bush at the start of the year, he was asked by the president: 'What reaction do you expect from the Iraqis to the entry of US forces into their cities?' To this, Professor Makiya replied reassuringly: 'The Iraqis will welcome US forces with flowers and sweets when they come in.'

Many of the current problems are temporary. Electricity and water supplies will have to be restored (electricity is vital in Iraq because the flatness of the Mesopotamian plain means that everything has to be pumped). Above all, an occupation authority will have to get round to paying salaries to government employees. The state is by far the biggest employer in Iraq and, scanty though these salaries are, they are vital for restoring the economy and the administration.

But if a US occupation develops long-term weaknesses this will not have a lot to do with looting, spectacular though it is, or the breakdown of the Iraqi administration. It will stem rather from whether Washington is, in effect, planning a classic colonial occupation, giving power only to Iraqis wholly dependent on the US. The signs are not very good. Asked about the visibly growing influence of the Shia clergy, a senior member of the US administration said: 'We don't want to allow Persian fundamentalism to gain any foothold. We want to find more moderate clerics and move them into positions of influence.'

Today, the US is convening a meeting in Baghdad of some 300 Iraqis to form the nucleus of an interim administration. Most are former exiles seen as American pawns by ordinary Iraqis. And looking at the names of some of the more dubious characters, it may be that the real looting of Iraq is still to come.

The US can probably control Iraq for the moment by garrisoning the main towns and getting the administration running again. But in the longer term it is very vulnerable. With the exception of Kuwait, none of Iraq's neighbours want a long-term American occupation of Iraq to succeed.

In the 1920s, Britain solved the problem of how to rule Iraq by returning power to the Sunni Muslims who had traditionally ruled. The US might like to do this, but since the Sunni make up only 20 per cent of the population this would inevitably mean a dictatorship. On the other hand, free elections would see the long-awaited triumph of the Shia which the US, fearful of an increase in Iranian influence, is so eager to avoid.

In their current triumphant mood, George Bush and Tony Blair show no sign of appreciating the depth or extent of the morass they have entered. Six months ago an Iraqi friend told me he was all in favour of the US going to war to get rid of Saddam, but he added: 'My only fear is that, before it starts, the US will realise that this war is much against its own best interests.'

18 June 2003

As he marches with a demonstration of unemployed former soldiers, Ryad Abdul Wahab draws up his shirt to show the stump of his right arm. 'I was wounded in the fighting at the airport during the war and now I can get no pension,' he says. 'How can I survive?'

Most of the demonstrators are officers from the 400,000-strong Iraqi Army dissolved several weeks ago by L. Paul Bremer, the US chief administrator. Many of them say they have nothing to live on and are being punished, though they had refused to fight for Saddam Hussein. 'We did not fight for Saddam but we will fight for our children,' says Major Kassim Ali, formerly an artillery officer. He says they want back pay, pensions and the re-establishment of the army. Several of the officers are old and only nominally part of Saddam Hussein's armed forces, but were not allowed to retire by the previous regime. Others say that during the war, US planes dropped leaflets on them promising fair treatment if they did not fight.

Bremer's disbandment of the regular army, the least politicised of Iraq's numerous security agencies, has been criticised for the social dislocation it is causing. Some of the officers at the demonstration even threaten suicide attacks on American soldiers.

As the protesters gather outside the arched gate of the main US head-quarters in central Baghdad, beside the bombed-out planning ministry, an American military police convoy drives up. Demonstrators bang on the sides of the vehicles. American soldiers open fire, and in an instant two demonstrators are dead.

20 June 2003

As American troops step up their hunt for Saddam Hussein, people in his home village of al-Awja, overlooking the Tigris north of Baghdad, view the fate of their most famous son with mixed feelings. On the wall of the gatehouse to Saddam's local palace somebody has written: 'It is your house Saddam and it will always flourish and we will guard it for ever.' But al-Awja is not a stronghold of pro-Saddam loyalists. Many of its 1,000 people suffered during his long reign or drew no benefit from living in the village where the former Iraqi leader was born in 1937.

Sheikh Ahmad Ghazi, the leader of the Albu Nasir tribe into which Saddam was born, says it is difficult to explain to Americans, and even Iraqis, that while some of his tribe flourished others were persecuted. 'He killed my own brother in 1995,' he says. A well-educated engineer who speaks fluent English, Sheikh Ahmad says that the village is the last place that Saddam or his immediate entourage would take refuge because of deep divisions within the tribe and the local community.

American military commanders clearly had a different view during the war. In an orchard below the low hill on which al-Awja stands is a long house where Sheikh Ahmad's father and predecessor as leader of the Albu Nasir, Ghazi Ahmad al-Khatab, was shot dead by US troops who arrived by helicopter on the night of 12 April. Blood still stains the floor where he fell. Ahmad Ghazi and three of his brothers were arrested and later released with apologies.

By the family's account Sheikh Ghazi was not armed when he opened the door to American soldiers, though given the fear of looting this sounds unlikely. Iraqi villagers have always carried weapons, but with the current looting they often have them close at hand. As a result, when American forces bang on a door after dark they are frequently met by a farmer with a rifle who thinks they are thieves, sometimes with fatal results for the occupant. Iraqis also talk about searches of the women's quarters in their homes, action seen as insulting and unacceptable.

Sheikh Ahmad sounds depressed and just occasionally amused by his difficulties in explaining the complexities of Iraqi politics and tribal life to successive American commanders in al-Awja. 'They seem to get most of their ideas of the Arab world from Hollywood,' he says. 'We have also had three different commanders here in six weeks so I have to start all over again with each one. They never seem to talk to each other. Since they don't pass on anything I've stopped talking to them.'

Aside from the abandoned palaces of Saddam and his family, al-Awja is little different from other Iraqi villages in the Sunni Muslim heartlands north of Baghdad. The columns of American armour on the roads seem like visitors from another planet. The slogan writers express regret for Saddam, but Sheikh Ahmad says that the real danger is the growing anger among local young men at the American occupation.

24 June 2003

American soldiers in Baghdad are not popular. Iraqis wonder why, with so many US soldiers in and around the capital, armed looters and thieves still prowl the streets. Last week, as the temperature soared to well over 100F, refrigerators and air-conditioning did not work because in many districts there are only one or two hours of electricity a day.

Above all, Baghdad is alive with frightening rumours because the Coalition Provisional Authority (CPA), the lumbering name of the US occupation administration, has somehow failed to get radio and television carrying credible information back on the air. One rumour, almost universally believed in Baghdad, is that gangs working for Kuwaitis are kidnapping Iraqi girls and taking them off to servitude in Kuwait. Forty kidnapped girls are said to have been discovered in a house in al-Mansur district, though nobody knows what street it was in.

The success or failure of the US occupation is still on a knife-edge. With the capture of Baghdad on 9 April, the US won an easy military victory but it has been unable to turn this into a political victory in the following 10 weeks. It might still do so but it faces many obstacles.

So far there have been only sporadic attacks by gunmen armed with automatic rifles and rocket-propelled grenade launchers. The blowing up of oil and gas pipelines in western Iraq may presage something more, but there is no co-ordinated guerrilla warfare. Armed resistance is confined to the Sunni Muslim heartlands in Baghdad and central Iraq. There have been no attacks in Kurdistan, where people are euphoric at the outcome of the war. They have regained Kirkuk and lands lost during 40 years of ethnic cleansing. They need the US to prevent Turkish intervention. Most important, there has been almost no resistance to the US in parts of Iraq dominated by the Shia Muslims, who make up at least 55 per cent of the population. They hope that their moment has come after centuries of oppression.

At the weekend I saw a small demonstration of Shia outside the al-Mansour hotel in Baghdad marching on the CPA headquarters housed inside Saddam Hussein's Republican Palace. The leader of the protest was Sheikh Ahmad al-Zirjawi al-Baghdadi, a Shia cleric in turban and dark robes, looking very much like Hollywood's idea of an Islamic fanatic foaming with anti-American rhetoric. In fact, he said: 'We are not asking for American troops to withdraw but for free elections.' This is the real problem for the US. It promised democracy for Iraq but it is frightened of the Shia representatives winning. It is therefore trying to delay elections until it thinks that people acceptable to Washington will get elected. This may be a long time coming.

Even if the US allows, prior to an Iraqi national election, a genuinely representative Iraqi political council with real power, it will be dealing with people it does not like. But if it does not do so, it will have increasing difficulties in ruling Iraq by military force alone.

24 July 2003

There used to be a mosaic of President George H. W. Bush on the floor at the entrance to the al-Rashid Hotel in Baghdad. It was placed there soon after the first Gulf War in 1991 and was a good likeness, though the artist gave Bush unnaturally jagged teeth and a slightly sinister grimace. The idea was that nobody would be able to get into the hotel, where most foreign visitors to Iraq stayed in the 1990s, without stepping on Bush's face. The mosaic did not long survive the capture of the city on 9 April and the take-over of the al-Rashid by US officials and soldiers. One American officer, patriotically determined not to place his foot on Bush's features, tried to step over the mosaic. The distance was too great. He strained his groin and had to be hospitalised. The mosaic was removed.

Almost all of the thousands of pictures of Saddam which used to line every main street in Baghdad have gone, though for some reason the one outside the burned-out remains of the old Mukhabarat (Intelligence) headquarters survives. My favourite was straight out of *The Sound of Music*: it showed Saddam on an Alpine hillside, wearing a tweed jacket, carrying an alpenstock and bending down to sniff a blue flower.

Other equally peculiar signs of Saddam's presence remain. The Iraqi Natural History Museum was thoroughly ransacked by looters, who even decapitated the dinosaur in the forecourt. In the middle of one large ground-floor gallery almost the only exhibit still intact is a stuffed white horse which, when living, belonged to Saddam. Wahad Adnan Mahmoud, a painter who also looks after the gallery, told me the horse had been given to the Iraqi leader in 1986 by the King of Morocco. The King had sent a message along with it saying he hoped that Saddam would ride the horse through the streets of Baghdad when Iraq won its war with Iran. Before this could happen, however, a dog bit the horse, and it died. Saddam issued a Republican Decree ordering the dog to be executed.

'I don't know why the looters didn't take the horse—they took everything else,' complained Mahmoud, who was in the wreckage of his office painting a picture of Baghdad in flames. 'It isn't even stuffed very well.' The horse, he added, was not the only dead animal which had been sent from Saddam's Republican Palace to be stuffed by the museum. One day an official from the Palace had arrived with a dead dolphin in the back of a truck. He said the leader wanted it stuffed. The museum staff protested that this was impossible because a dolphin's skin contained too much oil. Mahmoud laughed as he remembered the terrified expression on the official's face when told that Saddam's order could not be obeyed.

Saddam had three enthusiasms in the 1990s, two of which still affect the appearance of Baghdad. Soon after defeat in Kuwait he started obsessively building palaces for himself and his family. None of these is likely to be knocked down since they now serve as bases for the US Army and the CPA. Paul Bremer, the head of the CPA, has his headquarters in the enormous Republican Palace beside the Tigris, where he and his staff live in an isolation comparable to Saddam's. Then, in the mid-1990s, Saddam began to build enormous mosques, the largest of which, the Mother of Battles mosque at the old Muthana municipal airport, was only beginning to rise from its foundations when the regime collapsed. Saddam's third craze, beginning about three years ago, was more surprising. He started to write novels. He dictated them to his secretaries and they were published anonymously in cheap editions, but Iraqis were left in no doubt as to the author. The critical response was adulatory, the print runs enormous. After the fall of Baghdad, documents were found in the Mukhabarat headquarters instructing agents to buy the books and get their contacts to do the same. Copies of his most recent novel, *The Impregnable Fortress*, as well as an earlier volume called *Zabiba and the King*, are still for sale in the Friday book market on al-Mutanabbi Street.

They cannot do much about the palaces and mosques Saddam built, but the US Army and the CPA are obsessed with removing every mention of his name from Baghdad. You cannot enter the main children's hospital without walking through a stream of raw sewage, and on some days there is no electricity or water, but earlier this month two cranes were at work removing large green overhead signs for Saddam International Airport. The US officials now in charge of Iraq seem to believe that their problems will be over if all evidence of Saddam's existence is eliminated. This obsession explains in part the political failure of the US and Britain after their swift military victory. Their demonisation combined with Saddam's own personality cult to produce a picture of Iraqi society as being wholly dominated by one man. In fact, the regime's support base was always narrow—this was the reason for its exceptional cruelty.

Iraqis were never going to welcome the US and British Armies with cheering crowds hurling flowers. It is, nevertheless, extraordinary that in only three months the US has managed to generate such fury against its occupation. Guerrilla actions have so far been limited, but they are popular. In the middle of June two men drove up to US soldiers guarding a propane gas station near al-Dohra power station in south Baghdad and opened fire. One of the soldiers was shot through the neck and killed and the other was wounded in the arm. An hour or so later I asked the crowd standing around a pool of drying blood on the broken pavement what they thought of the shooting. They all said they approved of it, and one man said he was off to cook a chicken in celebration.

A month later the attacks have spread to the centre of Baghdad. I was waiting outside the National Museum, where the CPA had arranged a brief showing of the 3000-year-old golden treasure of Nimrud, whisked for the occasion from the vaults of the Central Bank, to demonstrate that life was getting back to normal. Suddenly there was a six-minute burst of firing on the other side of the museum. It is a measure of the chaos in Baghdad that this turned out to be the result of two quite separate incidents. The first was a funeral: as is normal in Iraq, people were firing their guns into the air as a sign of grief. The American troops on the roof of the museum thought they were under attack and shot back. But most of the gunfire was in response to somebody firing a rocket-propelled grenade into an American Humvee in Haifa Street, wounding several soldiers. The surviving soldiers had then opened fire indiscriminately and killed a passing driver. As the Americans withdrew, the crowd, dancing in jubilation, set fire to the already smouldering Humvee.

A week after I had been to look at Saddam's stuffed horse, Richard Wild, a young British freelance journalist, went to the Natural History Museum to get a story about its destruction by looters. He was a tall man with close-cropped blond hair and he was wearing a white shirt and khaki trousers. To an Iraqi he may have looked as if he were working for the CPA. As he stood in a crowd outside the museum a man walked up behind him and shot him in the back of the head, killing him instantly.

There are 55,000 US troops in and around Baghdad but they seem curiously vulnerable. They largely stick to their vehicles; there are very few foot-patrols. They establish checkpoints and search cars, but usually have no interpreters. 'Mou mushkila (no problem),' one driver said when asked to open the boot of his car. 'Don't contradict me,' a soldier shouted. Military vehicles are often stuck in horrendous traffic jams (because of the electricity shortage the traffic lights are not working) making them an easy target for grenades. Just before the attack in Haifa Street I was talking to an American soldier outside the National Museum. The tag on his shoulder read 'Old Ironsides.' I asked him what unit this referred to. He replied: 'The First Armoured Division, the finest armoured division in the world.' But tanks and heavy armour are not much use in Baghdad. A few hours later a sniper shot dead another soldier as he sat in his Bradley Fighting Vehicle by the gates of the museum.

Outside Baghdad the army has been conducting search missions in the villages and giving them such names as 'Desert Scorpion'. The press office puts out statements proudly listing the number of detainees and arms captured and suspicious amounts of money discovered. Villagers protest that they have always had weapons, and need them more than ever because of looters. They also have large amounts of cash, often in $100 bills. Iraqis have not kept much of their money in banks since Saddam closed them just before the first Gulf War. When they reopened the Iraqi dinar was worth only a fraction of its former value.

The guerrilla war does not approach the scale of that in Lebanon in 1983–84 or Northern Ireland in the 1970s and is mostly confined to Sunni Muslim areas, but it is growing in intensity. It is damaging to the US because press coverage can no longer be controlled. Every time a US soldier is shot a horde of television reporters and print journalists descend on the scene. The CPA is very conscious of the fact that it will be more difficult for George W. Bush to win re-election next year on the back of victory in Iraq when US television is still showing pictures of dead and wounded soldiers.

Many of the mistakes the US and British made after the war were very obvious. They allowed the Iraqi state to dissolve overnight. They ignored the mass looting for weeks. They took seriously the advice given by exiled Iraqi groups which had no support within the country. They allowed the civilians in the Pentagon systematically to marginalise the rest of the Administration in Washington. Above all, they were over-confident. 'They believed, because the war had been so easy for them, that they could do what they liked with Iraq,' an Iraqi friend tells me.

Before the invasion most Iraqis wanted to see an end to Saddam Hussein because of the calamities he had inflicted on them, including two disastrous wars. Impoverished by sanctions, they wanted a return to some sort of normality. Expectations were high: they did not see why, once Saddam was gone, they should not live as well as Kuwaitis or Bahrainis. Instead, in the ferocious heat of the summer they have limited electricity, an intermittent water supply and a petrol shortage. Looting has not stopped.

The lesson of the three-week war was that Saddam had little real support. It should have been possible to isolate the senior echelons of the Baath Party, the security and intelligence services and the tribal factions on whom Saddam relied. The Baath Party had about half a million members, but most joined because they could not get a job as a manager, a teacher or even a driver without being a member. Yet from their heavily defended new headquarters US officials issued an edict on 16 May ordering sweeping de-Baathification. Every former member of the Party felt threatened. A few weeks later, the army was disbanded without compensation (this decision was hurriedly reversed a month later as guerrilla attacks increased).

Bush and Blair found it much easier to deal with Iraq when everything that went wrong could be blamed on Saddam. In his weekly press conferences in the National Convention Centre opposite the al-Rashid Hotel, Paul Bremer speaks almost as if Saddam were still in charge. To mounting scepticism and occasional derision from journalists he regularly explains that the lack of electricity and water is the result of sabotage by members of the old regime. The guerrilla attacks, he says, are the last throw of a small number of 'desperate men' still loyal to Saddam. 'Those who refuse to embrace the new Iraq are clearly panicking.' Everything will come right when Saddam is killed or captured; though, contradicting himself, Bremer has also said that the guerrilla attacks are not centrally organised.

Before the war ended the US had danced nervously around the prospect of a provisional government. Even Stalin felt that an indigenous authority would be a useful veil to mask imperial rule when he invaded Poland in 1944, but in Iraq it was soon obvious that the US did not want to share power. When Abu Hatem, a resistance leader who had been fighting Saddam for 17 years, captured the city of Amara (the only Iraqi Arab city to fall to local insurgents) in southern Iraq on 7 April, the CIA ordered him to leave within the hour.

Another problem is that the only Iraqi opposition parties with any demonstrable support inside the country are both Kurdish: the Kurdistan Democratic Party and the Patriotic Union of Kurdistan, who have ruled their enclaves in northern Iraq for a decade. The others are all, by and large, dependent on foreign backers and are despised by most Iraqis. It is not just groups supported by the US, such as the Iraqi National Congress of Ahmed Chalabi or the Iraqi National Accord of Iyad Alawi, that are regarded with suspicion. So, too, is the Iranian-backed Supreme Council for Islamic Revolution in Iraq, led by Muhammad Baqr al-Hakim, which is trying to present itself as the representative of the Shia Muslims who make up the majority of the Iraqi population. When I visited Hakim's office in Najaf one of his guards spoke to me in Farsi before switching to Arabic.

By the end of May, Washington had decided that a provisional administration made up of Kurds and the exiled opposition would not help the occupation. This was certainly right. If the reputation of the opposition among Iraqis was low before the war it was further blackened by the enthusiasm with which they confiscated government buildings and cars. 'They are just looters in suits,' an Iraqi told me in disgust. According to a story in Baghdad (rumours here are always high on supportive detail), one opposition group has managed to seize 67 buildings and 120 vehicles and engaged in a shoot-out when the police tried to recover a car.

The alternative for the US—Saddamism without Saddam—is also difficult. The Iraqi state had largely dissolved in April. Other parts of it, like the army, had been dismantled. Saddam himself had not been captured or killed. And all the while it was becoming obvious that the US and Britain, with casualties mounting, had only limited control of the country. By early July, Bremer and the CPA were showing greater enthusiasm for an Iraqi interim administration—with a broader base than the old exiled opposition—which could reconstitute the police and civil government. The old imperial recipes for controlling an occupied country under the auspices of a client regime are particularly difficult to apply in Iraq: the country is too divided between ethnic, religious, tribal and political groups. But the US, with Britain tagging along behind, has found that direct rule by military force alone is failing. It was so much easier when they could blame everything on Saddam Hussein.

10 September 2003

A friend representing a French company in Washington recently went with some trepidation to Paris with the unwelcome news that he had been told by the Pentagon that there was absolutely no chance of his employers getting a contract in Iraq. He was not looking forward to reporting the total failure of his well-paid efforts, but to his relief the chairman greeted the dire news with prolonged laughter, saying: 'Don't worry. Let's just wait a year or two and then it will be American companies which won't be able to do business with the Iraqis.'

This could be discounted as the evil-minded French watching with delight as the Americans, with Tony Blair loyally chugging behind, sink deeper into the Iraqi quagmire. But the quite correct perception that the US has already failed in Iraq is becoming the common consensus in Iraq as well as much of the rest of the world.

It is a failure of historic proportions. The aim of the war in Iraq was to establish the US as the world superpower which could act unilaterally, virtually without allies, inside or outside Iraq. The timing of the conflict had nothing to do with fear of Saddam's weapons of mass destruction and everything to do with getting the war won in time for the run-up to next year's Presidential election in the US.

The US failure to win a conclusive victory in Iraq is like that of Britain in South Africa during the Boer War. Like the US, Britain went into the war filled with arrogant presumptions about an easy victory. As the conflict dragged on, with a constant trickle of casualties from attacks by the elusive Boers, nationalists from Dublin to Bombay drew the conclusion that the British Empire was not quite as tough as it looked.

In Washington as a visiting fellow at a think tank for the first six weeks of the year, I was continually struck by the ignorance and arrogance of the neo-cons, then at the height of their power. They had all the intolerant instincts of a weird American religious cult, impervious to any criticism of their fantasy picture of Iraq, the Middle East and the rest of the world. Iraqis willing to explain how their country really worked found appointments with senior officials mysteriously cancelled at the last moment, sometimes while they were sitting in the official's waiting room.

This should be the real charge against Tony Blair's government—not that it did not understand what was happening in Baghdad, but that it did not take on board the strange happenings in Washington. There is nothing peculiar about Britain supporting the US come what may, since this has been a priority of British foreign policy for nearly a century. But it should have been realised much earlier in London that this US government is very different from, and more dangerous than, any of its predecessors. The extent and irreversibility of the American failure is not yet appreciated outside Iraq.

11 September 2003

Somewhere in a secret hideout, probably on the Afghan–Pakistani border, Osama bin Laden must be smiling with quiet satisfaction. Two years ago today, members of his Islamic terrorist group al-Qa'ida crashed two planes and their terrified passengers into the Twin Towers of the World Trade Centre in New York and killed nearly 3,000 people. Two more hijacked planes crashed, one into the Pentagon killing 189 people and the fourth was brought down in Pennsylvania with 44 victims.

It was the bloodiest terrorist act in history and it has succeeded in setting the agenda for world politics ever since. Immediately after the atrocity, President Bush declared war on terrorism. This summer, his vice president, Dick Cheney, kept up the rhetoric, declaring that: 'One by one, in every corner of the world, we will hunt the terrorists down and destroy them.' But it is not a war that is going well.

It is not just that the US has failed to eliminate bin Laden, though it has killed or captured some of his senior lieutenants. Al-Qa'ida and similar groups are not like a regular army, which depends on highly trained officers and sophisticated military equipment. The men who flew themselves into the World Trade Centre and the Pentagon used carpet cutters to take over the planes. No, the reason why bin Laden is so pleased today is that he has succeeded in starting the war he always wanted, the war between the US and the Muslim world, and even if he is captured or killed tomorrow it will continue.

The conflicts in Afghanistan and Iraq have created a vast reservoir of recruits for his own and other terrorist organisations. But more than that, the Muslim world as a whole fears it is under attack and the militants are not deterred by the thought of getting caught. From Pakistan to Saudi Arabia, from Indonesia to Algeria, militant leaders are calling for the launch of a new international jihad against coalition forces, and fighters are pouring into Iraq.

This week, after a detailed analysis of the level of terrorist activity since 9/11, Professor Paul Rogers of Bradford University claimed that the US and Britain are actually losing the war on terror. 'Al-Qa'ida is growing in power,' he warned. President Bush and Tony Blair have fallen into a trap. Throughout history, terrorists have aimed to intimidate and draw attention to their cause. But they also have a subtler, less obvious intention. They want to provoke their victims into an overreaction, to tempt them into inflicting collective punishment on whole groups of people hitherto unsympathetic to the terrorists and their aims, and so win themselves new supporters.

In the wake of 9/11, the US needed to make sure that the terrorists who had organised the hijacking of the planes stayed isolated. The whole conspiracy to attack New York and Washington was probably known to fewer than 50 people. But instead, President Bush blamed Afghanistan, Iraq, Iran, Syria and the Palestinians for the tragedy, and threatened punishment against all of them. He would have been better advised to say who he thought was not responsible.

One Iraqi friend, an exile once sentenced to death by Saddam, and who has just returned from Baghdad, tells me: 'The Americans have made a terrible mistake. Islamic militants are flooding into the country because they think they can defeat the Americans in Iraq in the same way that they defeated the Russians in Afghanistan in the eighties. They don't really care about us Iraqis, but Iraq is now their chosen battleground against the US.'

Ambushes of US and British troops are being carried out by a whole range of groups, but there are definite signs that former members of

Saddam's security forces are linking up with Islamic militants from outside the country. Bomb attacks are becoming more lethal and better organised. The US, as Vice President Cheney claimed, may catch some terrorist leaders, but in the chaos of Iraq new ones are being created by the day. The fact is, whatever the claims being made, the US and Britain are not winning the war against terror.

27 October 2003

The thunder of a bomb echoes across Baghdad at about 8:30 a.m. on the first day of the Muslim holy month of Ramadan. It detonates outside the offices of the International Committee of the Red Cross. Seconds earlier, an ambulance packed with explosives had sped towards the building. 'I saw an ambulance coming very fast towards the barrier and it exploded,' says a witness. The blast kills two security guards and eight labourers passing in a lorry. Red Cross staff arriving for work weep in disbelief. Officials are in shock.

Minutes later, explosions reverberate at different points around Baghdad as suicide bombers blow themselves up outside three police stations. In the most lethal assault, at al-Bayaa police station in the al-Doura region, 15 people including an American soldier are killed. In the Shaab district in the north-east of the capital at least eight people die. Outside a fourth police station an unsuccessful bomber—later identified as Syrian—is dragged from his vehicle as he shouts: 'Death to the Iraqi police! You're all collaborators!'

At least 40 are left slaughtered and 220 injured in the bloodiest day in Baghdad since the overthrow of Saddam Hussein. The carnage signals a decisive moment in the Iraqi crisis. Three months ago, the US occupation seemed evenly balanced between success and failure. Today, it has become very hard to see how it can succeed.

'The more progress we make on the ground … the more desperate these killers become,' claims President Bush in response to the bombings. But the concrete face of al-Rashid Hotel—the most visible symbol of the US presence in Baghdad—is chipped and scarred from the previous day's attack when anti-American guerrillas fired a barrage of rockets from a home-made launcher disguised as an electric generator in a blue trailer.

The assault came at 6:10 a.m. as Paul Wolfowitz, the US deputy defence secretary and one of the architects of the invasion, was inside the hotel dressing for a breakfast meeting. Six to eight rockets struck between the seventh and eleventh floors. Guests were thrown from their beds by the blasts and, in one corridor, survivors had to wade through deep water from a burst pipe. In the minutes after the attack, American officials fled in their pyjamas and underpants. Wolfowitz is said to have run to safety, with alarms blaring, down a staircase filled with smoke. The attack killed an American colonel and wounded 15 people.

A shaken-looking Wolfowitz, whose room was on the twelfth floor, said after the attack: 'There are a few who refuse to accept the reality of a new and free Iraq. We will be unrelenting in our pursuit of them.' Iraqis interviewed in Baghdad have very different ideas about what is happening. All, without exception, approve of the attacks on the hotel and American soldiers, but not the suicide bombings because Iraqis are the victims. Omar Qais Zaki, 26, declares: 'I support the attack on al-Rashid but not the others, which only kill Iraqis. The Americans should leave immediately and we should have elections.' Ahmed, a car mechanic, says: 'I was happy when I heard about al-Rashid, but not these latest attacks.'

Meanwhile, the guerrilla attacks north of Baghdad in Sunni Muslim areas are increasing in number and in their sophistication. Crucially, over the past few months there has been a shift in Iraqi opinion that bodes ill for the future of the United States and its allies in Iraq. At the time of the overthrow of Saddam Hussein, Iraqis were evenly divided on whether they had been liberated or were facing an old-style colonial occupation. The majority had always hated Saddam Hussein's brutal regime. Just after the invasion, 43 per cent saw the US-led Allies as 'liberating forces'. A poll earlier this month showed that 15 per cent now see the Americans as liberators. The percentage of Iraqis who see them as occupiers has risen from 46 per cent to 67 per cent.

2 November 2003

A plume of dust and smoke rises from a field just outside Fallujah, west of Baghdad, where a giant American Chinook helicopter, crippled by a missile, has crashed and burned, killing 15 and wounding another 21 of the soldiers and crew on board. It is the worst single military disaster for the US in Iraq since the war to overthrow Saddam Hussein started in March.

The destruction of the helicopter should underline the speed with which the war in Iraq is intensifying: 16 US soldiers were killed in September, 33 in October and a further 16 in just the first two days of November. It is also spreading further north, to the cities of Mosul and Kirkuk. But even as I was driving to Fallujah, just before the helicopter was brought down, I heard on the radio President Bush repeat his old mantra that 'the Iraqi people understand that there are a handful of people who do not want to live in freedom.'

It is an extraordinarily active handful. I heard from a shopkeeper in the centre of Fallujah that a Chinook helicopter had been shot down on the other side of the Euphrates river, which flows through the town. It was only three or four miles away, but on the way we drove past the remains of a US truck which had been blown up two hours earlier by a bomb or rocket-propelled grenade. On the other side of a bridge over the river was a minibus taxi punctured by shrapnel, its interior sodden with blood. Locals claimed it had been hit by a US missile, which killed one passenger and wounded nine others.

The White House and the Pentagon seem unable to take on board how swiftly the US political and military position in Iraq is deteriorating. Even after the attack on the al-Rashid Hotel, narrowly missing Paul Wolfowitz, US generals in Baghdad are still contending to incredulous journalists that overall security in Iraq is improving. In his blindness to military reality Bush sounds more and more like the much-derided former Iraqi infor-mation minister, 'Comical Ali', still claiming glorious victories as the US Army entered Baghdad. Every attack is interpreted as evidence that the 'remnants' of Saddam's regime are becoming 'desperate' at the great prog-ress being made by the US in Iraq.

Two arguments are often produced to downplay the seriousness of the resistance. One is the 'remnants' theory: A small group of Saddam loyalists have created all this turmoil. This is a bit surprising, since the lesson of the war was that Saddam Hussein had few supporters prepared to fight for him. In fact, the 'remnants' of the old regime have become greater in number since the end of the war. The US occupation authority has been the main recruiting sergeant. It has behaved as if Saddam Hussein were a popular leader with a mass following. A friend, long in opposition to Saddam, tells me: 'Two of my brothers were murdered by Saddam, I fled abroad, but now they are going to fire four of my relatives because they were forced to join the Baath party to keep their jobs.'

Another comforting method of downplaying the resistance is to say it is all taking place in the 'Sunni triangle'. The word 'triangle' somehow implies that the area is finite and small. In fact, the Sunni Arabs of Iraq live in an area almost the size of England. Ghassan Atiyah, a distinguished Iraqi

historian and political activist, believes that 'if the Sunni Arabs feel they are
being made second-class citizens they will permanently destabilise Iraq, just
as the Kurds used to do.'

6 November 2003

The centre of the book trade in Baghdad is al-Mutanabbi Street, which
runs between the Tigris and Rashid Street, now shabby and decayed but
once the city's commercial heart. The bookshops are small, and open all
the time; on Friday there is a market, when vendors lay out their books in
Arabic and English on mats on the dusty and broken surface of the road.
Most are second-hand. In the 1990s, after the first Gulf War, I used to walk
around the district looking at books, often English classics once owned by
students. Difficult words were underlined and translated into Arabic in the
margin. There was plenty of stock as the Iraqi intelligentsia, progressively
ruined by sanctions, sold off their libraries.

The market was carefully monitored by a section of al-Amn al-Amm,
the General Security Service, led by Major Jammal Askar, a poet who used
to write verses in praise of Saddam. He oversaw the banning of books on
modern Iraq, mostly histories and memoirs written by exiles, and works by
Shia and Sunni clerics. Even so, books, often printed in Beirut, were smuggled in through Jordan, Syria and Turkey. 'You could bribe the officials at
the border to let in religious books, but not political books,' one bookseller
says. 'We used to take off the covers and replace them with the covers
of Baath Party books which they approved of.' Often only one copy was
brought in, photocopied a hundred or more times and then sold covertly.
The Amn al-Amm, its operations on the street led by a certain Captain
Khalid, launched repeated raids to find out who was selling them.

In 1999 my brother Andrew and I wrote a history of Iraq after the first
Gulf War called *Out of the Ashes: The Resurrection of Saddam Hussein*. It was
later republished in Britain as *Saddam Hussein: An American Obsession*. I
knew the regime would not like it because of its sympathetic treatment of
the Shia and Kurdish uprisings of 1991 and its account of the feuds within
the ruling family, and decided after publication that it would be wise to
keep out of Baghdad for a few years. When it became obvious that the
White House was determined to overthrow Saddam Hussein, I applied to
the Iraqi information ministry for a visa, although I was worried about how
safe it was to do so. Saddam Hussein was not short of critics, and possibly
the regime did not know or care what Andrew and I had written about

them. On the other hand, Saddam had hanged Farzad Bazoft, an *Observer* journalist, as a spy in 1990. When the Kurds arranged with Syria to let me cross the Tigris in a tin boat into Kurdish-controlled territory in northern Iraq, the problem resolved itself.

It turned out I was right to be nervous. After the fall of Baghdad, the new deputy mayor, a book collector, gave me a copy of *Out of the Ashes* in a copperplate long-hand translation into Arabic specially made by the Mukhabarat (Iraqi Intelligence). He said it had been found by looters in the house of Sabawi, Saddam's half-brother who was once the head of al-Amn al-Amm. It turned out that the book was well known to the booksellers in al-Mutanabbi Street and had sold well—mainly, they said, because 'it gave an account of the uprisings in 1991 and of the relationship between Saddam and the US.'

One Friday, halfway along al-Mutanabbi, I met Haidar Mohammed, a man in his mid-thirties with nervous, darting eyes, who had been the main seller of my book. He was known in the street as Haidar Majala, meaning Haidar 'Magazine', because he pretended that he was only interested in selling magazines. He said that he found life flat since the fall of Saddam, 'because in the old days, when I had to take a customer down an alleyway to secretly sell him a book and we both knew we could go to jail, life had a taste to it'. The first copy of *Out of the Ashes* he bought was an Arabic translation made in Beirut and smuggled into Iraq by a man called 'Fadhel', who other booksellers believed was later hanged. Haidar used a photocopier to make 50 copies and sold them to relatives and close friends for two dollars each. He then made another 200 copies and sold them quickly as well. He said: 'Once when a man who had bought the book was arrested in Kerbala I disappeared for three weeks, but he didn't give me away and only told them that he'd bought it on the street from a man he didn't know.'

Haidar, who had been selling books in Baghdad and Najaf since 1994, was finally arrested in November 2000, when he was caught by Captain Khalid with a book by Saad al-Bazzaz, an Iraqi editor, once a Saddam loyalist, who had gone into exile and published an exposé of the regime. 'I pretended I was a little simple and did not know what the book was about,' Haidar said ruefully. 'The judge accepted that my story was true so he only gave me two years in prison, though this was extended to three years when they found out I had deserted from the army.'

The booksellers of al-Mutanabbi are relieved that Major Askar and Captain Khalid have disappeared, but are wary of talking of the future.

These days they are selling books by Shia clerics as well as big pictures of Hussein and Abbas, the Shia martyrs. When I ask a group of booksellers standing beside Haidar what they think will happen, one says, without much confidence, that 'Saddam Hussein was difficult to overthrow, but the Americans will be easier to get rid of.' Iraqis have had difficulty in adjusting to the pace of events since the beginning of this year: the bombing of Baghdad, the fall of Saddam, the looting, the broiling summer without electricity, the banditry and now the sporadic guerrilla attacks and car bombs. New problems appear almost daily.

Paul Bremer claims, somewhat ludicrously, that life in Baghdad is back to normal. An energetic and arrogant man, who wears a smart New York suit with army boots protruding from the bottom of his trousers, he is inclined to speak of 'the extraordinary progress made since liberation'. With each car bomb or attack his tone gets shriller: 'The terrorists know that the Iraqi people and the coalition are succeeding in the reconstruction of Iraq.' Bremer is keen to sell Iraq as a success, and so, of course, is the US president, who mentioned recently that satellite television antennae are sprouting over Baghdad. It is true that the streets look cleaner and the heaps of rubbish are disappearing: 180,000 street cleaners have been hired at $3 a day. Some of them are assiduously painting curbstones white and yellow. The electricity supply is better and there are fewer power cuts than there were at the height of the summer heat. There are thousands of US-recruited police back on the streets, so Iraqis are less frightened of being robbed, raped or murdered than they were three months ago. They no longer lock themselves in their houses or refuse to send their daughters to school for fear of kidnappers. But they do not compare the situation today with what things were like during the first two terrible months after the US captured Baghdad: they compare it with life as it was 12 months ago under Saddam Hussein. And for most Iraqis life has not improved. For many it has got worse.

The overwhelming political and economic fact is that 70 per cent of the labour force—12 million people out of a total population of 25 million, according to the Ministry of Labour—is out of work. Engineers try to make a little money selling glasses of tea to passers-by from a table on the pavement. Men stand all day in the markets trying to sell a bunch of blackened bananas. As under Saddam Hussein, it is only the ration of basic foodstuffs provided almost free by the state that fends off starvation. There is a horrible desperation in the hunt for work. A Russian company asked a man who was trying to get a job as a driver about his qualifications. He said he felt he should get the job because, quite apart from his great experience as a driver, he had a live grenade in his pocket. He then showed the grenade to the Russian interviewing him and threatened to remove the pin unless he was immediately taken on.

By allowing the state to dissolve and disbanding the army, the US, in its ignorance, has brought about a revolutionary change in social and ethnic relations in the country. Everyone who was part of the Sunni-dominated Administration has lost out, which is not surprising; but the Government was the only big employer. 'The first mistake occurred when they disestablished the army and police forces,' says Nouri Jafer, the labour under-secretary in the interim government created by the US-appointed Governing Council. 'This created more unemployment because Saddam Hussein had more than a million in the security forces.' So far, the new US-trained army has just one battalion of 700 men in a force which will eventually grow to 40,000. Former conscripts and soldiers queue for hours trying to pick up a final pay-off of $40, and there are often riots. Even former members of the Intelligence service have demonstrated to demand their jobs back. One man, almost in tears, says he had travelled seven times from his home city of Kut, south of Baghdad, and has still not been paid. 'If the US would just pay the salaries of those who have recently lost their jobs I promise you that resistance attacks would go down by 50 per cent,' Nahed al-Ghazi, a sheikh in a village north of Baghdad, who has just had a grenade explode in the forecourt of his house because of his supposed pro-American sympathies, tells me.

Iraqis jokingly call those who have done well out of the collapse and occupation *hawasimi* or 'finalists'. This is a reference to Saddam's prewar claim that Iraqis were about to witness 'a final battle with the Americans'. Newly recruited policemen are hawasimi, said with a slight sneer. (The same word is used about those who are obviously much better off since the looting of Baghdad.) The US is hopeful that the new police force will be the front line against resistance attacks, but when I ask a policeman, who has just caught a car thief in al-Masbah Street, if he is doing anything to stop assaults on Americans, he replies: 'That isn't really our job. What we do is provide security for ordinary Iraqis.' When police in the town of Hawaijah, west of Kirkuk, shot dead a Fedayeen they were warned by local tribesmen to stick to their policing duties if they wanted to stay alive.

The changes in the physical appearance of central Baghdad since

mid-summer leave no doubt where power lies. Ever more elaborate fortifications are being built to defend Saddam Hussein's old Republican Palace
where Bremer and the CPA live and work, inside a sort of Forbidden City.
It is now surrounded by grey prefabricated concrete walls, with red painted
warnings forbidding drivers to stop next to them. The few entrances are
protected by tanks and rolls of razor wire. New notices have gone up saying
it is not permitted to swim in the Tigris outside the palace, presumably for
fear of underwater saboteurs. The British Embassy, abandoning its spacious
enclave, has fled inside the Rashid Hotel, its entrance guarded by Nepalese
soldiers. In future, it will work from a villa inside the Republican Palace.
The attack on the Baghdad Hotel in October led to a new frenzy of construction, with every hotel now sealed off by armed guards. The guards at
the hotel where I live say they do not like the concrete defences because
they give the impression that something suspicious is going on inside. Since
the latest bombings, the US Army has set up a multitude of checkpoints
around Baghdad, producing enormous queues of traffic.

It may not be enough. When there was an explosion in the foreign ministry, just outside the office of the General Council's interim foreign minister,
Hoshyar Zebari, it was first blamed on a rocket-propelled grenade. But it
turned out to have been caused by half a kilo of explosives with a timer—
which could have been left there only by a member of the foreign ministry
staff, about a thousand of whom were inherited from the old regime. 'We
have got the number of suspects down to 80,' one of Zebari's security men
says triumphantly.

The Americans in Baghdad live in conditions of extraordinary isolation.
An Iraqi friend spotted a group of visitors from the US holding a party in
a hotel at which the waiters were all wearing turbans reminiscent of the
Raj. He went up to one of them and said: 'I would like to shake you by the
hand.' Gratified, the American did so. 'Now', my friend said, 'you can go
home and say you met at least one real Iraqi.'

The guerrilla attacks are almost entirely confined to the Sunni heartlands north of Baghdad, though they are better planned than they were and
are spreading further north towards Kirkuk and Mosul. In early October
I went to Baiji, an oil refinery town with a population of 60,000, some
145 miles north of Baghdad, where I was told there had been an uprising.
I was sceptical, suspecting the account was exaggerated, but in the main
street a crowd of a thousand was holding up pictures of Saddam Hussein
and chanting: 'With our blood and with our spirit we shall die for you

Saddam.' The previous morning, the local Iraqi police had fired at demonstrators who were demanding the dismissal of the US-appointed police
chief and wounded four of them. More protesters gathered and burned
down the mayor's office. The police—300 of them—fled to a nearby US
base, where the American officers told them to go back or be sacked. The
police refused, saying they would be killed if they did so. The US military
command has been trying to leave these confrontations with protesters to
Iraqi police to deal with, but finally their tanks moved gingerly back into
Baiji, most areas of which remained in the hands of the protesters. In the
weeks since, there have been pin-prick guerrilla attacks on US troops with
home-made mortars, mines, bombs and Kalashnikovs.

The reasons behind the brief uprising in Baiji are common to all the
Iraqi provinces immediately north of Baghdad. There is anger over the loss
of jobs in the army, security forces and civil service. 'Half the teachers in
the schools have been dismissed because they were Baathists and there is no
one to teach our children,' one man complained. Prices have risen because
cheap Iraqi kerosene and bottled gas are being smuggled into Iran and
Turkey. Protesters set fire to two Turkish road tankers in the main street.
Above all, there is the day-to-day friction with the occupation forces. 'My
nephew Qusai went onto the roof to fix the television antenna and the US
soldiers shot him dead,' Faidh Hamid told me. A US patrol had beaten
an elderly man half to death with their rifle butts because they thought a
mortar had been fired from the window of his house—a Swedish journalist
embedded with the US patrol had watched in horror as the beating took
place. A 75-year-old merchant was trying to recover $16,000 in Iraqi dinars
and $4,500 in gold taken from his house in May during a US raid. He
showed me the petition he had sent to Baghdad: an official had scribbled
a note along the bottom saying the money was being permanently confiscated because a Fedayeen had been found in his house, something the
merchant denied.

The US has the military strength to retake a town like Baiji easily
enough. But the friction points between occupation forces and Iraqis are
so numerous and diverse that there will always be fresh crises. The US lacks
allies not seen as its pawns. In Baiji, the local office of the Iraqi National
Accord, one of the members of the Governing Council, had been set on
fire. There is a self-defeating crudity about the occupation's methods. US
troops routinely tie up those they detain, force them to lie on the ground
and put bags over their heads.

Saddam Hussein should not have been a hard act to follow. Iraqis know that he ruined their country with his disastrous wars against Iran and Kuwait. But in Baiji a clerk at the local registration office for births and deaths said he noticed that over the last couple of months parents of newborn babies had started to name them 'Saddam'.

15 December 2003

The American capture of Saddam Hussein, found hiding in a hole in the ground beneath a farm near Tikrit, marks the end of an era in Iraq. The country is littered with battered portraits of the former president. At the entrance to every Iraqi town is a plinth with his picture, his face now pock-marked with bullet holes or half-smashed by rifle butts, as he looks down on his ruined and occupied country.

In only one respect did Saddam succeed. He wanted to leave his mark on history, to make his name ring out across the world. Through the absurdities of his own personality cult at home and the sometimes equally exaggerated demonisation of his rule by his enemies abroad, the Iraqi leader's name will never be forgotten.

He destroyed Iraq. When he became president in 1979 he gained total control of a country with a well-educated population, an efficient adminis-tration and extensive oil reserves. In a quarter of a century, he impoverished his people, drove many of them into exile and left the Iraqi oilfields in the hands of foreign troops.

He was not without intelligence, but it was the intelligence of the secret policeman and at crucial moments it was almost always overwhelmed by his arrogance. His actions so dramatically affected Iraq, the Middle East and the world that it is easy to forget that he was in many ways a small-time operator whose political base within Iraq was always narrow.

Saddam had no noticeable redeeming features. The savagery of his regime was exacerbated by the divisions within Iraq, but he did what he could to make sure different Iraqi communities felt threatened by each other. In the weeks since the fall of Baghdad, however, Saddam may have drawn some pleasure from seeing the US so swiftly dissipate, in the eyes of Iraqis, any political capital it gained from his overthrow. His capture may further expose how difficult and dangerous it is to govern the country. The glee in Washington today resembles that felt by the US administration in April when the war was won more easily than any of its critics had supposed. But the subsequent occupation was harder than many predicted.

The US must now understand that Saddam himself probably had very little control over the guerrillas who have killed or wounded so many Americans and their allies in the last two months. The resistance cells seem to be loosely organised and mostly home-grown in the towns and villages of central Iraq. There is also the lesson of three wars—the Iran–Iraq War in 1980, the invasion of Kuwait in 1990 and the war this year—that Saddam had peculiarly bad military judgement.

His capture does have one benefit for the US and its allies. It is the first real success they have had since the fall of Baghdad and it will puncture the image that the US administration in Iraq is a sort of Inspector Clouseau figure, making mistake after mistake while confidently claiming victory at every turn. But the imprisonment of the former Iraqi leader does not solve the most serious US problem in Iraq, which is that it does not have local allies with sufficient strength to run the country.

Sometimes the US has tried to reverse its mistakes, but Paul Bremer's administration is a strange lumbering beast which usually only reacts slowly to events around it. For instance, a centrepiece of American policy is to create a new Iraqi army and police force loyal to the new regime. It is then extraordinary that somebody decided to pay the soldiers $70 a month for an exceptionally dangerous job.

The US troops and commanders scattered around Iraqi provincial cities and towns seem to have a much better idea of what is happening. For months they have told anybody who will listen that the Iraqi resistance is locally organised and not controlled from the top by Saddam. In theory the US should be winning this war. Its weakness—and this will continue despite the capture of Saddam—is that the leaders do not quite understand the nature of the war they are fighting. The guerrillas are not very strong. But they can inflict immense political pain in Washington with limited means, and they know it.

One of the curiosities about US and British attitudes to events in Iraq is that it is often based on the belief that ordinary Iraqis do not know what is happening. In fact, they are very sophisticated. For over a decade many have had nothing to do but listen to foreign radio broadcasts in Arabic from the BBC, Monte Carlo and Voice of America. The quality of news they listen to is probably higher than that heard by most people in Europe or the US.

Iraqis learned from an early stage after the fall of Baghdad that the only thing that had an impact on policymakers in Washington was violence.

This does not mean they all favoured or would take part in guerrilla war. But they knew that moderate opposition would get nowhere. Many Iraqis were rather in the position of Roman Catholics in Northern Ireland in the 1970s who strongly disliked the IRA, but had also noted that Westminster only listened to the grievances of their community when it was accompanied by violence.

Now that Saddam is imprisoned it will be impossible to blame Iraqi resistance on his machinations. It is easy to forget that he was a wonderful enemy to have as a target. He was easy to demonise but was militarily and politically incompetent. If the US and Britain exaggerate the impact of the capture of Saddam—as Tony Blair seems to be doing—then none of the fundamental problems in ruling Iraq will be solved, and the guerrilla war will only escalate.

FOUR

Resistance

Iraq, 2004

18 March 2004

Six months ago, as the number of guerrilla attacks and suicide bombings increased, an Iraqi friend in business in Baghdad used to comfort himself by saying: 'The Americans cannot afford to fail in Iraq.' But as the country gets closer to civil war his confidence has ebbed away. Nearly 200 Shia were killed by suicide bombers in and around the holy shrines in Karbala and Khadamiyah in Baghdad on 2 March. A month earlier, there had been an attack on Kurdish leaders and their followers at a festival in Arbil in Iraqi Kurdistan: 100 had died. Each atrocity outdoes its predecessor. In January it had been the turn of the 31 workers killed as they queued to enter the main US headquarters in Baghdad.

A quick way to assess American progress is to take the four-lane highway leading west from Baghdad to the Euphrates. It is a dreary stretch of road, built by Saddam Hussein at the height of the Iran–Iraq War as his main supply route. On the way out of Baghdad, the US Army has cut down or burned date palms and bushes which might give cover to guerrillas, but there are no other indications that the road might be dangerous. In the last nine months, however, more American soldiers have been killed here—or just off the highway, in the dishevelled truck-stop towns of Abu Ghraib, Fallujah, Kaldiyah and Ramadi—than in any other part of Iraq.

Earlier this year, the US military command claimed the number of attacks on its forces was down since the capture of Saddam Hussein in

December. I decided to drive the 70 miles to Ramadi to see if the road was getting any safer. We never got there. On the outskirts of Baghdad we ran into a stalled convoy of tanks and armoured personnel carriers loaded onto enormous vehicle transporters. A soldier stopped us. 'We discovered an IED on the road,' he said, 'and we are trying to defuse it.' Along with other Iraqi cars and trucks, we turned off the road and drove along a track between a stagnant canal and a rubbish dump.

After half an hour we arrived in Abu Ghraib (the site of Iraq's largest prison), in a market full of rickety stalls selling fruit and vegetables. I stepped out of the car to make a call on a Thuraya satellite phone. As I was talking, a US patrol drove by in their Humvees. Suddenly, the vehicles stopped. Half a dozen soldiers ran towards our car, pointing their guns at our chests. 'Get down on your knees and put your hands behind your head,' they screamed. We did both. One of them snatched my Thuraya. When Mohammed al-Khazraji, the driver, said something in Arabic, a soldier shouted: 'Shut the fuck up.' I said I was a British journalist. We waited on our knees until the soldiers lost interest and climbed back into a Humvee. As we drove out of Abu Ghraib we heard the voice of a preacher at a nearby mosque denouncing the occupation. 'The occupiers', he said, 'now attack everybody and make life impossible.'

A few miles further down the road, we reached the turn-off for the town of Fallujah, but it was blocked by US soldiers and members of the Iraqi Civil Defence Corps, one of the paramilitary organisations now being rapidly expanded. A plump Iraqi soldier, resting his hands on his submachine gun, said: 'The Americans are carrying out a big operation and there is a big battle with the mujahedin [jihadis] around a mosque in Fallujah.' He seemed to have little interest in these activities and pointed to a track that would allow us to enter Fallujah avoiding the cordon round the town.

This was not a particularly violent day on this stretch of road. A few days earlier, a Black Hawk medical evacuation helicopter had been shot down by a heat-seeking missile near Fallujah and all nine soldiers on board were killed. Many more die when supply trucks or soft-skinned Humvees are caught by roadside bombs, the notorious IEDs—known to the soldiers as 'convoy killers'—which usually consist of heavy artillery rounds, 155mm and 122mm shells with a detonator. Again and again these bombs have torn vehicles apart, often killing two or three soldiers. By the standards of Vietnam it is not a very big war, but it is now on the same level as guerrilla campaigns fought by Hezbollah in southern Lebanon in the 1990s, and from the US point of view things are not getting any better. The local insurgents in Fallujah are becoming more confident. In one attack in February they almost killed General John Abizaid, the US Middle East commander, and in another they over-ran the police headquarters, killing some 20 men.

The soldiers in the specialised units of the 82nd Airborne Division sound a little perplexed by the sort of war they are fighting. At a base called Volturno, hidden inside an old Baath Party recreation camp beside a lake, a platoon of combat engineers, in charge of clearing the road of mines, ruefully explains that they did not expect to be fighting this kind of war. In a dark hut, Staff Sgt Jeremy Anderson, leader of a squad of eight sappers, says he and his men were trained to deal with big conventional minefields such as those laid by the old Soviet Army. Nobody thought they would be dealing with the sort of amateur but lethal devices planted by guerrillas around Fallujah. Anderson says the only way he could get information about IEDs was by using an ageing army manual on 'booby traps in Vietnam'. Another sapper calls out: 'I never even heard of an IED before I came to Iraq.'

Outside the hut, Sgt Anderson shows off an old green-painted 155mm South African–made shell, whose TNT is wrapped around with plastic explosives; it produces razor-edged pieces of shrapnel eight to twelve inches long. The guerrillas bury several of these a few feet from the road with the nose of the shell removed and replaced with blasting caps. These are connected by wires to a battery, usually taken from a motorcycle. The bomb can then be detonated by means of a command wire three or four hundred metres long. Alternatively, the bombers can send a signal to the battery remotely by using a car door opener, the control for a child's toy or some types of mobile phone—which explains why the soldiers who stopped us when they saw me using a satellite phone had seemed so edgy: they had been told that Thurayas could be used to detonate a bomb under their feet.

Anderson displays a grudging respect for the versatility of the bomb-makers. One bomb was found attached to the underside of a bridge over the highway: that way it would explode downwards as a US convoy passed underneath. Another was wired to a solar panel which would detonate as soon as a US soldier brushed away the dirt shading it from the sun. The sappers walk gingerly along the verges of the roads. Anderson explains: 'We look for wires—anything that seems out of place.' They gently prod the sandy ground with short, silver-coloured wands. The wands, 18 inches long and looking like a conductor's baton, are made of titanium and are non-magnetic. They are curiously delicate and old-fashioned and in a way symbolic of the type of war the US is now fighting in Iraq.

Conventional mine detectors, intended to detect metal, do not work here because Iraqis use the side of the road as a rubbish dump. It is impossible to distinguish buried shells from discarded cans and other junk. The guerrillas have also started planting booby traps specifically designed to kill the sappers. 'Somebody has watched us at work,' Anderson says. 'They saw that we always pick up rocks and turn them over to make sure nothing is hidden underneath. So one day they tied a string to a rock rigged to an old water bottle with a power source inside attached to some old mortar rounds.'

The helicopter pilots who try to guard convoys around Fallujah are based ten miles from the town in an old Iraqi airbase at Habbaniyah. A detachment equipped with light Kiowa Warrior helicopters (US helicopters are all named after Indian tribes) is stationed near a hangar gutted by fire. The helicopters swoop and hover around the convoys or try to follow guerrillas on the ground. There is a steady trickle of losses.

The helicopter pilots and their gunners are not worried by being shot at with AK-47 submachine guns. Except at night, when they can see the tracer, they seldom know when they are under fire. One pilot suggests that for an Iraqi farmer on the ground 'it must be difficult to resist the temptation to shoot at us, like duck hunting.' A few minutes later, evidently thinking that his remark might be considered flippant, he asks urgently that it not be attributed to him. These days, the helicopters fly fast and low to avoid the missiles. A gunner in one of the Kiowas says: 'The helicopter flies at 100 feet, so by the time anyone on the ground can react it's gone.' Less comfortingly, he says the device on the roof for confusing heat-seeking missiles 'works 85 per cent of the time'. He does not add that the missiles, by forcing the helicopters to fly fast and low, make it very difficult for them to see anything on the ground.

When asked who he thinks is shooting at him, Major Thomas von Eschenbach, the commander of the squadron, repeats the official line. 'One group are former regime loyalists, with tribal loyalties to Saddam Hussein, and a second are foreign fighters who may be coming in from Syria.' The pilots themselves admit they see few Iraqis and then only from the air. A troop commander says: 'The men are mostly 5'6" to 5'10" tall and are between 150 to 180 pounds. The hardest part is picking out the bad guys. About half of Iraqis seem to drive white pick-ups.'

Von Eschenbach says that anybody could shoot at a helicopter with a rocket-propelled grenade launcher—it requires only ten minutes' training —but a surface-to-air missile is more complicated. He suspects foreign fighters are at work, though I point out that half a million former members of the Iraqi Army might also be involved. As for the proficiency of the guerrillas who are shooting down helicopters, von Eschenbach says: 'It's just like the Afghans did with the Russians … they find out our weaknesses.' Helicopters fly in pairs and the guerrillas always attack the second or 'trail' helicopter so there is nobody to see what is happening in the seconds before the missile strikes.

The US Army in Iraq has always been more vulnerable than it looks. Its high level of mechanisation means that it is very dependent on a continuing flow of supplies. These can be brought in only by road. If the Iraqis had placed bombs along the highway from Kuwait to Baghdad during the invasion last year, the advance would have been far slower and more costly; the last nine months have shown how easily the US Army, with a vast number of vehicles on the roads at any one time, can be attacked by guerrillas using crude explosive devices. Bases are difficult to defend against mortars. In almost 20 years, the Israeli Army in southern Lebanon, with an equivalent superiority to Hezbollah, found no answer to these tactics.

The American commanders respond that they have lost only 3,600 soldiers dead and wounded from hostile fire and accidents since the start of the war, not a high figure given the number of troops involved. But that misses the point. There are two types of guerrilla war. The first builds up guerrilla resistance step by step until a regular army is formed: the classic example is Mao Zedong in China. The second type involves sporadic attacks by a limited number of guerrillas, with the aim of putting irresistible political pressure on the enemy. This was the type of campaign waged by the IRA in Ireland in 1919–21, the Irgun in Palestine in the 1940s, EOKA under Grivas in Cyprus in the 1950s and the IRA again in Northern Ireland. It is this second type of war which the US is facing and does not quite know how to combat.

Things could get a lot worse. Most of the current guerrilla action is in the Sunni towns around Baghdad. It is less intense in the capital itself and in Mosul, the largest Sunni city, with a population of 1.6 million. Tony Blair and British foreign secretary Jack Straw have on occasion drawn comfort from this without, it seems, considering what would happen if the attacks spread to all the Sunni Arab parts of the country. A further difficulty is that the guerrillas belong to many different organisations without any central command.

Perhaps the most extraordinary aspect of the war is that the US does not really know who is behind the suicide bombing campaign which began last August with an attack on the Jordanian embassy. Since then anybody actually or potentially associated with the US occupation, the police, the UN, the Shia and the Kurds, has been liable to come under attack. There seems to be an endless supply of suicide bombers, wearing explosive belts or driving trucks packed with explosives. The US insists that the campaign is being carried out by foreigners, but logistics, safe houses and intelligence must be arranged by Iraqis, because non-Iraqi Arabs would be too visible to remain concealed for long.

Not all the US military commanders have been as heavy-handed as Paul Bremer and the CPA in Baghdad. In Mosul, General David Petraeus, the commander of the 101st Airborne Division, has been far more careful not to alienate the Sunni establishment in the city, which was a main recruiting ground for the Iraqi Army (there are 1,100 generals in Mosul because Saddam often paid off retiring officers with promotion). Exile parties like the Iraqi National Congress and the Iraqi National Accord, deeply resented in the capital for taking over jobs and businesses, have been kept at arm's length. There have been assassinations, suicide bombs and ambushes in Mosul, but not on the same scale as around Baghdad. Petraeus, who left Iraq in February after ten months in the country, said his most important advice to his successor was 'not to align too closely with one ethnic group, political party, tribe, religious group or social element'.

Washington is struggling to free itself from the trap into which it plunged so eagerly a year ago. Suddenly, Bremer and the CPA are desperately cultivating two men who until recently they treated with contempt: Ali al-Sistani, the Shia Grand Ayatollah, in the shrine city of Najaf, and Kofi Annan, the secretary-general of the UN. But too many mistakes were made in the first year of the occupation for a change of course to work now.

6 April 2004

The US Marines are fighting their way into the town of Fallujah on the Euphrates, 40 miles west of Baghdad, where a week ago four American civilian contractors were killed and their burnt and mutilated remains hung from the metal girders of a bridge over the Tigris. US commanders have pledged to conduct house-to-house searches to find and punish those responsible. So far five Marines are reported killed in the operation, but Iraqi casualties are unknown because ambulances are not being allowed to enter the town.

It is impossible to reach Fallujah. It has been sealed off by 1,200 Marines and two battalions of Iraqi security forces. The main road from Baghdad to Jordan, which passes close to Fallujah, is closed. US soldiers manning a razor-wire barrier wave vehicles onto a road which skirts the town. 'The city is surrounded,' says Lieutenant James Vanzant, a spokesman for the Marines. 'We want to make a very precise approach to this. We are looking for bad guys in town.'

Iraq is experiencing a crescendo of violence not seen since the end of the war to overthrow Saddam Hussein. Separate from the action in Fallujah, the war has entered a new stage as troops are also confronting Shia fighters in southern Iraq. Up to now almost all the attacks on the coalition have taken place in Sunni Muslim districts and towns north of Baghdad. But in the south the militia of Muqtada al-Sadr, a young Shia cleric, has taken to the streets. His group is well organised, and he has a committed core of supporters. His position depends on the reputation of his martyred father, Mohammed Sadiq al-Sadr, assassinated by Saddam in 1999.

Paul Bremer has miscalculated badly in seeking or stumbling into a confrontation with Sadr and his black-clad militia, the Mehdi Army. On 28 March Bremer suddenly closed Sadr's newspaper, *al-Hawza*, which Sadr interpreted as a move against him. Bremer then arrested Mustafa Yaqubi, Sadr's lieutenant in Najaf, which in turn provoked demonstrations and attacks on police stations and government buildings in Baghdad and southern Iraq.

The consequence is heavy fighting in Shia cities between supporters of Sadr and coalition troops. Sadr himself is believed to have moved to a house in an alleyway in Najaf, one of the two holiest shrines of Shia Muslims. It would be impossible for foreign troops to arrest him there without provoking a violent and more widespread Shia reaction. 'My fate will be either assassinated or arrested,' Sadr has said. His Mehdi Army has taken over the holy shrine of Imam Ali, whose golden dome rises in the centre of Najaf. In a statement, Sadr pledged: 'The US-led forces have the money, weapons and huge numbers but these things are not going to weaken our will because God is with us.'

According to Tony Blair, 'Muqtada al-Sadr does not represent the vast majority of Iraqi Shia. He represents a small band of extremists.' But the evident strength of Sadr's forces, making attacks in all the main Shia towns, shows that his men are committed and able to tap into a general feeling of hatred among Shia towards the CPA.

9 April 2004

We attempt to get to Fallujah by driving down the old road to Abu Ghraib. Two days ago this road was open. But when we come upon four tanks, their barrels pointed towards us, closing the road that runs behind Baghdad airport, we realise that the war has moved closer to Baghdad. In the distance we can see three columns of oily black smoke rising into the sky; local people tell us an American convoy was attacked a few hours earlier.

With the main highways blocked, we try to find another road or track to Fallujah. At this point we see trucks, piled high with relief supplies, one with a sign on the front saying 'al-Hayat Humanitarian Organisation'. It is an aid convoy carrying food and medicine to the besieged city. We decide to follow—they seem to know a route through a maze of country roads and tracks leading backwards and forwards over stagnant canals. Young men wave Iraqi flags from the backs of the trucks and chant patriotic songs; they are less than discreet about their presence. We drive down narrow tracks through shabby brown villages where people clap as we pass. Aiding Fallujah is obviously popular.

We weave around the countryside for what seems a very long time until we find ourselves close to the highway again. Nearby is a deserted building which I recognise because I have been there before. It is a milk factory which achieved international notoriety during the 1991 Gulf War when the US Air Force bombed the plant, claiming it was a production centre for biological weapons; the Iraqi government said that it only produced baby milk. This is Abu Ghraib. While we have circled around behind a US road block, we are disappointed not to have got further west.

Just as we reach the highway, a convoy of petrol tankers accompanied by US soldiers on Humvees drives past. Suddenly, there are staccato bursts of fire from Iraqi guerrillas on the other side of the road. Then comes the whoosh of RPG launchers. American soldiers on their Humvees immediately fire back with shuddering machine guns and M-16s. We rapidly drive off the road onto a piece of wasteland. We jump out of the car and lay on the ground with our faces pressed into the sand; other Iraqi drivers take cover near us. Bassil al-Kaissi, our driver, shouts at them: 'Take off your keffiyehs or the Americans will think you are mujahedin and kill you.'

Fortunately for us most of the firing from the insurgents is coming from the far side of the road and passing over our heads. Then somebody starts shooting at the US troops from our side of the road and their machine gunners open up.

At a pause in the firing we jump back into the car and drive off down a narrow road away from the fighting. We move slowly: I tell the driver not to raise dust and attract attention. At a small bridge over a canal several mujahedin run towards us carrying a heavy machine gun on a tripod and rocket-propelled grenade launchers. They stop on the bridge and listen to the shooting, which has started up again, seeming not to know where it is coming from. One of them shouts: 'What is happening?' Bassil, not wanting to arouse their suspicion by driving away too quickly, stops the car. 'We were trying to bring help to Fallujah,' he tells them, 'but those pigs opened fire on us.'

Abu Ghraib, on the western outskirts of Baghdad, is a town of scattered houses, abandoned factories and date palms which offers plenty of cover for guerrillas. The violence has spread from the Sunni cities of Fallujah and Ramadi to the fringes of the capital. The US Army has evidently not taken on board the way in which its week-long siege of Fallujah, where at least 280 people have been killed, is spreading rebellion in this part of Iraq, otherwise they would not have risked vulnerable petrol tankers on the exposed highway. Everywhere in Abu Ghraib there are freshly painted anti-American slogans on the walls. One reads: 'We shall knock on the gates of heaven with American skulls.' Another: 'Sunni Shia = Jihad against Occupation.'

11 April 2004

US civil and military leaders in Iraq have discovered this week that their authority is a house built on sand. It has crumbled in the face of poorly armed and ill-organised opposition in Fallujah and southern Iraq. The message is that the opponents of the US in Iraq are not very strong, but the coalition itself is very weak.

Not only are large parts of the country outside its control, the US is weaker in Iraq than it was a year ago. Its allies within the US-appointed Iraqi Governing Council (IGC), to which the US is supposedly going to hand over power on 30 June, are accusing it of 'genocide'. The IGC issued a statement demanding an end to military action and 'collective punishment'—a reference to

Fallujah. One of its members, Adnan Pachachi, the former Iraqi foreign minister, whose language is normally highly diplomatic, has denounced the siege, saying: 'It is not right to punish all the people of Fallujah, and we consider these operations by the Americans unacceptable and illegal.'

In Vietnam a US commander once said of a village: 'We had to destroy it in order to save it.' In Iraq the same might apply to Fallujah. It is true that since the war Fallujah has been the most militant and anti-American city in Iraq, but it is not entirely typical. Sunni by religion and highly tribal, it has a well-earned reputation among Iraqis as being a bastion for bandits. Iraqis in Baghdad, even those sympathetic to the resistance, used to speak of people in Fallujah pursuing their own private feud with the US.

Yet the US responded to the killing of the four US contractors with a medieval siege, one in which they initially refused to allow ambulances in or out. If the Americans really believed they were being attacked by a tiny minority, Iraqis ask, why were they attacking a city of 300,000 people? The result has been to turn Fallujah into a nationalist and religious symbol for all Iraqis. For the first time the armed resistance is becoming truly popular in Baghdad. Previously Iraqis often approved of it as the only way to put pressure on the US, but they were also wary of the guerrillas, because of fear of religious fanaticism or connections with Saddam's deeply unpopular regime.

The US made a similar mistake by driving Muqtada al-Sadr into a corner. He has never been able to mobilise many people in the past. During a confrontation with the authorities last October he was unable to put more than a couple of thousand marchers on the streets in Sadr City, supposedly his home base. He was an irritant for the CPA, but he never rivalled the influence of Shia clerical leaders such as Grand Ayatollah Ali al-Sistani. There were no real signs that Sadr's movement was going anywhere until Paul Bremer confronted him. This may have been a pre-emptive strike to get Sadr out of the picture before the nominal handover of power to the Governing Council on 30 June, but it has proved a disastrous misjudgement.

2 May 2004

Wisps of grey smoke were still rising from the wreckage of four Humvees caught by the blast of a bomb which killed two US soldiers and wounded another five. It seems they had been caught in a trap. When the soldiers smashed their way into an old brick house in the Waziriya district of Baghdad last week, they were raiding what they had been told was an insurgent bomb factory, only for it to erupt as they came through the door. The reaction of local people, as soon as the surviving American soldiers had departed, was to start a spontaneous street party.

A small boy climbed on top of a blackened and smouldering Humvee and triumphantly waved a white flag with an Islamic slogan hastily written on it. Some other young men were showing with fascinated pride a blood-soaked US uniform. Another group had found an abandoned military helmet, and had derisively placed it on the head of an elderly carthorse.

Watching the dancing, jeering crowd was Nada Abdullah Aboud, a middle-aged woman, dressed in black. She had a reason for hating Americans, though she claimed she did not do so. 'I do feel sorry for the young soldiers, though they killed my son,' she said quietly. 'They came such a long distance to die here.' It turned out that her son, Saad Mohammed, had been the translator for a senior Italian diplomat working for the CPA. She said: 'My son was driving with the Italian ambassador last September near Tikrit when an American soldier fired at the car and shot him through the heart.'

Saad Mohammed is one of a large but unknown number of Iraqis shot down by US troops over the past year. There seems to have been no rational reason why he had been killed. But the high toll of Iraqi civilians shot after ambushes or at checkpoints has given Iraqis the sense that, at bottom, American soldiers regard them as an inferior people whose lives are not worth very much.

7 May 2004

The publication of pictures from Abu Ghraib showing what may happen to Iraqi prisoners at the hands of their captors allows the outside world to see what Iraqis have known for some time: the occupation is very brutal. In Baghdad, stories have been circulating for months about systematic torture in the prisons. In the US the impact of the photographs is all the greater thanks to the administration's previous success in controlling news from Iraq. Last October I wrote a piece about US soldiers bulldozing date-palm groves near Balad, north of Baghdad, to punish local farmers after an ambush; I immediately received a flood of outraged emails from the US denying that American soldiers would do such a thing.

American civil and military leaders in Iraq live in a strange fantasy world. It is on display every day in a cavernous hall in the old Islamic Conference

Centre in Baghdad, where coalition spokesmen hold daily press conferences. The civil side is represented by Dan Senor of the CPA, a bony-faced,
dark-suited man, recently imported from the White House press office. He
makes little secret of the fact that his job is to present a picture of Iraq that
will get President Bush re-elected. He jogs around the heavily protected
US enclave, known as the Green Zone, wearing a T-shirt with 'Bush and
Cheney in 2004' written on it. Senor is not impressed by the Iraqi resistance: for him it will never amount to anything much more than a small
gang of al-Qa'ida terrorists and die-hard Saddamists, desperately and vainly
seeking to prevent the birth of a new Iraq.

Much zanier is Brigadier General Mark Kimmitt, the deputy director
for coalition operations, who specialises in steely-eyed determination. He
likes to illustrate his answers with homilies drawn from the home life of
the Kimmitt family. One day an Iraqi journalist complained that US helicopters were scaring children in Baghdad by roaring low and fast over the
rooftops. Kimmitt replied that he had spent most of his adult life 'either
on or near military bases, married to a woman who teaches in the schools',
and that on these bases 'you often hear the sound of tanks firing. You often
hear the sound of artillery rounds going off.' Yet Mrs Kimmitt, the general
continued proudly, had been able to keep her pupils calm despite the constant thundering of the guns by 'letting them understand that those booms
and those bangs were simply the sounds of freedom'.

Kimmitt urged the journalist to go home and explain to his children
that it was only thanks to the thundering guns, those sounds of freedom,
that they were able to 'enjoy a free life'. In fact, US helicopters have been
flying so fast and so low in the last six months to make it more difficult for
guerrillas to shoot them down.

Few Iraqis share the Kimmitt family's benign view of US air power. A
day after listening to the general, I visited Musak, a Christian accountant.
Normally he works in the Dohra electric power station, whose four tall
chimneys dominate the skyline in south Baghdad. He was at home because
the giant turbines have been closed down and the German engineers from
Siemens, who were supposed to install new turbines, have fled Baghdad
for fear of being kidnapped. The walls of al-Iskan, the lower-middle-class
district where Musak lives, are covered in slogans supporting the resistance.
Musak explained: 'A few weeks ago a man, nobody knows who, shot at a
helicopter with his Kalashnikov. The helicopter fired two rockets in return.
They hit the tent where a family were holding a wake for a dead relative,

killing two people and wounding 15.' After this, support for the insurgents increased in al-Iskan.

That the US military had based their entire strategy on a belief in their own propaganda only became clear last month, as local uprisings swept across Iraq. US commanders had convinced themselves that all the pin-prick guerrilla attacks came from Former Regime Loyalists and mysterious Foreign Fighters (FRLs or FFs in US military parlance). They spoke glow-ingly of the progress made by the new US-trained Iraqi police, army and paramilitary units. These forces, ultimately to number 200,000, were intended gradually to replace American troops.

The speed with which US plans for Iraq fell apart is astonishing, but the reason is plain: the US military and Paul Bremer provoked simultane-ous confrontations with Iraq's two main communities, the Shia and Sunni Arabs, who together make up 80 per cent of the population. As US control over large parts of Iraq began to slide, officials responded by refusing to believe what was happening. Only occasionally were there visible signs of panic. The CPA website is normally full of upbeat information about reconstruction projects and improvements in the electricity supply. It also has news about security, the chief preoccupation of the foreign business-men who make up most of its readership. As the crisis grew worse the CPA decided that the information was too alarming to report. A brief message on its website read, unpretentiously: 'For security reasons there are no security reports.'

Why has US rule in Iraq been so dysfunctional? Why did the US Marines have to call on a general from Saddam Hussein's Republican Guard to take responsibility for security in Fallujah when the Republican Guard had been so contemptuously dismissed by Bremer in May last year? Why was that the only way to bring the three-week siege to an end? A CNN/USA Today poll in March showed that 56 per cent of Iraqis want an immediate with-drawal of coalition forces—and that was before the uprisings.

Iraq is essentially controlled by the US military. The State Department was sidelined before the war. The uniformed military and the civilian CPA report separately to the Pentagon. The US Army devises and carries out its policies regardless of Bremer. In a panicky reaction to the guerrilla attacks, the CPA recently announced it was closing the biggest highways around Baghdad to civilian traffic. The tone of its statement was threatening. 'If civilians drive on the closed section of the highways they may be engaged with deadly force,' the CPA warned. In other words, they would be shot.

Within a few hours the US Army announced that it knew nothing of the CPA's decision and had no intention of enforcing it. Bremer was forced to drop the idea.

This is something more than the traditional split between civilians and the military. Bremer keeps decision-making within a tight circle. Senior members of the CPA say they know nothing beyond what they read in the newspapers. But important decisions, such as disbanding the Iraqi Army, are taken in Washington by Paul Wolfowitz and Co. The prime aim of the White House is for news from Iraq to look good in the run-up to the presidential election. The unbridled greed of firms bidding for CPA contracts and the privatising fervour of the neo-cons has led to damaging failures. For instance, the contract to set up a television station supporting the US was given to SAIC, a company popular with the Pentagon, but with no experience of television. As a result, Iraqis mostly get their news from Al Jazeera and Al Arabiya, both deeply hostile to the US occupation.

It was the US Marines who besieged Fallujah, turning the city into a nationalist symbol, but it was Bremer who initiated the confrontation with Muqtada al-Sadr, failing to realise how disillusioned the 15 or 16 million Iraqi Shia, a majority of the population, are with the occupation. They think the US wants to deny them power by postponing elections and using the Kurds to retain effective control of the country.

The Mehdi Army, Sadr's militia, are not very appealing. I ran into a group of them when I was trying to get to Najaf, where Sadr had taken refuge. They were guarding a checkpoint just outside the town of Kufa. I was wearing a red and white keffiyeh and sitting inconspicuously in the back of the car because foreigners had been shot and killed in the area. The Mehdi Army did not like me wearing a keffiyeh. There were a lot of things about me they did not like. They were intensely suspicious of my satellite phone, mobile and camera. At first they tried to push me into another car, then they decided to take ours. Three gunmen, clutching machine guns, their chests covered with ammunition bandoliers, crammed in. We followed another car, also filled with gunmen, to the green-domed Imam Ali mosque in the centre of Kufa—their headquarters.

Once we had parked outside the mosque the gunmen relaxed a little. One of them offered me a cigarette and I took it, though I had given up smoking. Most of them came from the slums of Sadr City in Baghdad. They spoke about defending Iraq from America and Israel and about the theft of Iraqi oil. Their slogans were nationalist rather than religious. They were fascinated by a copy of the *New Yorker* they found in the back of the car. One gunman pointed angrily at a small Stars and Stripes in an advertisement. Finally my mobile and my passport reappeared, though not my satellite phone, which I saw a black-clad gunman covertly pocket. It did not seem a good moment to demand it back.

Despite having an overwhelming military force available to take Fallujah and Najaf in April, the US did not dare do so. It became evident even in Washington that to crush the resistance in either city—not a difficult task against a few thousand lightly armed gunmen—would spread rather than end the rebellion.

19 May 2004

Soon after US occupation officials took over Saddam Hussein's palace complex in central Baghdad as their headquarters last year there was an alarming development. The lavatories in the palaces all became blocked and began to overflow. Mobile toilets were rapidly shipped into the country and installed in the palace gardens.

It turned out that American officials, often bright young things with good connections with the Bush administration in Washington, did not know that lavatories are used in a slightly different way in the Middle East compared to back home. In particular water fulfils the function largely performed by paper in the West. The water pipes in Saddam's palaces were not designed to deal with big quantities of paper and became clogged, with spectacularly unsavoury results.

It was the first of many mistakes made by the CPA, which has now ruled Iraq for a year based on inadequate local knowledge. It has been one of the most spectacularly incompetent regimes in history. If Paul Bremer decided important issues by flipping a coin he would surely have had better results. In Najaf, the Shia shrine city, the occupying forces even managed to appoint a Sunni governor, which was a bit like giving Rev Ian Paisley a position of responsibility overseeing the Vatican. Fortunately the governor did not last long in that role. He was arrested for kidnapping and is now in jail.

Downing Street and the White House are now both talking up the handover of sovereignty to Iraqis on 30 June and the creation of new Iraqi security forces. This is less a policy than a cynical public relations gimmick. The allies have been trying to build up the Iraqi security forces for over a year. But when the uprisings began last month, 40 per cent of the US-trained forces promptly deserted while 10 per cent mutinied and changed sides, according to the US Army. The reality, as Dr Mahmoud Othman, an independent member of the IGC says, is that Iraqis will not fight other Iraqis on behalf of a foreign power.

Of course the purpose of the exaggerated significance being given to the handover of sovereignty to an interim government is to pretend that now there will be a legitimate authority in Iraq. Over the past year, the CPA has repeatedly said it will delegate power to Iraqis. It has never happened and is unlikely to happen now. The US-appointed IGC was told it would be consulted on important security decisions only to wake up one morning to find US Marines besieging Fallujah.

19 June 2004

An Iraqi friend, who feared for his life because he was close to the Americans, used to live inside the Green Zone. One day he fell into conversation with an American soldier guarding one of the gates. The soldier said he was of Iraqi origin and could speak Arabic. He added that security was not quite as tight as it looked since prostitutes were regular visitors to the zone. My friend, a little alarmed, decided to investigate. He went to a house which was being used as a brothel. He says: 'In the toilet I found that the women were writing pro-Baath party, anti-American and patriotic slogans with their lipstick on the mirrors.' Their clients could not tell what they had written because it was in Arabic.

The story illustrates the way in which the CPA officials became wholly isolated from the real opinions of Iraqis, as remote as if they lived in a Martian spaceship which had temporarily touched down in the centre of Baghdad. The CPA may be the least successful organisation ever created by the US government. It is certainly one of the strangest. 'It is really like living in an open prison,' says one CPA official.

Much of the security is in the hands of private companies. One day I had an interview with an Iraqi minister inside the zone. We had arranged it over the phone. The meeting never took place. I was first asked who I was by a friendly Nepalese soldier, then questioned by a nervous Algerian and finally stopped by a paunchy security man who, from his accent, came from Mississippi or Alabama. 'We can't let in journalists,' he said in a suspicious and hostile tone. 'They are a security threat.' I asked exactly whom they had threatened. The security man said: 'They killed the president of Afghanistan.' It turned out he had read somewhere of Ahmed Shah Massood, the Afghan warlord, being assassinated by two Moroccans with Belgian passports pretending to be a television crew. I said these were hardly typical of the journalistic profession but he was unconvinced.

24 June 2004

It is probably one of the most dangerous jobs in the world. Colonel Abu Mohammed is the policeman in charge of defusing unexploded bombs in Baghdad, where the sound of explosions is so common that, unless the blast is very close, people no longer come to their doors to check what has blown up.

'I used to have 11 experts in defusing bombs here but now I am almost the only one because it is so dangerous,' says the colonel, a surprisingly cheerful bald man in his early 50s. 'Some of the others are dead or injured or were threatened into resigning.' It is easy to understand why so many of the surviving officers in the bomb squad have left the police force or transferred to other departments. It is not a well-paid job. The colonel says he makes about $370 a month. Until recently his men had no body armour to protect them from the blast. 'We asked the Americans for robots so we don't have to risk our lives but we haven't received any,' he says.

A police officer called Saleh Mehdi, 25, appears and shakes hands with his left hand. He explains that his right arm was blown off by a bomb on 25 December last year: 'First we got a call saying there was a roadside bomb in Palestine Street. I went there and defused it. Then there was another found three kilometres away and a third behind the Turkish embassy. Then we had to go back to Palestine Street because two more bombs had been discovered there.' Mehdi was standing a yard away from one of the bombs when it blew up. Probably somebody was watching as he got near and pressed a button on a remote control which detonated it. His right arm was torn off and his body peppered with shrapnel. He says: 'I had a mechanical arm fitted but it did not work. I was sent to Oman to get an electronic arm but it has not arrived.' He received no compensation.

The roadside bomb and the suicide bomb are the chosen instruments of those trying to end the occupation. It is a measure of the failure of the American military and civilian authorities in Iraq that the police who deal with many of the bombs in Baghdad are so ill-equipped.

5 July 2004

It is tempting to see the so-called handover of power from the US to the Iraqi interim government on 28 June as a fake. The few who attended the ceremony at which sovereignty was legally transferred—two days earlier than expected in a surprise move to prevent the occasion being spoilt by guerrilla attacks—had to pass through four American checkpoints. Iyad Allawi, the new prime minister, worked for years for MI6 and the CIA and is kept in power by 138,000 US troops. The ministers in the new government live in palatial villas inside a secure compound. Many of them have spent most of their lives outside Iraq.

The appointment of Allawi is itself a demonstration of how far the balance of power has swung against the US. Twelve months ago Paul Bremer was blithely talking about continuing the occupation for two years. Direct imperial rule seemed feasible to Washington. Young Republicans were sent off to rule Iraq like the offspring of British gentry dispatched to loot India in the 18th century. A 24-year-old Republican who applied for a job at the White House was instead sent to Iraq to reopen the Baghdad stock exchange. It stayed shut. US generals at their briefings routinely claimed that the number of hostile incidents was falling. I began to wonder why, if there were only 15 or 16 attacks a day on American soldiers, I seemed to see at least a quarter of them whenever I drove out of Baghdad. Then American soldiers in the field told me that they no longer reported guerrilla attacks unless there had been US casualties. It was a bureaucratic hassle to make out the reports and their commanders were keen to hear that resistance was petering out.

Twenty years ago I used to go to the open-air restaurants that lined Abu Nawas Street to eat mazgouf, fish from the Tigris grilled over a wood fire. The restaurants were badly affected when Saddam, to bolster his Islamic credentials, banned the public consumption of alcohol. After his overthrow, the owners hoped their customers would return. These days, Abu Nawas is deserted even in the middle of the day and used mainly by military vehicles. The street can be entered only from one end and there is a checkpoint intended to protect the Palestine and Sheraton Hotels, both of them full of foreigners, who know that Abu Nawas is too dangerous for them.

In the Shatt al-Arab restaurant on the bank of the Tigris dark grey fish swim in a pool decorated with blue tiles (the river is polluted now and the fish come from fish farms). The manager, Shahab al-Obeidi, says business is not good: three-quarters of his customers used to come in the evening but now he shuts at 6 p.m. because the nights are unsafe. Once he stayed open because he had a large table of customers who seemed to be enjoying themselves. 'When I gave them the bill they laughed and took out their pistols and fired them into the ceiling and through the windows,' he says, pointing to the numerous bullet holes.

Foreigners in Baghdad and other cities all now live in the Green Zone or other mini Green Zones. The concrete blocks, razor wire and guards spread in all directions. I no longer carry a camera in Baghdad because anybody taking photographs is suspected of carrying out reconnaissance for an attack. Paranoia runs high. A member of a newly arrived French camera crew caught in a traffic jam idly took a photograph of the enormous concrete blockade defending the street leading to the Baghdad Hotel, which Iraqis believe to be the CIA headquarters. Iraqi guards immediately arrested the crew and kept them in a prison cage for two nights.

The Baghdad Hotel is close to Saadoun Street, one of the city's main arteries. A few weeks ago the road was narrowed from four lanes to two in the section near the hotel. There is now a permanent traffic jam, and around thirty shops inside the hotel's *cordon sanitaire* face closure. 'My business has completely disappeared,' Nadim al-Hussaini says, sitting outside his empty shop. 'First 30 to 40 per cent when they put up the concrete barrier, and 100 per cent when they closed the road. I don't want to get blown up any more than the Americans do. But the real solution is simply for the Americans staying at the hotel to leave.'

Neither the suicide bombers nor the US Army care very much how many ordinary Iraqis get killed. The entrances to the Green Zone provide no protection for Iraqis queuing for jobs or to have their documents checked. They are frequently caught in bomb blasts. On 17 May a suicide bomber assassinated Izzedin Salim, the head of the IGC, as his fleet of cars was waiting to enter the Green Zone. An Iraqi minister told me that Salim might have survived if US soldiers at the gate had not delayed the convoy by complaining that some of the documents were not complete. There is an Iraqi conspiracy theory which sees foreign suicide bombers and the US acting in unison to prevent Iraq regaining its independence.

The suicide bombers have gone some way towards discrediting the resistance, which ought to be helpful to Allawi's interim government. Most Iraqis see the blue uniformed Iraqi police in their elderly white and blue patrol cars as a defence against crime rather than as allies of the occupation. The attacks on police stations are not popular. Even Muqtada al-Sadr told his militiamen to co-operate with the police in Sadr City, 'to deprive the terrorists and saboteurs of the chance to incite chaos and extreme lawlessness'. Some resistance groups in Fallujah complain that they are losing support because the bombers are killing Iraqis rather than Americans. Ministers in the new government speak of restoring order by 'cutting off the hands' and 'slitting the throats' of the insurgents. This is the sort of rhetoric once used by Saddam.

Iraqis are desperate for the return of some sort of security. Among the better-off there is a pervasive fear of kidnapping. Over the last year this has become a local industry, now so common that new words have been added to Iraqi thieves' slang: for example, a kidnap victim is *al-tali*, or 'the sheep'. I visit Qasim Sabty, a painter and sculptor who owns a gallery, to ask him about an exhibition of work depicting the torture at Abu Ghraib, but the first thing he talks about is kidnapping. 'So many of my relatives have been kidnapped,' he says. 'I fear I am going to be next.' He mentions another gallery owner who has just paid $100,000 for the return of her son. A businessman friend living in Jordan has just paid $60,000 to have his brother-in-law returned. Doctors are a favourite target. Operations are postponed because surgeons have fled the country. The owner of the dilapidated Shatt al-Arab restaurant disappeared to Syria after his son was kidnapped. I asked Lieutenant-Colonel Farouk Mahmoud, the deputy head of the police kidnap squad, the best way to avoid being kidnapped. 'Go abroad!' he said brightly, to laughter from his officers.

It is not only the well-off who feel threatened. Gangs of thieves hop on and off buses in Rashid Street in the city centre and rob passengers at gun- and knife-point. Ali Abdul Jabber, a bus driver, has been robbed three times. 'On the last occasion', he says, 'the thieves jumped on board because the doors have to be open in this hot weather. Two of them stood guard at the back while two others walked down the bus looking in people's handbags and stealing money and jewellery.' Jabber dared not turn round: he thought that if the thieves suspected he could identify them they would kill him. Nobody went to the police. 'The passengers didn't even discuss it among themselves because this sort of thing is so much part of daily life in Baghdad.' Most of them thought he was in league with the gang.

After the disasters of the past year the Americans know they cannot occupy Iraq, even in the short term, without the support of local allies. The problem is that most Iraqis would like Allawi and the interim government to get rid of the suicide bombers and kidnappers—and of the US occupation as well. But the US shows no sign of abandoning its plan to keep Iraq as a client state. It would have a weak army, devoted entirely to counter-insurgency. It would have no tanks, aircraft, missiles or artillery and would resemble a Latin American state of the 1960s with an army and security forces controlled largely by Washington. This was the message brought by Paul Wolfowitz when he turned up in Baghdad in June just before the supposed handover of power. The US will allow Iraq to rearm, but only against its own people. It was a tellingly low-profile visit. Wolfowitz and his entourage kept away from tall buildings.

14 September 2004

Pools of blood, broken glass and discarded shoes are spread across Haifa Street in Baghdad after a bomb exploded outside a police station, leaving a crater seven feet across. The blast tore through a crowd of young men who were trying to get jobs in the police force. Forty-seven people have been killed and at least 114 wounded.

Charred body parts hang from trees and birds killed by the blast lay scattered across the street in one of the city's busiest shopping districts, which has become a front line in the spreading insurrection against Iraq's US-backed government. The explosion was caused by a suicide bomber who blew up a car filled with artillery shells. 'There was a loud explosion and suddenly my body was covered in blood,' says Yassin Hamid, a 21-year-old student, as he lies in a nearby hospital. 'I decided to join the police to help my family.' Mahdi Mohammed, whose barber shop is close to the centre of the explosion, says: 'I could see burning people running in all directions.'

The attack is the latest of a new spasm of violence in Iraq. It demonstrates that the interim government of Iyad Allawi is failing to quell the insurgency or provide security for ordinary people. The attack has been claimed by the Tawhid and Jihad group of Abu Musab al-Zarqawi, the Islamic militant. A statement on an Islamic website says: 'A lion from the Brigades of Those Seeking Martyrdom succeeded in attacking the centre of volunteers for the renegade police apparatus.'

It is a measure of the level of violence in Baghdad that the car bomb was not the day's first explosion on Haifa Street. Taha Salem Shalash, 24, went to the police station at 7:30 a.m. looking for a job. 'Three mortar bombs landed close by and the police asked us to leave,' he says. 'They said there would be no interviews.' The job-seekers suspected, however, that the police might begin recruiting again. Some 250 men were standing in the street or drinking tea in cafes when the bomb exploded.

The willingness of young men to wait close to police stations, despite knowing they may be targeted, shows the desperate shortage of jobs in

Iraq. At least half the population is unemployed; a quarter live on less than $2 a day.

18 September 2004
300 civilian lives lost.
16 coalition troops killed.
17 foreign hostages held.
3 headless corpses found.
Battles rage in Fallujah, Basra, Hillah and Ramadi.
Kofi Annan declares the war illegal.
The US shifts $3.4 billion from reconstruction to security.
So ends one of the bleakest weeks in Iraq's grim recent history.

23 September 2004
In Iraq signs of disintegration are everywhere. Iraqis were cynical about how much real independence the interim government would have, but thought that nothing could be much worse than direct rule by Paul Bremer. There was a brief moment when Iyad Allawi tried to put some distance between himself and the Americans. He produced a plan which would have allowed Iraqi guerrillas who had killed US soldiers, thinking they were doing their patriotic duty, to be amnestied. The idea was to split the Sunni Muslim resistance, or at least show that the interim government was not entirely an American pawn. It was too much for Washington to stomach. The plan was watered down and soon forgotten.

Allawi started off with a very narrow political base in Iraq. He comes from a family that was wealthy under the monarchy, but he was a militant member of the Baath Party in the 1960s and early 1970s and appeals to former Baath Party members who lost their jobs under Bremer. At the same time, his own career and the movement to which he belonged, the Iraqi National Accord, had been fostered by MI6 and the CIA for many years. Iraqis are desperate for security, and for a few months they hoped the interim government might provide it. Allawi was determined to show he was a force to be reckoned with. In August he chose to confront Muqtada al-Sadr and his Mehdi Army militiamen in Najaf, but he could do this only by relying on the American army. After three weeks most of the city was in ruins, 400 people had been killed and 2,500 wounded, but, as with the earlier American operation in April, Allawi still had not eliminated Sadr or his men. No sooner had the battle in Najaf ended than the US Air Force started an intensified bombing campaign against the Sunni resistance west of Baghdad. Boasting of strikes against 'terrorists', the US military put out statements claiming dozens of insurgents had been killed. On one occasion, as a spokesman was saying the US military had conducted a 'precision' raid on Islamic militants in Fallujah, Iraqis were watching television pictures of a Red Crescent ambulance in the city torn apart by a US bomb that killed the driver, a paramedic and five patients.

It is strange to sit in Baghdad watching George Bush's stump speech about freedom being on the march in Iraq despite continuing troubles. It is a lot worse than that. Allawi and the interim government rule parts of Baghdad and some other cities. But there could be uprisings by the Shia in Basra or the Sunni in Mosul at any time. The government, probably with American prompting, has told the Ministry of Health to stop issuing figures for the number of Iraqi civilians killed and wounded every day. The government recruits more and more policemen, but in much of the country they stay alive by co-operating with the resistance. In Mosul province they even contribute a portion of their salary to the insurgents. The resistance gets more powerful each month but it is also increasingly split between the nationalists and the Islamic militants. Allawi might have been able to take advantage of this by wooing the nationalists. But he is seen by the resistance as a creature of the occupation. 'Allawi's visit to the US is the visit of an employee to his employer,' says Taher Abdel Karim, a computer engineer.

The insurgents are very fragmented and often belong to groups only 10 to 15 strong. Because they have no central organisation capable of giving orders and getting them obeyed it is unlikely that there will be a ceasefire while the military occupation continues. The most effective guerrilla units are now very expert. They recently tried to kill the governor of Baghdad, Ali al-Haidri. It was a sophisticated operation. Local shopkeepers say two men had been loitering near a car. When the convoy appeared one of them opened the boot, where a gunman was waiting to open fire. Two other gunmen ran into the street in front of the convoy. The driver of the governor's car tried to escape by driving down a side street but the ambush party had foreseen that and planted a large bomb beside the road. The explosion missed the governor by a second.

Iraq today is like Lebanon after the civil war. The US is still baffled by its failure to get control of the country after defeating Saddam Hussein so easily last year. The interim government is trying to re-create the Iraqi state.

Iran, Turkey, Syria, Jordan, Kuwait and Saudi Arabia all know that their future will in part be determined by what happens in Iraq. All have their allies within the country. There are multiple friction points. Many of the countries and parties involved in the struggle for Iraq are still feeling their own strength. They are all a long way from agreeing an end to the war or even a truce.

5 October 2004

The US campaign to eliminate 'no-go' areas under rebel control in Iraq is getting into full swing. American generals have triumphantly announced they have successfully taken over Samarra and killed 125 insurgents. They failed to mention that this is the third time they have captured this particular city on the Tigris river north of Baghdad in the past 18 months. Fallujah is being bombed every night and may soon be subjected to ground assault.

The creation of the no-go zones was largely the consequence of the way in which US strategy is dictated by the electoral needs of President Bush. The US Marines commander who was in charge of western Iraq in April says it was against his advice that Fallujah was first besieged on orders from above. The marine attack was then called off after a few days, again apparently on orders from the White House because it did not want Iraq leading the television news night after night.

I have spent most of the past year-and-a-half travelling in Iraq, and I have never known it so bad. The upsurge in rebel attacks is being portrayed in London and Washington as an attempt to sabotage the Iraqi elections due to take place in January. There is no reason to think that the impending polls in Iraq have any connection with the increasing violence. The insurrection is spreading each month under its own momentum. It does so because the dominant fact in Iraqi politics is the overwhelming unpopularity of the US occupation.

The Iraqi Sunni and Shia communities may have their differences, as do the Islamic militants and nationalists, but they hate the US Army more than they hate each other. One Shia leader told me how in his city, Kerbala, the Shia radical Muqtada al-Sadr is deeply unpopular. But when a US helicopter dropped leaflets in Arabic denouncing him, local people rushed out and burned them. They would not be told by a foreign invader what to think about one of their own.

11 December 2004

The first independent reports are emerging from Fallujah, which since 8 November has been subjected to a devastating US offensive by 10,000 US troops helped by British and Iraqi soldiers—the second major assault on Fallujah this year. It is a flattened city which is facing an unprecedented, permanent security crackdown and an uncertain future. The operation began just after the US presidential elections: its aim, to clear a city regarded by the Americans as a hotbed of insurgency.

More than 70 Marines have died, and 1,600 rebels. But no one knows the civilian casualty toll—this in a city which once numbered 300,000. Indeed, there are no estimates of how many people are still there. A Red Cross team—which entered without escort and left before curfew—met no residents, apart from engineers and technicians. The Red Cross reported that hundreds of dead bodies remain stacked inside a potato chip warehouse on the outskirts. Some of the bodies are too badly decomposed to be identified. Raw sewage runs through the streets. All this, and there are no humanitarian workers inside the city.

When the first of Fallujah's refugees are allowed to return, they will be funnelled through five checkpoints. Each will have their fingerprints taken, along with DNA samples and retina scans. Residents will be issued with badges with their home addresses on them, and it will be an offence not to wear it at all times. No civilian vehicles will be allowed in the city in an effort to thwart suicide bombers. One idea floated by the US is for all males in Fallujah to be compelled to join work battalions in which they will be paid to clear rubble and rebuild houses.

The battle for Fallujah has been largely successful from the US point of view, because the assault has not provoked the widespread nationalist reaction across Iraq seen in April, when the Americans first attacked the city. Many Shia Iraqis have come to see Fallujah as the headquarters of the extreme sectarian Sunni, whose suicide bombers have slaughtered mostly Shia police and army recruits. Many have been pleased to see Fallujah insurgents killed or dispersed.

But the taking of Fallujah may have less military affect than the US and the Iraqi interim government had hoped. The city's capture was supposed to break the back of the insurgency and open the way for people to take part in the Iraqi elections on 30 January. Yet, so far, there is little sign that resistance to the US and the interim government is weakening in Sunni Muslim districts in central and northern Iraq.

FIVE

Bombs and Ballots

Iraq, 2005

27 January 2005

The impending election of a 275-member National Assembly on 30 January is the result of pressure from Grand Ayatollah Ali al-Sistani, the 71-year-old cleric, who exercises such immense influence over the Shia community. US officials never mention today that in the months after the overthrow of Saddam Hussein they were opposed to an election, citing difficulties in identifying voters without a census and a lack of security. The real reason the US was so nervous was that it feared that Shia parties, particularly those very religious and close to Iran, would win a majority. It hoped instead to rule Iraq through direct imperial control supplemented by returning Iraqi exiles acceptable to Washington.

It did not work. Gradually, the arrogant neo-conservatives holed up in the Green Zone came to realise that the Grand Ayatollah, who seldom leaves his house down a narrow alley in Najaf, held them in the palm of his hand. Paul Bremer could travel all over the country but he never succeeded in meeting Sistani.

In June 2003 the cleric issued a *fatwa*, or religious ruling, saying those who framed Iraq's new constitution must be elected rather than selected by the US and the now defunct Iraq Governing Council. In November 2003 he stated that elections, not the elaborate, regional caucuses suggested by the US, should be used to choose a transitional government. As rebellion spread across the Sunni Muslim heartlands in northern and central Iraq the

US accepted that it had to reach an agreement with Sistani. Under great military pressure from Sunni Arabs, Washington could not afford to fight the Shia as well. It agreed to an election.

When the US invaded Iraq, the Shia clergy were determined not to repeat what they consider a historic mistake. After Britain had captured what became Iraq from the Turks in 1917, the Shia vigorously opposed the occupation. They rebelled in 1920, prompting the British to co-opt the Sunni Arabs to rule Iraq as they had under the Ottomans. The Shia have been excluded from power ever since.

Sistani's powerful influence was underlined last year. For the first time in six years, he left his house in Najaf to have medical treatment in London. While he was there, Muqtada al-Sadr's Mehdi Army fought fierce battles against the US Marines for control of Najaf. Much of the city was destroyed. But on his return the Grand Ayatollah was able to produce a peace agreement which saved the Shrine of Imam Ali from destruction.

Under his auspices, a largely Shia slate, or coalition, called the United Iraqi Alliance was put together for the election. It includes all the main parties which are predominantly Shia. It is expected to top the poll. The Shia want to demonstrate that they have the right to hold political power. But victory will not necessarily give them real authority. The National Assembly requires agreements between the three main communities, Shia, Kurd and Sunni, to reach a decision. The US remains the most powerful force in the country. The Sunni insurgents control swaths of territory. The Shia still have some way to go before they rule Iraq.

30 January 2005

Mohammed Mahmoud is a rare figure—a Sunni Muslim, living in Baghdad, who is prepared to say that he is going to vote in today's election, though he is not foolhardy enough to allow his photograph to be taken. Although the election is the closest Iraq has ever come to a free and fair poll, its shortcomings are impossible to ignore. Much of the country is in the grip of a bitterly fought insurgency, daily life is a catalogue of power failures and shortages, and millions of Mahmoud's fellow Sunni Arabs are either too afraid to vote or heeding the calls of their leaders to boycott.

Mahmoud is a middle-aged engineer who runs a stationery shop in central Baghdad's inner Karada district. Karada is famous in Baghdad for its strong sense of communal solidarity—when the rest of the city was being looted after the overthrow of Saddam Hussein, the banks and government offices were defended by locals. Most people in Karada are expected to vote, so Mahmoud can cast his ballot in comparative safety. Even if it is known that he has voted he will not, unlike people living in other districts of Baghdad, be in much danger. He is not typical, though, of the neighbourhood in which he lives and works: 90 per cent of people in Karada are Shia, and almost 10 per cent are Christian.

For all his determination to vote, Mahmoud does not think life will get much better. 'If you want to have a stable Iraq, you must have a real dialogue with the resistance here, the men who carry arms,' he says. 'Lots of my friends are not voting for this reason. They say that this is the most important thing for the country. They tell me that they think what is happening is just an American show to impress the international community. I am going to vote, but I think they should have delayed the election for three months so all communities in Iraq could take part.' While Kurds and Shia will vote, the abstention of most of the Sunni will permanently destabilise the country in his view. 'It is like making a table with only three legs,' he says. 'It will never stand up straight.'

3 February 2005

On the day of the election, 30 January the streets of Baghdad were clear of traffic. Families, mainly Shia, drifted down the main road in the Jadriyah district to the polling stations near the al-Hamra Hotel, where I live. The thump-thump of mortars in the distance did not affect the festive mood. The odd bicycle rattled past. For the first time in more than a year there was no danger of suicide car bombs. A blue and white police vehicle hooted at a small child kicking a ball. Children often play in the alleyway behind the hotel—their favourite game, played with plastic Kalashnikovs, is Americans vs. the resistance—but it had been a long time since I had seen any of them on the main road.

Jadriyah, a middle-class neighbourhood built on a large loop in the Tigris, is one of the safer parts of Baghdad. When it is warm enough to sit outside in the evenings, families eat kebabs and drink tea in makeshift restaurants beside the main road. But things are changing. Last month a suicide bomber blew himself up beside a large half-finished office building that served as a guard post for the Australian soldiers who protect their embassy. A nearby building was turned into a grey concrete sandwich by the blast, as one floor collapsed on top of another. 'He must have been one of the stupidest bombers in the world,' said Nabil, a businessman who was sitting on a chair in the street watching voters go by. 'He killed two people, both Iraqis. One of them was a mentally ill man everybody liked who'd never recovered from his son being killed in the Iran–Iraq War.'

A few hundred yards further down the road was a battered white kiosk where a middle-aged man was selling cigarettes. On the inside wall of the kiosk was a picture of him and his 14-year-old son. The boy was called Ali Abbas. He used to sell me cigarettes until I gave up smoking in December 2003. When another suicide bomber blew himself up in Jadriyah Street—his target was never clear—I had forgotten that the explosion was close to Ali's kiosk; I did not know that it had killed him.

The election is not likely to bring peace nearer. The resistance is still escalating in Sunni areas. The insurgents are getting more expert. The night before the election they fired a rocket into the US embassy in the heart of the heavily fortified Green Zone, killing two Americans. On the afternoon of the poll they shot down an RAF Hercules with a missile, killing ten men, the worst British loss in a single incident since the war began. US policy is gradually to replace American troops with a newly trained Iraqi police force and army. But Iraqis are terrified of being identified as working for the occupation. Shortly before the election, a man drove a Toyota car into Zaidoun Street, which contains several government buildings, including the office of the Iraqi National Accord, the party of Iyad Allawi. Challenged by police commandos in camouflage uniforms and black ski masks, the man detonated a bomb. 'Going by the remains of his face which we found later, we think he was a non-Iraqi Arab, maybe a Sudanese or from the Gulf,' the detective in charge of the case told me.

It was a routine suicide bombing. More telling about the state of security in Iraq was the attitude of the injured police commandos after they arrived in the Yarmouk hospital. Even as they lay in bed they clutched their submachine guns and refused to remove their ski masks in case they might be recognised and hunted down by insurgents. 'You mustn't take any photographs,' a masked commando shouted at two Iraqi photographers as he blocked the doorway into the ward where the policemen were being treated.

The election may have come too late. If it had happened in the months after the invasion, Iraqis would not have felt they were being occupied by an imperial power. Now a new political class—drawn from the unpopular exiled parties, long absent from Iraq and dependent on foreign intelligence services—has got used to power and is not going to give it up easily. Equally the resistance is too well entrenched in the Sunni Arab provinces of Iraq for it to be eradicated. An opinion poll last month showed that 53 per cent of the 5 million Sunni supported armed resistance.

The Western media coverage of the election was simple-minded, treating it as a horse race, with Iraq as the prize. Mahmoud Othman, a veteran Kurdish politician elected to the National Assembly, says that a new Iraqi government needs to do three things: open negotiations with the resistance, arrange a timetable for American withdrawal, and go some way towards ending the worsening economic crisis.

None of these is likely to happen soon because, regardless of the result of the election, real power in Iraq is still largely held by the US. The interim government cannot even hold a press conference unless it is protected by American machine-gunners inside the Green Zone. In the weeks before the election, the US embassy in Baghdad, which still operates from Saddam's old Republican Palace, the symbolic centre of power in Iraq, made clear to the Iraqi political leaders that there were two things the US could not accept: a Muslim cleric at the head of the new government, and any official demands for a timetable for American withdrawal. This veto, spoken or unspoken, remains in place. There is no doubt what Iraqi Arabs want. In a recent opinion poll, 82 per cent of Sunni said they want the US to leave as soon as an elected government is in place. More surprisingly, 69 per cent of Shia gave the same answer. Only the Kurds want the US to stay. 'You can't talk to the Americans,' Abu Ali Anwar says. 'I have no food, electricity or fuel. It was bad under Saddam but now it is ten times worse.'

A significant pointer to the real balance of power in Iraq is the speed with which the Sunni and Shia political leaders covertly bowed to US demands. The United Iraqi Alliance told voters that electing its candidates was the quickest way to end the occupation. The second item in its manifesto was a demand for a timetable for multinational withdrawal. Just before the election, the manifesto was withdrawn. When it re-emerged, the item about US withdrawal had disappeared. The Arabic version of Allawi's party website also called for 'a conditions-based withdrawal'; when the US complained, Allawi quickly gave a series of interviews saying that talk of a pull-out was premature.

The Shia and Sunni political parties have a dilemma. Whatever they say in public about ending the occupation, they know they can scarcely survive without it. The Brussels-based International Crisis Group said in a well-informed report in December that 'national elections scheduled for

January will change little unless they produce institutions that can address basic needs and prove their independence by distancing themselves from the US and reaching out to all political components.' This coincides with what Othman recommends but, whatever the make-up of the National Assembly, it is unlikely to produce a government which can do any of these things effectively.

The television and newspaper coverage of Iraq in the run-up to the poll gave the impression that Iraqis were spending their time talking about the outcome of the election. In fact, conversations are more likely to be about the economic crisis and the shortages. In January, for the first time, large areas of Baghdad had no drinking water. The electricity supply is poor. It is cold this winter: people are turning to kerosene heaters. But the fuel is in short supply, mostly coming from men who drive tanks of it around the streets on carts drawn by mangy horses. Much of Baghdad now depends on small generators, costing about £100 each, to produce enough electricity for lights and television. This increases the demand for petrol further.

The interim government, set up last June, has a reputation for extreme corruption. 'You can't get the smallest contract from them without bribery at every level,' an Iraqi businessman tells me. In Najaf during the election, it was impossible to buy petrol legally since the supply was diverted into the black market controlled by the local police. For all the billions of dollars supposedly spent on reconstruction, the only cranes to be seen on the skyline of Baghdad are a few rusty ones rising around two giant mosques that Saddam Hussein had been building. Some nine billion dollars spent under the US-controlled CPA in 2003–04 cannot be accounted for. Officials in the oil ministry are blamed for complex scams that divert petrol, intended to be sold to the Iraqi consumer at artificially low prices, to neighbouring countries where it is sold at market price. The officials pocket the difference. Even the mobile phone system is packing up. This was one of the few welcome innovations post-Saddam but now the phones very often do not work.

The government has shown itself incapable of dealing with the economy, or lack of it. Ministers are incompetent. Many lived abroad for decades and their families are still there. The amount of time they spend out of the country is a standing joke in Baghdad. One paper claimed to have established that on one day the entire cabinet was travelling on urgent business outside Iraq. Once safely in New York, London, Paris or Dubai, ministers are happy to give optimistic interviews about the state of Iraq: the insurgents, they say, are on the run. The Kurdish ministers are the exception: they have decades of political and administrative experience. After years of fighting Saddam Hussein, they are also less troubled by the constant attempts to assassinate them. Hoshyar Zebari, the foreign minister and a Kurdish leader long on the run from Saddam, seemed amused rather than worried that a torpedo, presumably looted from a naval arsenal, had been found in a truck near his house packed around with 880 kilos of artillery shells and explosives. The truck driver had lost his nerve at the last moment and run off.

A new Iraqi government may be more legitimate than the old one, since it will have been elected, but it will still be weak. It is to last only 11 months, after which there will be fresh elections for a National Assembly once a constitution has been passed by a referendum. The selection of a government this time round will be tortuous, requiring compromise between different communities, and may well produce paralysis. As in Lebanon it may institutionalise sectarian divisions. The deputies will first choose a president and vice president by a two-thirds majority. These must then agree unanimously on a choice of prime minister, who will in turn choose a government, which must then be confirmed by the assembly. This system was devised largely at the insistence of the Kurds, who want to have a veto on any decision that might reduce their quasi-independence.

Journalists traditionally approve of elections as a cure for all ills. The arrival of each voter at a polling station in a Sunni area was deemed another body blow to the insurgency. CNN interviewed a smiling policeman in the ruins of Fallujah, who said he had been pleasantly surprised by the number of people voting. It was the fourth time in a little over a year that a supposed turning point for the US and its local allies had been reached. The first was in December 2003, when Saddam Hussein was captured. Six months later sovereignty was formally handed back to a US-nominated Iraqi government amid media fanfares. Last November, after savage fighting, the US recaptured Fallujah and American generals claimed to have broken the back of the resistance. Expectations of a real change after the elections may turn out to be equally exaggerated. The Americans will stay; the war will go on.

14 February 2005

The final election results have confirmed the victory of the Shia coalition, or United Iraqi Alliance, cobbled together by Grand Ayatollah Ali al-Sistani, even if it was not the clean sweep some of its party leaders may have hoped for. The Kurds also fared well with a quarter of the votes.

The Sunni community very largely abstained. It is not only that a mere 2 per cent of people voted in Anbar province, but in Nineveh province, of which the capital is Mosul, the turnout was only 17 per cent, and most of these voters were probably Kurds. Optimistic forecasts that the Sunni vote might be higher than supposed turned out to be propaganda.

The Iraqi list of Iyad Allawi, the interim prime minister, at first seemed to have done better than expected. He was well financed by the US and Arab states such as the United Arab Emirates. He had the advantages of incumbency. He hoped to win the votes of secular Iraqis, particularly the Shia who fear the religious parties. In the event, Allawi's 14 per cent was a disappointment.

The almost inevitable result will be a Shia–Kurdish coalition. The Kurds are relieved that the Shia list did not get the two-thirds majority needed to form a government on its own. There will now be intense negotiations on who gets what job. The major Shia parties in the United Iraqi Alliance, the Supreme Council for Islamic Revolution in Iraq and Dawa, are in the bizarre position of relying partly on Iran and partly on the US for their real power. They also know that their victory owes more to Grand Ayatollah Sistani's support than to their own popularity.

The US now must deal with the sort of government it did not want to see elected. It must co-operate with some politicians that it was trying to arrest 18 months ago. The election is a step forward but it will produce a weak government with an inadequate army, battered security forces and a corrupt bureaucracy.

7 April 2005

The Shia leader Ibrahim al-Jaafari has been chosen as the prime minister of Iraq after prolonged wrangling between the victors in the election nine weeks ago. The solemnity of the moment of his appointment was marred when the new Iraqi president, the Kurdish leader Jalal Talabani, mysteriously left the ceremony. When he re-emerged he explained that he had momentarily forgotten the name of the prime minister whom he was appointing. Jaafari, the mild-mannered leader of the Islamic Dawa Party, did not look disturbed by Talabani's sudden memory loss. But other members of the United Iraqi Alliance saw it as a possible bad omen.

Jaafari, a physician exiled for two decades, first in Iran and then in

Britain, is considered to lack a forceful personality by other Iraqi political leaders and he has got the job of prime minister in part because he has fewer enemies than other candidates. In contrast the new president, Talabani, is a vastly experienced and powerful Kurd who evidently intends to play a prominent role in future, despite the office of president being a largely ceremonial one. His election marks an extraordinary reversal of fortune for the long-persecuted Kurds, and he is the first non-Arab president of an Arab state. People danced and waved the Kurdish flag in the streets of Kurdish towns and villages as the news of Talabani's selection was announced.

11 April 2005

Gunmen ordered 16 off-duty Iraqi soldiers out of a truck in Latafiya, south of Baghdad, at the weekend and killed them, but signs are growing that the slaughter of all Iraqis in the army or police, or civilians working for the government, is leading to divisions in the resistance. The split is between Islamic fanatics, willing to killing anybody remotely connected with the government, and Iraqi nationalists who want to concentrate on attacking US troops. Posters threatening extreme resistance fighters have appeared on walls in Ramadi, a Sunni Muslim city on the Euphrates river west of Baghdad. Insurgents in the city say that resistance to the Americans is being discredited by the kidnapping and killing of civilians.

The resistance has proved extraordinarily effective—far more so than the regular Iraqi Army during the war in 2003—killing 1,089 US soldiers and wounding some 10,000. The key to its effectiveness is that it has swum in a sea of popular support or acquiescence. However, the near universal antipathy to the occupation has enabled marginal, unpopular or criminal groups opposed to the US to flourish. Islamic fundamentalists, commonly called the Salafi or Wahhabi, have been able to establish themselves in Sunni Muslim districts. Baathist officials, army officers and security men were swiftly able to establish guerrilla cells.

The extreme Islamic groups, typified by that led by Abu Musab al-Zarqawi, see themselves fighting a world full of 'infidels', 'apostates' and 'crusaders' in which an Iraqi Shia or Christian is as worthy of death as a US soldier. When American forces damaged two mosques in Mosul in fighting, the resistance blew up two Iraqi Christian churches. The Sunni sectarianism of the Salafi has limited the nationalist appeal of the resistance and ensured that the Shia largely supported the destruction of Fallujah by the US Marines last November.

6 May 2005

The three months it took to cobble together a government in Iraq after January's election shows the depth of the divisions between the Shia, Sunni and Kurdish communities. In the north of the country the Sunni Arabs and the Kurds are close to civil war. Their savage skirmishes, around the oil city of Kirkuk and in the streets of Mosul, are generally unreported in Baghdad. The war of 2003 made the Kurds the north's dominant power. They are no longer penned in their mountains, or in their decrepit cities crowded with refugees from the 3,800 villages destroyed by Saddam Hussein. But their advance south is contested by the Sunni Arabs, everywhere on the retreat but able to stage daily suicide bomb attacks, ambushes and assassinations. On 4 May a man with explosives attached to his body blew himself up in a queue of young men trying to join the police in Arbil, killing 60 of them and wounding 150. Ghassan Attiyah, a political commentator in Baghdad, tells me: 'The Kurds were able to destabilise Iraq for half a century under Saddam Hussein and his predecessors. The Sunni Arabs are certainly strong enough to do the same thing if they want to.'

The Kurds have the upper hand militarily in Kirkuk and are not going to give it up. They are intent on reversing decades of Arabisation by forcing out the settlers from central and southern Iraq brought in by Saddam. I recently met a shaken-looking journalist from *Hawlati*, an independent Kurdish magazine, who had been instructed by his editor to leave the city. The local police had told him he would be killed if he did not get out or hire bodyguards. His editor, Asos Hardi, has spoken out against de-Arabisation: the Kurds, he says, must not do to the Arabs what Saddam did to the Kurds. Few Kurds agree with him, and it is easy to see why. In the swaths of open grassland around Kirkuk, a few stones or the outline of a wall are the only signs of where a village used to be before Saddam's Anfal campaign of collective punishment in 1987–88, when 779 Kurdish villages were bulldozed or blown up, along with their schools, clinics and mosques. 'They even cemented up the wells and killed the animals so nobody could come back,' Nouri Talabani, a professor of law who chronicled the destruction, tells me.

The Kurds want their land back. But they also want the Northern Oil Company, part of the Iraqi National Oil Company, which runs the oil fields west of Kirkuk. Talabani complains that until recently 'there were only 33 Kurds out of 10,000 people working for the oil company.' The Sunni insurgents are determined to keep striking at Iraqi oil exports. Some of the bloodiest fighting is along the oil pipeline which passes through a string of Arab villages in Kirkuk province. If the Kurds are to win autonomy from Baghdad, or anything close to independence, then they need a measure of control over the oil fields.

The sectarian geography of this no man's land between Arabs and Kurds is intricate. Kurdish control peters out in the west and south of the province. Around the town of Hawaijah, a notorious Baathist stronghold to the west, the farmers working in the fields are Arabs. When the US tried to sack Baath Party members here after the invasion, the local hospital almost closed down: all its doctors were members. The headmaster of a secondary school was fired for being a Baathist. His pupils offered to burn down the school in retaliation but he persuaded them not to. The new headmaster, sent from Kirkuk, was too frightened to take up his post. The situation is even more unstable in Mosul, a city of 1.75 million people on the Tigris. Some 70 per cent of its population are Arabs, mostly living on the west bank of the river; the rest are Kurds, who live mostly on the east bank. It is a traditional centre of Arab nationalism and religious fundamentalism. Saadi Pira, until recently the leader in Mosul of the Patriotic Union of Kurdistan, claims that 'Mosul was always the true centre of the resistance to the Americans, much more than Fallujah.' The Kurds in Mosul do not even bother to pretend that it is anything other than extremely dangerous.

To help me get into Mosul in reasonable safety, I am sent by the Kurdish government in Arbil into the Kurdish heartland to get protection from a battalion of the Iraqi National Guard. The commander, having at first complained that he could not spare any men, orders four heavily armed Peshmerga to travel with me in a pick-up truck. We drive to an army post on the outskirts of Mosul, where Lieutenant Colonel Jassim refuses to allow us into the city in a three-vehicle convoy with uniformed soldiers. Too conspicuous, he says: we will be a target for suicide bombers. A nondescript civilian car is procured; two soldiers are to accompany us, with Arab robes over their uniforms. The driver tries to stick to the Kurdish neighbourhoods, driving at high speed up and down alleyways. At one point, driving even faster past a row of large villas, he says: 'This area was allocated to senior army officers under Saddam and now they are all terrorists. There have been many attacks here.' As we get close to the old Baath Party headquarters, now taken over by the Kurdistan Democratic Party, a cloud of smoke and dust spurts into the air from an explosion a few hundred yards away. On the way back we see the mangled wreckage of a car bomb.

Khasro Goran, the deputy governor of Mosul and the leader of the KDP, claims that security in the city is much improved, though not perfect. The largest government security force in Nineveh province, of which Mosul is the capital, is the 14,000-strong, mainly Arab, blue-uniformed police. 'They are not much good at finding terrorists,' Goran says, 'because they are terrorists themselves.' He suspects them of being implicated in the assassination of the previous governor and has warned his own bodyguards against telling the police about his movements: they might try to assassinate him.

The police showed their real sympathies during an uprising on 11 November last year when the resistance entered Mosul in force. It happened a few days after the start of the US Marines' assault on Fallujah, and so was little noticed by the outside world. The Western media were either confined to their hotels in Baghdad for fear of being kidnapped or embedded with US Army units. While triumphant American reporters and generals trumpeted victory from Fallujah, the insurgents were able quietly to capture Mosul, which has a population five times as large. The police abandoned their barracks—some 30 of them are still empty six months later—and their commander fled. The resistance captured $40 million worth of arms and equipment. Weeks later the bodies of executed Iraqi soldiers were still turning up all over the city. Police loyalty has not improved since. Recently, a Kurdish unit of the Iraqi Army was ambushed west of the city, close to the Syrian border. The soldiers pursued their attackers, but only as far as the nearest police station, where they had found refuge. The Kurds say that both groups—insurgents and police—belong to the powerful Sunni Arab Shammar tribe.

US influence is on the retreat in Nineveh province, as it is in the rest of Iraq. There are few troops on the ground: no more than 6,000 American soldiers remain in an area with a population of nearly 3 million. For a year after the invasion, 21,000 men from the heavily equipped 101st Airborne Division had been stationed in Mosul. The division's commander, General David Petraeus, probably the most intelligent senior American officer in Iraq, reached a tentative understanding with the local Sunni Arab establishment. Thousands of former army officers took a public oath renouncing the Baath Party. The Kurds were furious that the Americans were truckling to Saddam's former lieutenants. Since then, the American military has changed tack, favouring the Kurds and hostile to the Sunni Arabs. But they have no choice: the Kurds are America's most important ally. In Mosul the

CIA depends on Kurdish intelligence. 'When the CIA tried to operate by themselves in the city last year they learned nothing,' a local observer says. 'These days the Kurds provide the agents and the Americans provide the money and together they are very effective.' But perhaps they are not effective enough. The Sunni Arabs of the north remain wholly alienated and will continue to give shelter to the resistance. Animosity between Kurds and Arabs in Mosul is deep. A Kurdish leader in Arbil says: 'Mosul is a time bomb waiting to explode.' Khasro Goran is more optimistic, but in passing he mentions that at the time of the election somebody had tried to assassinate him, killing one of his bodyguards and wounding two others.

The Kurds, almost to their own surprise, are the community which made the biggest gains after Saddam's fall: they hold Kirkuk; one of their leaders is president of Iraq; they enjoy a degree of autonomy close to independence. The US needs the Kurds, its only reliable allies in Iraq (though it would have been happy to let the Turkish Army march into Iraqi Kurdistan during the war, had Turkey allowed US divisions to be based in Turkey). But the Kurds fear that this may be as good as it gets. They dare not declare formal independence for fear of a Turkish invasion. The government in Baghdad will get stronger in time, and as it does so it may try to restore its authority over Kurdistan.

Politically and militarily strong for now, the Kurds are geographically isolated. It takes two days to travel back from Kirkuk to Baghdad: the two-hour road journey is too dangerous, and I have to go by way of Turkey. The only airport in Iraqi Kurdistan, at Arbil, is closed: the central government claims it is not properly equipped. Traffic between Iraq and Turkey passes over two bridges a few hundred yards apart on a fast-flowing river at Ibrahim Khalil. This might be the longest traffic jam in the world. Columns of trucks and petrol tankers waiting to cross the border stretch back 70 kilometres into Turkey. Sometimes drivers wait two and a half weeks to get across. Turkey, worried by the impact of events in Iraq on its own Kurdish population, tightens or relaxes the regulations for crossing the bridges to show the Iraqi Kurds that it controls their main link with the outside world.

As we leave northern Iraq we spend three and a half hours at the border while Turkish gendarmerie search each car. Afterwards, plainclothes intelligence officers come along and search everybody all over again. Among those waiting patiently on the bridge to leave the country is Dr Azad Khanaqa, a confident-looking Iraqi Kurd now living in Saudi Arabia. Formerly a microbiologist at Hannover University, he is an expert on the growing of truffles. He tells me he hopes to use his knowledge to revive the area where he grew up, east of Kirkuk. 'They destroyed everything,' Khanaqa says, 'my father's house in particular, with bulldozers and explosives.' He intends to plant olive, oak, cedar, hazelnut and walnut trees in the ruins. Among their roots the spores of the black truffle will be implanted, and in four or five years will grow into a sort of underground mushroom, selling for 1,400 euros a kilo. I like Khanaqa's plan: to introduce the truffle into a country-side better known for its minefields.

13 May 2005

In Iraq a barber works in a dangerous trade. Many have been murdered, beaten or forced to close their businesses by Islamic fanatics who accuse them of shaving off beards or giving Western-style haircuts. 'I did not take them seriously when they warned me against shaving off beards,' laments Mohammed Hassan al-Jebabi, once the owner of a barbershop in a Sunni town on the outskirts of Baghdad. 'One day six men arrived in a pick-up truck. They shot into the air and took me away. After 12 days they dumped me back in front of my shop with my arms and legs broken. They said next time they would cut off my hands.'

The Salafi or Wahhabi fundamentalists believe it is un-Islamic for men to shave or for barbers to employ an ancient method of hair removal using a thread. Even trimming beards is seen as a crime against religion. Most bar-bershops in Sunni or mixed Shia and Sunni districts of Baghdad now carry a notice in the window saying: 'We apologise to our customers but we are not shaving beards.' It became common a month ago and ended a fortnight in which barbershops were shut after the murder of Abbas, a hairdresser in the Sha'ab district. Three men arrived outside his shop in a car. One went in and said: 'We told you to stop.' He then shot Abbas.

The killing persuaded Abdullah Farhan not to shave any more beards. He says: 'Abbas was a friend of mine. They told me that Islam rejected the shaving off of beards, though I doubt it. Now our business is down 50 per cent.' Many barbers have closed. Zeidoun Kamal Abdullah in Haifa Street says he has not been threatened. But Khalid, a friend of his from the same district, was killed because he shaved beards and gave short-back-and-sides haircuts, which in Iraq is known as 'the marine haircut'.

The dangerous decision on wearing or not wearing a beard under-lines the chronic insecurity of life in Iraq today. Dangerous though it may be to shave off a beard it is by no means safe to wear one. While fundamentalists persecute the clean shaven, government forces are highly suspicious of excessive facial hair as a sign of extreme Islamic and insurgent sympathies.

13 July 2005

A street in al-Jedidah, a poor Shia neighbourhood of Baghdad, is filled with distraught relatives gathering up the dead and injured. Women scream in anger and rage. A suicide car bomber has killed 27 people and wounded 67, most of them children, after blowing himself up beside a US patrol. The children were crowding around the American vehicle to receive sweets from soldiers when they were caught by the blast. A child's bicycle lies on its side spattered with blood. All that remains of the bomber's car is a blackened engine block.

The explosion was so powerful that it set a nearby house on fire and damaged two others. The children who gathered around the US Humvee stood little chance. The bomb also killed one and wounded three American soldiers. The US military is likely to be blamed by Iraqis for attracting children close to their vehicles by giving away sweets. Last September, 35 children were killed by bombs which exploded as American troops were giving out sweets at a ceremony to celebrate the opening of a sewage plant in west Baghdad.

24 July 2005

The Duke of Wellington, warning hawkish politicians in Britain against ill-considered military intervention abroad, once said: 'Great nations do not have small wars.' He meant that supposedly limited conflicts can inflict terrible damage on powerful states. Having seen what a small war in Spain had done to Napoleon, he knew what he was talking about.

The war in Iraq is now joining the Boer War in 1899 and the Suez crisis in 1956 as ill-considered ventures that have done Britain more harm than good. It has demonstrably strengthened al-Qa'ida by providing it with a large pool of activists and sympathisers across the Muslim world it did not possess before the invasion of 2003. The war, which started out as a demonstration of US strength as the world's only superpower, has turned into a demonstration of weakness.

The suicide bombing campaign in Iraq is unique. Never before have so many fanatical young Muslims been willing to kill themselves, trying to destroy those whom they see as their enemies. It is this campaign which has now spread to Britain and Egypt. The Iraq war has radicalised a significant part of the Muslim world.

The shrill denials by Tony Blair and Jack Straw that hostility to the invasion of Iraq motivated the bombers are demonstrably untrue. The findings of an investigation, to be published soon, into 300 young Saudis, caught and interrogated by Saudi intelligence on their way to Iraq to fight or blow themselves up, shows that very few had any previous contact with al-Qa'ida or any other terrorist organisation previous to 2003. It was the invasion of Iraq which prompted their decision to die.

Some 36 Saudis who did blow themselves up in Iraq did so for similar reasons, according to the same study, commissioned by the Saudi government and carried out by a US-trained Saudi researcher, Nawaf Obaid, who was given permission to speak to Saudi intelligence officers. A separate Israeli study of 154 foreign fighters in Iraq, carried out by the Global Research in International Affairs Centre in Israel, also concluded that almost all had been radicalised by Iraq alone.

Before Iraq, those who undertook suicide bombings were a small, hunted group; since the invasion they have become a potent force, their ideology and tactics adopted by militant Islamic groups around the world. Their numbers may still not be very large but they are numerous enough to create mayhem in Iraq and anywhere else they strike, be it in London or Sharm el Sheikh.

The bombers have paralysed Baghdad. The detonations of the suicide bombs make my windows shake in their frames in my room in the al-Hamra hotel. Sometimes, thinking the glass is going to shatter, I take shelter behind a thick wall. The hotel is heavily guarded. At one time the man who looked for bombs under cars entering the compound with a mirror on the end of a stick carried a pistol in his right hand. He reckoned that if he did discover a suicide bomber he had a split second in which to shoot him in the head before the driver detonated his bomb.

For future historians Iraq will probably replace Vietnam as the stock example of the truth of Wellington's dictum about small wars escalating into big ones. Ironically, the US and Britain pretended in 2003 that Saddam ruled a powerful state capable of menacing his neighbours. Secretly they believed this was untrue and expected an easy victory. Now in 2005 they find to their horror that there are people in Iraq more truly dangerous than Saddam, and they are mired in an un-winnable conflict.

4 August 2005

Suicide bombs blow up with the regularity of an artillery barrage in Baghdad. I no longer always go up onto the roof of the hotel where I live to see the black smoke rising and to try to work out where the bomb went off. On a single day recently 12 suicide bombs exploded in the city, killing at least 30 people.

It is only when a bomb explodes in a place where I might have been or when the atrocity is particularly grotesque that I pay much attention. One day three bombers—one in a vehicle, two on foot—attacked the entrance to the Green Zone normally used by journalists attending press conferences. A surviving policeman said that one bomb was concealed in a coffin strapped to the roof of a van. The driver had got through a checkpoint by saying he was delivering a body to the police forensic laboratory.

Few of the suicide bombers are Iraqi (so they say), though the number may be increasing. But the organisation, the vehicles, the explosives, the detonators, the safe houses and the intelligence must all be home-grown. Hoshyar Zebari, the foreign minister, tells me that the Iraqi Army recently found a workshop capable of turning out seventy cars rigged to explode every day.

According to Iraqi government intelligence, bombers are given a primary target, but if they cannot reach it they drive around Baghdad looking for someone else to kill. They are always told never to come back. Some buildings have been hit again and again, the army recruitment centre at the old al-Muthana airport no fewer than seven times. Every time I drive past there I see hundreds of young men, dressed in white robes and flip-flops, probably from southern Iraq, waiting to be interviewed. The guards try to herd them away, shouting: 'You'll make yourselves targets.' But they are desperate for jobs and frightened of losing their place in the queue. A few weeks ago a young man started making a speech to the would-be recruits, complaining that they were being forced to wait while successful applicants were paying bribes. Nodding their heads in agreement, the volunteers gathered around the speaker. When a large enough crowd had assembled he pressed a switch and blew himself up, along with 25 of those listening to him.

There are near daily massacres of working-class Shia, but now the Shia have started to strike back. The bodies of Sunni are being found in rubbish dumps across Baghdad. 'I was told in Najaf by senior leaders that they have killed upwards of a thousand Sunni,' an Iraqi official says. Often the killers belong, at least nominally, to the government's paramilitary forces, including the police commandos. These commandos seem increasingly to be operating under the control of certain Shia, who may be members of the Badr Brigade, the military arm of the Supreme Council for the Islamic Revolution in Iraq and the country's largest militia, with up to 70,000 men.

The commandos, whose units have macho names such as Wolf Brigade and Lion Brigade, certainly look and act like a militia. They drive around in pick-up trucks, shooting into the air to clear the traffic, and are regarded with terror in Sunni districts. In one raid the commandos arrested nine Sunni Arabs who had taken a friend with a bullet wound in his leg to hospital. (The commandos claimed they were suspected insurgents, even though wounded resistance fighters generally keep away from hospitals.) The men were left in the back of a police vehicle which was parked in the sun with the air conditioning switched off: all were asphyxiated. Abu Musab al-Zarqawi, leader of the shadowy al-Qa'ida in Iraq, has announced that he is setting up a group called the Omar Brigade specifically to target the Badr militia.

Unlike the death squads that used to operate in Latin America, the Shia commandos rarely try to conceal their responsibility for killings. They arrive in full uniform, a garish green and yellow camouflage, at the homes of former Sunni officials and arrest them. A few days later the bodies— sometimes savagely tortured, with eyes gouged out and legs broken—turn up in the morgue. The Badr Brigade, which fought on the Iranian side in the Iran–Iraq War of 1980–88, is often said to be an arm of Iranian intelligence determined to settle old scores. Air force pilots believe they are being singled out for assassination because they are suspected of having bombed Iranian cities nearly 20 years ago. This may not be true, but fear of the death squads is certainly pushing the Sunni community as a whole towards sympathy with the insurgents, who are seen as armed fellow Sunni who might protect them.

More than two years after the US invasion the Iraqi state remains extraordinarily weak. At 5 a.m. on one day in mid-June, resistance fighters walked into Dohra, a large district of south Baghdad, and took it over: the local police disappeared. The insurgents retreated only when US helicopters arrived overhead. The army and police are often less well armed than the insurgents. Yet immense sums of money have been spent on training and equipment. 'The Ministry of Defence and the Ministry of the Interior spent $5.2 billion under the interim government of Iyad Allawi,' a senior official tells me, 'but we don't know what happened to the money.' He adds sorrowfully that he asked the interior ministry for 50 pistols for the presidential bodyguards; he was told they had none.

The most notorious scandal in Iraq at the moment is the government's purchase of 24 military helicopters as part of a $300 million deal with a Polish engineering company. They were paid for up front. When an Iraqi inspection team went to Poland, they found that the helicopters were 28-year-old Soviet Army machines that, according to the manufacturer, should have been put out of commission three years ago. The Iraqis are now trying to get their money back. The Ministry of Defence says it is investigating 40 questionable contracts, for everything from machine guns to armoured vehicles. One shipment of MP5 machine guns was received at a cost of $3,500 a gun: the guns turned out to be Egyptian copies that should have cost $200 each.

Defence procurement in the Middle East, as in much of the world, is corrupt. But in most countries usable equipment, however overpriced, does eventually turn up. In Iraq the corruption is on a different scale: often the money disappears entirely and nothing is received in return. For two years the Iraqi administration has been less a government than a racket. The corruption does not stop with defence. Laith Kubba, a senior aide to Ibrahim al-Jaafari, cites the case of 'a power station ordered at a cost of $500 million but the contract details covered just one sheet of paper. A ministerial committee refused to sign that contract so the minister sacked them and appointed a committee which would sign.' Salam al-Maliki, the transport minister, says: 'Everything has been stolen in the ministry bar its name.' Commuter buses were sold for spare parts and new trucks simply disappeared. Even the bed-sheets for the police guarding the ministry were stolen.

The looting of Baghdad which began in the days after Saddam's fall has never really ended. 'Security is our biggest problem and after that corruption,' says Kamaran Karadaghi, President Jalal Talabani's chief of staff. Another official warned me against investigating corruption. In Iraq, he said, more money had been stolen by a few people 'than a Colombian drug lord could make in a year'.

A few Iraqi officials have been suspended; a few arrest warrants have been issued. Several of the more dubious arms procurement deals were negotiated by Ziad Tareq Cattan, the former deputy defence minister. Returning to Iraq after 27 years in Europe, he was rapidly promoted by Paul Bremer. He was sacked in June and a court order for his arrest issued on 7 July. He is currently in Arbil in Iraqi Kurdistan and claims innocence. He argues that while he worked there the defence ministry was under the control of US generals: he could not have committed the alleged frauds without their knowledge. 'We could do nothing in the ministry without decisions from the generals,' Cattan was quoted as saying. 'We couldn't move a single soldier from east Baghdad to west Baghdad without their permission. We had to ask them, to plead with them for one machine gun.'

Nobody knows how many soldiers and policemen actually turn up for work. Mahmoud Othman, a Kurdish leader, says that an army unit supposedly numbering 2,200 men was sent to Kirkuk. The Kurds counted them: there were just 300 men in the unit. Nobody knew what had happened to the other 1,900. 'They say that there are 150,000 men in the army and police,' Othman says, 'but I believe the real figure is 40,000.' The rest either appear only to draw their pay or never existed in the first place. Establishing the real strength of the army is important because the US and Britain want to reduce the number of their troops. The British want to decrease the size of their force in the south from 8,500 to 3,000 over the next nine months. In cities such as Basra and Amara this means handing over power to the local Shia militias: the Badr Brigade and the Mehdi Army.

7 October 2005

The imminent referendum on a new Iraqi constitution is dividing the country. Sunni Arabs fear it will destroy Iraq by breaking it up into cantons. The Shia and Kurds hope it will give birth to a new Iraq in which they will hold power. The US has put intense pressure on negotiators to reach an agreement because it is desperate to prove to ever more sceptical American voters that Iraq is fast progressing towards democracy.

It is difficult to find many optimists in Baghdad. 'If the constitution passes then the Sunni will not accept it and if it fails the Kurds and the Shia will be very angry,' says Nabil, a driver waiting in a queue outside a petrol station near my hotel. Others have a more apocalyptic view. Hussein Kubba sees the federal constitution as a recipe 'for the break-up of Iraq and endless bloodshed: the south will be a Shia mini-state influenced by Iran and there will be Taliban-like control over the Sunni west. Baghdad will be a no-man's-land. Whatever happens with the referendum the constitution will never have legitimacy.'

It is a bizarre moment for Iraqis to vote on the rules of the system under which they will supposedly live for the foreseeable future. Agreement on a constitution implies a degree of consensus on the type of government the people want and the laws they will obey. But in Iraq Shia and Sunni Arabs cannot visit each other's heartlands in western or southern Iraq without taking the risk of being murdered. An Arab, Sunni or Shia, will be lucky to find a hotel room in a Kurdish city like Arbil or Sulaimaniyah, and even then will be viewed with suspicion.

A constitution also assumes a stable balance of power. But the relationship between the three main Iraqi communities and the foreign occupiers is not stable. The Kurds are at the peak of their power and want to freeze their gains under the constitution. The Shia are also gaining in power. In Iraq political authority has always been exercised through the security agencies. That is why, during the three months of negotiations to form a government after the January election, the Shia insisted on getting the interior ministry. Through it they control much of the police and the paramilitary police commandos. The Sunni are in theory the big losers since the overthrow of Saddam Hussein, but they are able to destabilise Iraq. The US, for its part, would obviously like to cut its losses but does not know how to.

For all the talk of the constitution, the mood in Baghdad is determined more by day-to-day considerations of survival. Everybody's nerves are on edge. As I came in from the airport on the main highway I had my eye on a car near me that was about fifty yards from a police car. A policeman obviously thought it was too close and opened fire. We could not see if he was shooting at the civilian car or in the air. We turned swiftly off the highway onto another road hoping it would be safer. But here there was another problem: a passing convoy of police commandos had heard the shooting. Once again we had to dodge down side streets: the notoriously trigger-happy commandos, thinking somebody was shooting at them, were about to open fire.

25 October 2005

A majority of Iraqis have voted for the new federal constitution, which will divide the country into three regions. The results show that the Sunni Arabs largely voted against the constitution while the Shia and Kurds voted in favour. Overall, 78 per cent of Iraqis voted 'yes' and 21 per cent voted 'no'.

The US and Britain as well as the Iraqi government will hope that the outcome will not be seen as a rebuff to the Sunni, driving them into the arms of the resistance. The constitution envisages a federal state in which Kurds and Shia will have important powers and the central government will be weakened. The Kurds will be able to maintain their own army in northern Iraq, local law will override federal law when the two are in conflict and oil developments will come under regional control. Existing oil fields will continue to be under the central government.

Many Sunni see the constitution as, in effect, marking the break-up of Iraq. But the country will now move towards an election on 15 December in which the Sunni, unlike in the election in January, are likely to participate.

26 October 2005

I no longer go to see the aftermath of suicide bombs, gun battles and assassinations in Baghdad. It is too dangerous. Instead the violence comes to me.

On the floor above the room in the hotel in Baghdad where I live is the office of Rory Carroll, the *Guardian* correspondent. Kidnapped by gunmen last Wednesday, he was happily released 36 hours later in a blaze of publicity.

Unknown to the outside world, a story without a happy ending happened the following day on the floor just below my room. This is the reception area of my block of the hotel where, behind a wooden counter, usually sits Abu Hussein, the friendly and efficient desk clerk. His son had a business collecting money from shopkeepers for whom he would buy scratch cards for mobile phones from a Baghdad cell-phone company. He would get a small commission from the shopkeepers and the company selling the scratch cards.

Somebody must have tipped off a kidnap gang that last Thursday Abu Hussein's son would be carrying upwards of $50,000 in cash to the phone company. He was abducted by two carloads of gunmen. At first they demanded a ransom, but he told them they had just stolen all his money. The kidnappers let him phone his father, adding that he would be released the following day in a certain square in Baghdad.

Abu Hussein went to pick him up. He saw a car draw up and his son get out of it and take several steps towards him. Then the kidnappers fired a burst of shots into his son's back and he fell down dead.

11 December 2005

Hamlet is not usually quoted in the mosques of Baghdad but in the al-Mohsinin mosque Imam Abdullah pauses dramatically in his address before telling worshippers that 'the question for the Sunni people is: to be, or not to be.' He is urging them to vote in the election for the National Assembly on 15 December. He argues the Sunni committed 'a very great error when they did not vote in the January election.' Their enemies had taken over the government. The prime minister permitted death squads to operate against the Sunni community.

The difference from the election in January is that this time Iraq's 5 million Sunni will vote in all but a few militant strongholds. Umm Nadam, a middle-aged housewife shopping in the Karada district of Baghdad, says: 'This is the last chance for the Sunni and we should not lose it.'

Every flat surface in Baghdad is covered in election posters. The grey concrete walls put up to stop suicide bombers provide ideal spaces for political messages. This time, going to vote should not be as perilous as in January when there were numerous attacks by bombers. Sunni insurgents are unlikely to risk blowing up their own people. The borders will be sealed. The airports will be shut. On election day, all vehicles will be banned from the streets.

Nobody doubts the importance of the poll. 'This time it is the real thing,' says an Iraqi politician after ticking off on his fingers the fictitious turning points trumpeted by the US and Britain since the overthrow of Saddam Hussein in 2003. The election will decide the composition of the National Assembly for the next four years. Iraq will have a permanent government rather than a temporary one.

21 December 2005

The first results from the parliamentary election last week show the country is dividing between Shia, Sunni and Kurdish regions. Religious fundamentalists now have the upper hand. Iyad Allawi, the secular and nationalist candidate backed by the US and Britain, endured a humiliating defeat. The election marks the final shipwreck of American and British hopes of establishing a pro-Western secular democracy in a united Iraq.

The Shia religious coalition has won a total victory in Baghdad and the south of Iraq. The Sunni Arab parties who openly or covertly support armed resistance to the US are likely to win large majorities in Sunni provinces. The Kurds have already achieved quasi-independence and their voting reflects that. All the successful parties have strength only within their own community. The Shia coalition succeeded because the Shia make up 60 per cent of Iraqis but won almost no votes among the Kurds or Sunni each of whom is about 20 per cent of the population. The Sunni and the Kurdish parties won no support outside their own communities.

Islamic fundamentalist movements are ever more powerful in both the Sunni and Shia communities. Ghassan Attiyah, an Iraqi commentator, says: 'In two and a half years Bush has succeeded in creating two new Talibans in Iraq.' The success of the United Iraqi Alliance, the coalition of Shia religious parties, has been far greater than expected according to preliminary results. Iran will be pleased that the parties it has supported have become the strongest political force. Ironically, President Bush is increasingly dependent within Iraq on the co-operation and restraint of the Iranian president Mahmoud Ahmadinejad.

Another victor in the election is the fiery nationalist cleric Muqtada al-Sadr. Bush cited the recapture of the holy city of Najaf from Sadr's Mehdi Army in August 2004 as an important success for the US Army. The US military said at the time it intended 'to kill or capture' Sadr. He will now be one of the most influential leaders within the coalition.

The election means a decisive switch from a secular Iraq to a country in which, outside Kurdistan, religious law will be paramount. 'People underestimate how religious Iraq has become,' says one Iraqi observer, adding: 'Iran is really a secular society with a religious leadership, but Iraq will be a religious society with a religious leadership.' Already most girls leaving schools in Baghdad wear headscarves. Women's rights in cases of divorce and inheritance are being eroded.

1 January 2006

It is difficult to avoid a sense of loss in Iraq. The territory on which I live here is constantly shrinking. In 2004 it became too dangerous to leave Baghdad by road. In 2005 the balance between undeniable risk and potential benefit had to be weighed before each journey out of the hotel.

The loss of which I am most conscious is that of my hotel room, number 106 on the first floor of the al-Hamra hotel in the Jadriyah district of Baghdad. It was torn apart by two suicide bombers who blew themselves up 50 yards away on 18 November. I was out of Iraq and my colleague Kim Sengupta was lying in bed reading a book when the bombs exploded, cutting him with flying glass and demolishing the room around him. I found it disorientating to move to a room in an undamaged part of the hotel. The conditions are not too bad. But I miss the place where I lived for so many months since the fall of Saddam. It was a little island of normality in the lethal chaos of Baghdad.

Of course, the losses of almost everybody else in Baghdad are much greater than my own. Many have lost their lives. One thousand bodies of people who have died by violence are brought each month to the melancholy cul-de-sac which houses the city morgue. But the extent of violence in Iraq is so great that it mutes one's emotions. One cannot really mourn for people one has never known when people one does know are being killed or injured.

SIX

Civil War

Iraq, 2006–07

22 February 2006

Iraq has taken a lethal step closer to civil war after a devastating attack on one of the country's holiest sites. The golden-domed Shia shrine at Samarra, north of Baghdad, has been destroyed, sparking a round of bloody sectarian retaliation. The Golden Mosque was attacked early in the morning when men dressed in police uniform tied up the guards and planted explosives. Two bombs were detonated. No one was killed but the historic mosque is badly damaged. The bomb attack has enraged the Shia who regard the shrine in the same way that Roman Catholics view St Peter's in Rome.

The shrine is very difficult to defend. The majority of people in Samarra are Sunni and in 2004 the city was taken by Islamic extremists before being recaptured by the Americans. Although I was searched the last time I visited the mosque it has large gateways through the outer wall into an inner courtyard, which armed men would find easy to storm. The shrine guards, who might detect a single bomber, were evidently not able to stop a unit of armed and determined men posing as police.

The destruction of the Golden Mosque will be an immense psychological blow to Iraqi Shia who have endured so much down the centuries. The shrine contains the tombs of the 10th and 11th imams, Ali al-Hadi who died AD 868 and his son Hassan Ali al-Askari who died AD 874. His son, the last of the 12 Shia imams, Mohammed al-Mahdi, disappeared and is known as the 'hidden imam'. Shia believe he is still alive and will bring justice to humanity.

In response to the bombing the Iraqi president, Jalal Talabani, called on Iraqis to 'stand hand in hand to prevent the danger of civil war'. He urged the formation of a national unity government that 'will bring stability to Iraq'. But there is little sign of stability. In retaliation for the attack some 50 Sunni mosques have already been burnt, blown up or taken over in Baghdad alone. At least three Sunni clerics are among 11 reported deaths nationwide.

Armed militiamen of the Mehdi Army have taken up positions on the streets of Baghdad and in the Shia cities of the south. Muqtada al-Sadr himself is returning quickly to Iraq after cancelling a meeting with the Lebanese president. One of his aides said: 'If the Iraqi government does not do its job to defend the Iraqi people we are ready to do so.'

As news spread of sectarian clashes and demonstrations, people in Baghdad rushed home before dark and some started to stock up on food. In Najaf, another Shia holy city, protesters chanted: 'Rise up Shia! Take revenge!' In one of the most serious acts of retaliation, Shia protesters set fire to a famous Sunni shrine on the outskirts of Basra. It contains the tomb of Talha bin-Obeid-Allah, a companion of the Prophet Mohammed.

The Shia clerical leader, Grand Ayatollah Ali al-Sistani, called for a week of mourning and has forbidden attacks on Sunni mosques, asking people to protest peacefully. He made a rare appearance on television, shown meeting in his house in Najaf three other grand ayatollahs to discuss the destruction of the mosque in Samarra. In the past Sistani's appeals for calm have been heeded despite a long series of atrocities by suicide bombers against the Shia which has left several thousand dead. There are signs that patience among the Shia is now growing thin.

In a number of respects civil war in Iraq has already begun. Many of the thousand bodies a month arriving in the morgue in Baghdad are of people killed for sectarian reasons. It is no longer safe for members of the three main communities to visit each other's parts of the country. Death squads targeting Sunni operate in Baghdad. Sunni are particularly terrified of the police commando brigades controlled by the interior ministry.

19 March 2006

Iraq is a country paralysed by fear. It is at its worst in Baghdad. Sectarian killings are commonplace. In the three days after the bombing of the Shia shrine in Samarra some 1,300 people, mostly Sunni, were picked up on the street or dragged from their cars and murdered. The dead bodies of four suspected suicide bombers were left dangling from a pylon in the Sadr slum. The scale of the violence is such that most of it is unreported. The country's former prime minister, Iyad Allawi, says that scores are dying every day: 'It is unfortunate that we are in civil war. We are losing each day, as an average, 50 to 60 people throughout the country, if not more. If this is not civil war, then God knows what civil war is.'

Unseen by the outside world, silent populations are on the move as frightened people flee neighbourhoods where their community is in a minority. Districts where Sunni and Shia lived together for decades if not centuries are suddenly being torn apart in a few days. In the al-Amel neighbourhood in west Baghdad, for instance, the two communities lived side by side until a few days ago, though Shia were in the majority. Then the Sunni started receiving envelopes pushed under their doors with a Kalashnikov bullet inside and a letter telling them to leave al-Amel immediately or be killed. It added that they must take all of their goods which they could carry and only return later to sell their houses. The reaction was immediate. The Sunni in al-Amel started barricading their streets. Several Shia families, believed to belong to the Shia party, the Supreme Council for Islamic Revolution in Iraq (SCIRI), were murdered later the same day the threatening letters were delivered. 'The local Sunni suspected those Shia of being behind the letters,' says an informant. 'Probably they called in the local resistance and asked them to kill the SCIRI people.' One effect of the escalating sectarian warfare is to strengthen the Sunni insurgency as their own community desperately looks to its defences.

Life in Baghdad has become far more dangerous than it was under Saddam Hussein. Every facet of daily living is affected. In the last few days, temperatures have started to soar and people would normally be buying summer clothes. But in the shopping district of al-Mansur last week few people were on the streets. Many shops were closed because their owners are too frightened to leave their homes.

Iraqi political parties have now spent three months since the election on 15 December trying to form a government. But ask Iraqis on the street what they want from their rulers and many reply: 'What government? It never does anything for us.' Supply of electricity, clean water and sewage disposal are all down from 2003. The only improvement is in electricity supply outside Baghdad but even this is periodic.

All Iraq is suffering, but Baghdad and the central provinces are turning into a slaughterhouse. In al-Khadra, a Sunni neighbourhood of west Baghdad, the insurgents are waging two wars at the same time, one against the Americans and the other against Shia militiamen, some of whom work for the Ministry of the Interior. Last week, Sunni guerrillas attacked a car which they claimed was carrying CIA agents in a road tunnel and killed those inside. Two days later, they ambushed a convoy of vehicles of the Badr Group, the Shia militia. Four of the militiamen were killed and petrol was poured over their bodies and set alight. Soon afterwards, a bus was spotted abandoned by a highway. At first it was thought it might contain a bomb. Instead it had a grislier cargo, the bodies of 18 Sunni tortured and killed.

6 April 2006

A friend of mine, a normally pacific man living in a middle-class Sunni district in west Baghdad, rings me. 'I am not leaving my home,' he says. 'The police commandos arrested 15 people from here last night including the local baker. I am sitting here in my house with a Kalashnikov and 60 bullets and if they come for me I am going to open fire.'

It is strange to hear President Bush and British defence secretary John Reid deny that a civil war is going on, given that so many bodies—all strangled, shot or hanged solely because of their religious allegiance—are being discovered every day. Car bombs exploded in the markets in the great Shia slum of Sadr City in early March. Several days later a group of children playing football in a field noticed a powerful stench. Police opened up a pit which contained the bodies of 27 men, probably all Sunni, stripped to their underpants; they had all been tortured and then shot in the head. Two and a half years ago, when the first suicide bomb targeting the Shia killed 85 people outside the shrine of Imam Ali in Najaf, there was no Shia retaliation. Since the Samarra bomb this restraint has definitively ended.

Iraqis often deceive themselves about the depth of the sectarian divisions in their country. They say, rightly, that there is much intermarriage between Sunni and Shia. But such marriages are most common among the educated middle class in Baghdad and, in any case, they have become less common since 2003, when sectarian differences widened after the Sunni rebelled against the occupation and the Shia did not. My Shia and Kurdish friends, who see themselves as wholly non-sectarian, sincerely believe that

the three-year-old Sunni rebellion is the work of a few jobless Baathist officials making common cause with Islamic fanatics imported from Saudi
Arabia. 'They are not real Iraqis,' they say. They refuse to accept, despite
the evidence of opinion polls, that the guerrillas are supported by most of
the 5-million-strong Sunni community. The Sunni and the Kurds, for their
part, see the Shia leaders as puppets manipulated by Iranian intelligence.
They will not take on board that the 15 or 16 million Shia, who make up
60 per cent of the population, will not give up their bid for power after
centuries of marginalisation. Kurdish hostility to Arabs is equally underestimated by both Shia and Sunni.

Across Iraq, the community-based allegiances of members of army and
police units are sapping the power of the state. As sectarian and ethnic war
escalates, people want militiamen from their own community defending
their street, regardless of whether or not they belong in theory to the army
or the police. In Sunni areas, the only people well enough armed to organise a defence are the resistance fighters, and the fear of Shia death squads
swells their ranks. In Shia areas, sectarian bombings and shootings lead to
greater reliance on the Mehdi Army of Muqtada al-Sadr. Meanwhile, the
number of American casualties has decreased to about one a day, compared
to two or three a day last year. The insurgents believe that the Americans
are going to leave whatever happens, as support for the war diminishes in
the US, and that attacks against US troops are therefore less urgent. But
in the Sunni heartlands north of Baghdad, resistance is as strong as it has
ever been. On 21 March, a hundred fighters armed with automatic rifles,
rocket-propelled grenade-launchers and mortars captured a police headquarters and stormed a jail in Muqdadiyah, 60 miles north of Baghdad.
By the time they withdrew they had killed 19 policemen, freed 33 prisoners and captured enough radio equipment to make the rest of the police
network insecure. Provincial authorities claim the Muqdadiyah police chief
was a resistance double-agent.

The moment when Iraq could be held together as a truly unified state
has probably passed. But a weak Iraq suits many inside and outside the
country and it will still remain a name on the map. American power is
steadily ebbing and the British forces are largely confined to their camps
around Basra. A 'national unity government' may be established but it will
not be national, will certainly be disunited and may govern very little. The
Iranians have been the main winners in the struggle for the country. The
US has turned out to be militarily and politically weaker than anybody

expected. The real question now is whether Iraq will break up with or without an all-out civil war.

24 April 2006

It has been four-and-a-half months since the parliamentary election on 15 December, when the Shia religious parties won almost half the seats. It has taken this length of time for the appointment of a new prime minister. Finally Nouri al-Maliki is replacing Ibrahim al-Jaafari, but Iraqis are wondering why the crisis could not have been resolved earlier, since the two men are politically identical leaders of the Dawa party.

In speaking of anything to do with the Iraqi government it is worth restating the limitations on its authority. 'It is the government of the Green Zone only,' a senior official tells me in exasperation. 'I swear to you there are some ministers who have never seen their own ministries, but just call their director-generals to bring documents to the zone so they can sign.'

Nevertheless, the dispute over who should be the next Iraqi prime minister does reveal the state of the different parties and countries now struggling to control the country. The political battle shows that the US is still not comfortable with the idea of Iraq being ruled by the Shia, who see US demands for the formation of a 'national unity government' as being a polite way of trying to dilute the Shia victory at the polls. Washington is clearly worried at the growth of Iranian influence and of the growing power of Muqtada al-Sadr.

There were plenty of reasons for getting rid of Jaafari. He was a notably ineffective prime minister. But criticism of Jaafari by President Jalal Talabani, the Kurdish leader supported by the US and UK, was interpreted by the Shia political leaders as an underhand attempt to roll back their takeover of the Iraqi state. In this they were largely correct. The crisis has gone on so long because the Shia coalition, the most powerful political force in Iraq, wanted to show that it could not be forced to give up its candidate. It also suspected that the US and Britain were hoping to split the Shia by rejecting their choice of prime minister.

The US and Britain now seem bereft of ideas about what to do next. Once again they vainly sought to promote their favourite Iraqi politician, Iyad Allawi, despite his dismal performance in government and at the polls. He may now have suffered his final political defeat, from which even his foreign friends will be unable to resuscitate him. The next government, which will serve for four years, is unlikely to be much better than the present one. The Shia parties are not going to give up their grip on the interior ministry, which commands more armed men than the defence ministry.

Zalmay Khalilzad, the US ambassador, has sought to boost Sunni political fortunes in the hope that this will drain support from the Sunni insurgency. There is no sign of this happening. Several Sunni politicians who claim to be linked to the armed resistance have been unable to prevent their own relatives being kidnapped and murdered in recent weeks. Washington should accept that Iraq, even in the form of a loose confederation, is going to be a Shia-ruled state. Trying to prevent this outcome only serves to destabilise the country further.

23 May 2006

Two months ago I met an Iraqi Army captain from Diyala, a province north-east of Baghdad which has a mixed Sunni, Shia and Kurdish population. He said Sunni and Shia were killing each other throughout the area. 'Whoever is in a minority runs,' he said. 'If forces are more equal they fight it out.' Diyala is well-watered compared to much of Iraq and has lush orchards. In the 1990s I used to visit villages along the Diyala river, where many of the farmers specialised in growing pomegranates. Then, their main concern was the breakdown of health services as a result of UN sanctions. In 2003, after the invasion, I returned to Baquba, the nondescript provincial capital, but before long the city became an early centre of armed resistance to the occupation and too dangerous to visit.

To find out what is happening there now, I decide to take advantage of the province's peculiar sectarian geography. In eastern Diyala there is a pocket of Kurdish territory, at the centre of which is the town of Khanaqin. I can get there safely, I think, by travelling south out of Kurdistan down the long strip of Kurdish-controlled land that runs along the Iranian border. It is too risky to go beyond Khanaqin, but if what I have been told is true, I am bound to find Kurdish and Shia refugees in Khanaqin who have fled there from Baquba and further west.

It turns out to be easy enough. I drive south from Sulaimaniyah through Iraq's only tunnel, past the lake at Derbendikan and along the Sirdar river, its valley a vivid green between the hills. A Kurdish official told me the road is 'absolutely safe', so long as I enter Khanaqin by crossing the river below a ramshackle town called Kalar and circling round. Under Saddam Hussein, most of Khanaqin's Kurdish inhabitants were forced to leave;

nearby villages were destroyed. They have now returned, along with a new wave of refugees fleeing from the Sunni death squads which are driving out both Kurds and Shia from the rest of Diyala.

In Khanaqin I meet Salar Hussein Rostam, a police lieutenant in charge of registering families fleeing from the rest of Iraq. 'I've received 200 families recently, most in the last week,' he says, gesturing to a great bundle of files beside him. 'They all got warnings telling them to go within 24 hours or be killed.' Kadm Darwish Ali, a Kurdish police officer who lived in Baquba for 20 years, says that he initially ignored warnings to leave. But after the explosion of violence that followed the destruction of the Shia al-Askari shrine in Samarra in February, the threats escalated. 'Everything got worse after Samarra,' Ali says. 'I had been threatened with death before but now I felt every time I appeared in the street I was likely to die.' He sent his family to Khanaqin a month ago and followed them soon afterwards. 'It will get worse and worse,' he says.

Sadeq Shawaz Hawaz and his brother Ahmed live with nine other relatives who also fled Baquba in a three-room hovel off a track with sewage running down the middle of it. Sadeq and Ahmed were fruit traders in the city's market, but several weeks ago a car with four men in it arrived at their house while they were at work. This was a Sunni district; the brothers were both Shia by religion and ethnically Kurdish. 'A tall man came to the door,' Ahmed's wife, Leila, says. He asked for the men of the family; she told him they were not there. 'We will get them,' he said, and left. A week later the same men were back, and ordered the family to leave before evening prayers. Not having any money, or anywhere else to live, the family clung on. But then there was a third visit: the tall man promised Leila's five-year-old daughter Zarah chocolates if she would tell him the names of the men of the family. At this point their nerve broke and they fled, leaving most of their belongings behind. 'Later I went back to try to get our furniture,' Ahmed says, 'but there was too much shooting and I was trapped in our house. I came away with nothing.'

4 June 2006

Iraq is so lethal for journalists because the threats are multiple. Travel without guards and you are less likely to be targeted, but vulnerable to kidnappers. Travel with guards or be embedded with US or Iraqi troops and you may be safe from kidnappers, but you are more likely to be hit by a roadside bomb.

In the past week British journalists Paul Douglas and James Brolan have been killed in a car bomb attack that left the CBS correspondent Kimberly Dozier critically injured. Nothing is more absurd than to imagine—as diplomats deep in the Green Zone slyly pretend—that journalists lurk in their hotel rooms or in the zone itself. If this were true then they would not have been kidnapped or killed in such numbers. Iraq is so dangerous for journalists because they have become the victims of the same lethal anarchy affecting everybody. Normal safeguards do not work. A wealthy banker from Basra living in Baghdad saw six of his bodyguards executed by men dressed as policemen before they kidnapped him.

It is worse for local journalists. They make up most of the casualty figures. It used to be that they were primarily in danger from US troops, but now they are being hunted down because the television stations or newspapers they represent are the enemy of one or other faction in Iraq. Few of their deaths are reported abroad. The latest to die was Ali Jaafar, a sports reporter and anchor for the state television al-Iraqiya, who was assassinated in the street in west Baghdad.

Iraq is far more dangerous than anywhere else I have worked. In Belfast and Beirut in the 1970s it was possible to get killed by accident but armed groups, however murderous, generally cultivated the media. It was only in 1984 that the political kidnappings of journalists started in Lebanon. In Chechnya, kidnap capital of the former Soviet Union, the Chechen resistance was conscious that holding journalists hostage was not going to help their cause and threatened to kill anybody who did so. But in Iraq the insurgents see all the foreign and Iraqi press as enemies to be seized or murdered. The armed resistance relies on the internet to broadcast its aims and publicise its victories, not on the Iraqi or foreign media.

At first the usual precautions taken by foreign journalists seemed to work in occupied Iraq. I was careful to have very good drivers who knew the roads well. I always kept an eye on oncoming traffic (no cars coming towards you means trouble ahead). But in 2004 it became clear I would have to be very careful when I went anywhere. I tried to make myself as invisible as possible. This meant sitting in the back of the car pretending to read an Arabic newspaper so nobody could see my face. I used an old car and did not wash it too often so it would not stand out in the Baghdad traffic. I started having a second car tailing mine to make sure we were not being followed and to have an extra pair of eyes. I did not have an armed guard, partly because of expense, but also because attacks by kidnappers are usually carried out by at least seven or eight armed men. A single guard with a gun would not be enough.

I no longer made appointments with people I did not know well. If I visited refugees from cities assaulted by US troops I did not stay long, perhaps only 20 minutes, or a time so short that I thought it would be difficult for anybody to organise a kidnap. I stopped taking the roads out of Baghdad. The most notorious of these was the airport road but in fact all the roads out of the capital were very dangerous. I also limited my visits to the Green Zone partly because its inhabitants were ill-informed about events in Iraq but also because its entrances were so frequently targeted by suicide bombers. A secondary hazard was that soldiers guarding the entrances were extremely nervous and likely to open fire at the least hint of danger. This was and is a general risk. Before the referendum on the constitution last October there was a tight curfew and a ban on all vehicles. An official gave me a pass to drive around but told me not to use it 'because any soldier or policeman who suspects you of being a suicide bomber will open fire long before you can show him your pass'.

The best routine for reporters in Iraq is to have no routine that anybody else can predict. This is easy enough to do because of the almost permanent traffic jam in Baghdad. The most dangerous moments always seem to me to be on entering or leaving the hotel. I used to drive through police checkpoints where we knew the police to make it more difficult for anybody who did not know them to follow us.

The heavily fortified Hamra is a peculiar hotel. The staff are very good, the rooms clean and better than many other hotels, the food appalling but in three years it has never given me food poisoning. I got used to eating in my room. Social life originally revolved around the swimming pool but as the years passed people spent more time in their rooms. This is a pity because all the correspondents are good value. Those still in Iraq three years into the war are those who have an intense interest in the story and feel that what is happening should be reported regardless of the risk to themselves. Competitiveness is drowned out by the general sense of threat and the needs of personal survival.

Is it still possible for a journalist to operate in Baghdad? Obviously it is more restricted than before. I go to see friends who have their own guards. I keep out of areas that I think are controlled by militias. When I interview people I go to queues of cars at gasoline stations where I can talk to bored drivers without getting out of my vehicle so nobody, aside from the person

I am talking to, knows that I am a foreigner. It is easier to see members of the government but their knowledge of what is happening is restricted. There are parts of Iraq where it is safer to operate, notably those controlled by the Kurds. This means going to the northern three Kurdish provinces and then going with Kurdish troops—sometimes part of the Iraqi Army— to towns and cities where they are based. This enables me to travel with some degree of safety across a large swath of northern Iraq.

The lack of information or misinformation coming out of Iraq in the early years of the war, particularly in the US, was often the result of editorial decisions reached in New York, not the inability of the correspondents on the spot to find out what was happening. I remember distraught American correspondents buckling on their body armour as, on orders from head office, they sallied out to report on 'the good news from Iraq'. It was only after Hurricane Katrina and criticism of the White House's Iraq policy by the US military and its political allies in the second half of 2005 that this control of the news became less flagrant. Right-wing websites claiming that news of American achievements in Iraq was being suppressed by the media fell silent.

9 June 2006

Abu Musab al-Zarqawi, the leader of al-Qa'ida in Iraq, has been killed by two 500-pound bombs dropped by a US fighter jet. US and Iraqi intelligence officials discovered Zarqawi's hideout after following his deputy, Abu Abdul-Rahman, to a meeting in a house near the city of Baquba, 40 miles north of Baghdad. It was the final act in what the US military describes as a 'painstaking' spying operation involving sources within Zarqawi's network of associates.

The explosion of the laser-guided bombs killed Zarqawi and seven of his lieutenants. Two photographs of his body show Zarqawi's eyes shut; his nostrils filled with blood; with gashes to his forehead and cheek. He was dragged dying from the ruins of his house by Iraqi police and strapped to a stretcher. 'Zarqawi did in fact survive the air strike,' says Major General William Caldwell, the US military spokesman. Covered in blood, he was alive for a few minutes after the Americans arrived and muttered a few unintelligible words. 'Zarqawi attempted to sort of turn away off the stretcher. They—everybody—re-secured him back on to the stretcher, but he died almost immediately thereafter from the wounds he received from the air strike.'

6 July 2006

The career of Abu Musab al-Zarqawi was very strange. He was an obscure figure until Colin Powell made him famous by denouncing him before the UN Security Council on 5 February 2003. Powell claimed that Zarqawi was not only a member of al-Qa'ida but linked to Saddam Hussein's regime. Neither allegation was true, but together they met the political need to pretend that the invasion of Iraq was part of the war on terror.

The US elevation of Zarqawi to the front rank of al-Qa'ida leaders was self-fulfilling. To many Iraqis and Muslims wanting to fight the US, he became a symbol of resistance. His notoriety made it easy for him to raise money. In December 2004, Osama bin Laden declared him head of al-Qa'ida in Iraq. 'The Islamists often seem to follow a script provided by their enemies,' Loretta Napoleoni writes in her excellent book on Zarqawi.

The continued exaggeration by the US of Zarqawi's role was carefully calculated. He was rarely referred to at US military briefings in Baghdad during the first months of guerrilla war; the guerrillas were supposedly remnants of Saddam Hussein's regime, assisted by a few foreign fighters, whose final elimination was expected by the day. It was only after Saddam Hussein was captured in December 2003 that Zarqawi became pre-eminent at American briefings. It was evident at the time that a decision had been taken to portray him as the explanation for all Iraq's ills. This was confirmed by US documents leaked earlier this year. 'Through aggressive Strategic Communications,' one confidential internal briefing asserted, 'Abu Musab al-Zarqawi now represents: Terrorism in Iraq/Foreign Fighters in Iraq/Suffering of Iraqi People (Infrastructure Attacks)/Denial of Iraqi Aspirations.' Brigadier General Mark Kimmitt, the US military spokesman in Baghdad, said that 'the Zarqawi PSYOP programme is the most successful information campaign to date.'

Like many apparently successful propaganda campaigns, it had an important drawback: Washington, the US civil officials in Baghdad and the US military came to believe their own hype. They behaved as if Zarqawi and a relatively limited number of insurgents were alone in opposing the occupation. In fact, almost all the 5 million Sunni Arabs in Iraq supported armed resistance. Such was the American emphasis on Zarqawi's activities that many Iraqis wondered if he really existed. Certainly, his importance was always exaggerated. Other Sunni insurgent groups liked to blame Zarqawi for their more bloodthirsty actions. But his recently formed Tandhim al-Qa'ida fi Bilad al-Rafidayn (al-Qa'ida's Organisation in Mesopotamia) certainly exists and is probably one of the three or four biggest insurgent groups.

For the last three years there has been a curious co-operation between the US and al-Qa'ida in promoting the Zarqawi myth. But his death will not necessarily lead to the unravelling of his group. He was the most vocal proponent of slaughtering Iraqi Shia, as well as American soldiers. But the civil war between Sunni and Shia now has its own momentum. Ethnic and sectarian cleansing is underway. It is not likely to be reversed.

It may no longer be so obviously in American interests to demonise the Sunni insurgents. Ever since Zilmay Khalilzad arrived in Baghdad as the US ambassador at the end of last summer, he has been cultivating the Sunni Arabs and limiting Shia control of the state. Khalilzad played the central role in getting rid of the previous prime minister, Ibrahim al-Jaafari. Baghdad conspiracy theorists suspect that, just as the US used Zarqawi to blacken the Sunni resistance as a whole, his departure will now make it easier for the US to do a deal with the insurgents.

20 July 2006

The number of Iraqi civilians being murdered or killed in the current fighting has been revealed for the first time by the UN. It is far higher than previous estimates. Some 3,149 people were killed in June alone, or over 100 a day—more in one month than the total death toll in Northern Ireland in 30 years of violence—and the figure will rise higher in July because of tit-for-tat massacres by Sunni and Shia Muslims.

The death toll has risen every month this year. Overall 14,000 civilians were killed in the first half of 2006. Ever since the invasion in 2003 the US military and later US-supported Iraqi governments have sought to conceal the number of Iraqi civilians being killed. Now, for the first time, the health ministry in Baghdad has told the UN Assistance Mission for Iraq, which publishes a bimonthly report on human rights, the exact death toll recorded by hospitals around the country. In the first six months of the year the number of Iraqi civilians dying violently rose by 77 per cent.

The UN report paints a picture of Iraqi society dissolving under the stress of cumulative violence. Nobody is safe. A tennis coach and two players were shot dead in Baghdad for wearing shorts. Militias threaten the families of homosexuals, stating 'they will begin killing family members unless men are handed over or killed by the family.' Sectarian differences are behind most killings. Assassinations are often carried out by the security forces themselves. On 3 June, for instance, 50 police cars surrounded the al-Arab mosque in Basra and killed 10 of the 20 people inside.

Kidnapping, often of children, is common and the victims are frequently killed regardless of whether or not they have paid a ransom. 'In one case the body of 12-year-old Osama was reportedly found by the Iraqi police in a plastic bag after his family paid a ransom of $30,000. The boy had been sexually assaulted by the kidnappers, before being hanged by his own clothing. The police captured members of this gang who confessed to raping and killing many boys and girls before Osama.'

21 July 2006

Parents dare not let their children wander the dangerous streets of Baghdad alone, but until a few days ago they could give them a treat by taking them to al-Jillawi's toyshop, the biggest and best in the city, its windows invitingly filled with Playstations, Barbie dolls and bicycles.

They go there no longer. Today the shop on 14 Ramadan Street in the once-affluent al-Mansur district is closed, with a black mourning flag draped across its front. The three sons and the teenage grandson of the owner, Mehdi al-Jillawi, were shutting down for the evening recently, bringing in bicycles and tricycles on display on the pavement in front of the shop. As they did so, two BMWs stopped close to them and several gunmen got out armed with assault rifles. They opened fire at point-blank range, killing the young men.

I take a drive through empty streets in the heart of the city, making a zigzag course to avoid police checkpoints that might be doubling as death squads. Few shops are open. Those still doing business are frantically trying to sell their stock. Iraqis are terrified in a way that I have never seen before, since I first visited Baghdad in 1978. Sectarian massacres happen almost daily. The UN says 6,000 civilians were slaughtered in May and June, but this month has been far worse. In many districts it has become difficult to buy bread because Sunni assassins have killed all the bakers, who are traditionally Shia.

On 9 July, Shia gunmen from the black-clad Mehdi Army entered the largely Sunni al-Jihad district in west Baghdad and killed 40 Sunni, after dragging them from their cars or stopping them at false checkpoints. Within hours the Sunni militias struck back, with car bombs killing more than 60 Shia. Many people now carry two sets of identity documents, one Sunni and one Shia. Mehdi Army fighters manning checkpoints know this and sometimes ask people claiming to be Shia questions about Shia theology. One Shia who passed this test was still killed because he was driving a car with number plates from Anbar, a Sunni province.

The Iraqi Army and police are themselves divided along sectarian lines. Recognising this, the Shia-controlled interior ministry ludicrously suggested that people challenge the ferocious police commanders and demand their identity cards in order to distinguish real police from death squads. It is hard to think of a surer way of getting oneself killed.

8 August 2006

Driving into Baghdad from the airport, we avoid most checkpoints by taking a serpentine route through the city. At one moment we roar along a highway and then, still at speed, we abruptly divert down an alleyway, weaving between heaps of rotting garbage. I have always known roughly where Sunni and Shia live in Baghdad, but I am now acquiring detailed knowledge of its sectarian geography. A small mistake could have lethal results. The cemeteries are full of Iraqis who were caught in the wrong district.

This vast city of 7 million people, almost the size of London, is breaking up into a dozen cities, each one of which is becoming a heavily armed Shia or Sunni stronghold. Every morning brings its terrible harvest of bodies. Many lie in the street for hours, bloating in the 120F heat.

I first came to Baghdad, one of the great cities of the world, in 1978, a year before Saddam Hussein assumed supreme power. It was never a pretty city, but I found it deeply attractive. The Baghdad I knew is dying. No doubt there will be a city of that name on the banks of the Tigris in the future. But its special magic, the fact that gave the city its peculiar allure, was its complex ethnic and religious mix of Shia, Sunni and Kurds. It is this diversity of cultures that is disappearing. Baghdad is joining other cosmopolitan cities in the Middle East—Alexandria in Egypt, Smyrna in Turkey and Beirut in Lebanon—which have been torn apart by sectarian and ethnic cleansing over the last century.

I do not want to romanticise the old Baghdad that is now passing away as a centre of multiethnic understanding and amity. The city has, on the contrary, an extraordinarily violent past. It was founded as a round city by Abu Ja'far al-Mansour, the second Abbasid caliph, in AD 762, on the fertile banks of the Tigris, where that river comes close to the Euphrates. At the centre of the trade routes between east and west, it soon became one of the richest cities in the world. Its luxurious palaces, merchant quarters and crowded quays were the backdrop for the tales in *The Thousand and One Nights*.

The Mongols sacked the city in 1258, the Ottomans held it for hundreds of years and the British for a few decades. Iraqis have an acute sense of their own history. Different communities have their heroes and villains. Eighteen months ago, 1,200 years after Caliph al-Mansour died, gunmen, probably Shia, attached explosives to his statue near Baghdad railway station and blew it to pieces.

At the time I first started to visit Iraq in the late 1970s, the prospects for the city looked good. Oil revenues were soaring and administration was effective. New roads, bridges, hotels, schools and hospitals were being built across the city. I did not immediately recognise the bloodthirstiness of the regime because there was a hiatus in Baghdad's war with the Kurds, and it was only the following year, in 1979, that Saddam executed one-third of his Revolution Command Council and took over supreme power. Foreign journalists were supposedly closely watched, but my minder from the Ministry of Information, a menacing figure in many correspondents' reports from Iraq, had managed to miss me at the airport and we spent several days looking for each other. Iraq was still one of the most secular countries in the Middle East. In Basra, the main complaint among Iraqis about Kuwaitis was that they were crossing the border and drinking the city dry of beer.

It turned out that I was not watching a new dawn in Baghdad, but its last days of peace and normality. Two years later, Saddam plunged into a disastrous war with Iran that lasted until 1988. The optimistic and well-educated young men I had met when I first visited the country were forced into the army. Yet the physical appearance of Baghdad survived intact until the six-week bombardment by US bombs and missiles in the Gulf War of 1991. Explosions tore apart the bridges, power stations and oil refineries. After the Gulf War UN sanctions relentlessly impoverished the people, and soon there were millions living on the edge of destitution. The government started cutting off the hands and ears of thieves and showing the results on television. Iraqi society became like a lump of wet sugar ready to dissolve as soon as Saddam's iron rule was ended. When that came, in April 2003, the ferocity of the looting after Saddam fled was astonishing. The savage destructiveness with which ministries, government offices, museums and even hospitals were torn apart by the poor of Baghdad was like a social revolution. It was as if they were taking revenge against the Iraqi state that had oppressed them for so long.

People who thought that occupation meant liberation were rapidly disillusioned when the US took over Saddam's palace complex and renamed it the Green Zone. It instantly became a symbol of foreign conquest. The appearance of central Baghdad then changed rapidly because of the suicide-bombing campaign. Enormous blast walls, made out of concrete sections looking like giant grey tombstones, snaked across the city. They sealed off streets and districts, and blocked so many roads that there was a permanent traffic jam in the centre of the city.

American and British officials have often complained over the past three years that the media never report the good news from Iraq. It is therefore worth recording that, by this July, traffic jams in Baghdad were no longer a problem. I used to budget 45 minutes to travel between my hotel and the Green Zone; now I can do it in 15 minutes. The reason, however, is scarcely to the credit of the Iraqi government or the US. The streets of Baghdad are astonishingly empty of cars and vehicles because people are either too frightened to go out, cannot afford the high price of petrol or have fled abroad. The occupation, sectarian warfare and collapse of the economy have destroyed Baghdad. It may rise again, but it will be a different city.

15 October 2006

It is seldom realised that the US and Britain have largely provoked the civil war that is raging across central Iraq. The fact that there is such a war in Iraq should no longer be in doubt, with the dramatic claim last week by American and Iraqi health researchers that the true figure of Iraqi civilians being killed goes as high as 15,000 a month.

Last month I was in Diyala, a mixed Sunni–Shia province of 1.5 million people north of Baghdad, where a weary-looking federal police commander threw up his hands when I asked him if there was a civil war. 'Of course there is,' he said. 'What else do you call it when 60 or 70 people are being killed in Diyala alone every week?' In fact, the true figure for this one province is probably higher. Many bodies are never found. I talked to one woman who fled the town she had lived all her life after her son, a taxi driver, had disappeared while delivering a washing machine. Many bodies are thrown into the Tigris or its tributaries and float down river until they are caught by the weirs south of Baghdad.

The question has to be, was this civil war always inevitable? There was always going to be friction and possibly violence between the three main communities in Iraq after the overthrow of Saddam Hussein. But the occupation of Iraq by US and British armies over the past three years has deepened the divide between these communities. A Sunni ex-army officer supporting the resistance now sees a Shia serving in the Iraqi Army or police force not just as the member of a different Islamic sect but as a traitor to his country who is actively collaborating with the hated invader.

The last excuse for the occupation was that at least it prevented civil war, but this it very visibly is not doing. On the contrary, it de-legitimises the Iraqi government, Army and police force, which are seen by Iraqis as pawns of the occupier. For instance, the main government intelligence service, essential in fighting a guerrilla war, has no Iraqi budget because it is entirely funded by the CIA.

5 November 2006

'When does the incompetence end and the crime begin?' asked an appalled German Chancellor in the First World War when the German Army commander said he intended to resume his bloody and doomed assaults on the French fortress city of Verdun. The same could be said of the disastrous policies of George Bush and Tony Blair in Iraq. The picture they paint of what is happening no longer resembles reality to any degree. They claim US and British troops are present because Iraqis want them there. But a detailed poll of Iraqi attitudes by WorldPublicOpinion.org shows that 71 per cent of Iraqis want the withdrawal of US-led forces within a year. No less than 74 per cent of Shia and 91 per cent of Sunni say they want American and British troops out. Only in Kurdistan, where there are few foreign troops, does a majority support the occupation. Hostility to the American and British troops has a direct and lethal consequence for the soldiers on the ground. The same poll shows that 92 per cent of Sunni and 62 per cent of Shia approve of attacks on US-led forces.

For the past three-and-a-half years in Iraq, one needed to close both eyes very hard or live in Baghdad's Green Zone not to see that the occupation was detested by most Iraqis. In the first year of the occupation it could be argued that Bush and Blair were simply incompetent: they did not understand Iraq, were misinformed by Iraqi exiles, or were simply ignorant and arrogant. But they must know that for two-and-a-half years they have controlled only islands of territory.

I used to think how absurd it was for me to risk my life by visiting the Green Zone, the entrances to which were among the most bombed targets in Iraq, to see diplomats who claimed that the butchery in Iraq was much exaggerated. But when I asked them if they would like to come and have lunch in my hotel outside the zone, they always threw up their hands in horror and said their security men would never allow it. The fantasy picture of Iraq purveyed by Bush and Blair is now being exposed. The Potemkin village they constructed to divert attention from what was really happening is finally going up in flames. But it is too late for the Iraqis, Americans and British who died because they were unwitting actors in this fiction, carefully concocted by the White House and Downing Street to show progress where there is frustration, and victory where there is only defeat.

30 December 2006

Saddam Hussein, a leader who launched two disastrous wars that reshaped the politics of the Middle East and ruined his country, has been hanged by the Iraqi authorities who replaced him. Had he never lived, the world would be a different place. He wanted to be a world-historical figure and in a way he achieved his ambition. But he did so through defeat and not victory.

Often compared to Stalin or Hitler, Saddam also had a streak of Inspector Clouseau. He made endless mistakes. He ruined Iraq. He took over a country rich in oil and with a well-educated population when he orchestrated a coup in 1968. By 1979 he became president and sole leader after killing a third of his ruling Revolution Command Council. A year later he plunged into a disastrous eight-year war with Iran in which half a million Iraqis were killed, wounded or captured. In 1990 he once again overplayed his hand by invading Kuwait.

He was cruel by nature. But he was also the product of a violent, deeply divided country. A Sunni himself, he always represented the minority of Iraq's population who only held power by force. I first saw Saddam Hussein making a speech on a distant platform in Baghdad in 1978. He was already known as 'The Strong Man of Iraq'. Saddam's response to any form of dissent was repression, usually far in excess of what was needed to achieve his ends. The specific crime he has been executed for is killing 148 people from the village of Dujail because of an attempt to kill him there in 1982, but the assassination bid was only a scattering of shots in the direction of his motorcade. The savagery of the retaliation aimed, very successfully, to spread terror.

Saddam was a convenient enemy, as the US and Britain found. Few opponents could have been as easy to demonise, because in many ways he was a real demon. His physical appearance was threatening, and so was his rhetoric. But doubly convenient for Washington and London, this menacing rhetoric was far from reality. The 'mother of all battles' he promised foreign invaders in 1990 never happened. Instead, there was an embarrassing rout.

If Iraqis had really identified with Saddam—as so many Germans identified with Hitler—then the task of the US and Britain in Iraq might have been easier. But to the surprise of the invaders, the serious fighting began after his flight. When he was captured by US troops in December 2003, it had no dampening effect on the insurgency, which grew steadily in strength.

The US made every effort to portray the trial of Saddam as an Iraqi-run affair, but the former leader was right in seeing it as orchestrated by Washington. If confirmation of this were needed, it came when the date for announcing his death sentence was moved to 5 November, so it could be the leading item on the news the day before the US midterm elections. In the event, the reality of 25,000 US soldiers killed and wounded in Iraq made more impression on American voters.

Many Iraqis will rejoice at the death of Saddam, while others will accept his estimate of himself as a symbol of his country, making the final patriotic sacrifice. But he is only one of 4,000 Iraqis who will die violently this month. The war has its own momentum, and Iraqis are too worried about staying alive themselves to lament or rejoice very long at the execution of the man who ruled them for a quarter of a century.

1 February 2007

Iraq is experiencing the biggest exodus in the Middle East since Palestinians were forced to flee in 1948 upon the creation of Israel. 'We were forced to leave our house six months ago and since then we have moved more than eight times,' says Abu Mustafa, a 56-year-old man from Baghdad. 'Sectarian violence has now even reached the displacement camps but we are tired of running away. Sometimes I have asked myself if it is not better to die than to live like a Bedouin all my life.'

Iraqis are on the run inside and outside the country. The UN High Commission for Refugees says 50,000 Iraqis a month are abandoning their homes. Stephanie Jaquemet, regional representative of the UNHCR, says that 2 million Iraqis have fled abroad and another 1.5–2 million are displaced within the country. They flee because they fear for their lives.

The most common destinations are Jordan and Syria, which have taken 1.6 million people. At first it was the better-off who fled, including half of Iraq's 34,000 doctors. Now it is the poor who are arriving in Amman and Damascus with little means of surviving. Only Syria has formally recognised a need for temporary protection for Iraqis. Others, including the US and UK, are loath to admit that one of the world's great man-made disasters is taking place. The UNHCR thinks every Iraqi should qualify as a refugee because of the extraordinary level of violence in the country.

7 February 2007

Helicopters buzz overhead near the town of Taji, 20 miles north-west of Baghdad, as flames and a huge plume of black smoke rise from the crash site of the fifth US helicopter to be shot down in just over two weeks. The helicopter was hit by an anti-aircraft missile, killing all seven people on board. The US forces in Iraq depend heavily on helicopters because patrols are frequently attacked by bombs beside the roads. In this area of Iraq, Sunni insurgents have always been strong.

'The helicopter was flying and passed over us, then we heard the firing of a missile,' says Mohammed al-Janabi, a farmer speaking less than half a mile from the wreckage of the twin-rotor C-46 troop carrier. 'The helicopter then turned into a ball of fire. It flew in a circle twice, then it went down.'

A claim of responsibility has been made by the Islamic State of Iraq, a new umbrella group of insurgents including al-Qa'ida in Iraq, who have said they shot down two other helicopters recently. The statement said the group would post a video of the downing of the helicopter on the internet.

US military losses in Iraq have been rising in recent weeks though the overall level of deaths has been remarkably steady, according to the Department of Defense. In 2004, 848 US soldiers were killed and 8,002 wounded; in 2005, 846 killed and 5,946 wounded; in 2006, 821 killed and 6,372 wounded. Almost all US casualties have been suffered in fighting the Sunni insurgents. President Bush's belligerent rhetoric in his State of the Union address in January, suggesting he is going to take on the Shia militias as well, could lead to a sharp rise in US losses. But Muqtada al-Sadr, the nationalist Shia cleric whom the Mehdi Army follows, is determined to avoid a military confrontation with US forces as they implement a new security plan through the much-publicised 'surge' in the numbers of troops in Baghdad. Sadrist officials say they would allow the US Army into their bastion of Sadr City, home to 2 million people, but this probably means the militiamen would just go underground.

12 February 2007

The United States is increasing its hostility towards Iran by accusing the 'highest levels' of the Iranian government of supplying sophisticated roadside bombs that have killed 170 US troops and wounded 620. The allegations are similar in tone and credibility to those made four years ago by the US government about Iraq possessing weapons of mass destruction in order to justify the invasion of Iraq.

Senior US defence officials in Baghdad, speaking on condition of anonymity, say they believe the bombs are manufactured in Iran and smuggled across the border to Shia militants in Iraq. The weapons, identified as 'explosive formed penetrators' (EFPs), are said to be capable of destroying an Abrams tank. The officials use aggressive rhetoric suggesting that Washington wants to ratchet up its confrontation with Tehran. It has not ruled out using armed force and has sent a second carrier task force to the Gulf. 'We assess that these activities are coming from senior levels of the Iranian government,' says an official, charging that the explosive devices come from the al-Quds Brigade and noting that it answers to Ayatollah Ali Khamenei, Iran's supreme leader. This is the first time the US has openly accused the Iranian government of being involved in sending weapons to Iraq that kill Americans.

The allegations by senior but unnamed US officials in Baghdad and Washington are bizarre. The US has been fighting a Sunni insurgency in Iraq since 2003 that is deeply hostile to Iran. The insurgent groups have repeatedly denounced the democratically elected Iraqi government as pawns of Iran. It is unlikely that the Sunni guerrillas have received significant quantities of military equipment from Tehran. Some 1,190 US soldiers have been killed by so-called improvised explosive devices (IEDs) in Iraq since the overthrow of Saddam Hussein. Such bombs were used by guerrillas during the Irish war of independence in 1919–21 against British patrols and convoys. They were commonly used in the Second World War, when 'shaped charges', similar in purpose to the EFPs of which the US is now complaining, were employed by all armies. The very name—explosive formed penetrators—may have been chosen to imply that a menacing new weapon has been developed.

It is likely that Shia militias have received weapons and money from Iran and possible that the Sunni insurgents have received some aid. But most Iraqi men possess weapons. Many millions of them received military training under Saddam Hussein. His well-supplied arsenals were all looted after his fall. No specialist on Iraq believes that Iran has ever been a serious promoter of the Sunni insurgency.

At the end of last year the Baker-Hamilton report, written by a bipartisan commission of Republicans and Democrats, suggested opening talks with Iran and Syria to resolve the Iraq crisis. Instead, President Bush has taken a precisely opposite line, blaming Iran and Syria for US losses in Iraq. In the past month Washington has arrested five Iranian officials in a long-established office in Arbil, the Kurdish capital. An Iranian diplomat was kidnapped in Baghdad, allegedly by members of an Iraqi military unit under US influence. President Bush had earlier said that Iranians deemed to be targeting US forces could be killed, which seemed to be opening the door to assassinations.

The US stance on the military capabilities of Iraqis today is the exact opposite of its position four years ago. Then, Bush and Blair claimed that Iraqis were technically advanced enough to produce long-range missiles and to be close to producing a nuclear device. Washington is now saying that Iraqis are too backward to produce an effective roadside bomb and must seek Iranian help.

22 February 2007

One by one the places I knew best in Baghdad are being destroyed. I used to visit the Friday bird market in the city centre. Iraqis like birds. The Ghazil market was a dishevelled but friendly place in front of an ancient mosque, with homemade cages containing canaries, songbirds, parrots, doves, pigeons and falcons. At 11 a.m. on 26 January a man arrived at the market carrying a cardboard box pierced with air-holes. He put the box down and told the birdsellers he was going to get a drink of water. A few moments later, the explosives inside the box detonated, killing 15 people and wounding 55 more. A few birds that survived the blast continued to chirrup in their cages. Bedraggled black Shia prayer flags hung from nearby shops. I have always thought of Ghazil as a mixed area, but whoever planned the attack must have believed it was a Shia neighbourhood and that few Sunni would be killed.

Everybody in Baghdad is frightened. There are few friends of mine left in the city. One day I got a phone call from Hussein, a businessman I have known since the US invasion, who had remained an optimist longer than most. He now spoke in a frightened voice, and from London. I had not heard from him for a while, he said, because he had been kidnapped last summer. He came from a well-known Shia family and was lucky to be alive. His kidnappers whipped him, and then 'came back to apologise because a cleric at their mosque told them it was wrong to whip anybody over 40 years of age'; he was released after handing over all his money. He was told to leave the country, which he did, but he has no residence permit and cannot stay in Britain or Jordan indefinitely. He does not know what to do.

Bombs, kidnappings and sectarian killings: these are what people talk about in Baghdad. There is not much Iraqis can do about these threats, except run away. I am always talking to people about how to get to Jordan or Syria, and about the chances of getting asylum in the UK or elsewhere in Europe. There are relatively safe areas inside Iraq to which the Shia can flee; the Sunni are in danger wherever they go unless they leave the country altogether.

In Baghdad the Shia are on the offensive. They are the majority in the city and control more territory than the Sunni. Adhamiyah, now the only solidly Sunni neighbourhood on the east side of the Tigris, is under regular mortar attack by Shia militiamen. As areas with mixed populations have disappeared each side has felt able to use heavy mortars against the other, safe in the knowledge that they will not hit members of their own community. Those who fire the mortars do not seem to care what they hit so long as it is in a district belonging to the opposing side. On 28 January, in the Sunni district of Adil in west Baghdad, two mortar bombs exploded in the courtyard of a girls' secondary school, killing five children and wounding 21. A 15-year-old who was hit in the legs described watching her friend Maha bleed to death. 'The shrapnel hit her in the eyes,' Ban Ismet said, 'and there was blood all over her face.' Atrocities like this provoke little reaction in Baghdad these days. A Sunni friend of mine remarked, without much interest or surprise: 'They were probably aiming for the mosque next to the school.' Adil is under attack by the Shia militiamen of Muqtada al-Sadr's Mehdi Army; they now hold Hurriyah, which used to be a mixed district.

In his State of the Union speech in January President Bush talked of eliminating militias, both Sunni and Shia, from all of Baghdad. The US Army and its Iraqi government allies, he said, would enter hostile areas, cleanse them of insurgents and militias and remain there to prevent their return. Just how dangerous Baghdad is for Americans was underlined last month when a helicopter belonging to the US security company Blackwater was shot down as it flew over the Sunni area of al-Fadhil close to the central market. The US Army immediately sent in a rescue team, but by the time it arrived four of the five members of the helicopter's crew had been executed by shots to the head (the fifth died in the crash); within hours their identity cards were being shown on insurgent websites.

The lack of US control is even more apparent in the provinces. Recently US and Iraqi commanders gave a self-congratulatory press conference on the situation in Baquba, the capital of the fruit-growing province of Diyala. 'The situation in Baquba', they claimed, 'is reassuring and under control'; nasty rumours, they said, were being 'circulated by bad people'. A few hours later insurgents stormed Baquba's mayoral office, kidnapped the mayor and blew up the building. The local council's response was to sack 1,500 members of the Diyala police force on grounds that they had failed to resist the insurgency. The council now complains that insurgents are in effective control of Baquba and that Nouri al-Maliki's government has sent them no help.

American confrontation with Iran makes little sense in terms of Iraqi politics. The most important elements in the Iraqi government are pro-Iranian, notably the Supreme Council for Islamic Revolution in Iraq (SCIRI), which used to be based in Iran. When I went to see one of its leaders in Najaf his guards spoke to me in Farsi. The Badr Organisation, SCIRI's well-organised militia, was set up by the Iranian Revolutionary Guards and fought on the Iranian side in the Iran–Iraq War. It is inconceivable that SCIRI would switch its allegiance from Iran to the US. It is worth noting that the Iraqi nationalist cleric Muqtada al-Sadr and the Mehdi Army, prominent on the list of those denounced by Washington as creatures of Iran, have traditionally been anti-Iranian.

Confrontation with Iran makes some sense in the context of the politics of the wider Middle East. In Sunni countries such as Saudi Arabia, Egypt and Jordan Bush is appealing to sectarian bigotry against the Shia in Iraq, Lebanon and elsewhere: a powerful sentiment among leaders and people alike. The Shia takeover of the Iraqi government in alliance with the Kurds is being portrayed as the sharp edge of Iranian imperialism. Sunni rulers realise that the success of Hezbollah, which had widespread popular support when it fought Israel to a standstill in Lebanon last year, shows up the impotence, incompetence and corruption of their own regimes. To avoid such damaging comparisons they are happy to join the US in stoking the anti-Shia and anti-Iranian flames.

The real reason for Bush's anti-Iranian policy may be its effects on American domestic politics. Ever since the overthrow of Saddam was first planned the White House has shown itself more interested in holding power in Washington than in Baghdad.

3 April 2007

A failed American attempt to abduct two senior Iranian security officers who were on an official visit to northern Iraq was the starting pistol for a crisis that, 10 weeks later, led to Iranians seizing 15 British sailors and Marines in the Gulf. Early on the morning of 11 January helicopter-borne US forces launched a raid on a long-established Iranian liaison office in the city of Arbil in Iraqi Kurdistan. They captured five relatively junior Iranian officials who the US accuses of being intelligence agents—and still holds.

In reality, the US attack had a far more ambitious objective. The aim of the raid, launched without informing the Kurdish authorities, was to seize two men at the very heart of the Iranian security establishment: Mohammed Jafari, the powerful deputy head of the Iranian National Security Council, and General Minojahar Frouzanda, the chief of intelligence of the Iranian Revolutionary Guard, according to Kurdish officials. The two men were in Kurdistan on an official visit during which they met the Iraqi president, Jalal Talabani, and later saw Massoud Barzani, the president of the Kurdistan Regional Government (KRG), at his mountain headquarters overlooking Arbil.

The attempt by the US to seize the two high-ranking Iranian security officers openly meeting with Iraqi leaders is somewhat as if Iran had tried to kidnap the heads of the CIA and MI6 while they were on an official visit to a country neighbouring Iran, such as Pakistan or Afghanistan.

US officials in Washington subsequently claimed that the five Iranian officials they did seize, who have not been seen since, were 'suspected of being closely tied to activities targeting Iraq and coalition forces'. That explanation never made much sense. No member of the US-led coalition has been killed in Arbil and there were no Sunni–Arab insurgents or Shia militiamen there.

The raid on Arbil took place within hours of President Bush making an address on 10 January in which he claimed: 'Iran is providing material support for attacks on American troops.' He identified Iran and Syria as America's main enemies in Iraq though the four-year-old guerrilla war against US-led forces is being conducted by the strongly anti-Iranian Sunni–Arab community. Jafari himself later complained about US allegations. 'So far, has there been a single Iranian among suicide bombers in the war-battered country?' he asked. 'Almost all who are involved in the suicide attacks are from Arab countries.'

Better understanding of the seriousness of the US action in Arbil—and the angry Iranian response to it—should have led Downing Street and the Ministry of Defence to realise that Iran was likely to retaliate against American or British forces such as highly vulnerable Navy search parties in the Gulf. The abortive Arbil raid provoked a dangerous escalation in the confrontation between the US and Iran which ultimately led to the capture of the 15 British sailors and Marines—apparently considered a more vulnerable coalition target than their US comrades.

12 April 2007

We drive at great speed across the Greater Zaab river, swollen with flood-water, and through the crumbling walls of ancient Nineveh, capital of the Assyrian Empire. We pass a large mound beneath which is the tomb of Jonah, who, having survived his unfortunate experience with the whale, was buried here. We are heading for the ancient city of Mosul. The majority of its 1.8 million people are Sunni Arabs and one third are Kurds, along with 25,000 Christians. Arabs and Kurds have been fighting for control of the city for four years.

We finally speed into the heavily fortified headquarters of Khasro Goran, the able and confident deputy governor of Mosul—a Kurd, and more powerful than the Arab governor. The building is a former Baath party centre on the left bank of Tigris river taken over by the Kurdistan Democratic Party, of which Goran is head in Mosul. Its elaborate defences, high concrete walls and watchtowers would do credit to a castle in a particularly disturbed part of medieval Europe. The sentries indicate to cars on a nearby roundabout that they are getting too close to the headquarters by firing bursts from their automatic rifles into the air.

Aside from wholly Kurdish units, the Iraqi government's security forces are thoroughly infiltrated. This is true in Mosul and throughout Iraq. It is a crucial point that Bush and Blair never seem to understand when they explain that they are training and equipping some 265,000 police and soldiers in Iraq. The real problem for Washington and London is that most of these men are loyal to their own communities before they are loyal to the government in Baghdad. In Mosul, the police are mostly Sunni Arab, while the two Iraqi Army divisions are largely Kurdish. Out of 20,000 police, Goran believes that half belong to or sympathise with the Sunni resistance. When Saddam Hussein was sentenced to death, one policeman stuck a picture of the former leader on his windscreen by way of protest. Many of the police come from the powerful and numerous al-Juburi tribe. This makes it politically very difficult to fire or demote them.

On 6 March, insurgents from the Islamic State in Iraq movement stormed Badoush prison north-west of Mosul. They freed 68 prisoners, of whom 57 were non-Iraqis. It was the biggest jailbreak in Iraq since the occupation started in 2003. Goran cynically points out that there are supposedly 1,200 guards at Badoush, of whom 400 to 500 were present during the attack, but did nothing to halt it. He suspects that many of the guards, who get their orders not from him but from the Ministry of Justice in Baghdad, colluded with the insurgents in the break-out.

The history of Mosul over the past four years has some lessons for resolving the conflict in Iraq in the long term. Many of the crass errors made in the first days of the occupation in Baghdad did not happen in Mosul. American and Kurdish commanders have often been able men. But the end result has been disastrously similar in both cities. Perhaps the lesson is that Iraqi communities mean exactly what they say and will fight to get it. This means that the Kurds are going to recover their lost lands; the Sunni are going to get the Americans out; and the Shia, as the majority, are determined to be the primary force in government.

I have always liked Mosul. It feels a more ancient city than Baghdad. I used to enjoy climbing the ancient stone streets in the Christian quarter too narrow and rutted by carts over the centuries for any car to enter. Even today, from Goran's heavily defended KDP headquarters, there is a wonderful view across the shimmering Tigris towards the old city, with its elegant minarets, on the west side of the river. But, Goran warns, 'If you went into the streets on your own you would be dead in 15 minutes.'

18 April 2007

In a day of infamy for Iraq almost 200 people have been killed by four car bombs that tore through crowded markets and streets leaving the ground covered in charred bodies and severed limbs. 'I saw dozens of dead bodies,' says a witness in Sadriyah, a mixed Shia–Kurdish neighbourhood in west Baghdad where 140 people died and 150 were injured. 'Some people were burned alive inside minibuses. Nobody could reach them after the explosion. There were pieces of flesh all over the place. Women were screaming and shouting for their loved ones who died.'

Sadriyah meat and vegetable market in the centre of Baghdad has already been the target of one of Baghdad's worst atrocities when a suicide bomber blew up a Mercedes truck on 3 February killing 137 people. There is no doubt that this second bombing is directed at killing as many Shia civilians as possible. About half an hour before the Sadriyah blast, another suicide bomber rammed a police checkpoint at the entrance to the great Shia bastion Sadr City in east Baghdad, killing 35 people and wounding 75, police say. Black smoke rose from blazing vehicles as people scrambled over the twisted wreckage of cars to try to rescue the wounded. In the Shia neighbourhood of Karada a parked car exploded, killing 10 people and wounding 15.

The escalation is discrediting the US security plan, implemented by a 'surge' in American troop numbers. Launched on 14 February, it is intended to give the Iraqi government greater control over the streets of Baghdad. The Mehdi Army Shia militia, blamed for operating death squads against Sunni civilians, has adopted a lower profile and avoided military confrontation with the US. 'The problem is that the Shia stopped killing so many Sunni but the Sunni are killing more Shia than ever,' said an Iraqi official before the attacks.

The success of the US security plan in Baghdad depends on fostering a belief by Iraqis that it is providing them with security. The Sunni insurgents and Shia militias grew in strength in the Iraqi capital in 2006 because their communities were terrified of bombers, death squads and kidnappers. The US Army, Iraqi Army and police will only win acceptance if they provide a superior level of security.

Prime Minister Nouri al-Maliki is seen as being unable to defend his own people. Hours before the bombs, Maliki said that Iraqi security forces would take full control of the whole country by the end of the year. But in a move that could weaken his position, six ministers supporting Sadr have just withdrawn from the government because of Maliki's failure to demand that the US set a timetable for the withdrawal of its troops.

24 April 2007

A group linked to al-Qa'ida has claimed responsibility for two suicide truck bombs that have killed nine US soldiers and wounded 20 in Diyala province in one of the deadliest attacks on American forces in the past year. 'Two knights from the Islamic State of Iraq ... driving booby-trapped trucks, hit the heart of the Crusader American headquarters in the region of Diyala,' says a statement from the group calling itself the Islamic State of Iraq, which was posted on the internet.

Residents in the Ameen area south of the provincial capital, Baquba, say the patrol base of the 82nd Airborne Division that was attacked is in an old primary school. In a sophisticated operation, gunmen opened fire on US snipers on the roof of the school. Then one suicide truck bomb blasted a gap in the concrete wall protecting the base, through which a second truck was able to pass before blowing up and causing the school building to collapse. The US military says that only one truck exploded.

9 May 2007

Many Sunni are becoming increasingly hostile to al-Qa'ida in Iraq. The murder of Juma'a, the headmaster of a primary school in the Ghaziliyah district of west Baghdad, explains why. Juma'a, a teacher in his forties with three daughters and one son, was told by members of al-Qa'ida in his Sunni neighbourhood to close his school. Other headmasters got the same message but also refused to comply. The demand from al-Qa'ida seems to have come because it sees schools as being under the control of the government.

Juma'a knew the danger he was running. A few months earlier, he was detained by another Sunni insurgent group as he queued for gasoline. The insurgents suspected he was carrying fake identity papers and was really a Shia. They held him for three days until he proved to them he was a Sunni. Two weeks later, he was kidnapped again. This time there was no release. Other headmasters were kidnapped at the same time and their bodies found soon after. Juma'a's family wanted to look in the Baghdad morgue, the Bab al-Modam, but faced a problem. The morgue is deemed by Sunni to be under the control of Shia militiaman who may kill or arrest Sunni looking for murdered relatives. Finally, Juma'a's sister-in-law, Wafa, and niece went to the morgue on the grounds that women are less likely to be attacked. They passed through a room filled with headless bodies and severed limbs and looked at photographs of the faces of the dead. In 15 minutes, they identified Juma'a, but they were not strong enough to transport his body home in a cheap wooden coffin.

The revolt in Iraq against the occupation has been confined hitherto to the 5-million-strong Sunni community. The growing unpopularity of al-Qa'ida in Iraq among the Sunni is partly a revulsion against its massacres of Shia by suicide bombers that lead to tit-for-tat killings of Sunni. It is also because al-Qa'ida kills Sunni who have only limited connections with the government. Those killed include minor officials in the agriculture ministry and garbage collectors. The murder of the latter is because it is convenient for al-Qa'ida to leave large heaps of rubbish uncollected on roadsides in which to hide mines. The most visible sign of the revolt against al-Qa'ida in Iraq is along the roads passing through the deserts of Anbar province to the west of Baghdad to Jordan and Syria. In recent weeks, the road to Syria has been controlled by members of the Abu Risha tribe, led by Mahmoud Abu Risha and supported by the US.

It may be that al-Qa'ida has overplayed its hand with the establishment of the Islamic State of Iraq, uniting groups sympathetic to al-Qa'ida. The Islamic State of Iraq soon began to purge resistance activists who disagreed with its line. Sunni families were forced to make contributions and send some of their young men to fight alongside the group.

The Iraqi insurgency is notoriously fragmented and its politics are shadowy. By one account, the Islamic State of Iraq got chased out of Mosul in the north soon after being formed and took refuge in the Himrin mountains south of Kirkuk. Though shaken, it remains effective under the leadership of Omar al-Baghdadi, in large part due to the involvement of well-trained officers from the Iraqi Army and, in particular, the Republican Guards.

13 July 2007

In Iraq as in the US there is a sense that with the 'surge' Washington is playing its last cards. 'I assume the US is going to start pulling out because 70 per cent of Americans and Congress want the troops to come home,' says Mahmoud Othman, a veteran Iraqi politician. 'The Americans are defeated. They haven't achieved any of their aims.'

There have been some real improvements over the past six months. Sectarian killings in Iraq have declined to 650 in June compared with 2,100 in January. So-called 'high-profile' bombings, including suicide bomb attacks on Shia markets, fell to 90 in June compared with 180 in

March. But it is doubtful if these are entirely or even mainly due to the US surge. The fall in sectarian killings, mostly of Sunni by Shia, may be largely the result of the Mehdi Army militia of Muqtada al-Sadr being told by their leader to curb their murder campaign.

It is also true that last year, after the attack on the Shia shrine in Samarra, there was a battle for Baghdad which the Shia won and the Sunni lost. Baghdad is more and more Shia-dominated and the Sunni are pinned into the south-west of the city and a few other enclaves. As Sunni and Shia are killed or driven out of mixed areas, there are fewer of them to kill. Some 4.2 million people in Iraq are now refugees, of whom about half have fled the country.

14 July 2007

An Iraqi photographer and a driver, working for the London-based news agency Reuters, have been killed by fire from a US helicopter in a Shia district of eastern Baghdad. Unlike many incidents in which Iraqis are killed by US soldiers, the manner of the Reuters staffers' deaths is known fairly precisely.

The US military says US and Iraqi forces engaged 'a hostile force' and, after coming under fire, called for air support that killed nine insurgents and two civilians. The police and witnesses tell a different story. A preliminary police report from al-Rashad police station says Namir Noor-Eldeen, 22, a Reuters photographer, and his driver Saeed Chmagh, 40, were killed along with nine others by a 'random American bombardment'. One witness, Karim Shindakh, says: 'The aircraft began striking randomly and people were wounded. A Kia [mini-van] arrived to take them away. They hit the Kia and killed ... the two journalists.' US soldiers then took away Noor-Eldeen's camera equipment. Television footage shows a hole in the roof of the van.

Six Reuters staff have now been killed in Iraq since 2003. Reuters has long complained of hostile action against its journalists by US troops. A letter from the agency's editor-in-chief, David Schlesinger, to Senator John Warner, the chairman of the Senate Armed Services Committee, dated 26 September 2005, complains of 'a long parade of disturbing incidents whereby professional journalists have been killed, wrongfully detained, and/or illegally abused by US forces in Iraq.'

Iraq has become an extraordinarily dangerous place for journalists, with 110 killed since the US-led invasion in 2003 along with 40 media support workers, more than 80 per cent of them Iraqi. The death toll of 110 in four years compares with 63 in the 20 years of the Vietnam War. The casualties among Iraqis working for the media are so high in part because Iraqi insurgents suspect journalists of working against them. But US forces have never, in practice, accepted that Iraqis taking film or video footage of combat are simply carrying out their job.

The killings also illustrate how many Iraqi civilians are killed by US troops spraying fire in all directions in thickly populated areas.

29 August 2007

Muqtada al-Sadr has suspended the activities of his powerful Mehdi Army militia for six months after clashes in the holy city of Kerbala killed 52 people and forced hundreds of thousands of pilgrims to flee. His spokesman, Sheikh Hazim al-Araji, said on state television that the aim is to 'rehabilitate' the militia, which is currently divided into factions. Significantly, Araji said that the Mehdi Army will no longer make attacks on US and other coalition forces. This may ease the pressure on British troops in Basra, who have come under repeated attack from the Mehdi Army.

The surprise move by Sadr eases fears that escalating battles between Shia militias were turning into an intra-Shia civil war. The Mehdi Army has been battling police and security forces in Kerbala that are largely manned by the Badr Organisation, the military wing of the Supreme Islamic Iraqi Council. In the hours before Sadr's statement there were widespread attacks on SIIC (Islamic Supreme Council of Iraq) offices in Baghdad and Shia cities in southern Iraq by Mehdi Army militiamen.

Sadr has long blamed factions of the Mehdi Army outside his control for attacking Sunni civilians and Iraqi government forces. Nevertheless, his decision to stand down his militia shows he does not want a confrontation with the SIIC and the US at this time. He is also in effect blaming his own militiamen for the fierce gun battles in Kerbala that erupted on Monday as a million or more Shia pilgrims poured into the city to celebrate the birth of Imam al-Mahdi, the last of the 12 Shia imams, in the 9th century. The pilgrimage, along with other ritual events, has normally been a show of unity and strength by the Shia community.

Confusion still surrounds the cause of the fighting, which began as government security forces tried to police the vast numbers of pilgrims trying to visit the shrines of Imam Hussein and Imam Abbas, the founding martyrs of the Shia faith who were killed in the battle of Kerbala in

AD 680. The police in Kerbala largely owe allegiance to the SIIC and are accused of shooting at pro-Sadrist pilgrims, who would have been accompanied by Sadrist or Mehdi Army militiamen for their own protection while marching to Kerbala. Security officials say that it was the Mehdi Army that opened fire on government security forces.

SEVEN

Drawdown

Iraq, 2007–10

3 September 2007

The withdrawal of British forces from Basra Palace marks the beginning of the end of one of the most futile campaigns ever fought by the British Army. Ostensibly, the British will be handing over control of Basra to Iraqi security forces. In reality, British soldiers control very little in Basra, and the Iraqi security forces are largely run by the Shia militias.

Soon after the British arrival, on 24 June 2003, British troops learnt a bloody lesson about the limits of their authority when six military policemen were trapped in a police headquarters between Basra and Amara. A day later I visited the grim little building where they had died. Armed men were still milling around outside. The British line was that there were 'rogue' policemen and, once they were eliminated, the Iraqi security forces would take command. In fact, the political parties and their mafia-like militias always controlled the institutions. When a young American reporter living in Basra bravely pointed this out in a comment article he was promptly murdered by the police.

Could any of this have been avoided? At an early stage, when the British had a large measure of control, there was a plan to discipline the militias by putting them in uniform. This idea of turning poachers into gamekeepers simply corrupted the police. The violence in Basra is not primarily against the occupation or over sectarian differences (the small Sunni minority has largely been driven out). The fighting has been and will be over local resources. The fragile balance of power is dominated by three groups: Fadhila, which controls the Oil Protection Force; the Supreme Islamic Iraqi Council, which dominates the intelligence service and police commando units; and the Mehdi Army, which runs much of the local police force, port authority and the Facilities Protection Force. One Iraqi truck driver said he had to bribe three different militia units stationed within a few kilometres of each other in order to proceed.

In terms of establishing an orderly government in Basra and a decent life for its people the British failure has been absolute.

11 December 2007

Has the US turned the tide in Baghdad? Does the fall in violence mean that the country is stabilising after more than four years of war? Or are we seeing only a temporary pause in the fighting?

American commentators claiming victory as a result of the surge—the 30,000 US troop reinforcements—are generally making the same mistake that they have made since the invasion of Iraq was first contemplated five years ago. They look at Iraq in over-simple terms and exaggerate the extent to which the US is making the political weather and is in control of events. The US is the most powerful single force in Iraq but by no means the only one. The shape of Iraqi politics has changed over the past year, though for reasons that have little to do with the surge and much to do with the battle for supremacy between the Sunni and Shia communities.

The Sunni Arabs of Iraq have turned against al-Qa'ida, partly because it tried to monopolise power, but primarily because it has brought their community close to catastrophe. The Sunni war against US occupation has gone surprisingly well for them since it began in 2003. It is a second war, the one led by al-Qa'ida against the Shia majority, which the Sunni have been losing, with disastrous results for themselves. 'The Sunni people now think they cannot fight two wars against the occupation and the government at the same time,' a Sunni friend in Baghdad tells me. 'We must be more realistic and accept the occupation for the moment.'

'The Battle for Baghdad,' as it is known in Iraq, was won by the Shia. They were always the majority in the capital but, by the end of 2006, they controlled 75 per cent of the city. The Sunni fled or were pressed back into a few enclaves, mostly in west Baghdad. In the wake of this defeat, there was less and less point in the Sunni trying to expel the Americans when the Sunni community was itself being evicted by the Shia from large parts of

Iraq. The Iraqi Sunni leaders had also miscalculated that an assault on their community by the Shia would provoke Arab Sunni states like Saudi Arabia and Egypt into giving them more support—this never materialised.

It was al-Qa'ida's slaughter of Shia civilians, whom it sees as heretics worthy of death, which brought disaster to the Sunni community. Bizarrely, even Osama bin Laden, who never had much influence over al-Qa'ida in Iraq, was reduced to advising his acolytes against extremism. Defeat in Baghdad and the extreme unpopularity of al-Qa'ida gave the impulse for the formation of al-Sahwa, meaning the Awakening, an 80,000-strong anti-al-Qa'ida Sunni militia, often under tribal leadership, which is armed and paid for by the US. Much of the non-al-Qa'ida Sunni insurgency has effectively changed sides. An important reason why al-Qa'ida has lost ground so swiftly is a split within its own ranks. The US military does not want to emphasise that many of the Sunni fighters now on the US payroll, who are misleadingly called 'concerned citizens', until recently belonged to al-Qa'ida and have the blood of a great many Iraqi civilians and American soldiers on their hands.

If the Sunni guerrillas were one source of violence in 2006, the other was the Mehdi Army led by Muqtada al-Sadr. This has been stood down because Sadr wants to purge it of elements he does not control, and wishes to avoid a military confrontation with his rivals within the Shia community if they are backed by the US Army. But the Mehdi Army would certainly fight if the Shia community came under attack or the Americans pressured it too hard.

American politicians continually throw up their hands in disgust that Iraqis cannot reconcile or agree on how to share power. But equally destabilising is the presence of a large US Army in Iraq and the uncertainty about what role the US will play in future. However much Iraqis may fight among themselves, a central political fact remains the unpopularity of the US-led occupation outside Kurdistan.

Nothing is resolved in Iraq.

26 January 2008

There are checkpoints everywhere in Iraq. I count 27 on the road from central Baghdad to Fallujah. These guard posts provide protection, but they are also a threat because there are so many of them that it is easy for kidnappers, criminals and militiamen to set up their own checkpoints in order to select likely victims. In this case I am not too worried, because my driver is a policeman from the area and there are another four well-armed police in a car behind.

We turn up a track, guided by militiamen, to the hidden headquarters of Abu Marouf, a former insurgent against the Americans who has changed sides and now leads 13,000 men against al-Qa'ida. They are part of al-Sahwa, the Sunni Awakening movement. Part of Abu Marouf's force is paid for by the Americans. Ordinary fighters are believed to receive $350 a month and officers $1,200, but some receive no salary.

Abu Marouf is an angry man, complaining that if he and his men do not get long-term jobs in the Iraqi security forces in three months then they will stop suppressing al-Qa'ida and perhaps reach a deal with them. 'If the Americans think they can use us to get rid of al-Qa'ida and then push us to one side, they are mistaken,' he says. I do not quite believe his threat to ally himself with al-Qa'ida because the group cut off his brother's head with an old-fashioned razor, and 450 members of his tribe, the Zubai, have been killed by them.

The rain is sleeting down and we have to skirt muddy puddles to get back to the car. We go to Fallujah, sealed off from the outside world since it was stormed by the US Marines in November 2004. We drive around an enormous queue of people waiting at the final checkpoint, and only get into the city because the chief of police, Colonel Feisal, another brother of Abu Marouf, vouches for us and has sent an escort.

People in Fallujah say, as they do in Baghdad, that life is getting better, by which they mean that the chances of staying alive have risen sharply in the past six months, because al-Qa'ida has been eliminated or driven underground. Asked what he was doing immediately before becoming chief of police, Colonel Feisal replies engagingly: 'I was fighting against the Americans.' Asked why he has changed sides he replies: 'When I compared the Americans to al-Qa'ida and the [Shia] militia, I chose the Americans.' He volunteers that the worst day of his life was when Saddam Hussein was overthrown in 2003.

15 February 2008

People in Baghdad are not passive victims of violence, but seek desperately to avoid their fate. In April 2004, I was almost killed by Shia militiamen of the Mehdi Army at a checkpoint at Kufa in southern Iraq. They said I was an American spy and were about to execute me and my driver, Bassim Abdul Rahman, when they decided at the last moment to check with their commander. 'I believe', Bassim said afterwards, 'that if Patrick had an American or an English passport [instead of an Irish one] they would have killed us all immediately.'

In the following years, I saw Bassim less and less. He is a Sunni, aged about 40, from west Baghdad. After the Battle for Baghdad in 2006 he could hardly work as a driver because the Shia controlled three-quarters of the capital. There were few places where a Sunni could drive in safety outside a handful of enclaves. What happened to Bassim was also to happening to millions of Iraqis who saw their lives ruined by successive calamities. As their world collapsed around them they were forced to take desperate measures to survive, obtain a job and make enough money to feed and educate their families.

At the time we had our encounter with the Mehdi Army in Kufa, Bassim was living in a house in the mixed Sunni–Shia area of Jihad in south-west Baghdad. He loved the house, which had a sitting room and two bedrooms, because he had built it himself in 2001. 'I didn't complete it because I didn't have enough money,' he says. 'But we were so happy to have our own home.' He was living there in the summer of 2006 with his wife Maha, 38, and his children Sarah, 13, Noor, eight, and Sama, three, when Shia militiamen took over Jihad. Bassim fled to Syria with his family and, when he returned to Jihad three months later, he found pictures of Muqtada al-Sadr pasted to the gate of his house.

Neighbours told Bassim to get out as fast as he could before the Mehdi Army militiamen came back and killed him. He drove with his family to his father-in-law's house in the tough Sunni district of al-Khadra, where he and his wife and three children were to live in a single small room. He did not dare go back to his old home, but he heard about it in the summer of 2007 from a friendly Shia neighbour who said it had been taken over by militiamen. 'They accused me', says Bassim, 'of being a high-rank officer in the former intelligence service and because of that they got a permit [from Sadr's office] to take it over.' Two Shia families moved in for a couple of months and, when they left, they took all his remaining belongings. They left the house unlocked, and soon the wooden doors and other fittings were gone. The permanent loss of Bassim's home, his only possession of any value apart from his car, was a terrible blow. 'I have nothing else to lose aside from my house,' he wrote to me in a sad letter in the autumn of 2007, 'and because of what happened I had a heart attack. I worked as a taxi driver for a few days, but I couldn't do it any longer because of the dangerous situation and I had no other way of earning a living. Finally, I sold my car and my wife's few gold things and I will try to go to Sweden even if I have to go illegally.'

I thought his plan to travel to Sweden was a terrible one, as Bassim spoke only Arabic and had not travelled outside Iraq, apart from a few trips to Syria and Jordan. But there was nothing I could do to dissuade him. I did not see or hear from him for six months, though I heard from his friends that his bid to reach Sweden had failed and that he was stuck in Kuala Lumpur. Then, on 1 February, he appeared at the door of my hotel room in Baghdad, looking shrunken and miserable, and told me of his strange and disastrous odyssey.

I had originally hoped that his plan to travel illegally to Sweden was a fantasy he would never try to realise, but everything he had said in his letter turned out to be true. He had sold his car, his wife's gold jewellery and some furniture for $6,500 and borrowed $1,500 from his sister and the same amount from friends. Of this, $6,900 was paid to Abu Mohammed, an Iraqi in Sweden, who provided Bassim and a friend called Ibrahim with Lithuanian passports (these turned out to be genuine, but one of Bassim's many fears over the next three months was that his passport was a fake and he would be thrown in jail). The two men went first to Damascus and then, instructed over the phone by Abu Mohammed in Sweden, they flew to Malaysia. This would seem to be the wrong direction, but Malaysia has the great advantage of being one of the few countries to give Iraqis entry visas at the airport. Bassim and Ibrahim took rooms at the cheapest hotel they could find in Kuala Lumpur.

They were then told by Abu Mohammed to get a plane to Cambodia and take a bus to Vietnam. Though their money was fast dwindling, they did so. Somehow, still speaking only Arabic, they made their way from Phnom Penh to Ho Chi Minh City. The plan was to get a ticket to Sweden by way of France (Bassim now thinks that this was a mistake and it would have been better to travel first to Lithuania, posing as citizens returning home, but this would have left the two Iraqis with the problem of explaining to officials there why they did not speak Lithuanian).

In the check-in queue at the airport in Vietnam on 5 January, Bassim was desperately worried he would be detected. He had staked all his remaining money and his family's future on getting to Sweden. In fact, he and Ibrahim had little chance of being allowed on to the plane. Too many Iraqis, claiming to be citizens of small East European states, had tried this route before.

Suspicious Vietnamese immigration officials took them to an investigation room where Bassim felt ill and asked for a glass of water, which was refused. He and Ibrahim continued to protest that they were Lithuanian citizens and demanded to be taken to the Lithuanian embassy, knowing full well that Lithuania is unrepresented in Vietnam. It was all in vain. The officials guessed that they were Iraqis. They sent Bassim and Ibrahim back to Cambodia. Half-starved because he did not like the local food—'I was used to Iraqi bread'—and with his money almost gone, Bassim made his way back to Kuala Lumpur by the end of January. He last saw his friend Ibrahim heading for Indonesia in a small boat.

Abu Mohammed in Sweden became elusive and, when finally contacted by phone after six days, admitted that 'for Iraqis, all the ways from Asia to Sweden are shut.' He did not offer to return Bassim's $6,900. Demoralised, and hearing that many Iraqi refugees trying to get to Europe through Indonesia simply disappeared, Bassim used his last few dollars to fly to Damascus and took a shared taxi across the desert to Baghdad. 'The journey took three months but it felt like 10 years,' he says. 'I have lost everything.'

Life in the Iraq to which Bassim has returned is said by foreigners and Iraqis alike to be getting better. In contrast to the spurious turning-points of the past, the most recent political changes in Iraq, which have led to the fall in American and Iraqi casualties, are quite real. But they differ significantly from the way in which they are portrayed in the outside world. Baghdad is safer, but it remains an extraordinarily dangerous place. In effect, the surge has frozen into place the Shia victory of 2006. The city is broken up into enclaves sealed off by concrete walls with only one entrance and exit. Areas that were once mixed are not being reoccupied by whichever community was driven out. Bassim can no more reclaim, or even visit, his house in the Jihad district of Baghdad than he could a year ago. He can still work as a taxi driver only in Sunni areas. The US military and the Iraqi government are wary of even trying to reverse sectarian cleansing because this might break the present fragile truce.

In the coming weeks, we will see the fifth anniversary of the invasion of Iraq. There will be much rancorous debate in the Western media about the success or failure of the surge and the US war effort here. But for millions of Iraqis like Bassim, the war has robbed them of their homes, their jobs and often their lives. It has brought them nothing but misery and ended their hopes of happiness. It has destroyed Iraq.

6 March 2008

On 16 February, Nouri al-Maliki went on a walkabout in central Baghdad to demonstrate how safe things have become. The precautions taken by his bodyguards suggested otherwise. This brief venture out of the Green Zone took place in the al-Mansur district of west Baghdad, an area of big houses and many embassies that has been heavily fought over by Sunni and Shia in the past year. 'I was in Mansur on Saturday afternoon', an Iraqi friend told me, 'when, at about 3:15 p.m., I noticed a strange movement in the street. A sudden flood of soldiers in green uniform, led by generals and colonels, were checking parked cars and buildings.' Minutes later a large convoy of vehicles arrived, with three US Army Humvees in front and behind, and, in the middle, five armoured four-wheel drives. They stopped in front of the al-Ruwaad ice-cream shop but for 15 minutes nobody got out of the vehicles as soldiers searched all the shops nearby. When the officials and their guards emerged Maliki was in the middle of them and began to walk around. 'Everybody was scared when they saw him because they thought his presence might lead to an attack,' my friend said. 'Some women began to run away and I thought it was too dangerous for me to stay. I heard that Maliki gave 500,000 Iraqi dinars (£200) each to a woman who said her husband had been killed in a bomb explosion and to a blind beggar.' Maliki also bought two suits from a well-known shop called Mario Zengotti, which promptly shut down, the owner presumably calculating that Baghdad is full of people who might kill him for selling clothes to the prime minister.

The shooting may have died down for the moment, but the killings of 2006 and early 2007 have left a legacy of hatred and fear. Even the most liberal-minded Sunni and Shia no longer feel at ease in each other's company. The story of one family from al-Khudat, a middle-class Sunni neighbourhood in west Baghdad, explains why the city is going to remain divided. The victims in this case were Shia, but what happened to them, and how they reacted to it, is typical of refugee families elsewhere in Iraq. The family had lived in al-Khudat for thirty years and was well liked by its Sunni neighbours. The father of the family died two years ago, leaving his 55-year-old widow, Umm Hadi, who had been a primary school teacher, to support their four sons and three daughters. Early in 2007 it became so dangerous for Shia in al-Khudat that the family fled to Syria after asking the neighbours to look after their house. Umm Hadi did not like it there. 'We thought we were just going for a short time,' she said. 'The Syrians mistreated us and charged us a lot of money, so we decided to come back to Baghdad.'

On Umm Hadi's return from Syria a year later, she and her family found that their house had been taken by a Sunni family from al-Amel, another embattled area; they refused to leave. Umm Hadi and her sons, all grown up, were too frightened to call the police or the Americans. Instead they moved to Hurriyah in north-west Baghdad, which once was mixed but is now controlled by the Mehdi Army and the Shia. Hadi, the eldest brother, who works as a carpenter, was dispirited when he was asked on 1 February what he intended to do. 'We were so surprised that our house was taken and that our dear neighbours allowed this to happen,' he said. 'There is nothing we can do to force these people to leave because they might retaliate by attacking me or my brothers or even blow up the house.' He was interrupted by his mother. Her face quivering with anger, Umm Hadi said she was not going to surrender so easily. 'It is true that we are poor people,' she said, 'but that does not mean that we are weak. We can call on our strong Shia arm'—apparently a reference to the Mehdi Army—'to get our house back. I have information that one of the sons of the family who took it is working in a petrol station. It would be a good message to send his dead body to them if they insist on staying.' At this point one of her sons tried to excuse her, saying that she had 'suffered a lot since we came back to Iraq; she is a kind woman and does not mean what she says.' A week later, on 8 February, the father of the Sunni family who had taken their house was found shot dead in his car in west Baghdad.

6 June 2008

America, we now know, is negotiating a security agreement to replace the present UN mandate. The agreement—effectively a treaty, but it will not go by that name because Bush does not want to submit it to Senate approval—would continue the occupation under a different guise. The US would keep possession of more than 50 bases; in each case a few Iraqi soldiers would man an outer perimeter so that the US can say the bases will be in Iraqi hands. American soldiers and contractors would have legal immunity. The US would be free to carry out operations against 'terrorists' without informing the Iraqi government; it would be able to carry out military campaigns as and when it feels like it. Some of the Iraqi negotiators have been horrified by the extent of the American demands. But whatever his private misgivings, Nouri al-Maliki, the Iraqi prime minister, believes that he cannot finally do without American backing. His coalition of Shia religious parties, Sunni representatives and Kurds feel the same way.

The Iraqi–American security agreement, which Bush wants signed by 31 July, comes just as the Iraqi government is trying to regain control of the country's largest cities. Since the end of March the government has launched three offensives, sending its army into Basra, Mosul and Sadr City in Baghdad. Thousands of government soldiers now patrol Shia districts once dominated by Muqtada al-Sadr's Mehdi Army. In the Sunni Arab city of Mosul, where more than a thousand people have been arrested, the government claims it is on the verge of crushing the last remnant of al-Qa'ida in Iraq. Maliki is trying to prove that the Iraqi state is back in business. The operations in Basra and Mosul were given bombastic names—Charge of the Knights and Roar of the Lion—in an attempt to underline Maliki's intention to make the Iraqi Army the strongest non-American military power in Iraq.

At first sight the government seems to be succeeding, despite early failures. The attack on the Mehdi Army in Basra on 25 March initially made no headway and Iraqi soldiers ran out of food after a couple of days. They also had to be heavily reinforced by US air strikes and British artillery fire, called in by American advisers. But a few weeks later, government soldiers were taking over districts held by the Mehdi Army. In Sadr City the Americans again bore the brunt of the fighting. In both Basra and Sadr City the clashes ended when Muqtada al-Sadr called his men off the streets under ceasefires brokered by the Iranians. At this point the Iraqi Army moved in without US help. Maliki may not have won the decisive military victory he claimed, but at the end of the fighting his government looked stronger than ever.

The main supporters of Maliki's government are the US and Iran. From the Iranian point of view the present Shia–Kurdish government in Baghdad is as good as it is going to get, although Iran does want to reduce American influence on Maliki. The fighting in March and April in Basra and Sadr City between the Mehdi Army and the Iraqi government was in each case brought to an end by Iranian mediation. This is open knowledge. To arrange the ceasefires in Basra and Baghdad, President Jalal Talabani twice went to the Iraq–Iran border to see Qassem Suleimani, the head of the Quds Brigade of the Iranian Revolutionary Guard, even though Bush has denounced the Quds Brigade as terrorists orchestrating attacks on US forces. When President Ahmadinejad of Iran came to Baghdad earlier this year his visit was announced in advance and his convoy drove unhindered through the streets. When Bush comes to Baghdad it is kept a secret until the last moment; he travels only by helicopter and has never ventured outside the Green Zone.

14 August 2008

Presidential candidate Barack Obama was lucky in the timing of a recent visit to Iraq. He arrived just after the prime minister, Nouri al-Maliki, had rejected a draft of a security agreement which would have preserved indefinitely the US right to conduct military operations inside the country. The Iraqi government was vague about when it wanted the final withdrawal of US troops, but its spokesman Ali al-Dabbagh declared that they should be gone by 2010; this fitted Obama's promise to withdraw 'one to two' combat brigades a month for 16 months. Suddenly, his rival John McCain's belief that US troops should stay until some undefined victory looked impractical and out of date.

The Iraqi government seemed almost surprised by its own decisiveness. It is by no means as confident as it pretends to be that it can survive without US backing, but it unexpectedly found itself riding a nationalist wave. America made a mistake in pushing for a military agreement with Iraq at the time it did. When the US presented its first draft in March, it envisaged simply continuing the occupation with itself as colonial overlord. The agreement was compared by Iraqis to the Anglo-Iraqi Treaty of 1930, under which Britain retained enough authority to discredit Iraqi governments, which were seen as puppets of the imperial power. 'What the Americans were offering us in terms of real sovereignty was even less than the British did eighty years ago,' one Iraqi leader says.

The failed attempt to reach an agreement helped crystallise Iraqi resentment over the occupation. The military bases, the immunity for US soldiers, the thousands of Iraqis held prisoner by the US, the ability of US troops to arrest Iraqis and carry out military operations at will: all of this would have been institutionalised and officially sanctioned had the agreement been signed. Nobody—not Maliki, not Washington—expected the nationalist backlash to be as fierce as it was.

Although the Sadrists have for the moment gone to ground following the military onslaught against them, their blend of Iraqi nationalism, religious revivalism and social populism still has widespread appeal, and it was largely because Maliki did not want to be seen as an American pawn that he objected so vigorously to the US agreement. The bitterness between Maliki and the Sadrists is considerable because it was their members of parliament who made him prime minister. Sadrist ministers withdrew from Maliki's government in 2007 because he had not insisted on a timeline for an American military withdrawal. Sadrist crowds demonstrate every Friday demanding that the troops leave. It is curious that Maliki's government is now asking for the same thing as Sadr.

Muqtada himself sits in his house in the holy city of Qom in Iran, where he says he is pursuing his religious studies. His strategy is not to be drawn into a fight before the Americans depart or draw down their forces. When crowds attending Sadrist-controlled mosques in Sadr City last month started to tear down barriers placed in the streets by the Iraqi Army, it was Sadrist preachers who begged them to go home and avoid a confrontation. Muqtada 'is not the kind of man', according to his spokesman Salah al-Obaidi, 'who plucks the fruit before it is ripe.' But the Iraqi government is keeping up the pressure while it still has the backing of American firepower. In Amara the Sadrist governor has been put under arrest, the province is effectively under martial law and even Sadrists who took advantage of an amnesty are being arrested.

There were also other forces at play in Maliki's rejection of Bush's agreement. The Iranians made it clear that they would not accept it. What proponents of the surge like McCain never understood was that its success, in so far that it was successful, depended on Iran's co-operation; the new agreement would have brought this to an end. Maliki's increasing willingness to stand up to the US may well be the result of a private assurance from Iran that he will not face an uprising by the Mehdi Army in southern Iraq if he does so. The struggle for power in Iraq is entering a new phase. The US may not have got the agreement it wanted, but it remains the dominant military power in the country and still largely controls the Iraqi Army. Whether Obama or McCain wins the presidential election in the US, the battle over who really rules in Baghdad will continue.

15 December 2008

The sight of the Iraqi reporter Muntazer al-Zaidi hurling his shoes at President Bush at a press conference in Baghdad will gladden the heart of any journalist forced to attend these tedious, useless and almost invariably obsequious events. 'This is a farewell kiss,' shouted Zaidi. 'This is from the widows, the orphans and those who were killed in Iraq.'

Thousands of Iraqis have poured into the streets of Baghdad in support of Zaidi. As the Iraqi journalist remained in detention for what authorities called 'a barbaric and ignominious act', a crowd in the capital pelted US troops with their shoes in one of many street protests called in support of the reporter's action. Transcending sectarian divisions, demonstrations backing the journalist were held in the Shia holy city of Najaf, but also in the Sunni city of Tikrit.

18 December 2008

On 27 November the Iraqi parliament voted by a large majority in favour of a security agreement with the US under which its 150,000 troops will withdraw from Iraqi cities, towns and villages by 30 June next year and from all of Iraq by 31 December, 2011. The Iraqi government will take over military responsibility for the Green Zone in Baghdad, the heart of American power in Iraq, in a few weeks' time. Private security companies will lose legal immunity. US military operations will only be carried out with Iraqi consent. No US military bases will remain after the last American troops leave in 2011 and in the interim the US military is banned from carrying out attacks on other countries from within Iraq.

The Status of Forces Agreement, as it is officially known, finally signed after eight months of rancorous negotiations, is categorical and unconditional. America's bid to act as the world's only super-power and to establish quasi-colonial control of Iraq, an attempt that began with the invasion of 2003, has ended in failure. Even Iran, which had denounced the first drafts of the deal, fearing that any agreement would enshrine a permanent US presence in Iraq, now says that it will officially back the new security pact after the referendum: a sure sign that America's main rival in the Middle East sees the accord as marking the end of the occupation and the end of any notion of Iraq being used as a launching-pad for military assaults on its neighbours.

Astonishingly, this momentous agreement was greeted with little surprise or interest outside Iraq. On the day that it was finally passed by the Iraqi parliament, international attention was focused on terrorist attacks in Mumbai. For some months, polls in the US have shown that the economic crisis has replaced the Iraqi war in the minds of American voters. In any case, Bush has declared so many spurious milestones to have been passed in Iraq over the years that when a real turning point is reached people are naturally sceptical about its significance. The White House is anyway so keen to keep quiet about what it has agreed in Iraq that it has not even published a copy of the Status of Forces Agreement in English. Some senior officials in the Pentagon privately criticise Bush for conceding so much, but the American media are fixated on the incoming Obama administration and no longer pay much attention to the doings of Bush and Co.

There were last-minute delays to the accord as the leaders of the Sunni Arab minority, seeing Nouri al-Maliki's Shia–Kurdish government about to fill the vacuum created by the US departure, wrung as many concessions as they could in return for their support. Around three-quarters of the 17,000 prisoners held by the Americans are Sunni and their leaders wanted them released or at least to have some guarantee that they would not be mistreated by the Iraqi security forces. They also asked for an end to de-Baathification, which is directed primarily at the Sunni community. Only the Shia cleric Muqtada al-Sadr held out against the accord, declaring it a betrayal of an independent Iraq. The ultra-patriotic opposition of the Sadrists has been important because it has made it difficult for the other Shia parties to agree to anything less than a complete American withdrawal if they wanted to avoid being portrayed as US puppets in the provincial elections at the end of next month, or the parliamentary elections later in the year.

The Status of Forces Agreement finally agreed is in almost every way the opposite of the one the US started to negotiate in March, which was largely an attempt to continue the occupation under similar terms to the UN mandate that expires at the end of the year. Washington overplayed its hand. The Iraqi government was growing stronger as a result of the end of the Sunni Arab uprising. The Iranians had helped restrain the Mehdi Army, allowing the government to regain control of Basra and Sadr City from the Shia militias. Maliki became more confident, realising that his military enemies were dispersing and that, in any case, the Americans had no real alternative but to support him.

The occupation has always been unpopular in Iraq. Foreign observers and some Iraqis are often misled by the hatred with which Iraqi communities regard each other into underestimating the strength of Iraqi nationalism. Once Maliki came to believe that he could survive without US military support he was able to spurn American proposals until an unconditional withdrawal was conceded. In any case, by the end of August it seemed quite likely that Obama, whose withdrawal timetable is not so different from Maliki's, would be the next president. Come next year's elections, Maliki can present himself as the man who ended the occupation. His critics, notably the Kurds, think that success has gone to his head, but there is no doubt that the new security agreement has strengthened him politically.

14 June 2009

There are few American patrols on the streets of Baghdad and soon there will be none. In just over two weeks, on 30 June, US military forces will withdraw from Iraqi cities. The occupation which began six years ago is ending. On every side there are signs of the decline of US influence.

When Nouri al-Maliki held a meeting with 300 top military commanders last week a US general who tried to attend was asked to leave. 'We apologise to you, but this is an Iraqi meeting and you're not invited,' he was told. Maliki, who was put into power by the US in 2006, spoke of the departure of the troops as if he had been leading an insurgency against them. 'Foreign forces have to withdraw from the cities totally,' he said in the course of an hour-long speech in which he mentioned America only once. 'This is a victory that should be celebrated in feasts and festivals.' Given that the US is Maliki's main ally, this seems to show an astonishing lack of gratitude on his part. But the knowledge that the US forces are to go is transforming the political landscape. It is no longer politic for any Iraqi leader to be identified with the American occupation.

23 June 2009

I sometimes think I should not come back to Baghdad because I am burdened by too many grisly stories. I wonder if another correspondent might be better able to write chirpy tales about how life here is getting better, as indeed, in a certain sense, it is. He or she, coming to Iraq afresh, would have no memories of friends killed and tortured and would respond sympathetically to feel-good stories pumped out by the Iraqi and US governments. But then I recall that most Iraqis are influenced by the same experiences as myself. Almost every Iraqi I know has lost one or more members of their family. The bodies of many of the dead have never been found.

14 August 2009

Two or three years ago, tattoo artists in Baghdad were working overtime giving distinctive tattoos to men who feared they would be killed in the

Sunni–Shia sectarian slaughter. Aware that the faces of so many who died were being mutilated, potential victims wanted their families to be able to identify their bodies through a special mark known only to close relatives. One man had an olive tree tattooed onto his body because his father had planted one on the day he was born. This grisly ritual is no longer taking place because Iraq is now a safer place than it was at the height of the sectarian bloodbath in 2005–07. Tattooists report that their clients are today seeking to be marked with the image of a falcon, tiger or dragon for solely decorative reasons. The point is that security in Iraq is improving, but from a very low base. Baghdad is safer than it used to be though this still leaves it as one of the most dangerous cities in the world, certainly worse than Kabul, with perhaps only Mogadishu in Somalia edging it into second place.

The two wars which convulsed Iraq after the overthrow of Saddam Hussein by the US military in 2003 are largely over. The first was by the Sunni Arabs against the American occupation and was waged from 2003 to about halfway through 2007. It was effectively ended by the outcome of a second conflict, this time the extraordinarily bloody civil war between Sunni and Shia. It was the Shia victory in this war, fought primarily in Baghdad and central Iraq, which forced the Sunni insurgents to end their guerrilla struggle against the Americans.

The American military withdrawal stabilises Iraq to a degree never admitted by protagonists of the original invasion. Foreign occupation deepened sectarian and ethnic hatreds because the three main Iraqi communities took radically different attitudes towards it. And it destabilised Iraq in a second way because it frightened Iraq's neighbours. This is scarcely surprising since the neo-cons in Washington openly sought regime change in Tehran and Damascus, as well as Baghdad. So long as an American land army was in Iraq, the country's neighbours were always going to foster Sunni and Shia guerrilla groups attacking US troops.

As the Americans depart, a danger is that the Sunni states will refuse to accept the first Shia-dominated government in the Arab world since the Fatimids, and that they will support Sunni resistance to it.

8 December, 2009

Car bombers have killed as many as 127 people in Baghdad in a series of attacks that have left the city's streets strewn with the wreckage of burning vehicles and the charred bodies of the dead. The five bombs, including three that were detonated by suicide bombers, exploded in succession across the Iraqi capital over the course of an hour this morning, targeting a mosque, a market, a government ministry, an educational college and a court. The sound of screams and police sirens followed the detonation of each bomb. Some 425 people were wounded.

The coordinated assault is likely to be the work of al-Qa'ida in Iraq, which has adopted the tactic of launching devastating bombing attacks about every six weeks to maximise political and psychological impact. One aim is to discredit the government's claim that it has greatly improved security in the last couple of years. Some 155 people were killed in the last big attack by bombers on 25 October and over 122 in an earlier assault in August.

28 February 2010

With a week to go until Iraq's legislative election, Prime Minister Nouri al-Maliki has denied that a decision to purge hundreds of candidates from the ballot is aimed at the minority Sunni population, despite evidence that the witch-hunt is being extended. 'It's not true that it targeted Sunni,' Maliki said. 'The decision was made because some of those were blatantly propagating Baath Party ideas.' He said that most of those banned are Shia. However, all the important politicians among those blacklisted are Sunni. The banning of some 500 candidates was unexpectedly announced at the start of the year. In the last few days it has been widened to include several hundred security and army officers, and about 1,000 provincial officials, according to sources in the Iraqi capital.

Despite the government's notorious failings, posters and banners all over Baghdad—now largely a Shia city—call for 'No return for the Baathist criminals' and 'Revenge on the Baathists who oppressed you'. There are only a few posters promising to do something about unemployment, electricity and services. The Shia political parties, including those running the government, have been trying to outdo each other in the toughness of their demands for a clampdown.

The political aim of the purge is probably to weaken the secular nationalist coalition called Iraqiya, led by former prime minister Iyad Allawi. The most prominent politician to be banned is Saleh al-Mutlaq. He leads the National Dialogue Front, which is the second largest Sunni faction in parliament, and is allied to Allawi. Sectarianism never came close to dying away over the last couple of years. But after playing the anti-Baathist card so vigorously during the election campaign, the Shia parties may have difficulty getting the sectarian genie back in the bottle, particularly if there are many more bombs in Baghdad.

28 March 2010

As people in Sunni areas of Baghdad heard the full results of the election, they ran through the streets firing their rifles into the air in celebration and triumphantly chanting the name of Iyad Allawi. His Iraqiya group won 91 seats, narrowly beating the State of Law group led by Nouri al-Maliki into second place with 89 seats. As interim prime minister in 2004–05 Allawi ran an administration chiefly notable for its incompetence and corruption, so his political rebirth is astonishing. It has happened because, whatever his failings then, the bloodbath that followed his rule was even worse, particularly for the Sunni community.

This is Allawi's strength, and his weakness. Though a secular Shia himself, his success was the result of a massive turn-out of Sunni voters, enabling him to sweep away the opposition in the Sunni-majority provinces north and west of Baghdad. He also did well in the capital, now very much Shia dominated, which means that many Shia were attracted by his nationalist and non-sectarian platform. But the political landscape of Iraq remains determined by sectarian and ethnic differences. For many Shia and Kurds the resurgence of the Sunni is threatening, and they will try to limit it by preventing Allawi forming a government with the top jobs going to his Sunni allies. The Kurds would have difficulty doing a deal with Allawi because over a third of his seats are in provinces disputed between Sunni Arab and Kurd.

Surprising as Allawi's triumph may be, it is also something of a mirage because the Shia vote was split between Maliki's State of Law and the Iraqi National Alliance (INA), which won 70 seats. The INA is made up of two Shia religious parties, the ISCI and the followers of Muqtada al-Sadr. The revival of the latter, who represent the Shia poor, has been the second upset of the election.

The two big Shia blocs—State of Law and the INA—are now in talks about a merger which would give them almost half the seats in parliament. A new government would only need the addition of the 43 seats of the main Kurdish party to give them a majority. The Kurds and the INA will probably ask for a new prime minister, replacing Maliki with whom both have quarrelled.

Maliki ought to have done better because he controls the state machinery, with its $60 billion a year in oil revenues and several million jobs. This power of patronage was not as effective as it should have been because so much of the Iraqi government is parasitic, no service being performed unless accompanied by a bribe.

25 April 2010

The Islamic State of Iraq has confirmed that two of its top leaders, Abu Omar al-Baghdadi and Abu Ayyub al-Masri, have been killed in an air strike. A statement said: 'After a long journey filled with sacrifices and fighting falsehood and its representatives, two knights have dismounted to join the group of martyrs. We announce that the Muslim nation has lost two of the leaders of jihad.'

Despite the death of the two men, the organisation has demonstrated that it still has the ability to explode car bombs all over Baghdad, including the well-guarded Shia slum of Sadr City. Bombings killed 72 people on 23 April. The apparently co-ordinated attack, which occurred over a two-hour timespan and included at least 10 bombs and roadside devices, was aimed exclusively at Shia civilians.

11 November 2010

The US is facing a decisive political defeat in Iraq over the formation of a new government, as its influence in the country sinks lower than at any time since the invasion of 2003. The US campaign to promote its favoured candidate, Iyad Allawi, as president appears to have failed spectacularly. Previously, the US also failed to install Allawi to the more powerful post of prime minister, in a power-sharing arrangement with Nouri al-Maliki. This hope was ended when the Shia political parties finally united behind Maliki last month after seven months of deadlock.

President Barack Obama, Vice President Joe Biden and Senator John McCain, who is in Baghdad leading a congressional delegation, have all lobbied the Kurdish leaders to give up the post of president in favour of Allawi, but without success. The incumbent, Kurdish leader Jalal Talabani, will be re-elected. The job of speaker of parliament is likely to go to Osama al-Nujaifi, a Sunni member of Iraqiya. The speaker has a powerful and high-profile position, since he calls parliament into session and largely controls its work. Appointing Nujaifi may go some way to satisfying the Sunni demand for a share in government.

The reuniting of the Shia bloc is seen as a political triumph for Iran. The stalemate was broken with the surprise choice by Muqtada al-Sadr and his followers to abandon their resistance to Maliki staying in his job. The Sadrists openly admit that they took their decision under heavy Iranian pressure. Syria, which has been even more distrustful of Maliki, also appears to have softened its opposition to him at Iranian prompting. Iran has out-manoeuvred the US in shaping the new government to its own liking. 'American hegemony in Iraq is over,' Ghassan al-Attiyah, a commentator and political scientist, says. 'US influence is falling by the day.'

PART III: AFGHAN REPRISE

in Iraq the occupation by the US, Britain and their allies was always going to be resisted by Sunni and Shia Arabs and supported fully only by the Kurds, whose territory was not occupied. Most Iraqis were glad to be rid of Saddam Hussein, but this did not mean they favoured foreign occupation and from the beginning this meant more war was near-inevitable.

The same was not true of Afghanistan where the return of the Taliban some five years after their defeat in 2001 was the result of avoidable errors by the Afghan government and its American backers. Why did they make so many mistakes? Part of the explanation was simple arrogance after what appeared to be an easy anti-Taliban victory. The White House saw that the war to overthrow the Taliban in 2001 had succeeded more swiftly and at less cost than anybody could have imagined, though this was deceptive. The Taliban did not fight to a finish—its men went back to their villages and its leadership fled across the border. But the central Afghan government of Hamid Karzai had little to build on in terms of trained, capable and honest personnel. The economic infrastructure was wrecked. Afghans saw too little improvement in their lives. The Pashtun, the largest Afghan community, was largely displaced from power and patronage.

The US looked to the warlords as local allies, though they were widely detested by ordinary Afghans. The Taliban's political appeal, aside from its religious bigotry and obscurantism, had always stemmed from its supposed opposition to warlordism. Deep disillusionment with the Karzai government followed and, when I started writing about and visiting Afghanistan again from 2008, I noticed that the dominant political feature was dislike or hatred of the government at all levels of society. A political vacuum was created that the Taliban swiftly moved to fill. The deputy UN envoy Peter Galbraith said that the weakness of the US and its allies in Afghanistan was the corruption and unpopularity of the Karzai government, adding 'we have no local partner.' He was promptly sacked for his pains.

A second crucial factor leading to the return of the Taliban was the support of Pakistan, or more particularly the intelligence arm of the Pakistani armed forces, the ISI. Its not very covert backing was central to the Taliban's ability to train, recruit and re-supply its forces. After 2001 the Pakistani military was at first cowed by the US, but when President George Bush invaded Iraq in 2003, its leaders perceived that his 'war on terror' was not entirely serious and had lost direction. They saw that they could resume their support for the Taliban movement that they had built up between 1994 and 2001. It was only in 2007 that the US began keeping tabs on links between the ISI and the Taliban. Some Americans saw that this failure to confront Pakistan meant inevitable failure in Afghanistan. These included Richard C Holbrooke, the US Special Representative to Afghanistan and Pakistan, who famously said: 'we may be fighting the wrong enemy in the wrong country.'

The result of these miscalculations was an estimated 50,000 to 70,000 dead Afghans and 3,400 dead foreign soldiers including 2,300 Americans and 450 British. The presence of foreign troops in support of a hated local faction and corrupt and violent Afghan security forces meant that America, Britain and others were provoking the insurrection that they were supposedly trying to suppress. If policy makers in Washington and London had been in the business of alienating or enraging Afghans they could hardly have done a better job. I kept in mind the softly spoken words of a former colonel in the Pakistan Army who was a Pashtun and had commanded Pashtun troops. He told me, as is recorded later in this chapter, that he was perplexed by the American and British effort to win over the hearts and minds of the Pashtun of southern Afghanistan because 'at the centre of Pashtun culture is a hatred of all foreigners.'

EIGHT

The Return of the Taliban

Afghanistan, 2009–12

3 May 2009

I spent the war which overthrew the Taliban in 2001 in a town called Jabal Saraj just north of Kabul. It was miserably poor and extremely dirty, but it was firmly held by the anti-Taliban Northern Alliance and a good place to wait for the start of the US-backed offensive. Jabal Saraj stands at the southern end of the Panjshir valley, a main opposition bastion under both the Communists and the Taliban. The town itself had been ravaged by war. The main bridge had been blown up and replaced by a bizarre temporary structure made out of captured Taliban armoured cars heaped on top of one other. The front line with the Taliban ran 20 miles to the south, the trenches cutting through the well-watered villages of the Shomali plain.

When I was there, the people of the Panjshir and Shomali plain were doing badly even by Afghan standards. Offensives and counter-offensives by the Taliban and anti-Taliban forces had made it almost impossible to live and work. Much of the population had fled. The fruit orchards and fields were full of lethal little anti-personnel mines and the irrigation system had been wrecked. On the Taliban side of the line, which ran through Bagram airport, the villages had been systematically blown up or burned and some 140,000 people turned into refugees.

Eight years later, the people of the Shomali plain and the Panjshir valley are among the not very numerous winners in the Afghan conflict since the fall of the Taliban. Having once lived in one of the most dangerous places in the country, they can now count their towns and villages as very safe. Victors in the war, they were well positioned to win jobs and contracts in the post-Taliban era. Yet the reasons why they have done well help to explain why so many other Afghans are doing badly.

I drive north out of Kabul to visit the places where I spent the war in 2001. In reality this is the only direction I could go, since all other routes are dangerous. I asked a member of the Afghan parliament from Bamyan, north-west of the capital, if it was safe to visit his province. 'There are two roads there and one is very dangerous because the Taliban control it,' he replied judiciously. 'The other road is safe so long as you have armed body-guards.' On the second route men dressed in police uniform had recently stopped and killed six drivers and guards in two vehicles carrying money for a local bank.

The road out of Kabul is very crowded. For many in the city it is the only one that can be used to spend a day in the countryside. It is also a crucial lifeline for US and NATO forces. Their military supply routes to Pakistan are vulnerable to the Taliban on both sides of the border. Ironically, the Pakistani truck drivers carrying equipment for western troops to fight the Taliban are allowed safe passage only because the transport companies pay the Taliban commanders not to attack them.

Charikar used to be a dismal, impoverished, half-empty market town near Bagram airbase, through which ran the Taliban front line. Today it is full of trucks carrying fruit and vegetables to the capital from the farms and orchards of the Shomali plain, while crowding the road going in the opposite direction are petrol tankers and huge container lorries going to Tajikistan and Uzbekistan. I had been in Bagram where General Baba Jan, an important Northern Alliance military commander in charge of the area, used to show journalists the Taliban positions from the half-ruined control tower of Bagram airport. I ask what had happened to the general and I am told he is doing well, having become security chief of Kabul and later of Herat in western Afghanistan in the post-Taliban era. He no longer has an official position, but is said to have won a highly lucrative contract to supply US forces in their Bagram headquarters.

After the fall of the almost entirely Pashtun Taliban, the Northern Alliance commanders, mostly Tajik and Uzbek, were best placed to enter the new ruling elite. I drive along the Salang valley, where the road from the Shomali plain winds steeply upwards through the Hindu Kush mountains to the Salang tunnel, which is the only all-weather road linking northern and southern Afghanistan. The scenery is magnificent. The Salang river has turned into a torrent as the mountain snow melts. There is a thunderstorm, and the dark cliff walls beside the road are illuminated by flashes of lightning. I used to come here in 2001 to visit General Bashir Salangi, a warlord who belonged to the Northern Alliance and controlled the Salang tunnel. Even in the treacherous world of Afghan politics, General Salangi had achieved fame by secretly doing a deal with the Taliban in 1997 to allow thousands of their fighters to swarm through the tunnel—a potential catastrophe for the Northern Alliance. General Salangi had then blown up the mouth of the tunnel, trapping the Taliban, whose men were promptly slaughtered by Northern Alliance troops waiting in ambush. Since 2001 General Salangi has flourished in a series of senior posts. The careers of generals Baba Jan and Salangi underline a complaint made to me by an observer in Kabul: 'Whoever is meant to be in charge of our government, we still seem to see the same old faces which we have known since the early 1990s.'

One big change on the roads north of Kabul is that the bridges have all been rebuilt. These, almost without exception, had been blown up in the wars. The rebuilding of the roads is not quite as complete, but they no longer look and feel like rocky river beds. Jabal Saraj is once more a prosperous truck-stop town. The bridge made out of old Taliban armoured personnel carriers has been replaced by a new concrete structure. Reconstruction of bridges and roads, at the centre of the US aid effort, has the additional advantage of allowing American military forces to move around more easily.

Could the prosperity of this part of Afghanistan be repeated in the rest of the country? It is not very likely. Rather to their own surprise, its people, thanks to the US intervention provoked by 9/11, turned out to be victors in the war with the Taliban.

10 May 2009

Herat in western Afghanistan is cut off from the rest of the planet. This was once one of the great cities of the world, an imperial capital drawing its wealth from trade along the Silk Road with Iran, the rest of Afghanistan and central Asia. Above the 800-year-old mosque in the city centre are minarets covered in blue and green mosaics which soar above one of the most magnificent monuments of the Islamic world. But today Herat is cut off even from the rest of Afghanistan. I flew here because it was too dangerous to come by road. We turned right out of the battered-looking airport because, had we turned left down the main road towards Kandahar, we would soon have been in Taliban-controlled territory. The road going east to Bamyan and Kabul is risky for the same reasons.

Herat itself is peaceful compared to the rest of Afghanistan. There are police in their dark grey uniforms and forage hats checking cars, but they do not look as if they are expecting trouble. There are more new buildings than in Kabul, but on many construction sites work seems to have stopped.

I meet Obaidullah Sidiqi, a local businessman, at a picnic lunch in a well-watered orchard, full of mulberry and apple trees and honeysuckle, which he owns not far from the airport road. An attractive aspect of Afghanistan never mentioned in war reporting is the Afghan love of flowers. Even in front line positions soldiers dig small trenches, fill them with water and plant geraniums. Sidiqi, after 16 years in construction, part of it for the Save the Children Fund and partly on his own account, explains that business in Herat faces unique difficulties. For instance, last year he had contracts under way which he could only visit in disguise. One was for the construction of a school in Shindand district in the south of Herat province, a Pashtun area where the Taliban are strong. Sidiqi, like most people in Herat, is a Tajik. The Taliban rebellion is confined to the Pashtun, the community to which 42 per cent of Afghans belong, while in the past the Tajiks, who make up 27 per cent of the population, have been the core of the anti-Taliban opposition. 'I wanted to see how work was going at the school, but I did not dare go as myself,' Sidiqi tells me. 'So I grew my beard longer and pretended to be one of my drivers.' He also had to go in disguise to visit a road his company is building in Badghis province to the north-east of Herat, again in an area where the Taliban are strong. In fact, not all the danger comes from the Taliban—though it is always blamed on them—as there are plenty of bandit gangs in the mountains.

Overall, Sidiqi says this year is better than last, though he does not sound completely confident that it is going to stay that way. He says that 200 local factories have shut, and Iran, where so many Afghans used to go to work, is issuing very few visas. Within Afghanistan there is pervasive corruption with the award of a contract usually determined by the size of the bribe offered to the officials in charge.

I am sympathetic to Sidiqi's difficulties in moving around the country except by plane, because I face the same problem. I came to Herat because last Monday, 4 May, US aircraft attacked several villages in the Bala Baluk district of Farah province, which is immediately to the south of Herat. The local governor and surviving villagers said that more than 120 civilians had been killed. The US military denied that anything like that number had died and, if they had, it was the Taliban who had done it by hurling grenades into houses.

The problem is that Bala Baluk is in a Pashtun area where the Taliban are reputed to be strong. It is too dangerous to go directly to Bala Baluk, so the next best thing is to find a survivor or an eyewitness. I thought that some of the worst injured might be in Herat hospital, as it is the best in the area. But there turn out to be only 14 wounded and these are in Farah hospital. This could mean that there are fewer dead than the Afghans say, or that the bombardment was so intense that all were killed.

Despite there being no survivors to meet I do find a reliable witness, a radio reporter called Farooq Faizy, who went to Bala Baluk soon after the attack happened. He says that police and soldiers nearby were frightened of the Taliban and told him it was too dangerous to go on, but he spoke to some village elders, telling them: 'Talk to us and we will tell the world.' He says he is none too sure who is in control of the three villages—Gerani, Gangabad and Khoujaha—that were hit and he is careful about what he says. But he did take some 70 or 80 photographs and they bear out the villagers' story: they show craters everywhere; villages plastered with bombs; bodies torn to shreds by the blasts; mass graves; no signs of damage from bullets, rockets or grenades.

I suspect that the US military's claim that the Taliban had run through the village hurling grenades, supposedly because they had not been paid their cut of profits from the opium poppy crop, was just a delaying tactic. Usually the US military delays admission of guilt until a story has gone cold and the media is no longer interested. 'First say "no story"', runs an old PR adage, 'and then say "old story."' By the end of the week the US was admitting that the grenade-throwing Taliban story was 'thinly sourced'. Another thesis was that fighting had taken place 500 metres from the villages, and the Taliban had retreated through them, leading to the air strikes. Farooq Faizy says he saw signs of fighting in the shape of two burned-out Afghan Army or police vehicles and a destroyed US Humvee, but they were seven or eight kilometres away from the site of the bombing. He had taken photographs showing the destroyed Afghan vehicles—Ford pick-ups with a machine gun mount over the bonnet. It seems likely that this was the fight that had led to the Afghan Army and their US advisers asking for air support. What the Americans never explain in Afghanistan or Iraq is why they are using weapons designed for world war three against villages that have not left the Middle Ages—which makes heavy civilian casualties inevitable.

11 May 2009

One of the most feared of the Afghan warlords, Faryadi Zardad, was notorious for robbing, raping, torturing and killing travellers on the road between Kabul and Jalalabad. He kept a savage assistant in a cave who would bite and rip the flesh of his victims; other captives were murdered or imprisoned until they died of their sufferings or bribes were paid for their release.

Uniquely among the warlords of Afghanistan, Zardad is in prison for his crimes. In 1998, as the Taliban over-ran Afghanistan, he fled to Britain on a fake passport. He was running a pizza restaurant in south London in 2000 when he was unmasked by the BBC, and in 2005 he was sentenced to 20 years in prison in Britain. Zardad must consider himself exceptionally unlucky. Other warlords, who were once his comrades in arms, are now part of the political elite in Kabul, prominent members of the government or multimillionaire owners of palatial houses in the capital.

At the time Zardad was torturing and killing at his much-feared checkpoint at Sarobi on the Kabul–Kandahar road in 1992–96, he was a valued military commander in the forces of Gulbuddin Hekmetyar, the leader of the fundamentalist Hizb-e-Islami party. Rockets and shells fired into Kabul by Hekmetyar's soldiers devastated the city and killed thousands of people before it was captured by the Taliban. More recently, Hekmetyar's forces, who are particularly strong in Logar province just south of the capital, have been fighting as allies of the Taliban. But in the latest twist in Afghan politics, in which leaders switch sides and betray each other as swiftly as any English duke in the Wars of the Roses, Hekmetyar is reportedly about to start negotiations to join the Afghan government of President Hamid Karzai. Under a power-sharing deal, his party would supposedly fill several ministerial posts and governorships in return for abandoning the Taliban. He himself would go into exile in Saudi Arabia for three years at the end of which the US would remove him from its list of 'most wanted' terrorists.

A deal between Hekmetyar and President Karzai's government is not impossible, although a government spokesman has denied it. But if Hekmetyar's party does enter the government, its members will find themselves surrounded by many familiar faces. Just before Karzai went to Washington to see President Barack Obama last week, he neatly divided the opposition, and almost certainly ensured his re-election as president, by selecting as his vice-presidential running-mate Mohammad Qasim Fahim, a powerful Tajik former warlord. Human Rights Watch protested that General Fahim had the blood of many Afghans on his hands, but Karzai stressed his courageous role in the war against the Soviet occupation.

One reason the Taliban were able to conquer most of Afghanistan in the 1990s, aside from the support of Pakistan, was by taking advantage of a popular reaction against warlords. Zardad ruled only a small area, but far more powerful rulers were just as cruel and corrupt as he was. Much of northern Afghanistan was ruled by the Uzbek general, Rashid Dostum, who had been part of the Communist regime and commanded a powerful army. At the time of the terrorist attacks on the US in 2001, warlords including General Dostum and General Fahim were fighting for their lives or were in exile. But within hours of 9/11, the US was looking for local allies to provide the ground troops which, backed by US airpower, advisers and money, would overthrow the Taliban in Kabul. In a couple of months, warlords, many from the main opposition grouping, the Northern Alliance, were the new rulers of Afghanistan. Few of them now wear uniform, but they have held power ever since. General Dostum has gone into luxurious exile in Istanbul after a murderous assault on a Turkmen leader, but he remains influential among his followers and owns a fine pink palace in the famously wealthy Kabul neighbourhood of Sherpoor.

Aside from Hekmetyar, most of the other warlords no longer exercise power through their private armies, but through a mafia-like control of jobs, security services, money, contracts and land. Had Zardad played his cards a little differently, and chosen his place of exile more carefully, he might now be looking forward to profitable government employment in Kabul.

28 May 2009

Compared to Baghdad, Kabul is quiet. Checkpoints are everywhere, manned by Afghan police in tattered uniforms, but the police look relaxed and their searches of people and cars are often perfunctory. Only at the southern exit from the city, around a well-fortified police post, do people appear anxious as they prepare to take the road to Kandahar. Many check their pockets nervously, perhaps to make sure they are not carrying anything to suggest they might have a link to the government or a foreign NGO. South of Kabul this could lead to summary execution by roving squads of

Taliban fighters, usually six to eight men who move swiftly across country on motorcycles and set up mobile checkpoints on the roads. Sometimes, as well as examining documents, they take mobile phones from travellers and redial recent calls. If the call is answered by a government office the owner may be killed on the spot.

Taliban rule is not total across southern Afghanistan, but much of the area has been a no-man's-land since 2006. Afghan truckers carrying supplies for US or NATO forces have to pay local security companies for protection or bribe their way through. Not all the gunmen on the roads are Taliban: some local commanders and bandits act independently, though probably under licence from the Taliban. One Western aid official in Kabul tells me that a 100-truck convoy travelling from Pakistan to the Dutch base in Uruzgan province paid $750,000 for safe passage. The figure sounds extravagant, but similar stories are told by the owners of local Afghan trucking companies, always a more accurate source of information on the Taliban's reach than Western diplomats or military officers. 'It got really bad 18 months ago,' Abdul Bayan of the Nawe Aryana transport company says. 'Now if I am carrying goods to a NATO base and we are going to Kandahar or any of the towns on the way, we travel in a convoy of 15 to 20 trucks protected by five SUVs, each with four armed guards. If we are going to Kandahar it costs me $1,000 for each truck.' If the Taliban capture a truck they either burn it or ask for $10,000 to $12,000 to release it unharmed. Since each truck is worth $70,000, Bayan always pays up. NATO and US officials, so keen to stress that the Taliban are part-financed by the profits of the opium and heroin trade, never mention that it also draws a healthy income from its stranglehold on the supply lines of Western forces. I ask Bayan if he has ever asked the Afghan Army or police to protect his convoys. He looks bewildered: 'Get protection from the soldiers and policemen? They can't even protect themselves, what can they do for me?'

Over the last few years the Afghan government, despite being supported by US air power and 70,000 foreign troops, has lost control of vast tracts of southern and eastern Afghanistan. Soon after the Taliban fell in 2001 I drove from Kabul to the fortress city of Ghazni and then on to Qalat, Kandahar and Helmand. The road, a terrible 300-mile-long rutted track of deep potholes and broken pieces of ancient tarmac, was dangerous, but it was still possible to get through. Eight years later the road itself is in much better shape, but the journey is far too risky for a foreigner to undertake. One of the security companies Abdul Bayan uses was attacked by Taliban in Qalat, an impoverished, dusty town in Zabul province; seven of its men were killed and three captured. Daoud Sultanzoy, an anti-government member of the Afghan parliament from Ghazni, says he no longer dares go back to the city he represents, though he is 'as much afraid of the government having me shot as I am of the Taliban'.

Support for the current Taliban uprising, just like support for the original takeover of Afghanistan in the 1990s, is limited by the movement's reliance on the Pashtun. 'I wish we could get away from the idea that all Pashtun are Taliban and all the Taliban are Pashtun,' Sultanzoy, a Pashtun, says. It is true that not all Pashtun are Taliban, but solidarity among the Pashtun and the Taliban's safe havens in Pashtun areas of Pakistan explain the movement's resilience in the face of what appeared to be total defeat in 2001. The Pashtun are the largest community in Afghanistan, but at 42 per cent of the population they are not quite a majority. The Taliban have no support among the Tajiks (27 per cent of Afghans), Hazara (9 per cent), Uzbeks (9 per cent), Aimak (4 per cent), Turkmens (3 per cent) or Baloch (2 per cent). There has always been hostility between these ethnic groups, but it was exacerbated by the massacres of the 1990s and the Taliban's refusal, during their years in power, to dilute their fanatical Sunni fundamentalism or share power with the non-Pashtun minorities. They did not compromise because they did not have to, until 9/11 and the American intervention transformed the balance of power.

'It's not that the Taliban is very strong', one Afghan politician says, 'but that the government is very weak.' President Hamid Karzai is criticised at home and abroad for relying on warlords, but he seems to have little choice. Though often derided as the 'mayor of Kabul', he manoeuvres deftly between Afghan warlords, government officials, community leaders and foreign patrons. His victory in August's presidential election looks inevitable. He has faced down Washington's hostility, which was very evident at the beginning of the year, when American officials spoke openly about the corruption and ineffectiveness of his administration. The US has since reluctantly come to see that it has no real alternative. Last month Karzai secured the withdrawal of the presidential candidacy of Gul Agha Sherzai, the governor of Nangarhar province and a former warlord, who was his only rival for the Pashtun vote. Given the need to have strong support from the Pashtun, none of the remaining candidates stands much of a chance. Karzai is not overwhelmingly popular, but opposition to him is divided. He controls the state apparatus and, ramshackle though this is, it gives him a crucial advantage in getting support from the local power brokers who will determine who wins the election.

As well as weak, the government is also very corrupt. In Transparency International's index of corruption, Afghanistan is almost as bad as it gets. 'The whole country is criminalised,' says Ashraf Ghani, the former finance minister and one of the presidential candidates unlikely to be elected. General Aminullah Amarkhail, who was fired from his job as head of security at Kabul airport for his excessive zeal and success in arresting heroin smugglers, speaks of wholesale looting rather than simple corruption. 'You have to pay $10,000 in bribes to get a job as a district police chief,' he says, 'and up to $150,000 to get a job as chief of police anywhere on the border—because there you can make a lot of money.' Two hours after arresting a notorious smuggler with eight bags of heroin on her, he received a phone call from the interior ministry ordering him to release her and give her her drugs back. She and her gang apparently had a contract to smuggle 1,000 kilos of heroin out of Afghanistan. More serious is the impact of corruption on the price of basic foodstuffs, which are more expensive in Afghanistan than in most of the rest of the world. According to the World Food Programme, wheat prices in April were 63 per cent higher than international prices, 'making food unaffordable to millions of Afghans'.

On the Transparency index Afghanistan comes just ahead of Iraq. But Iraq is an oil state with an annual budget of almost $60 billion. The Afghan government has very little money and donations from foreign governments make up 90 per cent of public expenditure. The police make about $120 a month. The only way they can feed their families is to take bribes. A private soldier in the Iraqi Army earns about $600 and an officer who has graduated from university far more. The political landscape of Afghanistan is shaped by the country's terrible poverty. This was true before the fall of the Taliban and it has been true ever since. Some 42 per cent of the population of 25 million earns less than $1 a day. The female literacy rate is 18 per cent, only 23 per cent of the population has access to clean water, and 40 to 70 per cent of the workforce is unemployed. (The wide variation shows the government's own uncertainty about the means by which millions of Afghans are trying to survive.) The failure of the Karzai government and its Western backers to make a dent in these desolating figures explains why so many Afghans are disillusioned with both.

In Iraq the Sunni insurrection began within weeks of the fall of Baghdad whereas most Afghans initially welcomed the arrival of foreign forces on the grounds that they were at least better than the Taliban and the warlords. But the latest opinion polls show Afghan confidence in both the US and the Afghan government plummeting. The number of Afghans who think the US is doing well has more than halved from 68 per cent in 2005 to 32 per cent. Support for the Taliban remains low but 36 per cent now blame the continuing violence on the US, NATO or the Afghan government; 27 per cent blame the Taliban.

In an attempt to emulate the supposed success of the surge in Iraq in 2007, the US is planning troop reinforcements, a so-called Afghan surge. The first of the extra forces promised by President Obama are beginning to arrive in southern Afghanistan. By the end of the year some 30,000 American soldiers will be added to the 32,000 already there. Their goal will be to train and expand the Afghan security forces, possibly raising their number to 400,000; to support the central government; and to provide protection for the civilian population. They should at least be able to open up the main roads linking the cities of southern Afghanistan. There is also to be a surge in civilian advisers, including lawyers and economists, to assist the government. Each of these, it has been estimated, will be paid between $250,000 and $500,000 and will live in an expensive house in Kabul protected at even greater cost by a security company. Afghan-Americans, some of whom have lived in the US for decades, are being hired to come back as translators at a salary of $225,000. Plenty of indigenous Afghans speak English but they are not trusted. Meanwhile in Farah province, in the west of the country, the Taliban are hiring unemployed young men, giving them a weapon and paying them $8 for each attack they make on local police checkpoints, thus minimising the risk to veteran Taliban fighters while inflicting losses on government forces.

Will the surge work? The problem for the US military is that whatever goodwill they have earned by building schools, roads and bridges can be quickly lost. A quarter of Afghans approve of the use of armed force against US or NATO forces, but this figure jumps to 44 per cent among those who have been shelled or bombed by them. There is growing hostility to the presence of foreign armies, particularly in Pashtun areas where fighting continues. Recipes for counter-insurgency, devised in very different circumstances in Iraq, may not have much relevance in Afghanistan. It will be politically and militarily very difficult to seal off the Taliban from their safe havens in Pakistan. 'The surge is a double-edged sword,' Sultanzoy says. 'If it instigates more violence, it will provoke more resistance.'

3 November 2009

The election in Afghanistan has turned into a disaster for all who promoted it. Hamid Karzai has been declared re-elected as president of the country for the next five years though his allies inside and outside Afghanistan know that he owes his success to open fraud. Instead of increasing his government's legitimacy, the poll has further de-legitimised it.

10 May 2010

Up to last week nobody paid much attention to the fighting in north-west Pakistan, though more soldiers and civilians have probably been dying there over the last year than in Iraq or Afghanistan. In reality, this corner of Pakistan along the Afghan border is the latest in a series of wars originally generated by the US response to 9/11. The first was the war in Afghanistan when the Taliban were overthrown in 2001, the second in Iraq after the invasion of 2003, and the third the renewed war in Afghanistan from about 2006. The fourth conflict is the present one in Pakistan and is as vicious as any of its predecessors, though so far the intensity of the violence has not been appreciated by the outside world.

Western governments and media for long looked at the fighting in the tribal areas along Pakistan's frontier with Afghanistan as a sideshow to the Afghan war. Washington congratulated itself on using pilotless drones to kill Taliban leaders, a tactic which resulted in no American casualties and apparently no political fallout in the US. This has now all changed, since Faisal Shahzad attempted to detonate a bomb in Times Square in New York last week. Within days the US press and television was camped outside the locked gate of his family's compound in Peshawar, the effective capital of the north-west frontier region, and were trying to interview his relatives in the streets of his ancestral village of Mohib Banda, outside the city.

The Pakistan Taliban had been saying that they would seek revenge for the drone attacks by striking directly at the US, but nobody took them seriously. Their first claim that they were behind the Times Square bomb was disbelieved as being beyond their capabilities. It is difficult to see why the idea of their involvement should have been treated with derision, since suicide bombers from the Pakistan Taliban are blowing themselves up every few days along the north-west frontier.

Shahzad told his interrogators that he received training in Waziristan, further south—though it cannot have been very serious given the ama-teurism of his later efforts. But a high degree of technical expertise is not necessary since even the most botched and ineffective bomb attack has a powerful political impact so long as it happens in the US, as was demonstrated by the Nigerian student who tried and failed to blow up a plane over Detroit at Christmas by detonating explosives in his underpants.

One outcome of the abortive Times Square attack is that it has drawn the attention of the world to the seriousness of the fighting in the Federally Administered Tribal Areas of Pakistan. Last year the violence there and in other parts of what until recently was called the North-West Frontier Province was enough to send 3.1 million refugees running for their lives. Many of these, particularly from the Swat valley, in the northern part of the province, have now gone home, but hundreds of thousands of others are now taking flight because of army assaults on Pakistan Taliban strongholds in the Federally Administered Tribal Areas. These mass movements of people in obscure places like Orakzai or Kurram are hardly noticed—even within Pakistan, where they are reported without much detail on the inside pages of the newspapers.

The Pakistani foreign minister, Makhdoom Qureshi, believes that what happened in New York was 'blowback' for the US drone strikes in Pakistan, which he says killed 700 Pakistani civilians last year. This may be true, but it is also hypocritical since the drones are launched from inside Pakistan and senior Pakistani security officials confirm that the information on the whereabouts of Taliban leaders, enabling the drones to target them, comes from the Pakistan Directorate for Inter-Services Intelligence (ISI) agents on the ground. Without the ISI involvement the drones would be ineffective.

The attacks of the Predator drones are highly publicised and Shahzad told his interrogators that they were one reason why he made his abortive attack on Times Square. But the drones only cause a limited number of casualties and most of the destruction in the North-West Frontier Province is the result of heavy fighting between the Pakistan Army and the local Pakistan Taliban. Villages are destroyed and whole districts emptied of their inhabitants as the army imposes government authority in the seven 'agencies' (sub-divisions) of the Federally Administered Tribal Areas where the Taliban formerly had its strongholds. The army is winning, but the Taliban is not retreating without a fight. Suicide bombings have become as frequent and as devastating as in Kandahar or Baghdad.

Last month I visited Bajaur, a well-watered and heavily populated hilly agency on the Afghan border north of Peshawar from which the army has driven the Taliban over the last two years. Colonel Nauman Saeed, the commander of the Bajaur Scouts, a 3,500-strong force made up of tribal levies, said that the Taliban have been defeated and driven out of Bajaur and into Afghanistan and will never be able to return. But the area looks as if it is wholly under military occupation, with checkpoints every few hundred yards, little traffic on the roads, and many shops closed in the villages. Colonel Saeed says that 12 villages have been completely destroyed.

It is the same story south of Peshawar. We drove down the main road running to Lakki Marwat, just east of Waziristan, where there continue to be frequent suicide bombings. One had demolished part of a village police station, killing seven people, just a few hours before we passed through. Locals were wary and there was an atmosphere of subdued menace. I was glad to be riding in a well-armoured civilian vehicle with bullet-proof glass, protected by the bodyguards of a powerful tribal leader, businessman and senator. 'I tell people that this vehicle will only stop pistol bullets,' explained a former army colonel who is head of this leader's security. 'In this area, if you tell them that your vehicle can stop an RPG round then they will fire something even heavier at you.'

The Pakistan Taliban has gone but nobody believes they have gone very far. 'People don't want to co-operate with the army, because they think the Taliban will find out and take revenge,' said one man from a nearby village. When one village, called Shah Hassan, asked the local Taliban to leave, they retaliated by sending a suicide bomber into a crowd of young men playing volleyball. He detonated his explosives and killed 100 people.

Civilians are being squeezed between two implacable forces. The army's tactic is to order the civilian population out of whatever district it is trying to clear of Taliban, and then freely use its artillery and air power on the assumption that all who remain are Taliban supporters. It is a policy heavy on destruction that would be widely reported by the media if it occurred in Iraq or Afghanistan. In Pakistan it does not attract much criticism because places like Waziristan are almost impossible for Pakistani or foreign journalists to reach as they are too dangerous except under the protection of the army. But travellers who do go there are aghast at the extent of the devastation. 'What I saw was the stuff nightmares are made of,' writes Ayzaz Wazir, a former Pakistani ambassador who travelled on a bus through South Waziristan. 'Houses, shops, madrassahs and even official buildings on the roadside stood in ruins or demolished. There was no sign of any human or animal life, except for a few cows wandering about in the deserted villages.'

Local people fear that the crisis facing them is about to get worse as the US is demanding that the Pakistan Army invade North Waziristan, a district that is a stronghold of the Afghan Taliban. Officials say this is going to happen, and construction companies are hard at work widening and improving the main military supply route leading to Waziristan. The US has long believed that closing down the Afghan Taliban's safe enclaves in Pakistan might be the trump card in winning the war in Afghanistan. No doubt the loss of the enclaves would be a blow to the insurgency, but the Pakistan–Afghanistan border is 2,600 kilometres long and officials repeatedly stress it cannot be sealed. Senior Pakistani officers also give the impression that moving against the Afghan Taliban is something they would only do with reluctance. Whereas they refer to the Pakistan Taliban as 'miscreants' who lack legitimacy and popular support, they see the Taliban in Afghanistan as a resistance movement defending the Pashtun community.

15 May 2010

The US and NATO commander in Afghanistan, General Stanley McChrystal, who was boasting of military progress only three months ago, confessed last week that 'nobody is winning'. His only claim now is that the Taliban have lost momentum compared with last year. General McChrystal's strategy is to use the extra troops of the surge to seize Taliban strongholds and, once cleared, hand them over to Afghan forces. But all the signs are that it is not working.

Starting in February, 15,000 US, British and Afghan troops started taking over the Taliban-held area of Marjah and Nad Ali in Helmand province. Dozens of embedded journalists trumpeted the significance of Operation Moshtarak or 'Together', as it was called, as the first fruits of General McChrystal's strategy. Three months on local people say that the Taliban still control the area at night. Shops are still closed and no schools have reopened. Education officials who returned at the height of the US-led offensive have fled again. The local governor says he has just one temporary teacher teaching 60 children in the ruins of a school. Aid is not arriving. The Taliban are replacing mines, the notorious IEDs, removed by US troops and often use the same holes to hide them in.

The semi-official Pakistani view is that the US, Britain and NATO forces have become entangled in a civil war in Afghanistan between the Pashtun community, represented by the Taliban, and their Tajik, Uzbek and Hazara opponents who dominate the Kabul government. They expect the Pashtun to go on fighting until they get a real share in power. One Pashtun, a former colonel in the Pakistan Army, says: 'It will be difficult for the Americans and British to win the hearts and minds of the people in southern Afghanistan since at the centre of Pashtun culture is a hatred of all foreigners.'

18 July 2010

Afghans have been listening attentively to the uncertain trumpet call in Washington since President Obama announced last year that he would first increase the number of US troops as part of an Afghan surge, and then reduce the level of forces in 2011. His idea was to break the momentum of the Taliban's advance, inflict serious damage on them in the areas of their strongest support in Helmand and Kandahar provinces, and then negotiate. But Afghans are ever eager to emerge on the winning side. The message they received was that the Americans and their allies were not going to stay too long. The Pakistani military and political elite drew similar conclusions and prepared themselves for the day when the American troops depart.

The US leadership is clearly divided on the merits of staying in Afghanistan, but cannot work out how to withdraw without too great a loss of face. It reached the same point over Iraq, but there the situation was easier. The anti-US insurgents came from the Sunni community—only 20 per cent of Iraqis—who were under intense pressure from the Shia government, the armed forces, militias and death squads. The insurgency in Afghanistan is drawn from the Pashtun community, 42 per cent of the population, which so far shows no sign of splitting. With Iraq, it was enough that US voters got the impression they had won. A retreat could be conducted with no US objectives achieved, but nobody could be accused of cutting and running. This was the achievement of General Petraeus, who, following the unceremonious removal of General McChrystal, is now the military commander in Afghanistan, where dressing up a withdrawal as some sort of success will be far more difficult.

27 July 2010

The sheer nastiness of the Afghan conflict is vividly conjured by the cumulative effect of the thousands of uncensored front line US military reports that have been released by WikiLeaks. The 'Afghan Files' explain why the Kabul government is getting weaker, and they make it still harder for the US and British governments to explain why they are fighting to preserve an Afghan government so rotten with corruption and brutality.

Much of what is now documented from official sources had already been exposed by journalists. But the 91,000 leaked reports paint a more detailed picture than ever before of life in contemporary Afghanistan. The reality of the Afghan war as described by front line US officers and officials is as bad or worse than anything reported by the media. And the value of many of these ground-level reports is that they have not been edited or censored by senior officials. They are honest about what Afghans really think of the US-led coalition.

It has been difficult hitherto to convey what words like 'brutality' and 'corruption' mean in their Afghan context. But some of the revelations go a long way to explaining why so many ordinary Afghans are driven into the hands of the Taliban. For instance, in Balkh province in northern Afghanistan, a report was made on 11 October, 2009 about soldiers and police mistreating local people who refused to co-operate in a search. A district police chief raped a 16-year-old girl and when a civilian protested, the police chief ordered his bodyguard to shoot him. The bodyguard refused and was himself killed by the police chief.

In the town of Gardez in September 2007, with the Taliban comeback in full swing, provincial council officials spoke frankly to an American civil affairs official about the way they thought things were going. 'The people of Afghanistan keep losing their trust in the government because of the high amount of corrupt government officials,' one said. 'The general view of the Afghans is that the current government is worse than the Taliban.' The US official recorded bleakly: 'The people will support the Anti-Coalition forces and the security condition will degenerate.'

Overall, the WikiLeaks dossier gives the impression of the US military machine floundering into war and only gradually realising the crippling weakness of the Afghan government. There is intermittent understanding on the ground that the presence of foreign occupation forces is itself the main recruiting sergeant of the Taliban. Above all, the documents convey a sense of bewilderment that the US military should be making such great efforts and achieving so little.

8 May 2011

Does the death of Osama bin Laden open the door for the US and UK to escape from the trap into which they have fallen in Afghanistan? At first sight, the presumed weakening of al-Qa'ida ought to strengthen the case for an American and British withdrawal. When President Obama ordered the dispatch of an extra 30,000 troops to Afghanistan in 2009, he declared that the goal was 'to deny safe-haven to al-Qa'ida and to deny the Taliban the ability to overthrow the Afghan government.'

The problem for Washington and London is that they have got so many people killed in Afghanistan and spent so much money that it is difficult for them to withdraw without something that can be dressed up as a victory. Could the death of Bin Laden be the sort of success that would allow Obama to claim that America's main objective has been achieved? Unfortunately, it probably is not going to happen.

One reason is that the war is not going terribly well. At the start of this year's fighting season the Taliban have launched as many attacks as last year. In Kandahar last month, they were able to free 500 prisoners from the city jail by digging a tunnel 1,000 feet long over five months without anybody finding out about it. An organisation that can do this is scarcely on its last legs. The message of recent months is that the surge in Afghanistan, of which so much was expected, has not worked. The Americans and British are meant to be training Afghan military and police units to take the place of foreign forces. It is never quite explained how Taliban fighters, without any formal military training, are able to battle the best-equipped armies in the world, while Afghan government troops require months of training before they can carry out the simplest military task.

There is going to be no military solution to the Afghan conflict, and negotiations with the Taliban will have to begin sooner or later, so why not now?

5 February 2012

The announcement that the US plans to end the combat role of its troops in Afghanistan earlier than expected, and before the end of next year, is a crucial milestone in the international forces' retreat from the country. Coming after the French decision to go early, the US move looks like part of a panicky rush for the exit. More important, Afghans like to bet on winners, and the US action will convince many that these are increasingly likely to be the Taliban and Pakistan rather than the Afghan government. No wonder NATO officials looked so anxious as they pretended that the US action had not come as a nasty surprise.

The decision, revealed by the US defence secretary, Leon Panetta, with deliberate casualness to journalists on his plane, is an admission of failure. The US has an army of 90,000 soldiers in Afghanistan and is spending $100 billion a year, but has still been unable to defeat 20,000–25,000 Taliban who receive very little or no pay. As in Iraq, departing US troops will leave behind a very different political and military landscape in Afghanistan from the one they hoped to create. In the Iraqi case, power is held by Shia religious parties closely linked to Iran, which is the opposite of what the Americans wanted to see when they captured Baghdad in 2003. In the Afghan case, the government of Hamid Karzai has waning authority as the US steps back. In both Iraq and Afghanistan, powerful US armies failed to impose their control.

America's wars launched in the aftermath of 9/11 led Washington to overplay its hand disastrously. This was not so obvious at the time as it is now. At first sight, both wars looked easy because they were against feeble, isolated enemies, unpopular in their own countries. But successful invasion is very different from successful occupation. In neither Baghdad nor Kabul did the US have an adequate local partner. No neighbouring countries wanted the occupations to succeed. Above all, the US underestimated the extent to which foreign occupation generates resistance.

It is an extraordinary turn-around that a decade after 9/11 the Americans are departing and the Taliban are back in business. A leaked NATO report on interrogations of 4,000 captured Taliban, al-Qa'ida, foreign fighters and civilians shows that Taliban prisoners are in a confident mood. They believe their popular support is growing, Afghan government officials secretly collaborate with them, and, once foreign troops are gone, they believe they are going to win. In reality, it is unlikely that they will, because the non-Pashtun communities, a majority of the population, will resist them. But the authors of the NATO report say 'Afghan civilians frequently prefer Taliban governance over Giroa [Government of the Islamic Republic of Afghanistan] usually as a result of government corruption, ethnic bias and lack of connection with local religious and tribal leaders.' This enables the Taliban easily to recruit more fighters to replace their casualties.

An American success in Afghanistan was impossible once the Pakistan Army had decided to give full backing to a return of the Taliban. The US faced the same strategic weakness as the Soviet Army during its Afghan campaign. However many setbacks the anti-Soviet mujahedin or the anti-American Taliban suffered, they could always retreat across the 1,600-mile-long border with Pakistan to rest, re-organise and re-equip. President Barack Obama was told during his first days in office that the heart of the military problems facing the US in Afghanistan lay in Pakistan, but Washington could never work out an effective way of dealing with it. The NATO report tellingly quotes a senior al-Qa'ida commander from Kunar province in eastern Afghanistan saying: 'Pakistan knows everything. They control everything. I can't [expletive] on a tree in Kunar without them watching. The Taliban are not Islam. The Taliban are Islamabad.'

The US has failed in Afghanistan. They will leave a deeply divided country in which reconciliation will be very difficult. The war may soon be over for the Americans, but not for the Afghans.

PART IV: THE ARAB SPRING

The term 'Arab Spring' is at the root of many misconceptions about what happened in the Middle East and North Africa in 2011 and in subsequent years. It is a term that leads to expectations of fresh flowers of democracy, tolerance and peace replacing brutal and dictatorial old regimes. It evokes memories of the Prague Spring and creates hopes that the shift away from the old police states in the Arab world will be as peaceful as at the time of the fall of Communism a quarter of a century ago.

Five years later people are all too conscious that is exactly what did not happen and many feel they were deceived back in 2011. The years since have seen gloomy headlines reading 'Arab Autumn' or 'Arab Winter', with suggestions that references to spring were phony or propagandistic to begin with. But this is to carry cynicism or disillusionment too far because the name 'Arab Spring' was correct in identifying some of the democratic and secular ingredients which went into creating the popular protests that overthrew, or put under intense pressure, regimes from Tunis to Sanaa and Damascus to Bahrain. Demonstrations in Tahrir Square in Cairo that overthrew Hosni Mubarak seemed to be the apotheosis of what was happening and there was nothing fake about them.

What was deceptive was the pretence designed for Western audiences and Western governments that they were seeing the most 'bourgeois' of revolutions led by people comfortably familiar with Facebook and iPhones. I remember driving through Derna in eastern Libya, a city notorious for supplying a large number of suicide bombers to Iraq in previous years, and seeing a white sheet billowing from a balcony with a denunciation of 'terrorism' written on it in grammatical English. Somebody knew that a lot of foreign journalists coming from Egypt to Benghazi were passing that way. Five years later ISIS is battling other jihadis for control of Derna.

Militant Islamism was one element going into the Arab Spring cocktail from the beginning. There was never a pure progressive revolution that was hijacked by Sunni reactionaries, but then no revolution is pure. Revolutions are always a combination of different and conflicting interests. There should have been nothing unexpected or objectionable about this: a demand for civil rights and free elections in Syria or Bahrain was bound to favour a disenfranchised Sunni majority in the first case and a disenfranchised Shia majority in the second. In Libya, the very date of the uprising commemorated the day in 2006 when 11 protesters in Benghazi were shot down as they stood outside the Italian Consulate protesting against an Italian minister wearing a T-shirt with a cartoon of the Prophet Mohammed on it. The supporters of the Arab Spring looked for a return to the past as well as a leap into the future. In Libya many carried the flag of the monarchy. When peaceful protests were frustrated, the militarisation of dissent followed soon thereafter as states collapsed into chaos or reverted to a reliance on the police cell and torture.

NINE

Mission Creep

Libya, 2011

I was sceptical from an early stage about the Arab Spring uprisings leading to the replacement of authoritarian regimes by secular democracies. Optimistic forecasts I was hearing in the first heady months of 2011 sounded suspiciously similar to what I had heard in Kabul after the fall of the Taliban in 2001 and in Baghdad after the overthrow of Saddam Hussein in 2003. In all three cases there was the same dangerous conviction on the part of the domestic opposition, outside powers and the international media that all ills could be attributed to the demonic old regime and a brave new world was being born. This seemed very simple minded: I was very conscious that these police states—be they in Egypt, Libya, Tunisia, Syria, Yemen or Bahrain—were the product as well as the exploiters of threats to their country's independence from abroad as well as social, sectarian and ethnic divisions at home. Journalists, who earn their bread by expressing themselves freely, were particularly prone to believe that free expression and honest elections were all that was needed to put things right.

Explanations of what one thought was happening in these countries were often misinterpreted as justification for odious and discredited regimes. In Libya, where the uprising started on 15 February 2011, I wrote about how the opposition was wholly dependent on NATO military support and would have been rapidly defeated by pro-Gaddafi forces without it. It followed from this that the opposition would not have the strength to fill the political vacuum inevitable if Gaddafi was to fall. I noted gloomily that Arab states, such as Saudi Arabia and the Gulf monarchies, who were pressing for foreign intervention against

Gaddafi, themselves held power by methods 'no less repressive' than the Libyan leader. It was his radicalism, muted though this was in his later years, not his authoritarianism that made them hate him.

This was an unpopular stance to take on Libya during the high tide of the Arab Spring, when foreign governments and media alike were uncritically lauding the opposition. The two sides in what was a genuine civil war were portrayed as white hats and black hats; rebel claims about government atrocities were credulously broadcast, though they frequently turned out to be concocted, while government denials were contemptuously dismissed. Human rights organisations like Amnesty International and Human Rights Watch were much more thorough than the media in checking these stories, though their detailed reports appeared long after the news agenda had moved on. Whatever their other failings, the rebels ran a slick and highly professional press campaign from their headquarters in Benghazi. Spokesmen efficiently fended off embarrassing questions and crowds waved placards bearing well thought out slogans in grammatical English in front of the television cameras.

My doubts about many aspects of the Libyan uprising, as it was presented to the world, are open to misinterpretation. There was nothing phony about people's anger against a man and a regime that had monopolised power over them for 43 years. As in other Arab military regimes turned police states, Gaddafi had once justified his rule as necessary to defend Libyan national interests against foreign states and oil companies. But as the decades passed these justifications became excuses for a Gaddafi family dictatorship that stifled all dissent. Just how claustrophobic it was to be a Libyan at this time was brought home to me by Ahmed Abdullah al-Ghadamsi, an intelligent, able and well-educated man whom I met by accident after the fall of Tripoli and who worked for me as a guide and assistant. He came from a family and a district in Tripoli that was always anti-Gaddafi and he had been on the edge of the resistance movement before we met. He was good at talking his way through checkpoints and winning the confidence of the suspicious militiamen who were manning them. We shared a feeling of exhilaration now that the old regime was gone. I remember Ahmed saying to me with amused exasperation that 'books used to be more difficult to bring into the country than weapons.' Seven weeks later he was dead. He had felt he must play some active role in the revolution, had volunteered as a fighter and was shot through the head in the last days of the civil war.

In the early months of the uprising, a good place to judge the rebel movement was close to the front line in the largely deserted town of Ajdabiya, two hours' drive south of Benghazi. Here rebel pick-ups and trucks, with heavy machine guns welded to the back, rushed backwards and forwards, the speed of their retreats so swift as to endanger any camera crews or reporters standing nearby. I had an ominous feeling, as I drove about Ajdabiya, Benghazi and the hinterland of Cyrenaica, that all would not turn out well. 'It would take a long time to reduce Libya to the level of Somalia,' I wrote on 13 April 2011, 'but civil conflicts and the hatreds they induce build up their own momentum once the shooting has begun. One of the good things about Libya is that so many young men—unlike Afghans and Iraqis of a similar age—do not know how to use a gun. This will not last.'

Nor did it. By August, Gaddafi had fled and I was in Tripoli touring the abandoned palaces, villas and prisons of the ruling family which had so recently abandoned them. I tried not to be a professional pessimist, pointing out hopefully that, unlike Iraqis and Afghans, Libyans had a high standard of living, were well educated and were not split by age-old ethnic and sectarian divisions. But even this upbeat summary concluded plaintively as I added: 'All the same, I wish the shooting outside my window would stop.'

It never really did stop. Tripoli was full of checkpoints that reminded me of Lebanon during the civil war of 1975 to 1990. The arrival of the new transitional government from Benghazi did not fill me with confidence since one of its first measures was to announce the end of the ban on polygamy introduced by Gaddafi. I had periodically visited Tripoli in the 1980s and 1990s and had noticed that, as in the oil states of the Gulf, most of the work was done by migrants from poor countries that were Libya's African neighbours. To find out what was happening in Libya I would go for a walk in the marketplace and fall into conversation with bored Ghanaians or Chadians, all migrants on their day off, who would tell me more about the real state of the country than any Libyan official or Western diplomat. But with the fall of Gaddafi, all black faces were regarded with suspicion by the new rulers as likely supporters of the fallen leader. They were often accused of being 'pro-Gaddafi mercenaries', interrogated, jailed and occasionally murdered. Life for the migrant and indigenous black population was to get steadily worse in the coming years as Libya disintegrated and by 2015 Ethiopian and Egyptian Christians were being executed by Islamic State's Libyan clone. Meanwhile, the West Europeans were reaping what they had sown by destroying the Libyan state: migrant labourers, who had once found jobs in Libyan markets and building sites, were now risking their lives as they sailed in over-crowded and unseaworthy boats in a desperate attempt to reach Europe.

*My fears about the 'Somalianisation' of Libya, first expressed in March
2011, had turned out to be all too true. Four years later Libya was ruled, in
so far as it was ruled at all, by two governments, one based in Tripoli and the
other in Tobruk, while real authority lay in the hands of militias which fought
each other for power and money. Demonstrators in the streets of Tripoli were
shot down by anti-aircraft machine guns whose large calibre bullets tore apart
the bodies of protesters; Tripoli International Airport was destroyed in fighting
between rival militias; torture was ubiquitous and the country split between
east and west. For all his quirky personality cult and monopoly of power, life in
Libya under Gaddafi had not been as bad as this.*

*The demonisation of Gaddafi had an unfortunate effect in ensuring the
opposition had no real programme other than his replacement by themselves.
Libyans were visibly relieved at the end of 2011 to find that they no longer
had to study the puerile nostrums of Gaddafi's 'Green Book'—in the knowledge
that, if you failed the exam devoted to this work, you had to retake the entire
course. But Libyans also found to their horror that they had lost a haphazard
but functioning state, personal security in the sense of being able to walk the
streets in safety and were at the mercy of predatory militiamen who were paid
out of Libya's diminished oil revenues.*

*I remember a fellow journalist upbraiding me politely in 2011 for stress-
ing the failings of the Libyan rebels, saying: 'Let's remember who are the good
guys.' A few months later, as the revolution turned sour, good and bad in Libya
were ever more difficult to tell apart. This was a common experience in the six
countries most affected by the Arab Spring. By 2015, three of these—Libya,
Syria and Yemen—were being ravaged by warfare and two others—Egypt
and Bahrain—were ruled by authoritarian governments more brutal and dictatorial than anything that had gone before. Only in Tunisia, where it had
all started, did an elected civilian government cling on, though increasingly
destabilised by massacres of foreign tourists by gunmen fresh from Islamic State
training camps in Libya.*

18 March 2011

Western nations will soon be engaged in a war in Libya with the noble aim
of protecting civilians. But the course of such a conflict is impossible to
predict. The UN Security Council has authorised the use of 'all necessary
measures', including aerial bombing, to avert a military victory by Colonel
Muammar Gaddafi. It is not at all clear what this authorisation will mean
in practice.

The Americans, the British and the French have come to understand that establishing a no-fly zone is not enough. Colonel Gaddafi's main strike force consists of tanks and infantry, so the inability to use aircraft might not be sufficient to stop him capturing Benghazi and eastern Libya. Given that most of the Libyan population lives in cities and towns close to the sea, air strikes on the main coast road might stop the regime's motley forces. But it is the tradition of wars in the Middle East that the first days of foreign involvement are always the best.

In Afghanistan and Iraq, there was clarity of objective—which was to overthrow the Taliban and Saddam Hussein, respectively. There is less clarity with Libya. Is the aim to defend the rebels in the east of the country? Will it extend to any surviving rebel strongholds in the west, such as Misrata, where there has been street fighting? Is the aim to get rid of Gaddafi? No-fly zones on their own may have an intimidatory effect, but this depends largely on the implied threat of air strikes.

The occasions when outside air power does work are when strike aircraft are directed by specialist teams of foreign soldiers on the ground, acting in co-operation with local militias. This caused the collapse of the Taliban in 2001 and of the Iraqi government forces in northern Iraq in 2003. The problem is that it is not clear who the US and Europe will be aiding in Libya. The most surprising development in this uprising is that it began with the defection of military units but these, until the last few days, have not appeared on the battlefield. Hillary Clinton, the US secretary of state, says what really changed her mind about intervening in Libya was the Arab League's statement calling for action. But the members of this somewhat discredited body are mostly autocracies which may dislike Gaddafi, but whose methods of government are no less repressive.

3 April 2011
In the restaurant of the Amal Africa hotel in Ajdabiya south of Benghazi, waiters have started to ask journalists to pay their bills before they eat. This urgency on the part of the hotel management reflects their bitter experience of seeing journalists—their only customers—abandon meals half-eaten and leave, bills unpaid, because of a sudden and unexpected advance by the pro-Gaddafi forces.

It is a bizarre little war. For several weeks, the world has watched a motley force of rebel militiamen and a so-far-unseen, but probably quite small, government force, race to-and-fro on the main road south of Benghazi.

The front line reporting is brave but gives the impression that this is a regular military campaign. In television studios and in newspapers, arrows on maps show the advance and retreat of pocket-sized forces over vast distances (the Libyan coastline is 2,000 kilometres long) as if the Afrika Corps and the 8th Army were battling it out. They capture and recapture 'strategic oil ports' and places that are just a scattering of houses.

Since yesterday, rebel fighters without training or weapons, together with the foreign media, are being sternly forbidden from driving to the front line. It must have become obvious to the rebel leaders in Benghazi that television pictures of their forces—essentially untrained gunmen in their pick-ups looking like extras from a *Mad Max* film—were damaging the credibility of the rebel cause in Europe and the US. The Libyan militiamen look like a rabble even by the lowly standards of militias in Lebanon, Iraq and Afghanistan.

Even well-organised militias are dangerous to do business with because they are prone to paranoia, believing they have been sniped at or spied on by some innocent civilian. I remember, during a war between Druze and Christians south of Beirut in 1983, trying to persuade a Druze fighter that a toasting fork he had found in a house was not specially designed to out the eyes of Druze prisoners. So strong were his suspicions that he had been planning to shoot the Christian householders.

The new propaganda line of the rebels' National Transitional Council is that professional soldiers, who have turned against Muammar Gaddafi over the last 40 years, will now take command and, in the words of one television reporter, 'lick into shape the rag-tag militiamen'. But the new military leadership, which Britain, France and to a decreasing extent the US will be supporting, inspires even less confidence than their men. The careers of several make them sound like characters out of the more sinister Graham Greene novels. They include men such as Colonel Khalifa Haftar, former commander of the Libyan Army in Chad who was captured and changed sides in 1988, setting up the anti-Gaddafi Libyan National Army reportedly with CIA and Saudi backing. For the last 20 years, he has been living quietly in Virginia before returning to Benghazi to lead the fight against Gaddafi. Even shadier is the background of Abdul Hakim al-Hasidi, a Libyan who fought against the US in Afghanistan, was arrested in Pakistan, imprisoned probably at Bagram, Afghanistan, and then mysteriously released. The US deputy secretary of state, James Steinberg, told congressmen he would speak of Hasidi's career only in a closed session.

Life in Libya always seems to have a farcical but dangerous element to it. The first time I went in the early 1980s was to see the Libyan Army withdraw from Chad. Somewhere in the southern desert, the vehicle I was in ran out of petrol in the middle of a minefield where we were stuck for hours. Later I was taken to see a model farm in an oasis which turned out to be abandoned. The only inhabitants were little green frogs hopping happily about amid the broken pipes and water-logged palm trees.

For many years, Gaddafi's aides, responding to the latest whim of the leader, would invite the foreign press over to interview him. These interviews seldom took place, and journalists would sit discontentedly in hotels waiting for their editors to let them go home. I found the best antidote to boredom was thick 19th century novels. To this day, Tripoli makes me think of Jane Austen, most of whose books I read lying on a bed in the Libya Palace Hotel.

The mistake in Libya was ever to become involved in trying to impose a no-fly zone. This was only going to have an effect if it turned into a no-drive zone, and this works best when the enemy is unwary enough to drive around in tanks and armoured vehicles and rely on heavy artillery that can be destroyed from the air. If foreign military force was to be used to save the people of Benghazi from massacre, it would have been better to impose a ceasefire from the beginning. This would have to be policed by foreign forces, but it was and is an achievable aim. It is politically more neutral and avoids charges of reborn imperialism. It has not happened because the not-so-covert aim from the start was to get rid of Gaddafi.

One advantage of Libya is that the failings became obvious quickly. Never has 'mission creep' crept so fast. The shortcomings of local allies are more obvious at an earlier stage than they were in Baghdad or Kabul. The difficulty in breaking the military stalemate opens the door to a cease-fire agreement and a resort to political and economic pressure to displace Gaddafi rather than the present ill-considered war.

7 April 2011

A good place to judge the balance of forces between Muammar Gaddafi and the rebels is the western entrance to the deserted town of Ajdabiya, south of Benghazi. The place is marked by a high archway and a wrecked cement sentry box containing scraps of rotting food. On its broken walls are pasted sad pictures of young men who have gone missing, with the phone numbers of their families underneath.

We arrive mid-morning, having been warned that it would be a mistake to get there too early: rebel fighters could still be asleep and it is possible to drive straight through the rebel lines, without knowing they are there, and into the front line of the pro-Gaddafi troops. This was an exaggeration. Some rebel soldiers in uniform are turning back militiamen and journalists, to the irritation of both. The soldiers clear the road for giant flat-bed trucks going up to the front with vehicle-mounted Katyusha rocket launchers, and a lethal-looking contraption welded to the back of a truck which is, in fact, a rocket firing pod that is normally fitted to the underside of aircraft. In the other direction a couple of dozen flat-bed trucks return from the front to which they have delivered some 20 tanks earlier in the morning.

There is an atmosphere of friendly confusion because we imagine that the front line is far down the road towards the oil town of Brega. It turns out to be a lot closer than that. Suddenly white civilian ambulances race past us. A soldier in one of them shouts that they have been bombed. He does not say by whom, but we assume it is a NATO 'friendly fire' mistake. Soon there are plumes of smoke in the distance as four or five shells or rockets land. Militiamen start streaming back towards Ajdabiya. We stop at a small hospital there where doctors have become used to examining patients while giving media interviews. They are full of self-righteous and not entirely reasonable rage about NATO bombing the rebels and not Gaddafi's men.

Any event in eastern Libya at the moment can become the occasion for a political rally. In this case the reception of the wounded as they are carried from the ambulances into the hospital is delayed by political speeches and chants of 'God is great'. Nor does the ordeal of the wounded end there. In hospitals throughout the Middle East families and friends consider they have a divine right to visit patients. In Ajdabiya hospital, sobbing soldiers crowd into a ward so that stretcher-bearers can hardly get in. Angry doctors manhandle the grieving fighters out of the room for a few minutes before they burst in again.

The NATO attack on the rebel tanks turns out to be much as the first survivors describe it. The rebels had moved up tanks, ageing Libyan Army T-54s that had been in storage for 30 years and half a dozen more modern T-72 tanks. They claim they had told NATO but it seems likely, given the general chaos in Benghazi, that they did not. Not surprisingly, the NATO pilots assumed that the tanks must belong to the government.

The incident on the Ajdabiya-Brega road is important because it shows that the rebels are not going to be a serious fighting force for months and possibly not even then. British prime minister David Cameron and French president Nicolas Sarkozy have entered a war into which they will inevitably be sucked deeper because the rebel enclave around Benghazi is completely dependent on outside military support.

The Gaddafi forces show ominous signs of adapting faster than their enemies. They fire accurate artillery barrages and attack out of the desert in the same sort of pick-up vehicles as the rebels. What holds them back is that they are at the end of long supply lines and they do not have enough men to hold the ground they take. The same is true of the anti-Gaddafi fighters. Though there are plenty of people willing to demonstrate in Benghazi there are surprisingly few militiamen at the front. These are often derided by the foreign press for their military ineptitude or lack of experience, but what is most striking is that there are not enough of them.

The roadside from Benghazi is littered with the burned-out remains of tanks and trucks dating from the last time Gaddafi came close to capturing the city. He may not try to do so again and, if he does, it will probably be in vehicles that are the same as those used by the rebels. If the Gaddafi forces do advance, there is nothing much to stop them. On the road between Ajdabiya and Benghazi there are no fall-back positions. Should the front cave in, NATO aircraft will have to try to tell a dirty white Gaddafi pick-up with machine gun in the back from a dirty white pro-democracy pick-up similarly armed.

Back in Benghazi, away from the chaos of the front, this is not the picture the rebel military commanders want to give. At a press conference, the joint chief of staff General Abdul Fattah Younis, former head of Gaddafi's special forces, seeks to give the impression that all is under control. Asked about the NATO bombing of the tanks, he says that 'accidents happen in war'. He describes the panicked flight of militiamen as a military manoeuvre to throw back a temporary advance by Gaddafi's troops. General Younis' air of calm is very soothing, and many in Benghazi who have not been near the front line wish to believe that what he says is true. But there is an undercurrent of fear in the city, and it would not take much to start a panic. Libyans are beginning to learn the ways of survival well known in countries such as Iraq and Lebanon, where war frequently turns part of the population into refugees. The Kurds, with grim experience of taking flight, have a saying: 'If you are going to run, then run early.' Wait too long and you cannot get out.

13 April 2011

The conflict between pro- and anti-Gaddafi forces in Libya could turn the country into another Somalia, according to Moussa Koussa, the former Libyan foreign minister who has fled to Britain. The ingredients are certainly there for a prolonged conflict. It no longer seems likely, as it did during the first few weeks of the Libyan uprising, that Muammar Gaddafi will soon be fleeing for his life from Tripoli or will be the victim of a coup by his own lieutenants. Instead Gaddafi appears to be stabilising his authority and may be there for months or even years. On the ground there is a military stalemate. Small forces from both sides have captured and recaptured the town of Ajdabiya over several weeks, but neither has been able to land a knock-out blow. At times there are more journalists than fighters on the front line.

Gaddafi has proved that he is the most powerful player in Libya. His troops may not be able to advance in the face of air strikes, but they also have not retreated pell-mell after heavy losses. The opposition leaders comfort themselves with the belief that Tripoli and the east of this vast country is bubbling with unrest that will ultimately boil over and force out Gaddafi and his family. It might happen that way, but there is little sign of it. The regime in Tripoli appears to have recovered its nerve and has the forces to crush any fresh local uprising. For the moment Libya is effectively partitioned with the dividing line running along the old frontier between the historic provinces of Cyrenaica and Tripolitania.

The strength of the National Transitional Council is its international political and military support. It is less good at organising a functioning government. As with other Arab uprisings, the opposition is particularly effective at mobilising demonstrations and winning the sympathy of the international media. Benghazi's old town hall, from the balcony of which Mussolini, Rommel and King Idris addressed crowds in the square below at different times, is now, very appropriately, occupied by the immensely influential satellite television channel Al Jazeera.

When an African Union delegation visited here this week to propose ceasefire terms, which did not include the departure of Gaddafi, the crowd of hostile demonstrators outside the hotel where the meeting was taking place seemed better organised than the rebel leaders inside. Banners in Arabic, English and French demanded that the dictator should go and asserted that Libya would not be partitioned. Protesters denied there would be any civil war in Libya because the struggle was between the Libyan people on one side and a hated dictator on the other. Unfortunately, the situation is not so clear cut. Gaddafi has a core of supporters fighting for him and they cannot all be dismissed—despite the claims of the rebels—as foreign mercenaries. The longer the conflict goes on, and Libyans are forced to take sides, the more it becomes a civil war.

It would take a long time to reduce Libya to the level of Somalia, but civil conflicts and the hatreds they induce build up their own momentum once the shooting has begun. One of the good things about Libya is that so many young men—unlike Afghans and Iraqis of a similar age—do not know how to use a gun. This will not last.

The opposition leaders in Benghazi hope that time is on their side and that the increasingly isolated regime will crumble from within as it faces irresistible pressure from abroad. Possibly they are right. But Iraqi opponents of Saddam Hussein thought much the same 20 years ago, and conflicts before and after his fall inspired hatreds that wrecked their country beyond repair. When this Libyan war started I was struck by the parallels with foreign intervention in Iraq and Afghanistan. Now, at close range, I find the similarities even more ominous. The West has joined somebody else's civil war, and it is a conflict in which Britain, France and the US must inevitably play a leading role. Without their support, the local partner would be defeated within 24 hours.

22 May 2011
Flames billow up from the hulks of eight Libyan Navy vessels destroyed by NATO air attacks as they lay in ports along the Libyan coast. Their destruction shows how Muammar Gaddafi is being squeezed militarily, but also the degree to which the US, France and Britain, and not the Libyan rebels, are now the main players in the struggle for power in Libya.

Probably Gaddafi will ultimately go down because he is too weak to withstand the forces arrayed against him. Failure to end his regime would be too humiliating and politically damaging for NATO after 2,700 air strikes. It is fair to assume that most Libyans also want Gaddafi to go. He clings on because he rules through his family, clan, tribe and allied tribes, combined with his ebbing control of the ramshackle Libyan government and military machine. Everything within the part of Libya he still controls depends on Gaddafi personally. Once he goes there will be a political vacuum that the opposition will scarcely be able to fill. The fall of the regime may usher in a new round of a long-running Libyan crisis that continues for years to come.

Three months after the start of the Libyan uprising Gaddafi's troops have failed to capture Misrata, but the rebels do not look capable of advancing towards Tripoli. They have broken the siege of Misrata partly because their militiamen now clutch hand radios and can call in NATO air strikes. The Libyan government and opposition forces are both weak. The fighting forces that have been clashing on the desert road between Brega and Ajdabiya, south of Benghazi, often number no more than a few hundred half-trained fighters. Gaddafi's troops, with which he tries to control this vast country, number only 10,000 to 15,000.

Could the war be ended earlier by negotiation? Here, again, the problem is the weakness of the organised opposition. If they have the backing of enhanced NATO military involvement they can take power. Without it, they cannot. They therefore have every incentive to demand that Gaddafi goes as a precondition for a ceasefire and negotiations. Since only Gaddafi can deliver a ceasefire and meaningful talks, this means the war will be fought to a finish. The departure of Gaddafi should be the aim of negotiations, not their starting point.

One surprising aspect of the conflict so far is that there has not been a greater effort to involve Algeria and Egypt, the two most powerful states in North Africa. This would make the departure of Gaddafi easier to negotiate and would make the whole Libyan adventure look less like European imperialism reborn. The aim of NATO intervention was supposedly to limit civilian casualties, but its leaders have blundered into a political strategy that makes a prolonged conflict and heavy civilian loss of life inevitable.

26 June 2011

In the first months of the Arab Spring, foreign journalists got well-merited credit for helping to foment and publicise popular uprisings against the region's despots. Satellite television stations such as Al Jazeera Arabic, in particular, struck at the roots of power in Arab police states by making official censorship irrelevant and by competing successfully against government propaganda.

Regimes threatened by change have, since those early days, paid backhanded compliments to the foreign media by throwing correspondents out of countries where they would like to report and by denying them visas to come back in. Trying to visit Yemen earlier this year, I was told that not only was there no chance of my being granted a journalist's visa, but that real tourists—amazingly there is a trickle of such people wanting to see the wonders of Yemen—were being turned back at Sanaa airport on the grounds that they must secretly be journalists. The Bahrain government has an even meaner trick: give a visa to a journalist at a Bahraini embassy abroad and deny him entry when his plane lands. It has taken time for this policy of near total exclusion to take hold, but it means that, today, foreign journalistic coverage of Syria, Yemen and, to a lesser extent, Bahrain is usually long-distance, reliant on cellphone film of demonstrations and riots which cannot be verified.

With so many countries out of bounds, journalists have flocked to Benghazi in Libya, which can be reached from Egypt without a visa. Alternatively they go to Tripoli, where the government allows a carefully monitored press corps to operate under strict supervision. Having arrived in these two cities, the ways in which the journalists report diverge sharply. Everybody reporting out of Tripoli expresses understandable scepticism about what government minders seek to show them as regards civilian casualties caused by NATO air strikes or demonstrations of support for Muammar Gaddafi. By way of contrast, the foreign press corps in Benghazi, capital of the rebel-held territory, shows surprising credulity towards more subtle but equally self-serving stories from the rebel government or its sympathisers.

Ever since the Libyan uprising started on 15 February, the foreign media have regurgitated stories of atrocities carried out by Gaddafi's forces. It is now becoming clear that reputable human rights organisations such as Amnesty International and Human Rights Watch have been unable to find evidence for the worst of these. For instance, they could find no credible witnesses to the mass rapes said to have been ordered by Gaddafi.

The crimes for which there is proof against Gaddafi are more prosaic, such as the bombardment of civilians in Misrata who have no way to escape. There is also proof of the shooting of unarmed protesters and people at funerals early on in the uprising. Amnesty estimates that some 100–110 people were killed in Benghazi and 59–64 in Baida, though it warns that some of the dead may have been government supporters.

The Libyan insurgents were adept at dealing with the press from the outset and this included skilful propaganda to put the blame for unexplained killings on the other side. One story, to which credence was given by the foreign media early on in Benghazi, was that eight to 10 government troops who refused to shoot protesters were executed by their own side. Their bodies were shown on television. But Donatella Rovera, senior crisis response adviser for Amnesty International, says there is strong evidence for a different explanation. She says amateur video shows them alive after they had been captured, suggesting it was the rebels who killed them.

It is a weakness of journalists that they give wide publicity to atrocities, evidence for which may be shaky when first revealed. But when the stories turn out to be untrue or exaggerated, they rate scarcely a mention. Atrocity stories develop a life of their own and have real, and sometimes fatal, consequences long after the basis for them is deflated. Earlier in the year in Benghazi I spoke to refugees, mostly oil workers from Brega, an oil port in the Gulf of Sirte which had been captured by Gaddafi forces. One of the reasons they had fled was that they believed their wives and daughters were in danger of being raped by foreign mercenaries. They knew about this threat from watching satellite television.

It is all credit to Amnesty International and Human Rights Watch that they have taken a sceptical attitude to atrocities until proven. Contrast this responsible attitude with that of Hillary Clinton or the prosecutor of the International Criminal Court, Luis Moreno Ocampo, who blithely suggested that Gaddafi was using rape as a weapon of war to punish the rebels. Equally irresponsible would be a decision by the ICC to prosecute Gaddafi and his lieutenants, thus making it far less likely that Gaddafi can be eased out of power without a fight to the finish. This systematic demonisation of Gaddafi—a brutal despot he may be, but not a monster on the scale of Saddam Hussein—also makes it difficult to negotiate a ceasefire with him, though he is the only man who can deliver one.

There is nothing particularly surprising about the rebels in Benghazi making things up or producing dubious witnesses to Gaddafi's crimes. They are fighting a war against a tyrant whom they fear and hate and they will understandably use black propaganda as a weapon of war. But it does show naivety on the part of the foreign media, who almost universally sympathise with the rebels, that they swallow whole so many atrocity stories fed to them by the rebel authorities and their supporters.

24 July 2011

A NATO pilot who bombed Ain Zara south of Tripoli earlier this month almost certainly did not know that his attack came almost exactly 100 years after the very same target had been hit by two small bombs dropped by an Italian plane in 1911. The Italian air raid was the first in history, carried out soon after Italy had invaded what later became Libya during one of the many carve-ups of the Ottoman Empire. The first ever military reconnaissance flight took a route near Benghazi in October, and on 1 November Sub-Lieutenant Giulio Gavotti became the first pilot to drop bombs. He swooped down on a Turkish camp at Ain Zara and dropped four 4.5-pound grenades from a leather bag in his cockpit. The Turks protested that Gavotti's bombs had hit a hospital and injured several civilians.

The pros and cons should have become swiftly apparent. It is not that air strikes are wholly futile. I was in Baghdad during the US bombing in 1991 and again during Desert Fox in 1998. Crouching on the floor of my hotel room was a testing experience as I watched columns of fire erupt around the city and the pathetic dribbles of anti-aircraft fire in return. On the other hand, being shelled in West Beirut during the civil wars was in some ways worse because it went on for longer and was completely haphazard. In Baghdad I hoped that the Americans were taking care about what they targeted, if only for reasons of PR, although my confidence was severely dented when they killed some 400 civilians in the Amariya shelter.

Frightening though it is being bombed, air forces often exaggerate what they can do. They are always less accurate than they claim; their effectiveness depends on good tactical intelligence. Bombing works best as a blunt instrument against civilians as a generalised punishment. Against well-prepared soldiers, such as Hezbollah's guerrillas, it is far less effective. Israel's disastrous 2006 venture in Lebanon probably rated as history's most ill-thought out air war until this year when France and Britain decided to ally themselves to an enthusiastic but ill-trained militia to overthrow Colonel Muammar Gaddafi.

31 July 2011

In keeping with the British Government's well-established record of comical ineptitude in dealing with Libya, William Hague, the foreign secretary, chose to recognise the rebel leaders in Benghazi as the legitimate government of the country at the very moment some of them may have been shooting or torturing to death their chief military commander.

The exact circumstances surrounding the killing of General Abdel Fattah Younis remain murky, but he appears to have been lured from his operational headquarters at the front and arrested. As Muammar Gaddafi's long-term defence and interior minister, who gave a crucial boost to the insurrection by defecting in February, he knew he was a target for assassination, but may have misjudged the likely identity of the assassins. Believing he was on his way to answer allegations of still being in touch with Gaddafi, he and two of his senior aides were murdered and their bodies burned. 'You killed him,' shouted some of his soldiers as they burst into the hotel where the National Transitional Council had been meeting. Probably they are right and it is difficult to believe claims by the Council that pro-Gaddafi gunmen had infiltrated Benghazi and assassinated the commander-in-chief.

Regardless of the circumstances of his death, the murder should begin to raise questions about who Britain and other foreign powers are backing as a replacement to Gaddafi in Libya. What regime will follow his long-delayed fall, when and if it happens? Will a new regime be able to control the country? Is there any reason to suppose that it will have general support, given the bitterness of the civil war? Will the rebels not be as reliant on foreign powers in peace as they have been in war?

Remember that neither Saddam Hussein nor the Taliban were popular in Iraq or Afghanistan at the time they were driven from power. But what followed in both cases was prolonged and murderous anarchy because of the weakness of their Western-backed replacements. Hague, displaying a striking ability to get Libya wrong, praised the National Transitional Council leaders, as he recognised them as the Libyan government, as showing 'increasing legitimacy, competence and success'. Presumably, his information came from the same source that led him months ago to inform journalists that Gaddafi was already on his way to Venezuela.

The Libyan rebels are even weaker than those in Afghanistan and Iraq where the Western-backed opposition had a core of loyal and well-trained fighters. In Afghanistan, these were the mostly Tajik forces of the Northern Alliance and in Iraq the Kurds had a well-organised and well-led army in the north of the country. In Libya, rebel forces have always been more meagre, inexperienced and often appear to be one side in hitherto obscure tribal confrontations which have turned into mini civil wars.

The nature of the civil war in Libya has been persistently underplayed by foreign governments. The enthusiasm in foreign capitals to recognise the mysterious self-appointed group in Benghazi as the leaders of Libya is probably motivated primarily by expectations of commercial concessions and a carve-up of oil fields. These were the understandable motives which led Tony Blair, Nicolas Sarkozy and so many others to kowtow humiliatingly to Gaddafi prior to the uprising, and to treat his bizarre personality cult with respect.

21 August 2011

The end of Muammar Gaddafi's 41 years in power appears to be in hand as the rebels close in on Tripoli, though it is not clear if the old regime will collapse without a fight for the capital. It still has the men and the material to draw out the conflict, but its supporters may decide that there is no reason to die for a lost cause.

It is an extraordinary situation. The National Transitional Council in Benghazi is now recognised by more than 30 foreign powers, including the US and Britain, as the government of Libya. But it is by no means clear that it is recognised as such by the rebel militiamen who are in the process of seizing the capital. The rebel fighters in Misrata, who fought so long to defend their city, say privately that they have no intention of obeying orders from the Council. Their intransigence may not last but it is one sign that the insurgents are deeply divided.

22 August 2011

The civil war in Libya went on longer than expected, but the fall of Tripoli has come faster than was forecast. While it is clear Colonel Muammar Gaddafi has lost power, it is not certain who has gained it. The anti-regime militiamen that are now streaming into the capital were united by a common enemy, but not much else.

There is another problem in ending the war. It has never been a straight trial of strength between two groups of Libyans because of the decisive role of NATO air strikes. The insurgents themselves admit that without the air war waged on their behalf—with 7,459 air strikes on pro-Gaddafi targets— they would be dead or in flight. The question, therefore, remains open as to how the rebels can peaceably convert their foreign-assisted victory on the battlefield into a stable peace acceptable to all parties in Libya. Even those celebrating in the streets of Tripoli and cheering the advancing rebel columns will expect their lives to get better, and will be disappointed if this does not happen.

27 August 2011

NATO planes are bombing Muammar Gaddafi's home town of Sirte, underlining the degree to which NATO fully joined the war against him over the past month. It was the use of highly trained spotters on the ground calling in air strikes on pro-Gaddafi defensive positions and bases which led to the surprisingly swift military victory and the fall of Tripoli last weekend.

On the road south of the capital, along which the rebels advanced, one can see buildings held by Gaddafi forces torn apart by NATO bombs and missiles. The sand barriers set up by the government troops to block the road look pathetically ineffective in the face of this type of destruction.

'We are all one family,' said a Libyan businessman hopefully to me yesterday as we drove through the empty streets of central Tripoli with staccato bursts of machine gun fire occasionally drowning our conversation. There are ominous reports of massacres of prisoners on both sides. The next six months, or year, will show just how much of a family Libyans really are.

Security in Tripoli remains fragile. (As I write this in a room overlooking the port there is suddenly the sound of shooting not far from the hotel and for a moment the electricity cuts out.) 'The only real looting has been of government cars and we are asking drivers to show documents to prove that they own the vehicles they are driving,' said one rebel leader. 'If they can't prove ownership, we confiscate the car.' In fact, his worries are a little premature since most people are not driving anywhere because of fear of snipers and a shortage of petrol.

The legacies of war may be difficult to overcome. But Libyans have a good chance of restoring peace and prosperity. They are not divided by communal and sectarian differences as in Afghanistan and Iraq. For all the complaints against Gaddafi and misuse of oil money, the standard of living and educational standards are high. There is not a marginalised section of the population, living on the edge of malnutrition, as do a third of Afghans. Oil revenues are high and the 6 million population small enough for them to benefit all. Unlike Iraq, there is no occupying foreign army.

All the same, I wish the shooting outside my window would stop.

29 August 2011

The new rulers of Libya, the National Transitional Council, have arrived in town. I know this because they just kicked me out of my painfully acquired hotel room when they took over the whole of the eighth floor of the Radisson Blu Hotel where I am staying.

My eviction does not elicit much sympathy from other journalists, many packed two or three to a room, when I explain I have been given another room and I have it all to myself. The previous occupant, who had not done much clearing up before he departed, left behind an Omani military yearbook and some torn-up notebooks. He may have been one of the elusive group of Arab military officers who gave technical advice to the rebels, assuring their victory.

Even so, I wish the unknown officer had not taken the room's only towel which I am unlikely to get replaced. Luxury hotel the Radisson in Tripoli may once have been with its 350 rooms and 40 or so suites, which were once looked after by 400 staff, but this number is now down to about 20 harassed young men and two or three women. These heroically try to cope with the hordes of journalists pleading for a room that have descended on Tripoli since the city fell last week and they now have to deal with more peremptory instructions from the National Transitional Council as well.

The lack of a towel is less serious than it sounds because there has been no water in the hotel or most other places in Tripoli since last Friday. Pro-Gaddafi forces have seized the water wells 600 kilometres to the south in the Sahara and turned off the pumps. They are also said to have run out of fuel and cannot flee any further. As a result, there is no water for toilets or showers in the hotel and bottled drinking water is scarce and expensive. Journalists carry water from the swimming pool in waste paper bins to flush the toilets.

This is the first big test of the National Transitional Council. It seems to have learned from the experience of Baghdad in 2003 that security has to be maintained and looting prevented. Those members of the Council not at the Radisson are living at former regime bases in Souq al-Jumaa, a large district of crumbling old buildings famous for its revolutionary fervour. Locals say spies could never penetrate their networks of extended families and they were first to rise up in August. There are checkpoints every couple of hundred yards in Souq al-Jumaa. The militiamen manning them are relaxed and, so far, surprisingly stoic about the humanitarian crisis engulfing the city. A militiaman nestling his Kalashnikov on his knee says that, in the district, 'there is no water, electricity for five hours a day, little cooking gas and the price of food has gone up two or three times.' Almost all shops are closed and when I try to buy water at one of the few that is open, they have run out. People are not desperate yet and water is being handed out in blue plastic jerry cans but it looks pitifully little in a city of 2 million.

Just why so many Libyans hated Muammar Gaddafi and his ghastly family is made chillingly, and at times hilariously, clear as their palaces are exposed to public view. His daughter Aisha seized a large plot of land in the Noflein district in Tripoli in 2005 and three years later moved into a compound with several luxury houses furnished with unsurpassable vulgarity and poor taste. In one sitting room there is a sofa with the cushions resting on a gigantic golden bare-breasted mermaid who appears to be holding a dark-red feather duster that is probably meant to be a fan. Mufat, a local man who has been put in charge of the complex, explains that when Aisha moved in 'all her neighbours with windows facing her palace were told to close them and never open them again. If they did so they would be in big trouble.' When her father visited her twice a year the whole district was closed down. Gaddafi may be gone but it will be some time before people in Tripoli begin to blame their new rulers for their troubles.

30 August 2011

Yassin Bahr, a tall thin Senegalese in torn blue jeans, volubly denies that he was ever a mercenary or fought for Muammar Gaddafi. Speaking in quick, nervous sentences, Bahr tries to convince a suspicious local militia leader in charge of the police station in the Faraj district of Tripoli that he is a building worker who has been arrested simply because of his skin colour. 'I liked Gaddafi, but I never fought for him,' Bahr says, adding that he had worked in Libya for three years laying tiles. But the Libyan rebels are hostile to black Africans in general. One of the militiamen in control of the police station says simply: 'Libyan people don't like people with dark skins, though some of them may be innocent.'

Going by Bahr's experience, any black African in Libya is open to summary arrest unless he can prove that he was not a member of Gaddafi's forces. Fathi, a building contractor who does not want to give his full name and is temporarily running the police station, wants to know why Bahr has a special residence permit that an immigrant worker would not normally obtain. 'You must have been fighting for Gaddafi to have a permit like this,' he says. Bahr says that three years earlier he had walked through the Sahara and crossed the Libyan border illegally with other West Africans looking for work. They had been picked up by the Libyan police, but he had eventually bribed them to get a residence permit. He had been watching television with nine other African immigrants when they were arrested; no arms were found in the house.

Racism against black Africans and Libyans with dark skin has long simmered in Libya. Before the war there were estimated to be a million illegal immigrants in the country, which has a population of 6 million and a workforce of 1.7 million. The war has deepened racial hostility. Since February, the insurgents, often supported by foreign powers, claimed that the battle was between Gaddafi and his family on the one side and the Libyan people on the other. Their explanation for the large pro-Gaddafi force was that they were all mercenaries, mostly from black Africa, whose only motive was money. Amnesty International says these allegations are largely unproven and, from the beginning of the conflict, many of those arrested or, in some cases, executed by the rebels were undocumented labourers caught in the wrong place at the wrong time.

Black African immigrants in the past benefited from Gaddafi's aspiration to be a pan-African leader. The position of illegal immigrants was always uncertain, but they were essential to the economy. With the fall of Gaddafi, those who have not already fled face persecution or even murder. Last weekend 30 bodies of mostly black men, several of them handcuffed and others already wounded, were found after an apparent mass execution at a roundabout near Gaddafi's Bab al-Aziziya headquarters.

Any interview with a prisoner must come with a health warning, since he or she is unlikely to speak freely about their treatment while still under arrest. Bahr confirms that he is being well treated, but he does look very frightened.

31 August 2011

Much of the government propaganda on Libyan state television during the six-month civil war was focused on claims that the rebellion was being led by Islamic militants. The aim was to frighten the US and NATO abroad and secular Libyans at home. But the allegations also had some credibility, since the most militant and experienced anti-Gaddafi organisation was the Libyan Islamic Fighting Group. It is Abdulhakim Belhaj, one of the founders of this group which fought a ferocious guerrilla campaign against the regime in the 1990s, who now commands the militia units in Tripoli. Belhaj, 45, a veteran of the Afghan war in the 1980s, is a leading jihadi who was arrested at American behest in Malaysia in 2003, tortured in Thailand and handed over to Libya in 2004. At that time US and Libyan intelligence were co-operating in eliminating Islamists and American officers allegedly took part in interrogations in Tripoli. Released along with other militants in 2010 by an over-confident regime, Belhaj was well placed to play a leading role in planning and carrying out the assault that captured Tripoli.

The anti-Western attitudes of Libyan Islamists have been changed by the knowledge that without NATO air strikes Muammar Gaddafi would have won the war. The long term aims of the Libyan Islamic Fighting Group may not have changed much, but, as with Islamists in most countries convulsed by the Arab Spring, they long ago recognised that they had to be allied to liberals and secularists to overthrow police states in Syria, Egypt, Tunisia and Libya. They also needed to distance themselves from al-Qa'ida to avoid being denigrated.

The Islamists may, for the moment, look stronger than they are because they alone could provide experienced guerrilla leaders and an organised network of sympathisers in Tripoli. These cells could scarcely maintain their existence before the rebellion started on 15 February, but thereafter they expanded rapidly.

4 September 2011

In Libya effective rebel military control is visibly outpacing the establishment of political stability. There are checkpoints everywhere in Tripoli and along the coast road east and west. Security is surprisingly good, given that the war in these heavily populated areas has only just ended. Even the rattle of gunfire from jubilant rebels shooting into the air is subsiding.

People in Tripoli are astonished, as if they cannot entirely believe their luck, that the six-month war ended so quickly and decisively. Local militia commanders were also surprised by this. Even in an area like Abu Salim, supposedly full of Gaddafi supporters, there was little fighting. Khalid, an accountant in a local bank carrying an assault rifle, says: 'We thought they were strong, but the fighting only went on for a couple of hours. A lot of people switched sides at the last moment.' He and other militiamen suspect that pro-Gaddafi fighters have retreated to farms on the edge of Abu Salim and are planning an operation to root them out.

Almost everybody in Tripoli now claims to have been working openly or secretly on the rebel side. Such unlikely claims have probably been made in every captured city down the ages. But all the evidence is that by the time the rebels broke through at Zawiyah in August and, to their surprise, found the road to the capital open and undefended, the morale of the pro-Gaddafi forces had collapsed. One former soldier described how he had abandoned his tank at Zawiyah when ordered to retreat in the face of a rebel assault from the Nafusa mountains, an uprising in Zawiyah itself, and NATO planes relentlessly smashing pro-Gaddafi defensive positions. He simply decided that the game was up and there was no point in waiting to be incinerated inside his tank. He took off his uniform and ran.

Inside Tripoli, regime supporters similarly concluded that there was no reason to die for a doomed cause. Issam, an Islamist truck owner in charge of a district in Souq al-Jumaa, says his men had few weapons at first, but obtained them by 'going house to house asking pro-Gaddafi people to hand over their arms and stay at home'. Nobody refused. Khalid in Abu Salim says he thought the turning point in the war had come when Gaddafi failed to capture Misrata in early summer and NATO intensified the bombing. After that, Gaddafi's men were on the retreat and it was easy to pick the ultimate winner.

6 September 2011

Here is an account by a Libyan, who did not want to disclose his name, of what it was like to be tortured by Libyan security. He says: 'I was blind-folded and taken upstairs. I was shocked with electricity and made to sit on broken glass. They were kicking and punching me until I confessed. I said "No".' This went on for over a week. One day the interrogators tied his hands behind his back and took him upstairs. He continues: 'They opened the door and I saw my son and wife. There were five or six members of security with masks. They tied me to a chair and one of them said: "Do you want to sign or should we torture them?"' According to the prisoner one of the interrogators took his 10-month-old son and put a wire on his hand and 'he screamed and his face turned red.' The little boy appeared to stop breathing. Soon afterwards the prisoner signed the confession demanded by Libyan security.

The testimony about the baby's torture in front of his father was recorded by Human Rights Watch in Tripoli in 2005. The same year the UK signed a Memorandum of Understanding accepting Libyan diplomatic assurances that torture would not be used against Libyan exiles repatriated from the UK to Libya. Few documents agreed to by a British government exude so much hypocrisy and cynicism.

Will the close co-operation on what amounted to farming out torture by the CIA and MI6 to Muammar Gaddafi and his interrogators be forgotten in the rush of events in Libya? Western intelligence services presumably hope so. The fragile and divided Libyan authorities may think twice before quarrelling with the very organisations whose aid over the past six months enabled them to defeat Gaddafi.

Last week I saw Abdelhakim Belhaj, the head of the military council controlling all militia brigades in Tripoli, and asked him about how he was arrested in Malaysia, tortured in Thailand and sent back for more torture and imprisonment in Abu Salim prison in Tripoli. Given the Libyan rebels' reliance on NATO air strikes, I thought it likely that Belhaj, a founder of the Libyan Islamic Fighting Group which had been accused of links to al-Qa'ida, would avoid talking about his rendition. Instead Belhaj showed that he was still a very angry man. He said he was considering suing those responsible.

It is good that Belhaj is not willing to cover up what happened to him, and that his story is confirmed by documents in Tripoli proving the cosy relationship between MI6, the CIA and Gaddafi. It should help to discredit the way in which the world's most disgusting and oppressive dictators have been able in the decade since 9/11 to claim that anybody opposing them was an Islamic fundamentalist linked to al-Qa'ida. The degradation of standards started almost immediately in Afghanistan after the fall of the Taliban with the denial of the status of prisoners of war being granted to captives. By 2003 the government of Uzbekistan boiled to death two prisoners and still got a US grant for its security services. It now turns out that several of the rebels who played a crucial role in overthrowing Gaddafi, and have been lauded as freedom fighters by Western leaders, were among those savagely tortured by MI6's friends in Abu Salim. This might just begin to turn the tide against the systematic mistreatment of prisoners which has become such a hallmark of the security world since 9/11.

5 November 2011

I first met Ahmed Abdullah al-Ghadamsi in Tripoli in August about seven weeks before he was killed in one of the last battles of the Libyan war.

I was staying in the Radisson Blu, a large hotel that overlooks the harbour and was overfilled with journalists who had poured into the Libyan capital after the rebels captured it. I had found a room with great difficulty and was upset when a young man knocked on the door and told me I would have to leave. He said, politely but firmly, that members of the National Transitional Council were arriving from Benghazi and needed several floors of the hotel for themselves and their bodyguards. He added that, fortunately, there was another room I could have and he would help me move there. As we packed up, he said his name was Ahmed, he had previously worked at the Radisson, and he had now come back to help the few remaining staff cope with the influx of visitors.

We talked about the fighting, the fall of Muammar Gaddafi and the future of Libya. Ahmed was fresh-faced, looked a little younger than his 32 years, spoke good English, was obviously highly educated, and did not seem too alarmed by the uncertainty of living in a city where the government had just collapsed and the rebels were only slowly asserting their grip. I asked him if he would come to work for me as guide and translator and, after a few moments' thought, he said he would.

I learnt later, after he was dead, that there was a good deal that Ahmed had not told me. He was born in 1978 and came from a family that had long detested Gaddafi. He had gone abroad to study in Norway for six years between 2002 and 2008, and it may have been this foreign travel which gave him an air of self-reliance and sophistication. He had learnt Norwegian and improved his English (study of which had been restricted by Gaddafi). On his return to Libya he had joined the staff of the luxury Radisson Blu, often visited by leading Libyan officials and members of Gaddafi's family, one of whom, al-Saadi Gaddafi, had a suite there. On 15 February this year the popular movement against long-established police states in the Arab world spread from Tunisia and Egypt to Libya. Ahmed was one of the first people to protest in the streets in Tripoli and was also one of the first from Fornaj, a district militantly anti-regime, to be detained. His younger brother Mohammed recalls that Ahmed 'was the first to be arrested in Fornaj on 20 February, but he was jailed for just two hours or less before his friends and the protesters broke into the police station and freed him'.

Gaddafi was able to regain control of the capital and almost all of western Libya with the important exceptions of Misrata and the Berber minority in the Nafusa mountains 100 miles south of Tripoli. Ahmed later told the Italian photographer Enrico Dagnino that he had wanted to get more involved with the anti-Gaddafi resistance and 'went to the Nafusa mountains, but the fighters didn't trust him and after a week or 10 days he went back to Tripoli and worked at smuggling in guns and gelignite'. He was soon wanted by Gaddafi's security forces because he became involved in a plan to blow up the floor at the Radisson Blu where al-Saadi Gaddafi was living, Ahmed's brother Mohammed said. Despite this he got married for the second time (his first wife was a Norwegian) on 1 July.

I think of Ahmed now as an exemplar of the people who are at the forefront of the Arab Awakening from Tunisia to Bahrain and Syria to Yemen. He was brave, energetic and eager to help others. A well-educated man, he felt limited and humiliated by the restrictions of Gaddafi's police state and ludicrous personality cult. 'Books used to be more difficult to bring into this country than weapons,' Ahmed told me. 'You had to leave them at the airport for two or three months so they could be checked.'

Ahmed was a very good guide for me in Tripoli. I did not know that he felt deeply frustrated that he had not been able to take a greater and more effective part in the anti-Gaddafi resistance and by now it seemed almost too late to do so. Tripoli had fallen more quickly than anybody expected and the fighting was far to the east around the Gaddafi loyalist heartlands of Bani Walid and Sirte. I left Tripoli soon afterwards, but I expected to see Ahmed when I returned.

In the event, the last stand of the Gaddafi loyalists went on much longer than anybody expected. Ahmed worked with Cécile Hennion of *Le Monde* and the photographer, Enrico Dagnino, for several weeks. His brother Mohammed says that at about this time Ahmed told his mother that he wanted to go to fight; she asked him not to. But Enrico ran into a militia commander from Benghazi called Adel Tharouni and asked if he could join him to cover the battle for Sirte, Gaddafi's home town. A few days later Enrico, Cécile and Ahmed flew to Benghazi. Enrico says: 'Ahmed insisted he wanted to come to Benghazi not for money, but because he was interested in what was happening in Sirte. He did not tell us he was planning to join the fighting.'

They drove to the rebel positions outside Sirte where they linked up with Adel Tharouni's fighters from Benghazi. They slept in the desert living off macaroni and driving up to the front line every day. The battle for Sirte was turning into one of the bloodiest and hardest fought of the Libyan war. Ahmed told the fighters that he wanted to join them, but at first they had doubts about him and did not give him a weapon. Their attitude changed when Ahmed endured a heavy bombardment without flinching and he was given a gun. He quickly became a friend of the rebels and their commander.

The fighting intensified and there was a continual drain of casualties as the anti-Gaddafi fighters pushed deeper into Sirte. 'The first time Ahmed got close to death was during the battle for the hotel,' says Enrico. 'We drove into an ambush and had to fight for our lives for two hours.' They were eventually rescued by another rebel unit with heavy weapons. On 7 October there was a heavy exchange of fire between mortars and rocket-propelled grenade launchers on both sides. As the group fell back at nightfall, a mortar bomb landed close, killing one man and wounding others. 'One of the wounded was Ahmed,' Enrico recalls. 'He was lightly wounded in the head and was in shock, but was back in the front line the next morning.'

The rebel fighters suffered severe losses. One of the first to be killed was called Fatee from Tobruk who was a friend of Enrico and Ahmed. He was carried back with a bullet through his head. Ahmed had tears in his eyes. The rebel commander ordered an attack to get at the snipers. The last Enrico saw of Ahmed was him leading five or six fighters into a district of Sirte called Medina. After a day of heavy fighting, Enrico had returned to the rebel camp when Tharouni came up to him and said, 'I am sorry about Ahmed.' He had been shot through the head by a sniper. Another fighter who tried to rescue him was also killed.

Ahmed was declared a martyr by his unit and his body was taken back to Tripoli. He had got his wish to fight in the revolution against Gaddafi, but he was never motivated by blood lust or a desire for revenge. 'He was a strange fighter,' says Enrico. 'I never saw him fire any bullets. He would shoot only to save his life, saying he wanted to capture Gaddafi loyalists and there was no need to kill anybody if you were not in danger.'

Ahmed Abdullah al-Ghadamsi, born Tripoli 31 December, 1978, died Sirte 9 October 2011.

TEN

The 'Somalianisation' of Libya

Libya, 2012–14

7 July 2012

Libyans are voting in their first democratic election to choose an interim national assembly to rule the country after the overthrow of Muammar Gaddafi. International interest in this crucial election has been sparse compared to the wall-to-wall coverage by the foreign media during the eight-month war.

Last week Amnesty International produced a devastating report—'Libya: Rule of Law or Rule of Militias?'—based on meticulous and lengthy investigations, portraying Libya as a country where violent and predatory militia gangs have become the real power in the land. They jail, torture and kill individuals and persecute whole communities that oppose them now, did so in the past, or simply get in their way. A few actions by these out-of-control militiamen have gained publicity, such as taking over Tripoli airport, shooting up the convoy of the British ambassador in Benghazi, and arresting staff members of the International Criminal Court. But the widespread arbitrary detention and torture of people picked up at checkpoint by the *thuwwar* (revolutionaries) is not publicised because the Libyan government wants to play them down, or people are frightened of criticising the perpetrators and becoming targets.

Take the case of Hasna Shaeeb, a 31-year-old woman abducted from her Tripoli home last October by men in military dress and taken to the former Islamic Endowment Office in the capital. She was accused of being a pro-Gaddafi loyalist and a sniper. She was forced to sit in a chair with her hands handcuffed behind her back and was given electric shocks to her right leg, private parts, and head. Guards threatened to bring her mother to the cell and rape her, and urine was poured over her. After she was freed from the chair, her torturers could not open her handcuffs with a key so they shot them off her, fragments of metal cutting into her flesh. On being released after three days, Shaeeb had a doctor confirm her injuries and complained to the authorities about what had happened to her. They did nothing, but she received a threatening phone call from the militiaman who first arrested her and shots were fired at her house.

Shaeeb's story is uncommon only in that she made an official complaint which many others are too frightened to do. They have reasons for their fear. The government estimates that it holds 3,000 detainees and the militias a further 4,000. The latter prisoners are almost invariably tortured to extract confessions. The Amnesty report says 'common methods of torture reported to the organisation include suspension in contorted positions and prolonged beatings with various objects including metal bars and chains, electric cables, wooden sticks, plastic hoses, water pipes, rifle-butts; and electric shocks.' Burning with cigarettes and hot metal is also used.

Diana Eltahawy, the Amnesty researcher who carried out many of the interviews on which the report is based, says that 'things are not getting better' and, what makes things worse, in May the ruling National Transitional Council passed a law giving immunity to the thuwwar for any act they carry out in defence of last year's revolution. The National Transitional Council has also decreed that interrogations by militias, though these very often involve torture, should carry legal weight.

Will a new government legitimised by the ballot box be able to rein in the militias and re-establish law and order? Or will Libya become like Lebanon during the civil war, when militias who had begun as defenders of their local community swiftly turned into gangsters running protection rackets? An advantage in Libya is that the population is almost entirely Sunni Muslim and there are not the same sectarian divisions as in Lebanon, Syria and Iraq. The Libyan government, unlike the Lebanese, has substantial oil revenues and could buy off the militias or build the state security forces to the point where they can establish order.

It might happen. For all the black propaganda of the recent war, Libya does not have the tradition of ferocious violence of Iraq and Syria. Gaddafi may have had a demented personality cult and run a nasty police state, but he never killed people on the scale of Saddam Hussein or Hafez al-Assad. The legacy of hatred is not quite so bad in Libya as in other countries where militias have established their rule. Many Libyans still hope that the thuwwar are only flourishing in the interregnum between the Gaddafi regime and a democratically elected successor government. Some still see the militiamen as heroes of the revolution (and many did fight heroically), even though it was NATO that destroyed the old regime.

A difficulty for foreign governments and media alike is that, having rejoiced in the overthrow of Gaddafi last year, they do not want bad news to besmirch their victory. Eltahawy says that part of the problem in getting people to pay attention to what is happening these days is that since the fall of Gaddafi 'Libya is always portrayed as a success story.'

3 September 2013

A little under two years ago, Philip Hammond, the defence secretary, urged British businessmen to begin 'packing their suitcases' and to fly to Libya to share in the reconstruction of the country and exploit an anticipated boom in natural resources. Yet now Libya has almost entirely stopped producing oil as the government loses control of much of the country to militia fighters.

Mutinying security men have taken over oil ports on the Mediterranean and are seeking to sell crude oil on the black market. Ali Zeidan, Libya's prime minister, has threatened to 'bomb from the air and the sea' any oil tanker trying to pick up the illicit crude from the oil terminal guards, who are mostly former rebels who have been on strike over low pay and alleged government corruption since July. In an escalating crisis little regarded hitherto outside the oil markets, output of Libya's prized high-quality crude oil has plunged from 1.4 million barrels a day earlier this year to just 160,000 barrels a day now. The strikers in the eastern region of Cyrenaica, which contains most of Libya's oil, are part of a broader movement seeking more autonomy and blaming the government for spending oil revenues in the west of the country.

Foreigners have mostly fled Benghazi since the American ambassador, Chris Stevens, was murdered in the US consulate by jihadi militiamen last September. Violence has worsened since then with Libya's military prosecutor Colonel Yussef Ali al-Asseifar, in charge of investigating assassinations of politicians, soldiers and journalists, himself assassinated by a bomb in his car on 29 August.

Libyans are increasingly at the mercy of militias which act outside the law. Popular protests against militiamen have been met with gunfire; 31 demonstrators were shot dead and many others wounded as they protested outside the barracks of the 'Libyan Shield Brigade' in Benghazi in June. Rule by local militias is also spreading anarchy around Tripoli. The interior minister, Mohammed al-Sheikh, resigned last month in frustration at being unable to do his job, saying in a memo sent to Zeidan that he blamed him for failing to build up the army and the police. He accused the government, which is largely dominated by the Muslim Brotherhood, of being weak and dependent on tribal support. Other critics point out that a war between two Libyan tribes, the Zawiya and the Wirrshifana, is going on just 15 miles from the prime minister's office.

10 October 2013

Seldom has the failure of a state been so openly and humiliatingly confirmed as happened in Libya this morning with the brief kidnapping of the prime minister Ali Zeidan. He was taken from his hotel in Tripoli by a militia allied to the government without a shot being fired. Despite his swift release, the message is very clear: Libya is imploding two years after the former Libyan leader Muammar Gaddafi was dragged from a drainage tunnel under a road and summarily shot.

The immediate cause for the prime minister's abduction was US secretary of state John Kerry's assertion that the Libyan government had prior information about the seizure of the al-Qa'ida suspect Abu Anas al-Libi at the weekend. Zeidan has now paid a price for his own compliance with the US and for Kerry's self-regarding boasts. A government that allows a foreign power to kidnap its own citizens on the streets of its capital is advertising to its people and the world that it can no longer fulfil the most basic function of any state, which is to protect its citizens.

Dramatic though the seizure of Zeidan is, it is in keeping with the course of events in Libya over the last two-and-a-half years. What is happening in Tripoli is a repeat of what had begun to happen earlier in Benghazi, the original centre of the uprising of 2011. As in the rest of Libya, the government's attempt to integrate the militias into its security forces has largely meant it paying armed men with their own agenda whom it does not control.

16 March 2014

The Libyan former prime minister Ali Zeidan fled last week after parliament voted him out of office. A North Korean–flagged oil tanker, the Morning Glory, illegally picked up a cargo of crude from rebels in the east of the country and sailed safely away, despite a government minister's threat that the vessel would be 'turned into a pile of metal' if it left port (the Libyan Navy blamed rough weather for its failure to stop the ship). Militias based in Misrata, western Libya, notorious for their violence and independence, have launched an offensive against the eastern rebels in what could be the opening shots in a civil war between western and eastern Libya. Without a central government with any real power, Libya is falling apart.

A striking feature of events in the past week is how little interest is being shown by leaders and countries which enthusiastically went to war in 2011 in the supposed interests of the Libyan people. President Barack Obama has since spoken proudly of his role in preventing a 'massacre' in Benghazi at that time. But when militiamen, whose victory NATO had assured, opened fire on a demonstration against their presence in Tripoli in November last year, killing at least 42 protesters and firing at children with anti-aircraft machine guns, there was scarcely a squeak of protest from Washington, London or Paris.

It is an old journalistic saying that if you want to find out government policy, imagine the worst thing they can do and then assume they are doing it. Such cynicism is not deserved in all cases, but it does seem to be a sure guide to Western policy towards Libya. This is not to defend Muammar Gaddafi, a maverick dictator who inflicted his puerile personality cult on his people. But the NATO powers that overthrew him—and by some accounts gave the orders to kill him—did not do so because he was a tyrannical ruler. It was rather because he pursued a quirkily nationalist agenda backed by a great deal of money which was at odds with Western policies in the Middle East. If the real objective of the war was to replace Gaddafi with a secular democracy, it is absurd that the West's regional allies in the conflict should have been theocratic absolute monarchies in Saudi Arabia and the Gulf.

Libyan militias hold 8,000 people in prisons, many of whom say they have been tortured. Some 40,000 people from the town of Tawergha south of Misrata have been driven from their homes which were destroyed. Libya is a land of regional, tribal, ethnic warlords who are often simply well-armed racketeers exploiting their power and the absence of an adequate police force. Nobody is safe: the head of Libya's military police was assassinated in Benghazi in October, while Libya's first post-Gaddafi prosecutor general was shot dead in Derna on 8 February. Sometimes the motive for the killing is obscure, such as the murder last week of an Indian doctor, also in Derna, which may lead to an exodus of 1,600 Indian doctors who have come to Libya since 2011 and on whom its health system depends.

Western and regional governments share responsibility for much that has happened in Libya, but so too should the media. The Libyan uprising was reported as a simple-minded clash between good and evil. The foreign media have dealt with the subsequent collapse of the Libyan state since 2011 mostly by ignoring it, though politicians have stopped referring to Libya as an exemplar of successful foreign intervention.

19 May 2014

Libya is tipping towards all-out civil war as rival militias take sides for and against an attempted coup led by a renegade general that has pushed the central government towards disintegration. Forces commanded by General Khalifa Haftar stormed the parliament building in Tripoli at the weekend, having earlier attacked Islamist militia camps in Benghazi. In a move likely to deepen the crisis, the army chief of staff, whose regular forces are weak and ill armed, called on Islamist-led militias to help preserve the government. Al-Qa'ida-type movements such as the Lions of Monotheism have pledged to resist General Haftar, a spokesman warning him on its website that 'you have entered a battle you will lose.'

The fighting has been the heaviest since the overthrow of Muammar Gaddafi in 2011 and there are signs that opposing militias and elements of the security forces in different parts of the country and with differing ideologies may be readying to fight a civil war. Paradoxically, both the militiamen attacking and defending the government are paid out of the national central budget.

Many people in Tripoli express sympathy with General Haftar's denunciations of the Islamic militias as the popular mood becomes increasingly desperate over the collapse of civil order and the state. But Haftar's forces are in practice just one more militia faction and dependent on his alliance with other militias. Nevertheless, Libyans express growing support for anybody who can restore order and public safety by whatever means necessary.

25 May 2014

Khalifa Haftar's slow-motion coup is gathering support but without making a decisive breakthrough. Surprise attacks by Haftar in Benghazi and Tripoli show that he has been able to gather more support than anybody had given him credit for from the Libyan armed forces and the militias; he was even able to deploy aircraft and helicopters against his opponents' positions. Thousands joined demonstrations across Libya on Friday in the biggest mass rallies since 2011 in support of Haftar, against the Islamic militias and in favour of the suspension of the Islamist-led parliament. Just how much foreign support he enjoys remains uncertain, but his denunciations of 'terrorism' and the Muslim Brotherhood are evidently geared to win the support of the US, Egypt and Saudi Arabia.

Will Libya go the same way as Egypt, where a vengeful old regime has been restored with the backing of the army and the all-embracing state machine? Or will different sides move from confrontation to all-out civil war, as in Syria? The present situation in Libya has elements of both scenarios but also has crucial differences because power has been so fragmented since the overthrow of Muammar Gaddafi in 2011. The opposition was never able to fill the vacuum left by his fall. Power is held primarily by rival militias, the most effective of which are based in Zintan and Misrata, which number an estimated 250,000, of whom a maximum of 30,000 fought against Gaddafi.

There are many centres of power: the Islamist parliament, its mandate looking shaky after postponing a new election to give itself a longer lifespan; a dysfunctional government that has appeased militias it is too weak to confront; Islamist groups and extreme Islamist groups; federalists and anti-federalists; surviving interests from the Gaddafi era. The incoherence of the numerous players in Libyan politics has spread disorder, but their very diversity means that so far nobody has been strong enough to risk a fight to the finish.

Thus the Qaaqaa and Sawaiq brigades from Zintan took over the parliament (the General National Congress) on behalf of Haftar a week ago but then withdrew. The speaker of parliament called in the Libya Central Shield from Misrata to defend the General National Congress and its forces arrived in Tripoli on Thursday but there was no fighting. The government is now calling for all these militias to leave the capital. In Benghazi, the complex struggle between the different factions is still being fought at the level of individual killings: last week the assistant commander of military

intelligence, Hamza al-Mahmoudi, was found shot dead. With no tradition of extreme violence, up to now Libya's road to ruin has been relatively
low on casualties, but this could change very swiftly if present stand-offs
switch to military confrontations.

The uprisings in Libya and elsewhere in the Middle East had deep and
unavoidable weaknesses from day one but some of these were self-inflicted.
They believed too much of their own propaganda and saw the ills of their
countries as being solely the result of the corruption and incompetence of
the old regimes. They had a black-and-white vision which demonised their
opponents and allowed no compromise after victory—last year, Libyans
who had worked for Gaddafi, even those who had turned against him years
ago, were told they were going to be sacked.

2 November 2014

Remember the time when Libya was being held up by the American,
British, French and Qatari governments as a striking example of benign
and successful foreign intervention? It is worth looking again at film of
David Cameron grandstanding as liberator in Benghazi in September 2011
as he applauds the overthrow of Muammar Gaddafi and tells the crowd
that 'your city was an example to the world as you threw off a dictator and
chose freedom.' Cameron has not been back to Benghazi, nor is he likely to
do so as warring militias reduce Libya to primal anarchy in which nobody
is safe. The majority of Libyans are demonstrably worse off today than they
were under Gaddafi, notwithstanding his authoritarian rule. The slaughter
is getting worse by the month and is engulfing the entire country.

'Your friends in Britain and France will stand with you as you build your
democracy,' pledged Cameron to the people of Benghazi. Three years later,
foreign governments have good reason to forget what they said and did in
Libya in 2011, because the aftermath of the overthrow of Gaddafi has been
so appalling. Without the rest of the world paying much attention, a civil
war has been raging in western Libya since 13 July between the Libya Dawn
coalition of militias, originally based in Misrata, and another militia group
centred on Zintan. A largely separate civil war between the forces of retired
General Khalifa Haftar and the Shura Council of Benghazi Revolutionaries
is being fought out in Benghazi. Government has collapsed.

It is easy enough to deride the neo-imperial posturing of David
Cameron and Nicolas Sarkozy, or to describe the abyss into which Libya
has fallen since 2011. The people whom that intervention propelled into

power have reduced a country that had been peaceful for more than half a century to a level of violence that is beginning to approach that of Syria, Iraq and Afghanistan. Whatever Western intentions, the result has been a disaster.

ELEVEN

Yemen in the Crossfire

Yemen, 2009–15

By the summer of 2015 some 80 per cent of Yemen's 25 million population was in need of food, drinking water and medical aid. A country—already the poorest in the Arab world—was being crushed by Saudi air strikes and a tight economic blockade sealing off the country from the rest of the world. In ground fighting, the Houthis, a Zaidi Shia rebel movement, remained largely in control as Yemen was ripped apart by a savage civil war that the rest of the world showed little interest in stopping.

Power in Yemen has always been divided between parties, regions and tribes, and presided over by a weak central government, though the country has never wholly fractured. But since the Saudi bombing campaign began Yemen has become part of a wider conflict, sucked into the regional confrontation between a Saudi-led Sunni coalition and its Iranian-led Shia counterpart. Yemenis understandably but vainly protest that Sunni–Shia relations in Yemen have never before been a dominant feature of the country's political landscape.

It is sad to recall that not so long ago the impact in Yemen of the Arab Spring uprising of 2011 was seen as benign. The largely peaceful transfer of power from long-serving President Ali Abdullah Saleh to his successor, Abed Rabbo Mansour Hadi, was held up as an example to other states facing similar problems. But the idea that a stable balance of power had been established was a delusion. The first time I went to Yemen in 1978 Saleh was newly established as president, but people in the Yemeni capital Sanaa did not give much for his chances, one woman winning a bet by saying that he might stay as long as six weeks. The true answer turned out to be 33 years and it was only in 2012 that

Hadi, his vice president for 17 years, replaced him. Yemeni politics are com-
plicated, but over the course of the next three years Yemen shared similarities
with Iraq after the overthrow of Saddam Hussein and Libya after Muammar
Gaddafi in that the removal of a powerful ruler, greeted at the time as a victory
for democracy, had in fact created a dangerous power vacuum but had otherwise
solved nothing.

Central government, always feeble in Yemen, was crippled. Worse, newly
appointed President Hadi swiftly adopted authoritarian ways but was never
fully in charge. Saleh might nominally have departed, but he and his family
still controlled many of the levers of power such as much of the Yemeni armed
forces. Hadi's new regime unwisely sought to exclude or marginalise too many
important players, notably supporters of Saleh and the Houthi movement which
could field tens of thousands of battle-hardened militiamen. Without support
from the army and under relentless attack from the Houthis, Hadi put up only
feeble resistance and eventually fled into exile in Saudi Arabia.

There are few gainers from this war aside from al-Qa'ida in the Arabian
Peninsula (AQAP), against whom the US has been using drones since 2002.
Washington periodically exults at having eliminated some AQAP leader, post-
humously described as a lethal threat to America. In practice, the drone war
has had little connection with the real world. AQAP today, deftly using the
opportunities provided by war, is stronger than ever.

31 December 2009
We are the Awaleq
Born of bitterness
We are the nails that go into the rock
We are the sparks of hell
He who defies us will be burned

This is the tribal chant of the powerful Awaleq tribe of Yemen, in which
they bid defiance to the world. Its angry tone conveys the flavour of Yemeni
life and it should give pause to those in the US who blithely suggest greater
American involvement in Yemen in the wake of the attempt to destroy a
US plane by a Nigerian student who says he received training there.

Yemen has always been a dangerous place. Wonderfully beautiful, the
mountainous north of the country is guerrilla paradise. The Yemenis are
exceptionally hospitable, though this has its limits. For instance, the Kazam
tribe east of Aden are generous to passing strangers, but deem the laws of

hospitality to lapse when the stranger leaves their tribal territory, at which time he becomes 'a good back to shoot at'.

The Awaleq and Kazam tribes are not exotic survivals on the margins of Yemeni society but are both politically important and influential. The strength of the central government in the capital, Sanaa, is limited and it generally avoids direct confrontations with tribal confederations, tribes, clans and powerful families. Almost everybody has a gun, usually at least an AK-47 assault rifle, but tribesmen often own heavier armament.

I have always loved the country. It is physically very beautiful with cut-stone villages perched on mountain tops on the sides of which are cut hundreds of terraces, making the country look like an exaggerated Tuscan landscape. Yemenis are intelligent, humorous, sociable and democratic, infinitely preferable as company to the arrogant and ignorant playboys of the Arab oil states in the rest of the Arabian Peninsula.

It is very much a country of direct action. Once when I was there a Chinese engineer was kidnapped as he drove along the main road linking Sanaa to Aden. The motives of the kidnappers were peculiar. It turned out they came from a beekeeping tribe (Yemen is famous for its honey) whose bees live in hives inside hollow logs placed on metal stilts to protect them from ants. The police had raided the tribe's village and had damaged hives for which the owners were demanding compensation. The government had been slow in paying up so the tribesmen had decided to draw attention to their grievance by kidnapping the next foreigner on the main road and this turned out to be the Chinese engineer.

Yemen is a mosaic of conflicting authorities, though this authority may be confined to a few villages. Larger communities include the Shia in the north of the country near Saada, with whom the government has been fighting a fierce little civil war. The unification of North and South Yemen in 1990 has never wholly gelled and the government is wary of southern secessionism. Its ability to buy off its opponents is also under threat as oil revenues fall, with the few oil fields beginning to run dry.

It is in this fascinating but dangerous land that President Barack Obama is planning to increase US political and military involvement. Joint operations will be carried out by the US and Yemeni military. There will be American drone attacks on hamlets where al-Qa'ida supposedly has its bases. There is ominous use by American politicians and commentators of the phrase 'failed state' in relation to Yemen, as if this somehow legitimises foreign intervention. It is extraordinary that the US political elite has never taken on board that its greatest defeats have been in just such 'failed states', not least Lebanon in 1982, when 240 US Marines were blown up; Somalia in the early 1990s when the body of a US helicopter pilot was dragged through the streets; Iraq after the overthrow of Saddam Hussein; and Afghanistan after the supposed fall of the Taliban.

Yemen has all the explosive ingredients of Lebanon, Somalia, Iraq and Afghanistan. But the arch-hawk Senator Joe Lieberman, chairman of the Senate Committee on Homeland Security, was happily confirming this week that the Green Berets and the US Special Forces are already there. He cited with approval an American official in Sanaa as telling him that, 'Iraq was yesterday's war. Afghanistan is today's war. If you don't act pre-emptively Yemen will be tomorrow's war.' In practice pre-emptive strikes are likely to bring a US military entanglement in Yemen even closer.

The US will get entangled because the Yemeni government will want to manipulate US action in its own interests and to preserve its wilting authority. It has long been trying to frame the Shia rebels in north Yemen as Iranian cats-paws in order to secure American and Saudi support. As for al-Qa'ida in the Arabian Peninsula, it probably only has a few hundred activists in Yemen, but the government of long-time Yemeni president Ali Abdullah Saleh will portray his diverse opponents as somehow linked to al-Qa'ida.

In Yemen the US will be intervening on one side in a country which is always in danger of sliding into a civil war. This has happened before. In Iraq the US was the supporter of the Shia Arabs and Kurds against the Sunni Arabs. In Afghanistan it is the ally of the Tajiks, Uzbeks and Hazara against the Pashtun community. Whatever the intentions of Washington, its participation in these civil conflicts destabilises the country because one side becomes labelled as the quisling supporter of a foreign invader. Communal and nationalist antipathies combine to create a lethal blend.

Despite sectarian, ethnic and tribal loyalties in the countries where the US has intervened in the Middle East, they usually have a strong sense of national identity. Yemenis are highly conscious of their own nationality and their identity as Arabs. One of the reasons the country is so miserably poor, with almost half its people trying to live on $2 a day, is that in 1990 Yemen refused to join the war against Iraq, and Saudi Arabia consequently expelled 850,000 Yemeni workers.

It is extraordinary to see the US begin to make the same mistakes in Yemen as it previously made in Afghanistan and Iraq. What it is doing is much to al-Qa'ida's advantage. The real strength of al-Qa'ida is not that it can 'train' a fanatical Nigerian student to sew explosives into his under-pants, but that it can provoke an exaggerated US response to every botched attack. Al-Qa'ida leaders openly admitted at the time of 9/11 that the aim of such operations is to provoke the US into direct military intervention in Muslim countries.

In Yemen the US is walking into the al-Qa'ida trap. Once there it will face the same dilemma it faces in Iraq and Afghanistan. It became impossible to exit these conflicts because the loss of face would be too great. Just as Washington saved banks and insurance giants from bankruptcy in 2008 because they were 'too big to fail', so these wars become too important to lose because to do so would damage the US claim to be the sole superpower.

In Iraq the US is getting out more easily than seemed likely at one stage because Washington has persuaded Americans that they won a non-existent success. The ultimate US exit from Afghanistan may eventually be along very similar lines. But the danger of claiming spurious victories is that such distortions of history make it impossible for the US to learn from past mistakes and instead it repeats them by fresh interventions in countries like Yemen.

10 January 2010

Al-Qa'ida has always had some activists in Yemen. In 2000, they rammed the USS Cole in Aden's harbour with a boat packed with explosives and ripped a hole in its hull, killing 17 American sailors. The Yemeni government agreed to a secret truce with the group, under which it was not pursued if it carried out no more attacks. In 2006, al-Qa'ida began to reorganise in Yemen when 23 of its militants escaped from Sanaa jail. And as al-Qa'ida members came under greater pressure in Saudi Arabia, some fled to Yemen and set up a joint Saudi–Yemeni movement, al-Qa'ida in the Arabian Peninsula (AQAP). The number of active members of AQAP in Yemen is small, only 200 to 300 lightly armed militants in a country of 22 million people.

It is easy to see why AQAP finds Yemen a hospitable place. It is not a country where the state expects to have a monopoly of violence or authority. There are an estimated 60 million weapons in Yemen, almost three times the population. Long before 9/11, I used to be intrigued by the Yemeni authorities' attitude to personal weapons as exemplified by security measures at Sanaa airport. These were very strict, with all luggage x-rayed before being allowed into the airport building and x-rayed again at each stage of its journey to the plane. Passengers were given frequent body searches until they reached the departure lounge, where, as in most airports, shops sold local handicrafts and curios to travellers. The difference in Sanaa airport was that many of these items turned out to be swords and long curved knives. Discovering to their horror that many passengers were carrying such weapons, Western airlines had to get their own flight crews to ask Yemenis, as they boarded the plane, if they were armed. Yemenis found it a strange question, but dutifully handed over their daggers to be placed in plastic bags in the hold of the aircraft.

The US and Britain are about to increase their support for a government which is highly unpopular and engaged in a series of actual or potential civil wars. The heaviest fighting so far has been with the Zaidi Shia insurgents just south of the border with Saudi Arabia. They claim they are fighting discrimination and are responding to President Ali Abdullah Saleh's dependence on Saudi Arabia and its extreme Sunni Wahhabism. President Saleh has been portraying the Shia rebels as pawns of Iran, although his government has produced no evidence for this.

The dilemma for the US and Britain is that, as they become more openly supportive of the Yemeni government, they will be targeted as its sponsors by its many enemies. The south of the country, independent until 1990 and defeated in a civil war in 1994, is seething with rebellion. Government forces shoot at protesters. There have been many shootings and arrests, and torture is endemic. 'They can make a zebra say it is a gazelle' is a chilling Yemeni saying of the government's interrogation methods.

Southern newspapers have been shut down, including *Al Ayyam*, which is the most widely read. Hisham Bashraheel, its 66-year-old editor, was arrested last Wednesday at his newspaper office in the Crater district of Aden, after a protest against its closure last May when the paper was accused of supporting separatism. Some 30 protesters and 20 guards had fought a battle with the police in which one policeman and one guard were killed. They later gave themselves up.

I met Bashraheel in the cluttered office of *Al Ayyam* some years ago when he was already engaged in daily skirmishes with the authorities. Sitting on a chair in his office was a man called Abdul Hakim Mahyub, with a long scar down the side of his face, to whom Bashraheel introduced me. He said Mahyub's story of how he came by the scar explained a lot about current tensions between north and south in Yemen. Mahyub said he was a teacher in Aden and several weeks earlier he had an argument with a man laying pipes outside his school. As is common in Yemen, the pipe-layer had a knife in his belt. In the course of the argument, he drew it and stabbed Mahyub in the face, cutting through his cheek and into his tongue. His speech was affected and he found it difficult to continue teaching, but the reason he had come to Al Ayyam to complain was that he had just heard that the man who stabbed him, who came from Marib in northern Yemen, had been released by an official from the same province. Bashraheel said that favouritism towards northerners was becoming very common, but for publishing Mahyub's story he risked being accused of 'separatism' and stirring up hostility between north and south.

The US and Britain will face a similar difficulty in Yemen as they already do in Afghanistan. They will be supporting an unpopular and corrupt government. It is not that al-Qa'ida is strong, but that it is swimming in sympathetic waters because the government is weak. The government can see the danger of being labelled as an American pawn if it is too openly welcoming to foreign military aid. 'Any intervention or direct military action by the US could strengthen the al-Qa'ida network, not weaken it,' the deputy prime minister for defence and security affairs, Rashad al-Alimi, said last week. The government would have liked to take all the aid it could get but without telling anybody.

All this sounds like Afghanistan. And there is a further way in which the two countries resemble each other. Just as Pakistan believes it is crucially affected by what happens in Afghanistan, so Saudi Arabia regards the future of Yemen as a vital interest. Saudi Arabia is by far the most important foreign power in Yemen, providing $2 billion in budget support, but its interest has always been in a weak government in Sanaa over which it can exercise some control.

The only way that the US and Britain could squeeze out al-Qa'ida from Yemen entirely is by strengthening the armed forces to the point at which the central government could take over parts of the country it has not ruled for decades. But this would provoke communities that exist in a state of semi-independence from the state. As in Afghanistan, foreign intervention in Yemen would soon create a counter-reaction of which al-Qa'ida would be able to take advantage.

22 March 2011

It looks as if Yemen will be the third country in the Arab world after Tunisia and Egypt to see a change of regime as a result of Arab Spring street protests. President Ali Abdullah Saleh is visibly failing to cling on to power. Following a massacre of demonstrators by pro-government snipers in Sanaa last Friday, in which 52 died and 250 were wounded, military commanders are defecting and sending their tanks to protect protesters in the streets. The 'Friday Massacre' has not intimidated the opposition, but has led to many senior officials deserting the government. As military units take different sides there is the possibility of civil war, though the Yemeni elite has long experience of defusing armed confrontations. President Saleh and his family could fight it out, and have placed tanks to protect the presidential palace, but the odds against them are stacking up.

Saleh's errors since demonstrations started in Yemen in early February are very similar to President Hosni Mubarak's in Egypt. He offered change and said he would not run again for the presidency, but refused to step down. The regime used thugs to intimidate its opponents, and made the unlikely claim that it was the young demonstrators who were doing the shooting. It tried to get control of the local and foreign press. This culminated in the massacre last Friday that has probably ensured that President Saleh will go in the short rather than the long term.

1 October 2011

The killing of Anwar al-Awlaki by a US drone in Yemen is significant, unlike that of other al-Qa'ida operatives, because he was one the few effective propagandists in the group. He did not direct bomb makers, but his sermons inspired Muslims to violent action. No other figure in al-Qa'ida had the same power with words as US-born, Yemen-based Awlaki, who could speak in fluent English. In his YouTube lectures he talks with an easygoing and confident clarity.

In 2010, his words led a 21-year-old student in Britain called Roshonara Choudhry to stab and wound a member of parliament who had supported the Iraq war. She later told police that she had decided to act, without consulting anybody, after listening to Awlaki's lectures on the internet for 100 hours. 'I told no one. No one else would have understood,' she said.

A further reason for the US to be pleased by Awlaki's death is that the group to which he was affiliated, AQAP, was genuinely interested in striking at US targets. It may seem self-evident that al-Qa'ida is chiefly devoted to a holy war against non-Muslim great powers, but it is by no means the case, even if this was the aim of Osama bin Laden and Ayman al-Zawahiri. The most powerful al-Qa'ida franchisees, notably in Iraq and, to a lesser extent, Pakistan, have shown much more interest in attacking local targets, often Shia whom they see as heretics, than the US. But al-Qa'ida in Yemen has always been orientated towards assaults on US targets. It was from his base in Yemen that Awlaki influenced Major Nidal Malik Hassan, the army psychiatrist who carried out the shootings at the US Army base at Fort Hood, Texas, in which 13 people were killed in 2009.

Al-Qa'ida will probably be less weakened by the death of al-Awlaki than would be expected, mainly because it was never the structured guerrilla army that was portrayed by the Pentagon, CIA and the media. It has by now a highly depleted leadership cadre, but its significance in recent years has mostly been symbolic.

There was much optimism earlier in the year, as regimes toppled in Egypt and Tunisia, that al-Qa'ida would wither away. Islamists in North Africa now had many other options for action than taking up arms and, if they did take arms, it may not have been against the US and its friends. The indestructibility of dictators such as President Hosni Mubarak no longer seemed to be guaranteed by Washington and there was less reason to strike at US targets than 10 years earlier. This argument is partly true. There is less and less incentive for local insurgencies to adopt the al-Qa'ida franchise and many reasons for them not to invite US hostility. Al-Qa'ida's former allies in Libya are now part of the NATO-backed government in Tripoli. Al-Qa'ida itself is far less popular than it once was in countries such as Jordan after it started making attacks within the country against Jordanians.

At the same time, President Obama's full-blown support for Israel and the US military presence in Afghanistan means that the anti-American motivation of Jihadi groups will not disappear. Al-Qa'ida itself may become weaker and weaker, but its tactics and also its aims may start to be adopted by other, less identifiable, groups.

5 April 2015

The Saudi-led military intervention in Yemen, which the Saudi Air Force began bombing on 26 March, is code named Operation Decisive Storm. This is probably an indication of what Saudi Arabia and its allies would like to happen, rather than what will actually occur. Foreign states that go to war in Yemen usually come to regret it.

The Saudis are portraying their devastating air war as being provoked by the advance through Yemen of the Houthis, who belong to a Shia branch known as the Zaidi sect. In September, the Houthis captured the capital

Sanaa and have been pushing south against Sunni tribes ever since. The Yemeni government, always weak, has virtually collapsed, with President Abed Rabbo Mansour Hadi—who took over the presidency after Ali Abdullah Saleh ceded power in February 2012—exercising little authority since the Houthis took the capital.

The Saudis characterise the Houthis as Iranian-backed Shia Zaidis trying to take over the country. Much of this is propaganda. About a third of Yemenis are reckoned to belong to the Zaidi sect, which dominated the country for 1,000 years before the revolution of 1962. But the Zaidis are very different Shia from those in Iran and Iraq, and are not always seen by the Shia in other countries as part of their religious community. In the past, there has been little Sunni–Shia sectarianism in Yemen, but the Saudi determination to frame the conflict in sectarian terms may be self-fulfilling. By leading a Sunni coalition, Saudi Arabia will internationalise the Yemen conflict and emphasise its sectarian dimension.

The confrontation between Sunni and Shia, and between Saudi Arabia with its allies and Iran with its allies, is becoming deeper and more militarised. Conflicts cross-infect and exacerbate each other, preventing solutions to individual issues. Thus Saudi intervention in Yemen reduces the chance of a US–Iranian agreement on Tehran's nuclear programme and sanctions. The US position becomes even more convoluted: it is supporting Sunni powers and opposing Iranian allies in Yemen but doing the reverse in Iraq.

A decisive outcome is the least likely prospect for Yemen, just as it has long been in Iraq and Afghanistan. A political feature common to all three countries is that power is divided between so many players it is impossible to defeat or placate them all for very long.

12 April 2015

The ghost of Osama bin Laden will be chuckling this month as he watches the movements he inspired conquer swaths of the Middle East. He will be particularly gratified to see fighters from AQAP storm into Al Mukalla, the capital of Yemen's eastern province of Hadhramaut from which the bin Laden family originated before making their fortune in Saudi Arabia. Yemeni government soldiers abandoned their bases, leaving US Humvees and other military equipment. Earlier, AQAP had seized the central prison in the city and freed 300 prisoners, including Khaled Batarfi, one of the most important jihadi leaders in Yemen.

It is a measure of the severity of the multiple crises engulfing the region that AQAP, previously said by the US to be the most dangerous branch of al-Qa'ida, can capture a provincial capital without attracting more than cursory attention in the outside world. How different it was on 2 May 2011 when President Obama and much of his administration had themselves pictured watching the helicopter raid on Abbottabad, Pakistan where bin Laden was killed. The grandstanding gave the impression that his death meant that the perpetrators of 9/11 had finally been defeated. But look at the map today as unitary Muslim states dissolve or weaken from the north-west frontier of Pakistan to the north-east corner of Nigeria. The beneficiaries are al-Qa'ida or al-Qa'ida inspired groups which are growing in power and influence. The US and its allies recognise this, but cannot work out how to prevent it.

'It's always easier to conduct counter-terrorism when there's a stable government in place,' said the US defence secretary Ashton Carter, rather plaintively, last week. 'That circumstance obviously doesn't exist in Yemen.' You can say that again. Carter sounded a little put out that 'terrorists' have not chosen well-ordered countries such as Denmark or Canada in which to base themselves, and are instead operating in anarchic places like Yemen, Iraq, Syria, Libya and Somalia where there is no government to stop them. Suddenly, the drone war supposedly targeting leaders and supporters of al-Qa'ida in Yemen, Pakistan and Somalia is exposed as the politically convenient irrelevance it always was. In fact, it was worse than an irrelevance, because the use of drones, and periodic announcements about the great success they were having, masked America's failure to develop an effective policy for destroying al-Qa'ida in the years since 9/11.

For all the billions of dollars spent on security, the tedious searches at airports, the restrictions on civil liberties, tolerance of torture—not to mention the wars in Iraq and Afghanistan—the so-called 'war on terror' is being very publicly lost. The heirs of 9/11 are far stronger than ever. There are now seven wars going on in Muslim countries between Pakistan and Nigeria and in all of them al-Qa'ida-type movements are gaining in strength or are already strong. These movements are not being targeted effectively despite their many enemies. This failure can best be explained by a saying popular a few months ago among Western politicians and diplomats to explain their policy in Syria and Iraq: 'The enemy of my enemy is not necessarily my friend.' Few of those who pronounced these glib words had thought them through or appreciated that, if this was indeed the policy of the US, Britain and their allies, then there is no way the Islamic State,

Jabhat al-Nusra or AQAP can be defeated. In Yemen, the Houthis are the strongest military force opposing AQAP, but since the US supports Saudi Arabia in its air campaign against the Houthis it is ensuring a situation in which AQAP will be able to expand.

23 April 2015

The course of the Saudi air war has been very similar to successive Israeli bombardments of Lebanon and Gaza over the past 20 years. First, there are bloodcurdling claims of how the enemy will be defeated by airpower alone. Then, it becomes clear that air strikes are doing a lot of damage to civilians —944 Yemenis have been killed and 3,487 wounded so far, according to the World Health Organisation—but are not having a decisive impact on opposing military forces. Finally, there are mounting demands for an end to the air war from foreign countries, notably the US, which has aided the Saudi Air Force with intelligence and logistics.

Saudi Arabia is facing frustration at its lack of real achievement. The Houthis have not been forced to retreat at any point. They have full control of Sanaa and are fighting in Aden. They have many opponents inside Yemen, but in Sanaa and the northern part of the country people are appalled by the damage and casualties caused by what they see as indiscriminate air strikes. By fleeing to Saudi Arabia and endorsing the bombing, President Abed Rabbo Mansur Hadi, the man whom the Saudis are supposedly trying to restore to power, has discredited himself.

It had never been quite clear what the Saudis intended to achieve by this campaign that seems to be an exaggerated response to factional battles within Yemen. They claim that the Houthis are the proxies of Iran but this is widely seen as propaganda or an exaggeration, though it may be self-fulfilling since, under pressure, the Houthis will look for foreign allies. A further motive may be domestic Saudi politics as the new King Salman and his son Mohammed, the defence minister and chief of the royal court, look for a small successful war to compensate for the frustration of Saudi policy in Iraq and Syria where Iran has outmanoeuvred its regional rival. Iran has provided political and humanitarian support to the Houthis, but both Tehran and the rebels deny it has armed them.

The crisis in Yemen has got a lot worse as a result of the Saudi air war. Yemen has always been only loosely controlled from the centre and the war has exacerbated and militarised divisions. Protagonists are not always what they seem. Fighters reported as being supporters of President Hadi in Aden appear rather to be south Yemeni separatists who want to reverse the unity with the north agreed to in 1990.

26 April 2015

Yemeni politics is notoriously complicated and exotic, with shifting alliances in which former enemies embrace and old friends make strenuous efforts to kill each other. The reality of what is currently happening in Yemen is very different from the way it is presented. The Saudis allege that they are crushing a takeover of Yemen by the Houthi Shia militia backed by Iran, and intend to return the legitimate president, Abed Rabbo Mansour Hadi, to power. In fact, the Houthis' seizure of so much of Yemen over the past year has little to do with Iran. It has much more to do with their alliance with their old enemy, former president Ali Abdullah Saleh, who still controls much of the Yemeni Army. This enabled the Houthis, whose strongholds are in the north of the country, to capture Sanaa easily last September, which UN experts note 'was guarded by no less than 100,000 Republican Guards and Reserve Forces, most of them loyal to the former president'.

The Saudi air campaign is geared more to inflicting severe damage on the units of the Yemen Army loyal to Saleh than it is to weakening the Houthis. The Houthi militiamen are experienced fighters, their military skills and ability to withstand air attack honed between 2004 and 2010, when they fought off six offensives launched by Saleh, who was then in power and closely allied to Saudi Arabia. It was only after Saleh was ousted from office in 2012 that he reconciled with the Houthis. The Saudi war aim is to break this alliance between the Houthis and the Saleh-controlled military units by destroying the army's bases and heavy weapons. The more lightly armed Houthis are less likely to be hard-hit by air strikes, but without the support or neutrality of the regular army they will be over-stretched in the provinces south of Sanaa. In Aden, they are fighting not so much Hadi-supporters, but southern separatists.

The problem with the Saudi strategy is the same as that with most military plans. The 19th-century German chief of staff, General Helmuth von Moltke, said that in war 'no plan survives contact with the enemy.' The same warning was pithily restated more recently by the American boxer Mike Tyson, who said that 'everybody has a plan until they get punched in the mouth.'

The danger for Saudi Arabia is that wars build up an uncontrollable momentum that transforms the political landscape in which they are conceived. Had the Saudis not intervened in Yemen, it is unlikely that in the long term the Houthis would have been able to dominate the country because they are opposed by so many regions, parties and tribes. Yemen is too divided for any single faction to win an outright victory. But the air war has been justified by Saudi Arabia to its own citizens and the Sunni world as a counter-attack against Iranian and Shia aggression. It will not be easy for Saudi Arabia to back off from these exaggerated claims to reach the sort of compromises required if Yemen is to return to peace.

AQAP has been one of the main beneficiaries of the militarisation of Yemeni politics, because it can present itself as the shock troops of the Sunni community and its fighters are no longer under pressure from the regular army. As many Iraqis, Syrians and Afghans have discovered to their cost, Sunni–Shia sectarian hatred and fear is often only one massacre away.

Yemen was in crisis even before the present conflict. According to UN agencies, malnutrition in Yemen is about the same as in much of sub-Saharan Africa and only half the population has access to clean water. The country imports 90 per cent of the grains used for food, but no ships are coming in because its ports are blockaded by the Saudis or caught up in the fighting. In any case it is difficult to move food supplies because of a chronic shortage of fuel. Lack of electricity means that essential medicines in hospitals cannot be stored.

This is not a short-term problem—Yemen is finally falling apart, but it may take a long time doing so, which means that there will be a vacuum of power. Yemen has endured many wars that the rest of the world has ignored, but this one may well prove uncontainable.

TWELVE

Sectarian Venom

Bahrain, 2011

In early April 2011 I was in Cairo trying to decide if I should go to Benghazi or Bahrain, both of which had been convulsed by the Arab Spring. Benghazi and eastern Libya had been seized by rebels trying to overthrow Muammar Gaddafi, while in Bahrain the ruling Sunni al-Khalifa monarchy, backed by Saudi troops, had moved on 15 March to crush mass protests by the island's Shia majority demanding democratic reform. There had been killings, mass arrests and torture. The focal point and symbol of the demonstrations, the Pearl Monument, had been demolished by bulldozers. Western powers, so shocked at possible reprisals by Gaddafi against the Libyan opposition, were largely mute when it came to repression in Bahrain, which they considered to be part of the Saudi sphere of influence.

After debating with myself about which direction to travel, I made the long drive to Benghazi, where the uprising was still in full swing, rather than Bahrain, where Sunni counter-revolution was evidently triumphant. Not that that there had ever been a revolution, but the al-Khalifas and their security forces behaved as if there had, torturing respected doctors in their 50s in a bid to get them to admit that they were agents of Iran. Sectarian hatred between Sunni and Shia became more envenomed across the Middle East and beyond over the next four years, but in Bahrain it was there from the beginning. Shia mosques, religious meeting houses and holy sites were razed to the ground. Riots continued in Shia villages and suburbs of the capital Manama after the initial crackdown, but the balance of power was so much in favour of the al-Kalifas and the security forces that there was never any doubt about the outcome.

I wrote a series of articles about a young woman, the poet Ayat al-Gormezi, who had been jailed and tortured for reciting a poem that allegedly insulted the Bahraini King. It was an opportunity to personalise and dramatise the pervasive mistreatment of anybody deemed to be a dissenter. Ayat was eventually released and in August I finally visited Bahrain, which was becoming increasingly difficult for journalists to enter, during a brief liberal interlude when an international report on the events of the uprising was published. I was struck by the almost palpable sense of Sunni–Shia hatred. The government was bringing in foreign Sunni from Pakistan, Jordan, Yemen and Iraq to man the security forces and fast-tracking their Bahraini citizenship. Job discrimination was growing and I met young Shia professionals who believed that they had no choice but to emigrate if they wanted employment. State sponsored demographic change was underway.

The protesters in Bahrain suffered from the disadvantage that I was not the only journalist in 2011 and later to decide that, interesting though Bahrain was, there were other more important stories to be covered in countries like Libya, Iraq and Syria. Over the next four years individuals in Bahrain might be shot or mistreated, but this was overshadowed by the slaughter taking place in Iraq and Syria and, from early 2015, in Yemen. The US and Britain were relieved to find that they were not under much pressure to explain their tolerance of repression in Bahrain, where they hypocritically claimed to be supporting a reform process that nobody else believed was taking place.

Events in Bahrain might be ignored in the West, but they did help further poison relations between Sunni and Shia in the Islamic world. In Iraq and Iran the ongoing Shia street protests were widely covered on television. The clampdown on all opponents of the status quo grew ever more severe, with Sheikh Ali Salman, the leader of al-Wafq, the main opposition, jailed in 2015. There was growing evidence that Islamic State had established cells among hardline Sunni members of the Bahrain security forces. As elsewhere in the Middle East, the effect of the Arab Spring was to provoke a reaction that much increased the level of oppression and violence.

2 June 2011

'We are the people who will kill humiliation and assassinate misery,' a film captures Ayat al-Gormezi telling a cheering crowd of protesters in Pearl Square in February. 'We are the people who will destroy the foundation of injustice.' The 20-year-old poet and student addresses King Hamad bin Isa al-Khalifa directly and says to him: 'Don't you hear their cries, don't you hear their screams?' As she finishes, the crowd shouts: 'Down with Hamad.'

Ayat's call for change was no more radical than that heard in the streets of Tunis, Cairo and Benghazi at about the same time. But her reference to the king might explain the fury shown by the Bahraini security forces who, going by photographs of the scene, smashed up her bedroom when they raided her parents' house and could not find her. Ayat was forced to turn herself in when masked policemen threatened to kill her brothers unless she did so. One policeman shouted at her father to 'tell us where Ayat is or we will kill each of your sons in front of your eyes.'

Masked police and special riot police later took Ayat away, telling her mother that her daughter would be interrogated. She has not been seen since her arrest two months ago, though her mother did talk to her once by phone and Ayat said that she had been forced to sign a false confession. Her mother has since been told that her daughter has been in a military hospital after being tortured. She is due to go on trial today before a military tribunal, her mother says.

11 June 2011

Bahraini security forces beat the detained poet Ayat al-Gormezi across the face with electric cable and forced her to clean with her bare hands lavatories just used by police, members of her family say in a graphic account of the torture and humiliation suffered by those rounded up in the Gulf nation's crackdown on dissent.

The trainee teacher, who spent nine days in a tiny cell with the air conditioning turned to freezing, is due back in court this weekend on charges of inciting hatred, insulting the king and illegal assembly, and her family fears she may suffer further mistreatment in custody amid threats of another round of interrogation. Ayat's family only learned about her mistreatment, amounting to torture, when she spoke to them at her arraignment earlier this month. 'When she reached the interrogation centre in Manama she was put in the very small cell and kept there for nine days,' her mother, Sa'ada Hassan Ahmed, says. 'The beatings with electric cable made her lips swell up.' At times, Ayat thought the air conditioning in the cell was emitting some form of gas, which made her feel she was suffocating. Throughout this period the police made no real attempt to interrogate her.

Her family say the days after Ayat was taken away was a period of intense psychological torture. 'We knew nothing about what had happened to her though we heard rumours that she had been raped or killed,' her brother Yousif Mohammed says. Her mother went from police station to police station asking for news of Ayat, but learned nothing. Sa'ada was finally told by the police that she should file a missing persons report, though she complained that this was absurd since it was the police who had detained her daughter.

After nine days, Ayat was moved to Isa prison and, 15 days after she was first taken away, she was allowed to make a phone call to her parents telling them that she was alive. The physical torture stopped, but she was kept under psychological pressure. 'At some point', her mother says, 'she was forced to sign a document but she was blindfolded and did not know what it said.'

She was told to clean up other cells and the corridor of the bloc she was in but was allowed no contact with other prisoners. On several occasions she was taken back to the interrogation centre where she had first been held and a video was taken of her giving her name and saying that she was a Shia and she hated Sunni.

Asked for further details of Ayat's interrogation in Isa prison, her mother says she does not know because the family did not have long enough to talk when they met during the arraignment. They were told the previous day to bring a lawyer, though it is unclear how freely he was able to talk to his client. While Ayat was meeting her family during the arraignment, a policeman overheard her giving details of her mistreatment. He said that if she continued to do so, she would be returned to the interrogation centre and tortured again.

12 June 2011

Poet Ayat al-Gormezi has been sentenced to one year in prison. She was jailed by a security court without any legal argument or her lawyer being allowed to speak, according to a family member present at the trial. Her brother, Yousif Mohammed, says that her treatment in prison has improved in recent days, in contrast to the extreme mistreatment she received when she was first detained at the end of March. He attributes the change in the authorities' behaviour to the international publicity given to her case. The family has lodged an appeal against the sentence.

13 July 2011

Ayat al-Gormezi, jailed and tortured for reading a poem critical of the government at a pro-democracy rally, has been suddenly released—though her sentence has not been revoked. The international outcry over the mistreatment of the student probably led the government to free her. Ayat was greeted by cheering crowds in her neighbourhood near Hamad town outside the capital after her unexpected release. Her family say they are delighted that she is free although they are worried about her future. They fear that she might be re-arrested, as she has not been pardoned and her release was not the result of an appeal against her one-year sentence.

18 July 2011

Hers was the voice of a revolution. Released from prison last week, the 20-year-old poet Ayat al-Gormezi, a symbol of resistance for pro-democracy protesters, claims she was tortured in prison by a female member of Bahrain's royal family. Ayat says she was beaten with a baton by a woman whom prison guards identified as a member of the ruling al-Khalifa family. While her interrogators had tried to blindfold her, she says, she was able to see 'a woman of about 40 in civilian clothes who was beating me on the head with a baton.' Ayat later described her interrogator to guards, who, she says, promptly named the woman as being one of the al-Khalifas with a senior position in the Bahraini security service. Ayat adds: 'I was taken many times to her office for fresh beatings. She would say: "You should be proud of the al-Khalifas. They are not going to leave this country. It is their country."' The guards explained it was not the woman's regular job, but she had volunteered to question political detainees.

Ayat says she was most terrified by continuing threats from her interrogators that she would be sexually assaulted or raped. All the while, she was beaten on the head and the body until she lost consciousness. 'Many of the guards were Yemenis and Jordanians,' she says. The recruitment of members of the Bahraini security forces from foreign Sunni states is one of the grievances of Bahrain's Shia majority, which says it is excluded from such jobs.

Ayat does not regret reading her poem in Pearl Square, the centre of Bahrain's democratic protests in February and March. 'What I said was not a personal attack on the King or the prime minister, but I was just expressing what the people want. I have written poetry since I was a child, but not about politics. I did not think it was dangerous at the time. I was just expressing my opinion.'

Anybody supporting the protests was in danger of detention and torture. Ayat's family sent her to stay with relatives, which she 'did not want to do. But after two weeks the security forces threatened my family and I had to give myself up. As I was taken away in a car, my family were told to pick me up at a police station the following day, so they thought it was not serious.'

But her mistreatment started immediately. She says: 'There were four men and one woman in the car, all wearing balaclavas. They beat me and shouted: "You are going to be sexually assaulted! This is the last day of your life!" They also made anti-Shia remarks. I was terrified of being sexually assaulted or raped, but not of being beaten.'

The vehicle she was in, escorted by the army and police, did not immediately go to the interrogation centre but drove around Bahrain. Another woman, whom Ayat says was a member of the teachers' organisation, was arrested and put in the boot of the car. Eventually, it reached the interrogation centre, which evidently doubled as a prison. Ayat says the beatings never stopped: 'Once they told me to open my mouth and spat in it.'

The first night she was put in a tiny cell: 'It smelled awful and I could not sleep because of the screams of a man being tortured in the next cell.' The second night she was placed in another cell with the two vents for air conditioning producing freezing air. She was taken out for regular beatings. 'I was very frightened,' she says, 'but I did not think they would kill me because every time I lost consciousness from the beatings, they called a doctor.'

Surprisingly, for the first four or five days, the interrogators did not ask Ayat about reading out her poem in Pearl Square. They abused the Shia in general, saying they were 'bastards' and not properly married (the accusation stems from the Shia institution of temporary marriage and is often used as an insult by Sunni). 'When they did ask me about the poem, they kept saying: "Who asked you to write it? Who paid you to write it?"' They insisted she must have been ordered to write the poem by Shia leaders in Bahrain or was a member of a political group, which she denies. The interrogators also kept saying she must owe allegiance to Iran. An obsessive belief that Shia demands for equal rights in Bahrain must be orchestrated by Tehran has long been a central feature of Sunni conspiracy theorists. 'They kept asking me: "Why are you loyal to Iran? Why are you not loyal to your own country?" I said it was nothing to do with Iran. I am a Bahraini and I was only trying to express what the people want.'

After nine days, Ayat was taken to a second prison in Isa town in Bahrain. For a week she was in solitary confinement and was given medication so the signs of her beatings were less visible. She was then taken to a more general prison where physical mistreatment stopped and there were four other women. 'After 16 days they let me talk to my family,' she says. 'It was meant to be for three minutes but they let me talk for 10. Once they took me back to the first interrogation centre to record a video apologising to the King.' International protests and ensuing bad publicity for the Bahraini monarchy led to her treatment improving, according to her family. Last week she was called to an office in the prison and told she was to be released on the condition that she would not take part in any other protests.

20 July 2011

Allegations of torture against the Bahraini security forces made by the student poet Ayat al-Gormezi are to be investigated by a special committee of the interior ministry. Ayat's family say she was called to give a statement to the committee set up by the interior minister in response to my article about how she was treated in prison after her detention on 30 March.

3 August 2011

A young man, his face masked by a red cloth so that only his eyes are visible, strides at the head of a crowd of protesters down the street in the Shia village of Nuwaidrat in Bahrain. The people behind him look as if they expect a confrontation with the police. Some wave red-and-white Bahraini flags which have become the symbol of the pro-democracy protesters. 'Soon the police will start shooting,' warns an onlooker as two police vehicles screech to a halt at the entrance to the village. Soon afterwards we hear the thump of tear-gas canisters being fired.

Signs of revolt simmering just beneath the surface are everywhere in the island kingdom of Bahrain, five months after protesters first demanded reform. Inspired by the Arab Awakening, thousands of demonstrators took over Pearl Square in the centre of Manama, the capital. A month later, on 15 March, government security forces, backed by a military contingent from Saudi Arabia, drove out the protesters, bulldozed the square and launched a pogrom of extraordinary ferocity against the majority Shia community, which had supported the protests.

Bahrainis, both Shia and Sunni, are still traumatised. 'I was expecting the government to thank us for treating so many people during the crisis,' recalls one doctor of previously moderate political views, who instead found himself subjected to beatings and sleep deprivation.

A 64-year-old man, active in defence of human rights, named Mohammed Hassan Jawad, who is still in jail, gave details to his family about how interrogators had tortured him with electric shocks to his genitals, legs, ears and hands. They made him bow down before a picture of the Bahraini King, Hamad bin Isa al-Khalifa, and told him to open his mouth so they could spit in it, adding that 'unless you swallow the spit we will urinate in your mouth instead.' His family, allowed to see him for only brief supervised periods, noticed that his toenails were dead and black from the electric shocks.

Bahrain, with a population of 1.2 million, half of them Arabs, should have been the one place in the Arab world where compromise was possible between rulers and ruled, and between Sunni and Shia. Instead it has joined places like Beirut and Jerusalem, with communities polarised and hate and suspicion filling the air. The shock of what happened is all the greater because Bahrain regards itself as one of the most liberal and best-educated countries in the Gulf. Unlike nearby Saudi Arabia, women drive cars and hold important government jobs.

The simple explanation for the human disaster that is consuming Bahraini society is that the government over-reacted. The al-Khalifas felt their rule was under threat as long-established despots across the Arab world were overthrown. They treated moderate reformers as if they were professional revolutionaries. Without any evidence, the authorities demonised Iran as the hidden hand behind the demand by the Shia for an end to discrimination. 'The Sunni community here was told that it faced an existential threat and equal citizenship for Shia meant an end to the Sunni,' one Shia political activist says. They believed it.

Bahrain has always been divided between the Sunni ruling elite, centred on the al-Khalifa royal family, and the Shia, but since March this has turned into something closer to an anti-Shia pogrom. Evidence of official sectarianism is widespread. After watching the beginning of a riot in Nuwaidrat we drive to a quieter part of the village where 10 Shia mosques were destroyed three months ago. A local man, who is writing a history of Shia mosques and holy sites in the neighbourhood and does not want his name published, points to a heap of rubble saying 'this used to be the Momin mosque where 200 to 300 people worshipped. There has been a mosque here for 400 years.' He describes how, on 19 April, military and police surrounded the area and moved in with construction equipment. By the time they withdrew, 10 out of 17 Shia mosques in Nuwaidrat had been levelled. Mosques were not alone in being targeted. Shia revere the burial places of their holy men, but in two places in Nuwaidrat the graves have been dug up by soldiers or police. The local historian points to a hole in the ground, saying this was the site of the grave of a Shia holy man called Mohammed Abu Kharis, who died 200 years ago. 'They dug up his bones and threw them away,' he says.

The official explanation of the destruction of at least 35 Shia mosques and religious sites is that they had been built without permission. It seems unlikely that the government could suddenly have been possessed by an overwhelming desire to use the army and police to enforce building regulations. Many Shia suspect that the Saudis were behind the destruction, since this is in the tradition of Wahhabism, the fundamentalist version of Sunni Islam prevalent in Saudi Arabia. One Shia leader has a different explanation, believing that the purpose of government-backed sectarianism is to intimidate the Shia community.

Official policy may not be so carefully calculated. Lubna Selaibeekh, spokesperson for the Ministry of Education, says she is 'appalled' by claims that students were being denied scholarship funding because they were Shia or had taken part in protests. She says that students in UK who lost state funding because they joined demonstrations had got it back again. 'There was an announcement but it was suspended.' She agrees that 6,500 out of 12,000 teachers in Bahrain took part in a strike to support the demonstrators at Pearl Square, but says only those who broke civil-service rules would face punishment. She asserts that the ministry has 'no statistics on who is a Shia or who is a Sunni.'

The government may claim not to keep sectarian statistics, but its opponents certainly do. Nabeel Rajab, head of the Bahrain Centre for Human Rights, has precise figures about discrimination showing that 'in 2003, 18 per cent of top jobs in Bahrain were held by Shia; today [it] is 8 to 9 per cent.' He believes the government is seeking to change the demography of the island by sacking Shia and bringing in and naturalising Sunni from Pakistan, Jordan, Yemen and other Sunni-majority countries. He says the 'government is creating the ingredients for a civil war' because the more the Shia are marginalised, the angrier and more extreme they will become as 'they have nothing to lose.'

Some 2,500 Shia have been sacked, though King Hamad has promised they will get their jobs back. It may not be that easy. Hussain, an IT specialist in the partially state-owned Batelco telecommunications company, was one of those who lost their jobs. He says that there is now a layer of Sunni officials who do not want Shia to return. 'They are treating us like Red Indians in America,' he says. 'We are the majority now but maybe not for long. I'm looking for a job in Qatar or Dubai.'

King Hamad claims to have offered compromise and national dialogue, but this still hovers uneasily between real concessions and PR. The 'national dialogue' forum that has just ended was heavily promoted by the government but turned out to be an unrepresentative talking shop. 'The dialogue was a monologue,' says Abdul Jalil Khalil Ibrahim, a negotiator for the main Shia party al-Wifaq, which withdrew from the dialogue. He says his party won a majority of all votes in the last election for the largely powerless Council of Representatives, but had just five members out of 320 attending the national dialogue.

8 August 2011

Is there a fatal connection between the initial letter 'B' and places torn apart by struggles for power between different religious communities? I started as a journalist in Belfast in the early 1970s when the city was convulsed by sectarian warfare between Catholics and Protestants. In later years, I moved to Beirut to cover the many-sided civil war, at the heart of which was the conflict between Muslims and Maronites. After 2003, I spent long months in Baghdad, writing about the fighting between Shia and Sunni which culminated in the slaughter of 2006–07.

Even so, it is surprising to find Bahrain added to the list of places polarised and traumatised by sectarian differences, in this case between Shia and Sunni. Among those similarly puzzled is Cherif Bassiouni, the highly distinguished Egyptian-American legal scholar, who has been asked by King Hamad bin Isa al-Khalifa to lead an inquiry into the events which followed the start of the Arab Awakening on 14 February. Compared to Iraq or Libya, Bassiouni notes that the casualties were light—about 33 dead—'but this relatively small number has had a traumatic effect on society.' He describes the two sides as producing wholly different accounts of what happened. He says 'it is like a murder scene where you have the dead body, but nobody can agree if the bullet came from the right or the left.'

He is convinced he has the backing of the King and the Crown Prince for an inquiry which will be somewhere between a fact-finding investigation and a truth commission. He suspects that in order to reverse sectarian polarisation, a purge of the security forces may be needed as well as a government-backed programme for reconciliation.

Many Shia believe that the King will be unable or unwilling to deliver on his commitments to Bassiouni. Alaa Shehabi, the wife of a jailed Shia businessman, says: 'It is a big problem if the King didn't know what was happening, and a bigger problem if he did know and is feigning ignorance.' Many Sunni, for their part, object to concessions to what they see as an evil Iranian-orchestrated conspiracy.

One does not have to go far in Bahrain to find out why the Shia are so angry. In Graham Greene's *Our Man in Havana*, his fictional Cuban police chief Captain Segura distinguishes between two classes of people, the torturable and the untorturable. It is not a distinction that has made much impression on the Bahraini security forces, going by their wholesale repression. Every part of Shia society was targeted—mosques and religious meeting places were bulldozed. Frantic families searched for relatives who had disappeared into police and army custody and were not heard of for weeks.

Some human-rights activists were expecting to be arrested, but were amazed and shocked by the brutality with which they were treated. Zainab Abdul-Hadi al-Khawaja had suspected that her father, Abdul-Hadi al-Khawaja, a human-rights activist, would be detained and he had told his family he was willing to go voluntarily. Instead, a band of masked police broke into his house at 3 a.m. and dragged him downstairs, breaking his jaw as they did so. His interrogators continued to beat him on his fractured jaw and threatened him with rape unless he confessed. When Zainab saw him weeks later in military court, where he was sentenced to life imprisonment, his face was so badly swollen that he told his family: 'I cannot even smile at you anymore.'

Zainab and her father are among the few of those mistreated who are willing to say what happened on the record. Others give me appalling accounts before saying anxiously: 'Please don't give my name or any detail which would let the police know that I talked to you.'

Any expression of sympathy for the protesters invited punishment. As Zainab is speaking to me in a coffee shop in Manama, the capital of Bahrain, a woman and child come to sit opposite us. The woman says she worked for years in a government ministry dealing with the special needs of the disabled, but she has just been suspended. One count against her is that she cried on the phone when talking to a senior official, saying: 'It is wrong what is happening to the Shia in Bahrain.'

Government officials and members of the Sunni community have a strikingly different picture of what happened in Bahrain. 'There are almost totally different narratives,' Bassiouni tells me. Mariam Ahmed al-Jalahra, assistant under-secretary at the Ministry of Health, describes how the Salmaniya Medical Complex was taken over by doctors sympathetic to the protesters. 'What happened was beyond disaster,' she says, adding that patients were put in danger and had to be moved to other hospitals. She herself was stopped at the hospital gates by protesters, though she was allowed to proceed when her driver identified her as a doctor. 'This was something scary,' she says. She denies that any doctor is being punished for treating injured protesters, but says that those who broke rules should suffer sanctions.

What comes across in talking with Jalahra and other Sunni is an exaggerated sense of victimhood in the face of mostly minor infringements of the law by the protesters. Two Sunni consultants from the 1,000-bed Salmaniya Medical Complex separately told me that they were very worried that they had been put on a 'shame list' because they disagreed with fellow doctors, almost all Shia. Again there is a lack of a sense of proportion. When I ask Sunni doctors what they think of allegations, for which there is strong evidence, that their Shia colleagues have been tortured, they reply blandly that the matter is under investigation and, in any case, they doubt that mistreatment in prisons is as bad as reported.

What did the interrogators want to find out from the consultants at Salmaniya which led to them being mistreated so badly? One doctor, still in detention, told his wife that he had been compelled to stand up for three weeks so the blood vessels and veins in his legs compacted. In miniature, the interrogators behaved like their predecessors during the show trials in Moscow in the 1930s, determined to extract confessions by any means that would support the unlikely official narrative of foreign-inspired plots and conspiracies. 'It was bizarre,' says one consultant who was badly beaten over four days. 'They wanted to prove all the violence came from the protesters or the hospital. They wanted us to say that we had taken blood from the hospital blood bank and thrown it over protesters to exaggerate their injuries.'

Finding evidence that the hospital and its staff were somehow linked to Iran was a priority. In one room in Salmaniya the police found a device they said came from Iran and was worth 52,000 dinar (£84,475), according to a price tag still on it. 'They could not say what the device was for, but they kept saying it was collecting information for the Iranians,' says the consultant.

Many doctors and teachers have now been released but others have been sentenced or are confined without charge. These include Rula al-Saffar, the head of the Nursing Society, and Jalila al-Salman, of the Bahrain Teachers' Society, who are both now on hunger strike. A further 2,500 people have been sacked, often with no reason. Almost all of them are Shia.

I go with Nabil Rajab, head of the Bahrain Centre for Human Rights, to the home of Abdul-Aziz Juma Ayad, a 38-year-old soldier who had been 20 years in the army and had died while under detention. His family says he had refused to act as an army sniper at Pearl Square and had been tortured with electric shocks to make him say he was importing weapons from Iran.

The al-Khalifas are in a strong military position. The army and police are dominated by Bahraini and foreign Sunni. The ruling elite is backed by Saudi Arabia, which is frightened of Shia dissent spreading to the Shia of its eastern province. The US has demanded the government moderate its repression, hinting that it might move its Fifth Fleet from its Bahrain base to somewhere else in the Gulf, but this sounds like an empty threat.

By targeting the Shia community and deepening its sense of alienation, the government is institutionalising instability on the island. The little state will become more reliant on Saudi Arabia and, as in Belfast or Beirut, religious loyalties and divisions will determine life and politics. Is it too late for the consequences of arrests, torture, killings, sackings and mosque demolitions to be reversed by government-backed conciliation? This might still just be possible but the genie of sectarian conflict, once released, never returns easily to its bottle.

PART V: SYRIA: REVOLUTION AND COUNTER-REVOLUTION

Every few months there are reports in the media that one side in the Syrian civil war is about to come out on top and its opponent is facing long-term defeat. The impending fall of the Syrian government was conventional wisdom from 2011 to 2013, though for most of this time President Bashar al-Assad held all 14 Syrian provincial capitals before losing one, Raqqa in north-east Syria, in the latter year. World leaders likewise spoke of Assad and his government going down like Muammar Gaddafi in 2011 and the Alawite community, to which the Syrian leadership largely belongs, fleeing to their ancestral villages in the mountains above Latakia. Some Western commentators gleefully speculated about where Assad and his family might take refuge.

Then, from about the summer of 2013, expert interpreters of what was happening in Syria did an about-turn and began to stress the staying power of the Assad regime. It had not only failed to collapse, but its armed forces were recapturing important territory in western Syria, including the Old City of Homs and positions close to the Lebanese border. By 2014 there was talk of the Syrian Army recapturing the rebel-held part of Aleppo, once Syria's largest city.

It never happened: in the second half of 2014 and the first half of 2015, a Syrian Army that looked increasingly exhausted and fought out was being driven back in the east by the Islamic State and in the west by Jabhat al-Nusra, the al-Qa'ida affiliate, and Ahrar al-Sham, another Sunni jihadi movement. Again there was talk about how the regime might be crumbling, though there was by now much anxiety at this prospect among Western governments because it was clear that the Syrian military opposition had become wholly dominated by ISIS and al-Qa'ida clones. There was no significant moderate armed opposition surviving and, when the US tried to build one up, it was ruthlessly crushed by Jabhat al-Nusra, which kidnapped or killed its members as they crossed into Syria. It was widely suspected that Turkish intelligence had tipped off the jihadis.

Predictions of defeat and victory have been exaggerated for several reasons. One is that there is a genuine civil war in Syria in which large bodies of people on both sides believe they are fighting for their lives. Many in Damascus do not much like the Assad government, but, if ISIS or al-Nusra win, they and their families are likely to be killed or compelled to flee. Those at risk are not only Alawites, Christians, Druze and Kurds, but include Sunni Arabs who make up the majority of the Syrian Army. In rebel-held areas, people may similarly be fearful of extreme Sunni Jihadis, but they fancy their chances of survival better under ISIS than under the Syrian Army or pro-government militias. So far, there is a sort of balance of hatred and terror which makes it unlikely that anyone in Syria will win a complete victory.

There is a further factor that keeps the war going and prevents a decisive win. The Syrian government and the rebels are not masters of the situation in their own country since the shape of the political landscape is determined by foreign powers with diverse and contradictory aims. The US would like Assad to go, but not if ISIS or al-Nusra replaces him. Turkey regards ISIS, the Syrian Kurds and the Assad government as enemies whom it would like to see defeated. Saudi Arabia and the Gulf monarchies have a somewhat similar approach. But Russia, Iran and Hezbollah are determined that Assad should survive and consider that it would be a disaster for them if he failed to do so. If Assad suffers a setback then they will increase their support.

These internal and external pressures counter-balance each other, which means that the horror story for the Syrian people will go on until the regional players decide that nobody is going to win and bring it to a stop.

THIRTEEN

From Revolution to Sectarian War

Syria, 2011–13

25 March 2011

Syrian troops have opened fire on demonstrators as protests sweep the country on an unprecedented scale with tens of thousands challenging the rule of the Assad family. In the southern city of Deraa, where the protest movement started a week ago, troops shot at demonstrators who set fire to a statue of the late President Hafez al-Assad, whose son Bashar has ruled Syria since 2000. Witnesses say that 50,000 people rallied in Assad Square in Deraa chanting 'Freedom! Freedom!' as they waved Syrian flags and olive branches. Demonstrators first demanded reform of the regime, but increasingly call for a revolution.

The focus of the Arab uprising has switched to Syria over the past week since police arrested a dozen children in Deraa for writing anti-government graffiti on a wall. Security services have tried to crush the protesters by force, killing 37 of them in a mosque on Wednesday. State television made the unlikely claim that the mosque was the headquarters of a kidnap gang and showed machine guns leaning against a wall and a table with neat bundles of bank notes on it.

Today in the town of Sanamein, near Deraa, security forces are reported to have killed 20 people after Friday prayers as they protested against the regime and killings by the security services. In Hama, north of Damascus, people ran through the streets shouting 'freedom is ringing out!'—a slogan used in popular uprisings in the Arab world over the past three months.

Police with batons reacted harshly and swiftly in breaking up small demonstrations in the capital, Damascus, including one in the ancient Umayyad Mosque. Dozens of people who chanted slogans in support of the people of Deraa were dragged away by police. In Tel, near Damascus, a thousand people rallied, calling the Assad family 'thieves', and there have been rallies in most other Syrian cities.

The protests are the biggest domestic challenge to the Assad family since the early 1980s, when President Hafez al-Assad crushed a Sunni revolt centred on Hama where at least 10,000 people were killed in 1982. The current protests are secular in tone, but Deraa and Hama are Sunni strongholds resentful of the influence of the Alawites, a heterodox Shia sect to which 12 per cent of Syrians belong, including Assad and many members of the ruling elite.

12 June 2011

The Arab awakening is turning into the Arab nightmare. In Syria, thousands of troops are assaulting the northern town of Jisr al-Shughour where the government claims 120 of its soldiers and police were killed last week. Leaving aside exactly how they died, the government in Damascus is making it lethally clear that in future its opponents, peaceful or not, will be treated as if they were armed gunmen. An extraordinary aspect of the Syrian uprisings is that people go on demonstrating in their tens of thousands despite so many being shot down. But some are evidently coming to believe that their only alternative is to fight back.

12 February 2012

As Syrian Army tanks mass around Homs and its artillery pounds Sunni districts of the city, Syria is slipping into the first stages of a sectarian civil war. This conflict could be as bloody as anything seen in Iraq between 2006 and 2007 or as long as the civil war in Lebanon from 1975 to 1990. The two words that best describe the current process in Syria are 'Lebanisation' and 'militarisation'; neither bodes well for Syria's people.

In Homs, death squads from the Sunni and Alawites are starting to seek out victims from each other's communities. Sunni say they are being massacred by shellfire; Alawites demand that their Sunni neighbours be bombarded even more heavily. Syria was never a homogenous country and is becoming less so by the day.

But that alone will not bring down President Bashar al-Assad, so anti-government forces are concluding that the only way to do this is by militarising the resistance. In practice, this is unlikely to do more than increase sectarian bloodletting. Untrained militias and Syrian Army deserters cannot stop armoured columns. Most probably insurgent leaders know this and their real intention is to do enough militarily to provide political cover for creeping international intervention on their side. This might be sold as a NATO-protected safe haven for insurgents and refugees in north-west Syria, but in fact would be a declaration of war.

Short of a serious split in the Syrian Army, the opposition forces' best chance of success is to lure outside powers into such a venture. They want a repeat performance of what happened in Libya. But Syria is not Libya, its powerful armed forces have not yet disintegrated, and, most important, it is not isolated internationally to anything like the same degree as Gaddafi was.

Of course, international leaders know this. Their foreign and intelligence services will have told them how different the two countries are. Yet the example of Libya may have misled them into writing off Assad prematurely. Months ago, the Israeli defence minister, Ehud Barak, was saying Syria's regime would go within weeks. King Abdullah II of Jordan said that, if he was Assad, he would step down, but later sounded as if he regretted his outspokenness. By December, the US state department was saying that Assad was 'a dead man walking'. But it has not happened. By any realistic calculation, Assad might well last into 2014. Glib references to his isolation are exaggerated. The vote on 4 February in the UN Security Council condemning him and asking him to turn over power to his deputy was vetoed by Russia and China. Moscow feels that it was swindled last year when the Security Council vote on protecting the civilians of Benghazi turned into permission for NATO to wage all-out war to overthrow Gaddafi.

At one level, the crisis in Syria is a popular uprising against a brutal, corrupt police state. There is no doubting the protesters' courage. But power in Syria is distributed along sectarian lines, just as it was in the recent past in Iraq, Lebanon and Ireland. Even supposing an anti-sectarian opposition, democracy in Syria means a loss of power for the Alawites and their allies and a gain for the Sunni. Given that Sunni make up three-quarters of Syria's 24 million population, their enfranchisement might appear to be no bad thing. Unfortunately, many of the government's most committed opponents evidently have more fundamental changes in mind than a fairer distribution of power between communities. Core areas of the insurgency, where the Sunni are in the overwhelming majority, increasingly see Alawites, Shia and Christians as heretics to be eliminated.

Television reporting and much print journalism is skewed towards portraying an evil government oppressing a heroic people. Evidence that other forces may be at work is ignored. An example of this came on Friday when two suicide bombers struck security compounds in Aleppo, killing 28 people and wounding 235 others. The obvious explanation was that Sunni suicide bombers, mostly operating through al-Qa'ida in Mesopotamia, who have been attacking Shia-dominated security forces in Iraq, are now doing the same in Syria. But, fearing their moderate image might be tarnished, spokesmen for the opposition swiftly said that the suicide bombings were a cunning attempt by the Syrian security forces to discredit the opposition by blowing themselves up. The BBC, Al Jazeera and most newspapers happily gave uncritical coverage to opposition denials of responsibility or said it was an open question as to who was behind the bombings.

As in Libya last year, the rebels invariably get a positive press. The increasingly sectarian nature of the conflict is understated. Syria is rushing headlong into a conflict that will tear the country's communities apart.

27 May 2012

Parts of Syria are convulsed by civil war, while in other areas life continues almost as normal. At the same moment as more than 30 children had their throats cut and dozens of civilians were killed by shelling in Houla in central Syria on Friday, people in Damascus were picnicking on the slopes of Mount Qassioun overlooking the capital.

Kofi Annan, the UN–Arab League envoy, returns to Damascus in the next couple of days to attempt to give more substance to a so-called ceasefire that began on 12 April. This now looks like a critical visit, as the Houla slaughter makes Syria once again the centre of international attention and a possible target for some form of foreign intervention.

The ceasefire was only sporadically implemented from the beginning. The government has always had more interest in its successful implementation, which would stabilise its authority, than the insurgents, who need to keep the pot of rebellion boiling. The UN monitoring team says that during the ceasefire 'the level of offensive military operations by the government significantly decreased' while there has been 'an increase in militant attacks and targeted killings'. But any credit the Syrian government might be hoping for in showing restraint will disappear if the Houla atrocities are confirmed.

Not that anybody in Syria expects a quick solution to the crisis in which a mosaic of different interests and factions are battling to control the country. 'My picture of Syrian society is that 30 per cent of people are militantly against the government, 30 per cent are for them, and 40 per cent don't like anybody very much,' says a Christian in Damascus. A diplomat believes people are much more polarised than six months ago into pro-government, anti-government and 'what I term the anti-anti-government, the people who dislike the regime, but equally fear the opposition'. The government has been exploiting this by targeting its non-violent opponents 'so they can say it is a choice between us and guys with long beards. People want change, but they are frightened it might be for the worse.'

Conversations with liberally minded critics of the regime in Damascus reflect these differences. 'If I made even the most peaceful protest I would be immediately arrested,' says one woman in frustration. 'The exiled opposition leaders have not developed a serious plan to reassure the minorities [Alawites, Christians, Druze, Kurds], though they are the main supporters of the government,' adds a businessman whose business is collapsing, forcing him to live off his savings.

Could the present stalemate change as a result of the death of all those people in Houla on Friday? Internationally, the atrocity, if confirmed in detail, will increase pressure for foreign support for the insurgency and tighter sanctions on Syria. Weapons from Saudi Arabia are now reportedly reaching the rebels and their degree of co-ordination in the fighting at Rastan is greater than a few months ago.

Both the government and the armed opposition have become stronger in the past six months and neither side sees much reason to compromise. It feels like the beginning of a long war.

30 December 2012

'Shame on you!' boomed the voice of a Syrian intellectual in my phone half an hour after I had returned from Damascus to Beirut. He was so incoherent in his rage that it was difficult to know his precise objections, but my sin seemed to be that I had been in Damascus, talked to members of the Syrian government and concluded that it was not going to collapse anytime soon. Our conversation was not of a high intellectual calibre. After an acerbic exchange, I asked why, if he felt so strongly, did he 'not stop being rude to people like me, go to Aleppo and fight beside the rebels instead of spending all your time in the cafés of Beirut?' Shortly afterwards, there was a mutual clicking-off of mobiles.

Driving the short distance between Damascus and Beirut is like shifting from one planet to another. What seems obvious and commonsensical in the Syrian capital becomes controversial and a minority viewpoint over the border in Lebanon. The difference in perceptions is explained partly by the way the international and regional media describe the war. There are few foreign journalists in the Syrian capital because it is difficult to get visas. By way of contrast, the rebels have a highly sophisticated media operation— often also foreign-based—proffering immediate details of every incident, often backed up by compelling, if selective, YouTube footage.

Understandably, the rebel version of events is heavily biased towards their own side and demonises the Syrian government. More surprising is the willingness of the international media, based often in Beirut but also in London and New York, to regurgitate with so little scepticism what is essentially good-quality propaganda. It is as if, prior to the US presidential election in November, foreign journalists had been unable to obtain visas to enter the US and had instead decided to rely on Republican Party militants for their information on the campaign—moreover, Republican activists based in Mexico and Canada.

17 March 2013

We are going to do it again. The British effort to get the EU arms embargo amended so it can supply weapons to the Syrian insurgents is justified by self-serving falsifications about the situation on the ground similar to those used to garner support for the invasion of Iraq 10 years ago. A spurt of suspiciously timed claims by unnamed diplomats last week suggested that British and French arms should be sent to the rebels because Russia and Iran had increased their supply of weapons to the Syrian government. This had disturbed the military balance of power between insurgent and government forces to the advantage of the former. A British official denounced the 'perversity' of this, saying that these new arms made it impossible for opposition forces to protect civilians.

Giving more arms to the rebels is not the way to end the war and will only give them hope that, if they refuse any negotiations with the government, the Western powers backed by their Arab allies will finally be driven to decisive military intervention on their behalf. The weapons will apparently go to 'moderate' factions of the insurgency. But a striking development in the fighting over the past six months has been the rise of Jabhat al-Nusra, built around a core of experienced fighters from al-Qa'ida in Iraq, as the most effective rebel military force. Its fighters, along with other jihadi groups, are ever more prominent in the struggle for northern and eastern Syria, while the Free Syrian Army has been pushed to one side. The Free Syrian Army drew much of its support from the poor Sunni of the country towns and villages. The middle class of Aleppo, which might have preferred Assad to stay in power, opts for Jabhat al-Nusra over Western-backed groups because it keeps some sort of order and does not steal. 'The Free Syrian Army are thieves,' shout protesters in rebel-held parts of Aleppo. 'We want the Islamic Army.'

Another aspect to the rise of al-Nusra ought to give pause to those in Britain and France planning to arm the opposition with the aim of ending the war more swiftly. Their strangely contradictory argument is that it is important to end the war if Syria is not to be wholly destroyed, and the way to do this is give enough arms to the insurgents so that they can win a decisive victory. Not only is there no sign of this happening soon, but a long war is very much in the interests of al-Nusra. Its literature makes the point that the longer the conflict goes on, the stronger the jihadis will become because they are better soldiers than their more moderate, but less effective, allies. Nevertheless, they need time to establish themselves in the countryside in areas where they are weak.

Arab diplomats say that, after two years of fighting, the rebels 'have still not been able to take a single city and there have been no major defections to them by whole units from the government forces.' This may be changing. On 4 March, the city of Raqqa on the Euphrates in eastern Syria fell to the rebels, the first provincial capital to be captured by them. But it is very significant that Raqqa fell entirely to jihadi forces led by al-Nusra using captured armoured vehicles. The Free Syrian Army appears to have played little role in the taking of the city.

The fall of Raqqa has another consequence. As eastern Syria comes increasingly under the control of the jihadi Sunni fighters, the border with Iraq is becoming a fiction. Al-Qa'ida in Iraq can move backwards and forwards across the frontier, where the population is solidly Sunni on both sides, with no impediment. This is bad news for the stability of Iraq as well as Syria.

The dimensions of the crisis have still not sunk in. Soon, if it has not happened already, the area of Sunni Arab insurgency will stretch from Fallujah up the Euphrates to Aleppo and on to the shores of the Mediterranean. It is wishful thinking to imagine that, even if weapons in large quantities are channelled to 'moderate' Syrian rebels, this is going to make much difference at this stage. Assad's government is not going to collapse like a house of cards as Western leaders were hopefully prophesying up to a few months ago. Only negotiations can end this war, and fresh supplies of arms will put off the day they start.

23 May 2013

Television has a great appetite for the drama of war, for pictures of missiles exploding over Middle Eastern cities amid the sparkle of anti-aircraft fire. Print journalism cannot compete with these images, but they are rarely typical of what is happening. This problem is much worse in Syria than it used to be in Iraq or Afghanistan (in 2001) because the most arresting pictures out of Syria appear first on YouTube and are, for the most part, provided by political activists. They are then run on television news with health warnings to the effect that the station cannot vouch for their veracity, but viewers assume that the station would not be running the film if it did not believe it was real. Actual eyewitnesses are becoming hard to find, since even people living a few streets from the fighting in Damascus now get most of their information from the internet or television.

Not all YouTube evidence is suspect. Though easily fabricated, it performs certain tasks well. It can show that atrocities have taken place, and even authenticate them: in the case of a pro-government militia massacring rebel villagers, for instance, or rebel commanders mutilating and executing government soldiers. Without a video of him doing so, who would have believed that a rebel commander had cut open a dead government soldier and eaten his heart? Pictures of physical destruction are less reliable because they focus on the worst damage, giving the impression—which may or may not be true—that a whole district is in ruins. What YouTube cannot tell you is who is winning the war.

In reality no one is. Over the last year a military stalemate has prevailed, with each side launching offensives in the areas where they are strongest. Both sides have had definite but limited successes. In recent weeks government forces have opened up the road that leads west from Homs to the Mediterranean coast and the road from Damascus south to the Jordanian border. They have expanded the territory they hold around the capital and trained a militia of 60,000, the National Defence Force, to guard positions once held by the Syrian Army.

This strategy of retrenchment and consolidation is not new. About six months ago the army stopped trying to keep control of outlying positions and focused instead on defending the main population centres and the routes linking them. These pre-planned withdrawals took place at the same time as real losses on the battlefield, and were misinterpreted outside Syria as a sign that the regime was imploding. The strategy was indeed a sign of military weakness, but by concentrating its forces in certain areas the government was able to launch counter-attacks at vital points.

From an early stage in the Syrian uprising the US, NATO, Israel and the Sunni Arab states openly exulted at the blow that would soon be dealt to Iran and to Hezbollah in Lebanon: Assad's imminent fall would deprive them of their most important ally in the Arab world. Sunni leaders saw the uprising not as a triumph of democracy but as the beginning of a campaign directed at Shia or Shia-dominated states. Hezbollah and Iran believe they have no alternative but to fight and that it is better to get on with it while they still have friends in power in Damascus. 'If the enemy attacks us', Hossein Taeb, a high-ranking intelligence officer in the Iranian Revolutionary Guard, recently said, 'and seeks to take over Syria or Khuzestan [an Iranian province] the priority is to maintain Syria, because if we maintain Syria we can take back Khuzestan. But if we lose Syria we won't be able to hold Tehran.'

Hassan Nasrallah, the leader of Hezbollah, made it very clear in a speech on 30 April that the Lebanese Shia also see Syria as a battleground where they cannot afford a defeat. 'Syria', he said, 'has real friends in the region and the world who will not let Syria fall into the hands of America, Israel or takfiri groups.' He believes the very survival of the Shia is at stake. For many in the Middle East this sounded like a declaration of war: a significant one, given Hezbollah's experience in fighting a guerrilla war against the Israelis in Lebanon. The impact of its skill in irregular warfare has already been witnessed in the fighting at Qusayr and Homs, just beyond Lebanon's northern border. 'It probably is unrealistic to expect Lebanese actors to take a step back,' a study by the International Crisis Group concludes. 'Syria's fate, they feel, is their own, and the stakes are too high for them to keep to the side-line.'

The Syrian civil war is spreading. This, not well-publicised advances or withdrawals on the battlefield, is the most important new development. Political leaders in the region see the dangers more intensely than the rest of the world. 'Neither the opposition nor the regime can finish the other off,' Nouri al-Maliki, the Iraqi prime minister, said earlier this year. 'If the opposition is victorious, there will be a civil war in Lebanon, divisions in Jordan, and a sectarian war in Iraq.' Of these countries, the most vulnerable is Lebanon, given the division between Sunni and Shia, a weak state, porous borders and proximity to heavily populated areas of Syria. A country of 4 million people has already taken in half a million Syrian refugees, most of them Sunni. In Iraq, the Syrian civil war has reignited a sectarian conflict that never entirely ended. The destabilising of his country that Maliki predicted in the event of an opposition victory has already begun.

The feeling that the future of whole states is in doubt is growing across the Middle East—for the first time since Britain and France carved up the remains of the Ottoman Empire after the First World War. 'It is the end of Sykes-Picot,' I am told repeatedly in Iraq; the reference is to the agreement of 1916 which divided up the spoils between Britain and France and was the basis for later treaties. Some are jubilant at the collapse of the old order, notably the 30 million Kurds who were left without a state of their own after the Ottoman collapse and are now spread across Iraq, Turkey, Iran and Syria. They feel their moment has come: they are close to independence in Iraq and are striking a deal with the Turkish government for political rights and civil equality. The 2.2 million Kurds in northern Syria, 10 per cent of the population, have assumed control of their towns and villages and are likely to demand a high degree of autonomy from any post-war Syrian government.

What will the new order in the Middle East look like? This should be Turkey's great moment in the region: it has a powerful military, a prospering economy and a well-established government. It is allied to Saudi Arabia and Qatar in supporting the Syrian opposition and is on good terms with the US. But these are dangerous waters in which to fish. There are signs that the violence is spilling over Turkey's 510-mile frontier with Syria, across which insurgent groups advance and retreat at will. On 11 May, two bombs in a Turkish border town killed 49 people, almost all Turkish. An angry crowd of Turks marched down the main street chanting 'kill the Syrians' as they assaulted Syrian shopkeepers.

When the US invaded Iraq in 2003 it changed the overall balance of power and destabilised every country in the region. The same thing is happening again, except that the impact of the Syrian war is likely to be less easily contained. Already the frontier dividing the western deserts of Iraq from the eastern deserts of Syria is ceasing to have any physical reality. In April, al-Qa'ida in Iraq embarrassed the rebels' Western supporters by revealing that it had founded, reinforced with experienced fighters and devoted half its budget to supporting al-Nusra, militarily the most effective rebel group. When Syrian soldiers fled into Iraq in March they were ambushed by al-Qa'ida and 48 of them were killed before they could return to Syrian territory.

There is virtually no state in the region without some stake in the conflict. Jordan, though nervous of a jihadi victory in Syria, is allowing arms shipments from Saudi Arabia to reach rebels in southern Syria by road. Qatar has reportedly spent $3 billion on supporting the rebels over the last two years and has offered $50,000 to every Syrian Army defector and his family. In co-ordination with the CIA it has sent 70 military flights to Turkey with arms and equipment for the insurgents. The Tunisian government says that 800 Tunisians are fighting on the rebel side but security sources are quoted as saying the real figure is closer to 2,000.

Fear of widespread disorder and instability is pushing the US, Russia, Iran and others to talk of a diplomatic solution to the conflict. Some sort of peace conference may take place in Geneva over the next month, with the aim at least of stopping things getting worse. But while there is an appetite for diplomacy, nobody knows what a solution would look like. It is hard to imagine a real agreement being reached when there are so many players with conflicting interests.

Five distinct conflicts have become tangled together in Syria: a popular uprising against a dictatorship, which is also a sectarian battle between Sunni and Alawites; a regional struggle between Shia and Sunni, which is also a decades-old conflict between an Iranian-led grouping and Iran's traditional enemies, notably the US and Saudi Arabia. Finally, at another level, there is a reborn Cold War confrontation: Russia and China versus the West. The conflict is full of unexpected and absurd contradictions, such as a purportedly democratic and secular Syrian opposition being funded by the absolute monarchies of the Gulf who are also fundamentalist Sunni.

By savagely repressing demonstrations two years ago Assad helped turn mass protests into an insurrection which has torn Syria apart. He is probably correct in predicting that diplomacy will fail, that his opponents inside and outside Syria are too divided to agree on a peace deal. He may also be right in believing that greater foreign intervention 'is a clear probability'.

The quagmire is turning out to be even deeper and more dangerous than it was in Iraq.

2 June 2013

The best hope for an end to the killing in Syria is for the US and Russia to push both sides in the conflict to agree a ceasefire in which each holds the territory it currently controls. In a civil war of such savagery, diplomacy with any ambition to determine who holds power in future will founder because both sides believe they can still win. Mutual hatred is too great for any long-term deal on sharing power. A ceasefire would have to be policed on the ground by a UN observer force. I recall the much-maligned UN Supervision Mission in Syria in 2012 arranging a ceasefire in the hardcore rebel town of Douma on the outskirts of Damascus. It did not stop all the shooting but many Syrians lived who would otherwise have died.

The White House has said in the past few days that its top priority in Syria is to impose regime change, but this is a recipe for a very long conflict. Why should Assad and his government surrender when they are more than holding their own on the battlefield? Moreover, Washington appears to have shut the door on the idea of Iran, a main player, attending the peace conference in Geneva. This again is unrealistic if the aim of negotiations is to end the fighting.

There may be a more sinister reason why the US has started setting the bar so high for talks. Washington's involvement is greater than appears because so much of it goes through Qatar, with the CIA determining who gets arms and money sent via Turkey. This would also explain why Britain and France are so keen to send the rebels weapons.

The explanation for the actions of the Western states may be that they do not want the war to end except as a victory for their allies. This certainly is the view of many in the Middle East, such as Mowaffak al-Rubaie, the former Iraqi national security adviser, who says the civil war 'is the best option for the West and Israel because it knocks out Syria as an opponent of their policies and keeps Iran busy. Hezbollah is preoccupied by Syria and not with Israel. Turkey's idea of a new Ottoman empire is gone with the wind.' This is a cynical but probably correct explanation for why the US, Britain, France and the Sunni monarchies do not want the war to end until they can declare victory.

23 June 2013

The second of two mortar bombs killed Ghassan al-Khouly as he stood guard last Thursday at an ancient gate into the Christian quarter of the Old City of Damascus. It exploded right beside him, killing him instantly, dark bloodstains and a small heap of stones today marking where he died.

Ghassan al-Khouly, an unemployed labourer who specialised in tiling floors, was one of the latest of an estimated 93,000 Syrians to have died since the start of the civil war in March 2011. Other than the fact he was a Greek Orthodox Christian, his experiences were not very different from those of many other Syrians caught up in the war.

I started to learn about the life and death of Ghassan after I heard four rifle shots fired at regular intervals while I was walking to the great Umayyad Mosque in the Old City just before Friday prayers. It did not sound like a gunfight, and it turned out the shots had been fired by an honour guard bringing a body home for the funeral later in the afternoon. I learned the name of the dead man but was told that it was not a good moment to see his widow and her two sons. But if I wanted to know what had happened I should talk to Barakat al-Shamas, who was standing guard with Ghassan and had been wounded in the same incident but was just back from hospital.

Ghassan and Barakat had both been in the National Defence Force, a 60,000-strong militia organisation that has been publicised abroad as being a ferocious pro-government paramilitary organisation, freshly trained to turn the tide of war in Syria. The National Defence Force may contain such units but in the Old City of Damascus its members are very much like the Home Guard in Britain in 1940. Everybody between the ages of 20 and 65 is meant to join, and many are quite elderly.

I meet Barakat, not looking at all intimidated by his experiences, surrounded by friends sitting in the guest room of his house. As he extends his right hand, which is covered with a blood-stained bandage, it is as if he has forgotten for a moment that he cannot shake hands with anybody. He says: 'I heard the sound of a shell coming in and I threw myself on the ground. When I got up I saw there was so much blood that I knew Ghassan must be dead.' Barakat was wounded with a piece of shrapnel penetrating his right hand as well as his neck and left leg.

I am surprised by the age of the two men who had been doing sentry duty: Barakat says he is 65 and Ghassan, the dead man, was 10 years younger. A photograph of Ghassan is on his death notice announcing funeral arrangements which has been pasted to walls in the Old City. The picture has the de-personalised look of head-and-shoulders ID photos, but shows a narrow-faced serious-looking man with a black moustache.

The rebels regularly fire mortars into districts of Damascus they do not control. This is difficult to stop because the rebels jump out of a car, take a mortar and a shell from the boot, fire it and are gone in a few minutes. This is their reply to government artillery which fires constantly at rebel-held districts. Ghassan and Barakat could not do much about the mortar attacks, but they were meant to stop rebels infiltrating through the Bab al-Sharqi, the Eastern Gate, into the Old City. 'Old men are better at this because they know everybody who lives here and can pick out strangers,' says a local observer.

'Our shift was meant to end at 2 p.m.,' recalls Barakat. He and Ghassan had moved to the north side of the gate to stay in the shade. It was then that the mortar bombs came down, one on either side of the gate. They did not leave much of a crater in the hard ground, but, aside from hitting the two guards, the shrapnel peppered an empty school bus and smashed its windscreen. Nobody can be certain where the mortar was fired from but they think it might have been Eastern Ghouta, a rebel stronghold to the east of Damascus under pressure from government forces. The mortar fire is the rebels' way of showing they are still in business.

I go to see Ghassan's widow, Nour al-Sabek, in the family house where she is living with her two sons, Shadi and Sherbel. As people come to pay their respects, the family sit near a large picture of the dead man. I ask Nour why her husband joined the National Defence Force since it paid almost no money. She replies that he loved his country and was frightened for his church, his children and his friends. Others say there are about 600 Christians in the neighbourhood who joined the National Defence Force and eight have been killed by mortars, snipers and bombs.

Nour says that until two years ago Ghassan was fully employed but when the rebels came all that was finished. They hold outer suburbs of Damascus where most of the new construction was, and as a Christian he did not dare go there. Everybody who is not a Sunni Muslim Arab assumes they are in danger of being killed, kidnapped or robbed in rebel-held areas. Forced to stay in the centre of the city he tried to eke out a living by doing odd jobs fixing electrical wiring, setting up satellite dishes and flooring. His family became poorer. A friend is worried that now Nour will have nothing to live on; her close relatives and friends have also lost their jobs. There is discussion among family members about the probability of Nour getting a lump sum from the government and a pension because her husband has been martyred. They think this likely, going by past experience, but not absolutely certain.

As we speak there is the booming of outgoing artillery in the background but nobody pays any attention to it since this has been typical background noise in Damascus for the past year. There is not much talk of general politics until Ebtisam, a thin, short, nervous-looking woman who is the sister of the dead man, asks me: 'Why does your country send weapons to Syria? Without foreign support we would finish the rebels.' She says that in the past she could walk home in the middle of the night, 'but now I must ask my brother to pick me up'.

Everybody who has gathered to mourn Ghassan al-Khouly says how good relations between Muslims and Christians were in Syria before the revolt. This has not always been true historically, since between 5,000 and 10,000 Christians were massacred in Damascus over eight days in 1860. But somebody remarks that there were more Muslims than Christians in Ghassan's funeral procession. His sons remain silent while their older relatives talk about their dead father. But just before I leave, Shadi, aged 13 and looking grief-stricken, suddenly says in a loud voice: 'The people and the world loved Ghassan al-Khouly.'

28 June 2013

Khalid is too frightened of travelling the 100 miles from Homs to Damascus to ask officials if they know what happened to his three sons, who disappeared 16 months ago as government troops over-ran the rebel stronghold of Baba Amr. He has not heard anything from them since and does not know if they are alive or dead, though he has repeatedly asked the authorities in Homs, Syria's third-largest city, about them.

Khalid, a thick-set man of 60 with grizzled white hair, who used to be a construction worker until he injured his back, says he dare not make the journey to Damascus because 'as soon as the soldiers at the checkpoints on the road see I come from a place like Baba Amr, with a reputation for supporting the rebels, they are likely to arrest me.' He explains that he cannot risk being detained because he has a wife and four daughters who rely on him. He is the last man left in his family since his sons went missing.

Syria is full of parents trying to keep their children alive or simply seeking to find out if they are already dead. It is as if both sides in the civil war are in a competition to see who can commit the worst atrocities. A few days before speaking to Khalid I saw a picture on the internet of a fresh-faced 23-year-old soldier called Youssef Kais Abdin from near the port city of Latakia. He had been kidnapped a week earlier by the al-Qa'ida-affiliated Jabhat al-Nusra while serving in the north-east of Syria, close to the Iraqi border. The next his parents heard of Youssef was a call from their son's mobile at 4 a.m. from al-Nusra telling them to look for a picture of their son online. When they did so, they saw his decapitated body in a pool of blood with his severed head placed on top of it.

The Syrian conflict is a civil war with all the horrors traditionally inflicted in such struggles wherever they are fought, be it Syria today or Russia, Spain, Greece, Lebanon or Iraq in the past. Evidence that both sides have committed supporters prepared to fight to the death is borne out by the estimate of some 100,000 dead published this week by the pro-rebel Syrian Observatory for Human Rights. It concludes that fatal casualties come almost equally from the two sides in the civil war: broadly 25,000 of them government soldiers, 17,000 pro-government militia, 36,000 civilians and 14,000 rebel fighters, though the last two figures in particular are probably understated.

Homs, an ancient city at the centre of a province with a population of 2 million, is a good place to judge the course of the war. It was an early scene of anti-government action in 2011 in the course of which peaceful protests turned into irregular but devastating warfare. Most of Homs today is controlled by the Syrian Army, aside from a few important areas including the Old City in the centre, which is held by rebels. Some 400,000 people have fled from here and are now scattered across the rest of the city. The houses they leave behind are occupied by opposition fighters, a fair number of whom are non-Syrian jihadi volunteers intent on waging holy war. 'It is very difficult to talk to the Salafi [Islamic fundamentalists] in the Old City,' says Monsignor Michel Naaman, a Syriac Catholic priest who used to live there and who has sought to mediate and arrange ceasefires between the Free Syrian Army and government forces.

But the political geography of Homs is not just divided between pro- and anti-government forces but has grey areas of uncertain or disputed control, where hundreds of thousands of people are trying to survive pressures from both sides. They live in an atmosphere poisoned by fear of a kind I have not seen since Baghdad at the height of the sectarian civil war in 2006–07.

Where else in the world would not just vulnerable refugees but army generals surrounded by armed guards make me promise not to reveal their names for fear that they and their families might be targeted for retaliation?

Homs is full of people who are refugees within their own city. Some flee because they are in areas that support the rebels and others because they are known to work for the government. Most simply want to get to a place of safety. In Homs this often means taking refuge in a school where the government provides food, water and the basics of life. At one school (the person in charge asks me not to identify it) I speak to Abu Nidal who worked in Homs' water and sanitation department. He comes from Baba Amr and left there for two months during the heavy fighting in 2012 when the Syrian Army stormed it. 'We went back and stayed six or seven months but [in March this year] the rebels came back, the situation was very bad and we had to leave again.' He says Baba Amr is now empty. When I drive past it the entrance to the district is blocked by rubble and there is nobody to be seen on the road beyond.

The fact that people in Homs have become inured to living in a constant state of terror does not make their suffering any better. 'It must be very dangerous to be a young man of military age here in Syria,' I say to a group of refugees, leading them to laugh dryly and respond: 'No, you are wrong. They kill men in their 60s and 70s as well!' I ask if they expect things to get better and they dolefully shake their heads.

As for Khalid and his hopeless search for his three missing sons, he says, 'I wish the Free Syrian Army and the government would leave ordinary people out of it and go and fight each other.'

25 August 2013

The priority for Syrian foreign policy for the past two-and-a-half years has been to avoid foreign military intervention on behalf of the rebels. By the same token, the opposition has tried by every means to secure armed intervention by the US and its allies sufficient to win the war.

The action by the Syrian government most likely to push an unwilling White House into military involvement has been the open use of chemical weapons against civilians. Damascus has furiously denied in the past that it has used them and proof has been lacking. Rebel accusations might have been fabricated and claims by Western governments were tainted by propaganda.

Experts specialising in chemical weapons had hitherto expressed scepticism, even derision, at supposed proofs of chemical weapons use in the media. CBRNe World, a journal specialising in chemical and biological weapons, asked of one alleged sarin gas attack: 'Could it be real—possibly. Could it be misdiagnosed and something other than sarin—possibly. Could it be fake—possibly.' Considering the question two months ago of whether chemical weapons had been used in Syria, Professor Julian Perry Robinson of Sussex University, a renowned expert, concluded: 'Onlookers can as yet believe the reporting only if they are willing to trust unsubstantiated assertion or incomplete evidence.'

So it is difficult to think of any action by the Damascus government more self-destructive than the Syrian Army launching a massive chemical-weapons attack on rebel-held districts in its own capital. Yet the evidence is piling up that this is exactly what happened last Wednesday, 21 August—that the Syrian Army fired rockets or shells containing poison gas which killed hundreds of people in Ghouta, in the east of Damascus. The opposition may be capable of manufacturing evidence of government atrocities, but it is highly unlikely it could do so on such a large scale as this.

There is now a strong possibility of a US military response, such as missile strikes from outside Syrian airspace on Syrian military units or bases from which the chemical weapons may have been launched. No doubt Obama would like to keep out of a full-scale intervention, as he made clear last week, saying of the wars in Iraq and Afghanistan that people who 'call for immediate action, jumping into stuff that does not turn out well, gets us mired in very difficult situations, can result in us being drawn into very expensive, difficult, costly interventions that actually breed more resentment in the region'. Nevertheless, the blatancy of the poison-gas attacks will make it difficult and damaging for him not to react militarily.

If the Syrian leadership knew that chemical weapons were going to be used, what could be their motive? They may be so convinced of American weakness and so confident of the backing of Russia and Iran that they feel they can ignore international condemnation. They may have seen Egypt's security forces shoot down hundreds of Muslim Brotherhood supporters on 14 August and thought, 'If they can get away with it, so can we.' Even so, the benefits of such an operation were always going to be outweighed by political costs abroad.

What will be the impact of the chemical-weapons attack within Syria? It will frighten people further in rebel areas and will show the utter ruthlessness of the government, something scarcely in doubt. But the action is also a sign of weakness, suggesting the Syrian Army cannot capture with conventional arms districts such as Jobar close to the centre of Damascus. Plenty of Syrian officials can see the criminal stupidity of using chemical weapons, so experts are asking if some state faction might want to sabotage possible peace talks by deploying them. A problem with this scenario is nobody else has noticed peace talks getting anywhere.

The Syrian government denies it had anything to do with the gas attack, but it has not given a credible account of what did happen. Initially, there was disbelief that it would do something so patently against its own interests, but all the evidence so far is that it has done just that.

28 August 2013

Should they happen, Western missile strikes on Syria will raise the political temperature in the whole region. What is unclear is whether the increased temperature will be temporary or permanent. Whatever the justification for the action by the US and its allies, it will be seen across the world as another American-led military intervention in the wider Middle East in the tradition of Iraq, Afghanistan, Somalia, Libya and Lebanon over the last 35 years.

British and French military actions are being justified by David Cameron and François Hollande on purely moral grounds as an act of retribution for the use of poison gas against civilians in Damascus and to prevent it happening again. This may go down well with domestic audiences but it will find few believers in the Middle East. The former US national security adviser Zbigniew Brzezinski was reported as saying: 'I am struck by how eager Great Britain and France appear to be in favour of military action. And I am also mindful of the fact that both of these two powers are former imperialist, colonialist powers in the region.' The air strikes will only confirm suspicions of British and French motives.

Will air strikes help spread the Syrian conflict to other countries in the region? The important point here is to take on board how far it has already spread and the degree to which it is already destabilising Syria's neighbours. The Islamic State of Iraq and the Levant, which fights in both Iraq and Syria, has already become stronger thanks to the war, and is responsible for bombings in Iraq more intense than anything seen since 2008. The same organisation is responsible for ethnically cleansing Syrian Kurds in northeast Syria, 40,000 of whom have already fled to the autonomous Kurdistan Regional Government in northern Iraq. If the Assad government becomes weaker, then the Islamic State, al-Nusra Front and other jihadis—the most effective rebel fighting forces—will be strengthened.

President Obama faces a problem in his effort to decide on military action vigorous enough to show US military strength but not so strong that it radically changes the balance of power on the ground in Syria. He wants a broad-ranging coalition but some of its members such as Saudi Arabia, Qatar and Turkey want to go much further than him in a campaign to overthrow the government in Damascus. Whatever happens, the balance of forces will be disturbed, affecting not only the struggle within Syria but regional confrontation between Sunni and Shia and between Saudi Arabia and Iran.

FOURTEEN

Syrian Catastrophe

Syria, 2013–14

14 December 2013

The final bankruptcy of American and British policy in Syria came 10 days ago as Islamic Front, a Saudi-backed Sunni jihadi group, over-ran the headquarters of the Supreme Military Council of the Free Syrian Army at Bab al-Hawa on the Syrian side of the border with Turkey. The Free Syrian Army and the Syrian National Coalition, groups that the US and Britain have been pretending for years are at the heart of Syrian military and political opposition, have been discredited. The remaining Free Syrian Army fighters are in flight, have changed sides, or are devoting all their efforts to surviving the onslaught from jihadi or al-Qa'ida-linked brigades.

The US and Britain stopped the delivery of non-lethal aid to the supply depot at Bab al-Hawa as the implications of the disaster sank in. The West's favourite rebel commander, General Salim Idris, is on the run between Turkey and Qatar, his former chief supporter and paymaster. Turkey closed the border, the other side of which is now controlled by the Islamic Front. The so-called moderate wing of the Syrian insurgency has very limited influence, but its representatives are still being urged by Washington and London to attend the peace conference in Geneva on 22 January to negotiate Bashar al-Assad's departure from power.

Confusion over what is happening is so great that Western leaders may not pay as much of a political price at home as they should for the failure of their Syrian policy. But it is worth recalling that the Syrian National

Coalition and the Free Syrian Army are the same people for whom the US and UK almost went to war in August, and whom they saw as candidates to replace Assad in power in Damascus. The recent debacle shows how right public opinion in both countries was to reject military intervention.

Who are the winners in the new situation? One is Assad because the opposition to him—which started as a popular uprising against a cruel, corrupt and oppressive dictatorship in 2011—has become a fragmented movement dominated by al-Qa'ida umbrella organisation the Islamic State of Iraq and the Levant, the other al-Qa'ida franchisee, the al-Nusra Front, and the Islamic Front, consisting of six or seven large rebel military formations numbering an estimated 50,000 fighters whose uniting factor is Saudi money and an extreme Sunni ideology similar to Saudi Arabia's version of Islam. The Saudis see the Islamic Front as capable of fighting pro-Assad forces as well as ISIS, but Riyadh's objections to the latter appear to be based on its independence of Saudi control rather than revulsion at its record of slaughtering Shia, Alawi, Christians, Armenians, Kurds, Turkomans or any dissenting Sunni.

The allegation of Saudi control is becoming easier to substantiate. Until a year ago, the Saudis stayed somewhat in the background when it came to funding the Syrian rebels, in which the leading role was played by Qatar in association with Turkey. But the failure of the rebels to win and US anger that the Qataris and Turks had allowed much of the aid to go to jihadis led to an important change this summer, when Saudi Arabia took over from Qatar as chief supporter of the rebels.

An interesting example of just how hands-on this Saudi direction has become is illustrated by a fascinating interview given by a top defector from the Free Syrian Army to ISIS, Saddam al-Jamal. Commander of the Liwa Allah Akbar battalion, he was until recently the top Free Syrian Army commander in eastern Syria, much of which is under rebel control. Questioned by his new ally, according to a translation by the Brown Moses Blog, he recalls that 'we used to meet with the apostates of Qatar and Saudi Arabia and with the infidels of Western nations such as America and France in order to receive arms and ammo or cash.' He says Western intelligence operatives have of late been worried about the growing influence of al-Qa'ida affiliates and repeatedly asked him why he was growing a beard.

Jamal gives an account of a recent three-day meeting between the Free Syrian Army commanders from northern and eastern Syria with Western,

Saudi, Qatari, Emirati and Jordanian intelligence operatives. This appears to have been soon after the Saudis took over the Syria file from the Qataris. He says the Free Syrian Army commanders, including General Idris, had a meeting with Prince Salman bin Sultan, the Saudi deputy defence minister. Jamal says that Prince Salman 'asked those who had plans to attack Assad positions to present their needs for arms, ammo and money'.

The picture that Jamal paints is of a Free Syrian Army that was a complete pawn to foreign intelligence agencies, which is one reason why he defected. The Saudis subsequently decided that the Free Syrian Army would not serve their purposes, and were frustrated by America backing away from war in Syria and confrontation with Iran. They set about using their limitless funds to attract into alliances rebel brigades such as the Islamic Front which would be Sunni fundamentalist, committed to the overthrow of Assad, against political negotiations, but distinct from al-Qa'ida. In reality, it looks highly unlikely that Saudi money will be enough to bring down or even significantly weaken Assad though it may be enough to keep a war going for years.

The old, supposedly moderate, opposition has been marginalised. Its plan since 2011 has been to force a full-scale Western military intervention as in Libya in 2011 and, when this did not happen, it lacked an alternative strategy. The US, Britain and France do not have many options left except to try to control the jihadi Frankenstein's monster that they helped create in Syria and which is already helping destabilise Iraq and Lebanon. Turkey may soon regret having given free passage to so many jihadis on their way to Syria. Ankara could close its 500-mile border with Syria or filter those who cross it. But Turkish policy in Syria and Iraq has been so dysfunctional in the past three years that it may be too late to correct the consequences of its erroneous conviction that Assad would fall.

The Geneva II peace conference on Syria looks as if it will be born dead. In so far as the Free Syrian Army and its civilian counterparts ever represented anyone in Syria they do so no longer. The armed opposition is dominated by Saudi-sponsored Islamist brigades on the one hand and by al-Qa'ida affiliates on the other. All US, British and French miscalculations have produced in Syria is a re-run of Afghanistan in the 1980s, creating a situation the ruinous consequences of which have yet to appear. As jihadis in Syria realise they are not going to win, they may well look for targets closer to home.

26 January 2014

I was just thinking that Damascus was a lot quieter than six months ago when there was the crash of a mortar bomb exploding a few hundred yards away. Fired from a rebel area, it had landed in Bab Touma, a Christian part of the Old City, where I am staying. It turns out not to have killed anybody, unlike the last time I was here, when a couple of mortar rounds landing in Straight Street killed four people.

'Things have not changed much since last summer,' says a local businessman. 'The biggest change is that people are more used to living in a permanent state of war in which survival is the main objective in life. After all, we are entering the fourth year of fighting.' He also admits that there are fewer exchanges of fire between government and opposition districts in which the Syrian Army uses by far the heavier weapons. But he does not expect the present military deadlock to change radically and he adds: 'We do not expect much from the Geneva II talks.'

The fighting has eased somewhat around Damascus in recent weeks. This is in large part because the rebels are fully engaged in fighting their own 'war within the civil war', pitting a disparate coalition of rebels against ISIS in a struggle that killed 1,395 people in the first three weeks of January. ISIS has retaken the one rebel-held provincial capital, Raqqa, and is insisting that women wear the niqab, the all-enveloping cloak and veil, and has banned music, pictures and cigarettes.

The government has gained a little from the rebel groups murdering each other and, such is the intensity of hatreds within Syria, has probably lost little credit domestically from the disclosure of pictures allegedly showing 11,000 prisoners tortured or starved to death. Syrians on both sides are inured to atrocities. But the depth of division within the opposition is now so great that it is difficult to see how its negotiating team in Geneva could deliver on practical questions such as ceasefires, prisoner exchanges and the delivery of aid. Indeed, the rebel negotiators would risk execution as traitors if they set foot in much of rebel-held north and east Syria.

But the government also has its weaknesses: it has not taken advantage of the rebel civil war to advance, except in a few areas around Aleppo and limited parts of Damascus. One explanation for this might be that it does not want to threaten the rebels and unite them while they are doing the government's work for it by killing each other. But it is also true that the government's forces are already over-stretched, without enough troops and not capable of launching offensives on very many different fronts. There is evidence for this in that Jabhat al-Nusra has reportedly captured, for the second time, the ancient Christian town of Maloula. This is just off the crucial main road north from Damascus to Syria's third city, Homs, and the fact that the government cannot permanently secure this important route shows that it is not strong enough to counter-attack. The Homs–Damascus road was also shut for 17 days recently when the opposition's forces took the town of Nabk halfway along it.

The government has been besieging rebel-held districts in the capital with the aim of starving them out. Some, such as Barzeh in Damascus, are once again partially under government control after deals in which heavy and sometimes light weapons are handed over by rebels. But these agreements are fragile because terms, such as those to do with freeing prisoners, may not be abided by. Some rebel bastions such as Douma, north-east of Damascus, have big reserves of food to hold out for a long time. In most of these much-fought-over districts, the population has largely fled and shows no signs of returning. The people who left are sleeping rough in parks or are crammed into apartments, while just across the border in Lebanon businessmen are charging $200 a month in rent for tents in which Bedouin and seasonal labourers once lived.

28 January 2014
It is not easy to get to the industrial town of Adra, even though it is close to Damascus. We take a highway through the mountains west of the capital and then suddenly drive off it onto a precipitous earth track. In front of us is an enormous orange truck with a trailer carrying a bulldozer. The bulldozer turns out to be one of several making tracks through the scrub and heaping banks of earth offer some protection from rifle fire. 'Drive fast because there are many snipers about,' says an army officer escorting our small convoy.

Our destination is the giant cement plant which a former worker, now a refugee, says once employed 937 workers and produced 3,000 to 4,000 tonnes of cement a day. It now looks like an enormous, dead mechanical monster with pathetic clotheslines carrying refugees' washing strung between big concrete columns. Nearby is a small party of displaced people from Adra looking bedraggled and depressed. They say the army brought them bread but they are short of everything else.

Adra, with its cement, steel and car plants, has now become one more Syrian town where the army and rebels confront each other but neither side has the strength to win a decisive victory. As they skirmish, locals either flee or cower in their houses with little or no electricity or water.

'They came through the main sewer at 4:30 a.m. and caught us by surprise,' says a Syrian soldier, who gives his name as Abu Ali, describing the rebel capture of part of the town. 'They chose a cold day in December to attack when there was snow and you could not see more than two feet in front of you.' The rebels who stormed the workers' housing complex on 11 December belonged to two much-feared jihadi groups, Jabhat al-Nusra, the official al-Qa'ida affiliate in Syria, and the Jaysh al-Islam. Khalal al-Helmi, a frail-looking 63-year-old retired employee of the oil ministry, says: 'Three men came into our building and shouted "Go down to the basement." We were down there three days.'

What went on in the streets of Adra immediately after the rebel occupation appears to add another grisly page to the list of atrocities in the Syrian civil war. Survivors say at least 32 members of religious minorities—Alawi, Christians, Druze and Shia—were killed immediately or taken away by gunmen who went from house to house with lists of names. They are also reported to have killed doctors and nurses in a clinic and workers in a bakery who were thrown into their own ovens. Given that the jihadis still hold this part of Adra, the exact details cannot be checked, but survivors have no doubt that a massacre took place.

There may be doubts about the exact number of people murdered in Adra but not about the suffering of those who have fled to the industrial zone. It is cold even in the middle of the day and the Syrian Arab Red Crescent has issued a statement saying it is 'deeply concerned about the plight of the Adra residents who fled the area'. It has distributed 31,000 blankets and 7,000 mattresses and is trying to provide clean water to 30,000 people. Adra is now surrounded by sand and rubble with occasional Syrian Army outposts on top. Even so, the exact position of the front line is worryingly uncertain. At one point, two Syrian Army soldiers seem to mistake us for the enemy and fire a couple of shots. A soldier in the vehicle in front of us jumps onto a heap of rocks and waves furiously in the direction from which the firing came.

29 January 2014

Syria is dotted with sieges and blockades of cities, towns and districts which in some cases are producing mass starvation. The politics of starvation are complex and open to manipulation for propaganda purposes. The problem stems primarily from the government forces' strategy of sealing off areas that have been captured by the armed opposition and not letting people or goods in or out. Electricity and water is usually cut off, then the Syrian Army bombards the area from the air and with artillery, leading to a mass exodus of refugees. This approach has the advantage from the government point of view of avoiding house-to-house fighting in which their best troops would suffer heavy attrition. The most high profile example of this strategy is in the Old City of Homs where between 2,500 and 4,000 civilians are besieged along with several thousand rebel fighters.

Every siege and blockade in Syria involves suffering for the victims but otherwise each situation is distinct. At Yarmouk, the Palestinian area in Damascus once called 'Little Palestine', Fuad, a Syrian Palestinian music teacher tries to help bring food to the 20,000 people besieged inside by the Syrian government. 'Bread is a dream for children inside Yarmouk Camp,' he says. Standing by a barrier of sand and rubble that blocks an entrance to the camp, he adds that 'people have been trapped in there for 185 days and are sick because they are eating weeds we used to feed our animals.' The siege of Yarmouk is only one element in the disaster that has hit the half-million Palestinians in Syria. Fuad, who is trying to emigrate to Egypt, says 'it is a second al-Nakba for us'—the first al-Nakba, or catastrophe, being the Palestinian expulsion in 1948 from what became the state of Israel. All the Palestinians in Syria are caught up in this new disaster because their camps after 1948 were usually built on the outskirts of cities such as Damascus and Aleppo. They were therefore right in the path of Syrian rebel forces advancing from the countryside in 2012 and five camps have some presence of the armed opposition. Palestinians living in a swath of camps in south Damascus fled first to Yarmouk and then fled again when the rebels took most of it over.

Elsewhere in Syria siege tactics are not only employed by the government side: unnoticed by the outside world, the largest single community currently besieged and on the edge of starvation lives in Zahraa and Nubl, two Shia towns west of Aleppo With a combined population of 45,000. In this case the besiegers are Sunni rebels who accuse the Shia townspeople of supporting the government and are seeking to starve them into submission.

4 February 2014

The sound of shellfire booms every few seconds from the besieged Old City of Homs. The rebels, surrounded in the densely packed quarter, reply with mortars of their own. Each of them detonates with a sharp crack, shaking the walls of the building I am in, a kilometre from the front line. In between shell bursts the regular chatter of machine guns rings out, lasting for at least six hours before subsiding in the early hours of the morning.

The intensity of the fighting in the battered city of Homs is greater than anything the people here have experienced in months. The city is one of the centres of the original uprising and has seen some of the most destructive fighting. Even when there is no fighting the city is tense. The streets clear as soon as darkness falls, unlike Damascus where the shops stay open late and heavy traffic in the government-held centre does not subside until after 8 p.m.

A few hours before the shooting intensified, I spoke to Captain Mohammed, who said his front line position in the Bab al-Sebaa district was 30 metres from where the rebels were dug in. 'We are completely surrounding them. There is fighting every day but they can't get out.' He guessed that the rebels—whom the government side invariably refers to as 'terrorists'—numbered over 1,000 fighters.

Captain Mohammed said he had been fighting in Homs for two-and-a-half years and turned up his right trouser leg to show where he had been wounded by a sniper's bullet. He thought the enemy was penned into the warren of streets that make up the Old City but they had made use of tunnels to get access to the outside world. He said that 'some months ago they came through a tunnel that came out behind where our men were positioned and attacked them from behind, but we killed them all.' He claimed that for all the international furor about starvation in the Old City 'they are not short of food, but weapons and ammunition.'

Whatever the Syrian government, under increasing international pressure to allow humanitarian aid into Homs, may want, army commanders on the spot like Captain Mohammed are reluctant to allow their enemies, whom they have been fighting for years, off the hook. Contrary to his belief, aid officials are convinced that people in the Old City are starving.

9 February 2014

It is a terrible story but it throws a grim light on the terrors of the Syrian war. It is told at first in a calm, precise voice by Nusair Mahla, a middle-aged government employee, until he finally has to choke back tears as he speaks of the last moments of his sister Maysoun Hala and her husband Nizar along with their two children, Karim and Bishr. He says that many other Syrians have suffered similar tragedies, but in few cases is it known so precisely what the victims themselves thought about their fate.

Nusair, a neatly dressed man in a brown suit, says the first he knew about his sister's family being in danger was an early morning phone call. He recalls it came after 6:30 a.m. and was from neighbours who said that insurgents, whom he invariably calls 'terrorists', had entered the industrial town of Adra 12 miles north of Damascus and were taking hostages. This happened on 11 December when fighters from Jabhat al-Nusra and the Islamic Front, another jihadi group, captured the main employees' residential complex at Adra using an old sewer to outflank government forces.

Nusair recalls: 'I immediately called my sister and told her to get out and come to my house in Mezze.' Nizar worked as a public relations specialist for the state oil company while Maysoun had qualified as an engineer at Damascus University and was a housing manager at Adra. As state employees they were at risk of being killed by jihadi rebels, but what made their execution certain was that, though very secular in lifestyle, they belonged to the Alawite sect.

In the event, the jihadis who had taken Adra believed that state employment or membership of any religious minority—Alawite, Christian, Druze—was enough to merit death. Maysoun told her brother that she did not dare follow his advice to leave her apartment building because the rebels were 'in front of the door of the building and they are also on the rooftops'. Even so, Nusair suggested she go with the two children, Karim, 16, and Bishr, five, and maybe the jihadis would let them pass.

She answered that 'they look so terrifying and I am afraid. I was looking out the window and I saw the terrorists killed one of the National Defence Force with a big knife.' Maysoun explained to Nusair that she and Nizar planned to try to wedge the door of their apartment shut. But if this failed and the jihadis broke in, then the whole family had taken a momentous resolution: rather than face torture and inevitable death at the hands of Jabhat al-Nusra, they would die as a family by detonating grenades that Nizar had somehow acquired (he does not seem to have had a gun).

The rest of the day was chaos, according to Nusair. All the relatives of the trapped family were calling them on landlines and mobiles to try to comfort them. At about midnight, Nusair's 25-year-old son William, who lives in Aleppo, called his aunt and asked about the situation. Maysoun replied: 'They are trying to get into the house.' William heard two gunshots. Maysoun repeated that if the rebels got in the family would blow themselves up. Then she cried out: 'They are inside the house, William, they are inside the house! We should say goodbye. Please forgive us.' Then he heard an explosion.

Nusair breaks off telling the story and puts his hands over his eyes as he tries to suppress his sobs. After a few moments he goes on to say that William phoned him and said: 'They are now in the hands of God.' Nusair called the landline and mobiles of the family in the apartment in Adra and there was no reply. He stayed at home with his own family in Damascus and told them: 'We can't do anything. They are now martyrs.'

Nusair gives some background about Nizar and Maysoun: 'They were a wonderful family. They were like a small democracy. Anything they wanted to do they discussed and, even if five-year-old Bishr was against doing something, they didn't do it.' Nizar was very secular—'I used to call him a secular extremist'—and pictures of the family together show Karim with long hair and his mother with her hair dyed blond and without a headscarf. She had been working hard trying to get ready housing for refugees from Douma, a rebel stronghold not far from Adra. Much of this emergency accommodation was in a half-built residential complex with no glass in the windows and no furniture. Nusair, evidently very close to his sister, says: 'I used to call her every night and she would say, "I am so tired preparing these houses that aren't ready for people to live in."'

The story does not end with the explosion and the apparent death of the family. At 3 a.m. the next day, Nusair got a call from Nizar's brother who said: 'Nizar just called me but the line was cut.' Nusair immediately called the Adra apartment on the landline and it was answered. He asked: 'What happened, Nizar?' Nizar replied in a slurred voice as if in pain: 'Bishr died and Maysoun and Karim are badly injured and bleeding. They are not moving. It is too late for me but please try to do something for them.' Nusair talked and tried to say encouraging things but, he says, 'finally the phone must have fallen from his hand. Those were the last words I heard him say.'

As to what happened next, Nusair says the details are unclear. Some neighbours in Adra said in the single telephone call they were able to make that they had gone to the apartment and found Nizar, Karim and Bishr dead, but that Maysoun was alive, although her leg was severed. They took her to their apartment.

Then comes a final horrible twist to the story. Nusair's daughter Senna is at school in Damascus. Some of the children whose parents were able to escape from Adra are now being taught there. She asked one of them if he knew Maysoun. He said: 'She was the woman with one leg cut off they [the insurgents] dragged behind a car.' Nusair says that Senna fainted as soon as she heard this.

The cruelties of the Syrian civil war get worse by the week. Each side belittles its own atrocities and claims them as retaliation for something even worse done by their enemies. Nusair explains why his sister, brother-in-law and their children decided to kill themselves: he says they believed that 'the jihadis would kill the youngest child in front of the mother and rape the mother in front of the husband. They would torture the men and then kill them all anyway. Better to die by their own hand.'

The story of how Nizar and Maysoun's family died together is well known in Damascus. The many Syrians who work for the government or belong to minorities wonder what they would do if the jihadis were at their door. It is tragedies like this one that provide the fuel for an ever more savage civil war.

23 February 2014

The political winds in the Middle East are changing but they still bring crisis and war. The two most important developments so far this year are the failure of the Geneva II peace talks and Saudi Arabia's replacement of its intelligence chief, Prince Bandar bin Sultan, as director of Syrian policy, with a member of the royal family notably close to the US and hostile to al-Qa'ida.

The reasons for the failure at Geneva are obvious enough and so are the consequences. The US secretary of state, John Kerry, made it clear from the beginning that Washington wants peace negotiations to be primarily about 'transition' and the end of the government of President Bashar al-Assad. But, since Assad's army controls most population centres and main roads in Syria, this radical change in the balance of power will not happen until the rebels stop losing and start winning on the battlefield.

The rebels have failed to overthrow the government, though the government appears incapable of defeating them. This explains the second important development of the year, which is the sidelining of Prince Bandar, who, as the head of Saudi intelligence, was in charge of directing, supplying and financing the rebels. This role has now been taken over by the interior minister, Prince Mohammed bin Nayef, who has been in charge of actions against al-Qa'ida inside the kingdom and is considered one of the most pro-US of the royal family's inner circle. Also assuming a role in determining Saudi policy towards Syria is Prince Miteb bin Abdullah, King Abdullah's third son and head of the Saudi National Guard.

The appointment of Prince Mohammed may mean less emphasis on military assault on Syria and more diplomatic pressure on Russia, Iran and Hezbollah to abandon Assad. One of the big mistakes of the opposition and its backers has been to allow the question of who rules in Damascus to become part of the hot and cold war between Iran and its enemies, and between Shia and Sunni, conflicts that have been going on since the Iranian revolution in 1979. Saudi Arabia could try to de-escalate some of these conflicts, but so far there is little sign of it doing so. Sadly, none of the ingredients for a long war in Syria has disappeared.

8 March 2014

In every war there is a city, a town, a mountain, a river or a road that all sides see as crucial if they are going to win, or at least avoid defeat. In the Syrian civil war, it is the road linking Damascus to Homs, Syria's third city, 100 miles to the north, which then goes west for 64 miles until it reaches the port city of Tartous on the Mediterranean coast. The route is so important because it connects the parts of Syria held by the government. If it is ever cut off permanently, it will be a crippling blow to the rule of President Bashar al-Assad.

It is a road I have got to know far too well in the past two years. When I think about driving it, I feel a tightening of the muscles in my stomach. There is nothing suicidal about the journey, but the risk is always there, and even after I have discussed the dangers involved with my careful, highly-informed and courageous driver George, a Syrian Christian, I wonder if there is something nasty ahead we do not know about.

We watch for signs that will give us advanced warning of danger, such as a lack of traffic coming towards us on the other side of the road, which could mean vehicles are being stopped by some trouble we cannot yet see. A good flow of traffic probably means that all is well, particularly if there are a lot of buses, since Syrian bus drivers go everywhere and are skilled in assessing risks. Heavy vehicles loaded high with valuable goods are also excellent news, because the driver would not be risking his cargo if he thought it might be stolen or destroyed.

I was last on this road in early February and I knew it had been closed for 17 days a month earlier after rebels captured most of the town of

Nabk, halfway to Homs. But George's mother comes from Nabk and he assures me that government troops are firmly back in control and there is no need to worry. Not everybody has been so positive: an experienced foreign journalist advised me to fly to Latakia on the coast in north-west Syria and then drive south to Homs. He said that if I was going to drive to Homs from Damascus it was worth hiring a second car to drive behind my own to make sure I was not followed. He had got through all right, but the second car had been stolen by armed bandits on the way back to Damascus.

It is the first few miles of the main highway north which make me most nervous. They go past districts such as Qaboun, Harasta, Barzeh and Douma that were or are rebel strongholds, but have been ravaged by artillery fire or systematically bulldozed. Viewed from the car window, I see a landscape of ruins with broken walls and concrete floors sandwiched on top of each other. Most of the time there is nobody to be seen as we speed past mile after mile of ruins, but that does not mean that a sniper is not looking at us through the sights of his rifle. The car showrooms that used to line this road are now burnt out and abandoned. The Mercedes building was a focus for rebel resistance and has taken a terrible battering.

We drive very fast and only stop once at a government checkpoint under a bridge. These are regular troops in uniform and not the National Defence Force militia, because the area is still a potential battleground. As in most places in Syria there is an intricate jigsaw puzzle of zones held by forces loyal to the government and zones controlled by rebels. Even this over-simplifies the situation on the ground, because in places like Barzeh there is a negotiated ceasefire, with rebel Free Syrian Army fighters and government soldiers jointly manning checkpoints, while inside Barzeh armed Free Syrian Army men are still in charge.

The military geography of Syria often follows its sectarian geography. We drive past tall buildings which are undamaged where most of the inhabitants are Alawites. As we exit the northern outskirts of Damascus, George looks more relaxed and says encouragingly, 'That is 80 per cent of the dangerous parts of this journey over.' Somehow, I do not feel comforted. A little to my surprise, he is not too worried about the proximity of Maloula, a Christian village built in a spectacular ravine in the mountains just off the road to the west that we had visited last summer. These days, all the Christians have fled and it is partly in the hands of Jabhat al-Nusra, which has gunmen in buildings and caves overlooking the town. It would not take much for these jihadis to push down from the mountain and block the road.

A strange aspect of the war in this part of Syria is how close the combatants are to each other. In a few cases there are negotiated ceasefires, but others seem to be local truces (or a live-and-let-live understanding between the adversaries) that are always fragile. This is particularly true of the part of the road which George and I are about to drive down, because clearly visible on a hill off to the left is the town of Yabroud, which is held by Jabhat al-Nusra, but mysteriously still has a large population of Christians who have not fled. Some deal is evidently in operation, but nobody quite knows what it is. The deal does not apply to strangers, and somebody fired a shot at us 18 months ago in just this area; the bullet whistled by uncomfortably close to our car. The Syrian Army has been bombarding Yabroud, but this does not necessarily mean it will launch a ground assault. The government is short of combat troops and uses them sparingly, usually to keep open roads vital to itself, or to block routes important to the rebels' supply network.

A few miles beyond Yabroud, Nabk is firmly back in government hands and the authorities are having a victory celebration in the undamaged centre of the town. We turn off the main road to have a look. I am not a great fan of this type of demonstration, with school children playing the main part, because local people are under the gun and do not have any alternative but to take part. The rally does show, however, that the government is pretty confident that it is in control. I also learn an interesting fact: the National Defence Force militiamen policing the demonstration were previously members of the rebel Free Syrian Army until a couple of months ago. They simply switched sides, though nobody knows on what terms.

We spend the night in Homs and then turn west, taking the road to Tartous, a city where there are many Alawites and which is firmly in the government camp. As we leave Homs, on our right is a big area of tall modern buildings called al-Wa'ar, whose 400,000 inhabitants are Sunni and where Sunni from the rest of Homs have taken refuge. Wa'ar is blockaded and it is difficult to get in or out, though it is not quite so tightly besieged as the Old City of Homs. This is an important strategic area. Homs' oil refinery is just to the south of the road and has been hit by mortar fire, though not badly damaged. I watch as a Syrian Army tank manoeuvres on the road before firing a shell into Wa'ar.

A little further west the road passes through the Homs Gap, with low mountains on either side of the highway, making this a much-fought-over route down the centuries. Control of the Homs Gap is why the Knights Hospitallers spent so much money in the 13th century building the Krak des Chevaliers, the greatest of the Crusader castles, with its massive towers and huge concentric masonry walls. I try to pick out the fortress on its distant hill and suddenly its white stones are illuminated by a shaft of sunlight—like a castle in a Renaissance painting. I am sorry I cannot get closer, but it is held by rebels based in two Sunni villages at its base, Zahra and Hosn. The villages have been blockaded for months, but what makes Zahra important are the oil and gas pipes, as well as the electricity lines that go through it—the rebels have been blowing them up.

By the time we reach the end of the road it is evident that in this part of Syria the government is expanding its control and the rebels are under pressure. But the expansion is slow and the army is overstretched. The road is more secure than it was six months ago, but it is still vulnerable to a sudden attack. The journey is also a reminder that Syria is more than ever a patchwork of different circumstances, depending on the military situation and which sects predominate. Much of what I heard in Beirut and Damascus about what is happening turns out to be mistaken, and media reporting has been full of certainties that melt away in the face of reality. In Syria, more than most places, only eyewitness information is worth much.

PART VI: BIRTH OF A CALIPHATE

In early June 2014 I was attending a conference in the Jordanian capital Amman about the war in Syria. I was arguing that the most important development in Syria was the rise of the Islamic State of Iraq and the Levant, which was freely carrying out military operations in an enormous area reaching from the Iranian border almost to the Mediterranean. The jihadi militants had captured Fallujah, 40 miles west of Baghdad, in January and the 350,000-strong Iraqi Army had been unable to launch a successful counter-attack and win it back. I sensed a certain restrained impatience among the Syrian experts who listened politely to what I had to say, but by and large did not seem to take my point very seriously. I had had a somewhat similar response at two conferences I had attended in London earlier in the year and I was beginning to wonder if there was something in the situation that I was missing. I stayed on in Amman for a day after the conference to see an Iraqi friend and noticed stories on the news-wires reporting that ISIS were attacking Samarra, Mosul, Baquba, Ramadi and Tikrit. This was in keeping with ISIS tactics, which were to launch a series of diversionary attacks with a couple of hundred fighters in motorised columns, before striking suddenly and very hard at single target. I wondered if this was the start of a general offensive by the jihadis and wrote a piece about it for The Independent *which the paper put on the front page.*

I had a more than usually strong personal interest for finding out how the situation in Iraq was developing because I was due to go there on 15 June. I wanted to see if I should modify my position as a permanent Cassandra, always saying that ISIS was rapidly gaining in strength and the Baghdad government was far weaker than anyone realised. I knew the Iraqi Army was dysfunctional and I was writing a book to be called The Return of the Jihadis *based on some lectures I had given in New York. At Christmas, I had made Abu Bakr al-Baghdadi, the ISIS leader, my newspaper's Middle East man of the year for 2013. But even so, I was astonished on getting back to London to hear that ISIS had taken Mosul and the Iraqi Army had disintegrated and was in flight.*

I travelled to Baghdad as previously arranged and was a little concerned to find that the official who was to confirm my entry visa had not yet arrived at the airport. When he belatedly did so, he explained that there were extra security measures on the road from the city centre to the airport. While I was waiting, I saw an old friend, Ammar al-Shahbander, an active opponent of Saddam Hussein who now ran the Baghdad branch of the Institute for War and Peace Reporting, which trained Iraqi journalists and published their works on its website. Ammar must have been on the same plane as me, but I had not previously noticed him. He invited me to come to stay in his apartment which was in the same building as his institute. It was a little safer than other places I might stay because it was in a well-protected area in east Baghdad. I thanked him, but said I would stick to my original plan to stay in a hotel where I would be freer to move about.

I rapidly found that this was riskier than I had expected as Baghdad's 7 million people waited to see if ISIS was going to attack the capital. There were checkpoints all over the city at which the army and police were reinforced by dangerous looking intelligence men in civilian clothes and Shia militiamen of uncertain loyalties. I imagined that the sense of fear in Baghdad, and the disbelief that the military disaster could be quite as bad as it looked, must be similar to what people in Paris felt in 1940 when they heard that the German Army had broken through and was racing across northern France.

I was staying in the Coral, a pleasantly modern hotel that I had used before, though this time round I was a little alarmed to find that I was the only guest. Sitting alone in the coffee shop, I watched through a plate glass window as a couple of security guards lolled in plastic chairs outside, their Kalashnikovs dangling from their hands. They did not seem much of a protection and I decided to take up Ammar's offer of a bed in his apartment and a place to work in his office. It was a good place to be during those critical days because the IWPR staff were monitoring Iraqi and foreign television as well as local websites and were highly informed about the real situation on the ground. Ammar, a cheerful, burly, prematurely balding man aged about 40, had been through so many crises in Iraq that he was unfazed by this one, though he could see that a civil war of great viciousness had begun. I liked him because he was highly intelligent, well informed and sceptical about whatever bit of conventional wisdom was going round in Baghdad at the time. Yet he was never cheaply cynical and, like myself, was fascinated by the extraordinary twists and turns of Iraqi politics.

As used to be said of Russians during Soviet times, Iraqis under a certain age could not help having led interesting and dangerous lives and Ammar's life had been more interesting and dangerous than most.

The weeks after the fall of Mosul were full of dangers: Baghdad is a Shia-majority city, but there were Sunni enclaves that might rise up at the same time as ISIS columns, flushed with victory after taking Mosul and Tikrit, attacked from outside. There were rumours of an assault on the Green Zone. Many ministers and MPs had fled to Jordan. Ammar did not think ISIS could attack successfully, but even so I found him examining a Kalashnikov carefully and commenting that the sights needed adjusting. We watched television together with some hilarity as Iraqi official spokesmen claimed a string of imaginary victories of which pictures were never available. Ammar shook his head in disbelief and said that Iraqis needed visual evidence of what they were being told, otherwise they would watch foreign channels unsympathetic to the Iraqi government.

I left Baghdad after a few weeks. It was not an easy place from which to report because government officials and army officers were of little use as informants since they themselves did not know what was happening. If they sounded as if they did, I reminded myself that these same people had just been responsible for one of the biggest and most humiliating military defeats in history. It was difficult to get to the front line in any direction because soldiers and militiamen were automatically turning back foreign journalists, even when they carried letters from senior commanders guaranteeing their access to the front. Worse, nobody knew where the front line really was, and I did not want to wander into no-man's-land on the outskirts of the capital and run into an ISIS patrol. An army officer took a group of journalists, of which I was not one, towards Abu Ghraib, the site of the famous prison just to the west of Baghdad. The idea was to dispel rumours that ISIS had captured it, but the government's attempt to restore confidence was discredited when the officer in charge of the press party adamantly refused to enter Abu Ghraib himself.

The situation in Baghdad did not improve despite a change of government from Prime Minister Nouri al-Maliki to Haider al-Abadi, of whom great things were expected. I covered the fighting and developments inside the newly declared Islamic State or Caliphate from the quarter or more of Iraq under the authority of the Kurdistan Regional Government. This now had a 650-mile frontier with ISIS and personal security was better than in Baghdad. I visited the Shia holy cities of Najaf and Kerbala where the religious authorities were tightly in control. When I did return to Baghdad I was planning to see if I could stay once again with Ammar, who I knew was one of the best-informed people

in the city. I was in Arbil, the Kurdish capital, on 2 May 2015 when I heard
that there had been car bombings in Karada and idly thought that this was
close to the IWPR office where I had been staying. A few minutes later, I saw
on the newswires that Ammar was dead. He had gone to an evening concert in
Karada, a district that was relatively safe by the standards of Baghdad. When
it ended, he and a friend had walked to a nearby café and it was as they left
a little later that a car bomb had exploded beside them. Ammar was killed
instantly by shrapnel lodged in his heart.

FIFTEEN

Ten Years On

Iraq, 2013

3 March 2013

Iraq is disintegrating as a country under the pressure of a mounting political, social and economic crisis, say Iraqi leaders. They add that 10 years after the US invasion and occupation the conflict between the three main communities—Shia, Sunni and Kurd—is deepening to a point just short of civil war. 'There is zero trust between Iraqi leaders,' says an Iraqi politician in daily contact with them. But like many of those I interview in Iraq, he does not want to be identified by name.

The escalating crisis in Iraq since the end of 2011 has largely been ignored by the rest of the world because international attention has been focused on Syria, the Arab uprisings and domestic economic troubles. The US and the UK have sought to play down overwhelming evidence that their invasion and occupation has produced one of the most dysfunctional and crooked governments in the world. Iraq has been violent and unstable for so long that Iraqis and foreigners alike have become desensitised to omens suggesting that, bad as the situation has been, it may be about to get a great deal worse.

The record of failure of post-Saddam governments, given the financial resources available, is astounding. One of the reasons many Iraqis welcomed the fall of Saddam in 2003, whatever their feelings about foreign occupation, was that they thought that his successors would restore normal life after years of sanctions and war. To their astonishment and fury this has not happened, though Iraq now enjoys $100 billion a year in oil revenues. In Baghdad there is scarcely a new civilian building to be seen and most of the new construction is heavily fortified police or military outposts. In Basra, at the heart of the oil fields, there are pools of sewage and heaps of uncollected rubbish in the streets on which herds of goats forage.

I was in Baghdad at the end of January when there were a couple of days of heavy rain. For years, contractors—Iraqi and foreign—have supposedly been building a new sewage system for the Iraqi capital but none of the water was disappearing down the drains. I drove for miles in east Baghdad through streets flooded with grey, murky water, diluted with sewage. I only turned round in Sadr City, the Shia working-class bastion, when the flood waters became too deep to drive through. Shirouk Abayachi, an adviser to the Ministry of Water Resources, explained to me that 'since 2003, $7 billion has been spent to build a new sewage system for Baghdad, but either the sewers weren't built or they were built very badly.' She said the worst flooding had been where in theory there were new sewage pipes, while those built in the 1980s worked better, concluding that 'corruption is the key to all this.'

Theft of public money and incompetence on a gargantuan scale means the government fails to provide adequate electricity, clean water or sanitation. One-third of the labour force is unemployed and, when you include those under-employed, the figure is over half. Even those who do have a job have often obtained it by bribery. 'I feared seven or eight years ago that Iraq would become like Nigeria,' says one former minister, 'but in fact it is far worse.' He cites as evidence a $1.3 billion contract for an electricity project signed by a minister with a Canadian company that had only a nominal existence—and a German company that was bankrupt.

Iraqis looked for improved personal security and the rule of law after Saddam, but again this has not materialised. The violence is much less than during the mass slaughter of 2006 and 2007 when upwards of 3,000 Iraqis were being butchered every month. But Baghdad and central Iraq remains one of the most dangerous places on earth in terms of bombings, assassinations and kidnappings. It is not just political violence that darkens lives, but a breakdown of civil society that leaves people often looking to tribal justice in preference to police or official courts. One woman says: 'If you have a traffic accident, what matters is not whether you were right or wrong but what tribe you belong to.'

The same sense of insecurity in the face of arbitrary government taints political life. If there is not quite the same fear as under Saddam, it often feels as if this is only because the security forces are less efficient, not because they are any less cruel or corrupt. The rule of Nouri al-Maliki, prime minister since 2006, has become a near dictatorship with highly developed means of repression, such as secret prisons, and pervasive use of torture. He has sought to monopolise control over the army, intelligence service, government apparatus and budget, making sure that his supporters get the lion's share of jobs and contracts. His State of Law Coalition won only 24 per cent of the votes in the 2010 election—2.8 million votes out of 19 million registered voters—but he has ruled as if he had received an overwhelming mandate.

Dr Mahmoud Othman, a veteran Kurdish leader and member of parliament, gives an excoriating analysis of what is wrong with present-day Iraq. 'It is a failed state,' he says. 'The country is run by gangs [within the government] and gangs are more important than law. Maliki rules because he is head of the armed forces. Iraq is run by force, but force does not mean that those exercising it are in control.'

Saddam Hussein and the US both found to their cost that Iraq can never be ruled by compulsion alone, something Maliki has been slow to learn. The power of religious and ethnic communities is too great for successful coercion by the state and is underpinned by Iraqis' loyalty to tribes, clans and extended families. When the Americans were leaving Iraq their main concern was that they would leave behind a security vacuum. But this was to mistake the nature of Iraqi politics. 'The new [post-Saddam Hussein] Iraq has been built on the consensus of three communities: the Kurds, the Shia and the Sunni,' says one Iraqi leader, previously optimistic about the future of the country. 'This political consensus has fractured.' He believes there is still some chance of repairing the damage, but, if this fails, he says, 'the end of Iraq and the division of the country will be inevitable.'

Iraqis who fought for years against Saddam Hussein, blaming most of Iraq's ills on his regime, today express bitter disillusionment with his successors. Mustafa al-Khadimi, a veteran opponent of Saddam's rule, says: 'I feel saddened and disappointed. I have given my life to destroying the old system and have seen members of my family and friends killed. Now I watch Iraq treated like a cake to be cut up between our politicians.' Others, equally despairing, criticise Maliki for exacerbating and exploiting political divisions to keep power in his hands. As the pre-eminent leader of the Shia, three-fifths of the population, he alarms them by suggesting that their political dominance is under threat from the Sunni, a fifth of Iraqis, once in charge under Saddam but now marginalised. Last year, Maliki sought to unite Sunni and Shia Arabs against the Kurds, another fifth of the population, by massing troops and threatening to invade Kurdish-controlled but disputed areas.

What makes these escalating conflicts so bizarre and damaging to Iraq is that they are fought by combatants who are part of the same power-sharing government. But because they do not co-operate—and indeed hate and fear each other—government itself is paralysed. The administrative apparatus has in any case been degraded by the departure of able officials abroad and the allocation of jobs solely through political patronage rather than experience or ability—membership of al-Dawa, the ruling Shia religious party, often being the essential qualification. One study of Iraqi officials revealed that on average they put in just 17 minutes of productive work during the day. These toxic elements combine to produce a corrupt, self-serving and ineffective government. But its failings have been there a long time and might not in themselves have produced a new crisis. Party patronage may be a crude and unfair way of distributing oil wealth, but it benefits a lot of people. Iraqis may be enraged by the lack of public services such as electricity or health care, but they have suffered these shortages for a long time. By 2011 Iraq had achieved a bloody and unsatisfactory stability that might have endured longer had it not been rocked by important changes in the political balance of power inside and outside Iraq.

The last American troops left at the end of 2011 and President Barack Obama made clear by his actions that he did not intend to be inveigled back into the Iraqi political morass. Polls showed American voters had a deep distaste for any involvement in Iraq. American influence plummeted. But the Iraqi political system was in large part a US creation and many of its leaders owed their careers to US backing. This includes Maliki, who was appointed as prime minister by the US ambassador, and Zalmay Khalilzad, because he was one of the few Shia politicians acceptable to the US and Iran. Both countries, though they fight each other for influence in Iraq, have a common interest in stabilising the post-Saddam settlement. When Maliki was reappointed prime minister in 2010 an Iraqi official called me to comment sarcastically that 'the Great Satan [US] and The Axis of Evil [Iran] have come together and given us a new prime minister.' With the

US departure there disappeared a major force for persuading Iraqi leaders to agree to share power.

In their last years there, the Americans had learned how to play Iraqi political games effectively. In 2007 during the so-called surge they had offered protection to the Sunni in return for an end to military action against US troops (al-Qa'ida continued to attack the Shia civilians and Iraqi government forces). It was always a temporary arrangement, regarded with suspicion by the Shia-dominated government in Baghdad. Just as the last US soldiers were leaving Iraq, Maliki forced his Sunni vice president Tariq al-Hashemi to flee to Kurdistan and he was later sentenced to death.

The Sunni suffered shattering defeats with the overthrow of Saddam Hussein, the formation of a Shia–Kurdish government and the loss of the sectarian civil war. But the conflict in Syria marked a change for the better in Sunni fortunes. They have been emboldened by the bid for power of Syria's Sunni majority just across the border from their own heartlands in Anbar and Nineveh provinces. They are encouraged by Sunni states backing Sunni rebels in Syria and sympathising with Sunni demonstrators in Iraq. Since late December, 2012, Iraqi Sunni have peacefully protested against discrimination in all its forms. Maliki and his senior officials appear to be finally taking on board the significance of Sunni protests and the strength of the Sunni counter-offensive against the Shia in the Middle East. Maliki predicted last week that 'if the opposition [in Syria] is victorious, there will be civil war in Lebanon, divisions in Jordan and a sectarian war in Iraq.'

The US departure, the Syrian crisis and the Sunni protests are all destabilising Iraq. The Kurds and the Shia religious leadership—the Marji'iyyah—regard Maliki and his government with distrust, but the very divisions of Iraq that weaken central governments also make it difficult to get rid of those in power, because their opponents are themselves so divided. Opposed to Maliki they may be, but they cannot agree on a successor.

The Shia are themselves divided. Muqtada al-Sadr, the populist nationalist cleric who fought the US occupation, has called for the removal of Maliki and has praised the demonstrators in Anbar. This is important because his well-organised political movement used to have a military wing, the Mehdi Army, feared and execrated by Sunni for carrying out atrocities against them. Muqtada recently said: 'Maliki's entire policy is offensive to the Shia because it portrays them as a tyrannous majority in the eyes of the Kurds and Sunni.'

Iraq is one of the great political minefields of the world. It is full of
ancient and modern battlefields where great empires have been humbled or
destroyed. Saddam Hussein claimed to have built up an army of 1 million
men in 1991, only to see it evaporate or mutiny. Much the same happened
in 2003. The US Army marched into Baghdad full of arrogant contempt
for what Iraqis said or did. Within a year the US military controlled only
islands of territory in a country they thought they had conquered.

Maliki may employ a million men in different branches of the Iraqi security forces. In most countries this would guarantee government control,
but in practice Maliki only has full authority in about half the national
territory. He has no power in the northern third of the country held by
the Kurds and increasingly limited influence in Sunni areas. This does not
mean the government is collapsing. It still has money, jobs, the army, intelligence services and electoral legitimacy. Qusay Abdul Wahab al-Suhail,
the Sadrist deputy speaker of parliament, says that the problem in Iraq is
that all parties have some degree of strength and therefore see no need to
compromise with opponents. The result is a permanent political stalemate
or paralysis.

Whatever the US and British invasion and occupation of Iraq 10 years
ago was meant to achieve it has not created a peaceful and prosperous
country. If an Iraqi was arrested before 2003 for a political offence he could
expect to be tortured unless he immediately confessed, and this is still the
case. The one improvement is that he stands less chance of being executed.

Ordinary Iraqis are pessimistic or ambivalent about the future. Professor
Yahya Abbas says: 'If you ask my students "What do you want?" About
95 per cent will answer "I want to leave Iraq."'

5 March 2013

'Iraq or Maliki! Iraq or Maliki!' shout Sunni Arab demonstrators as they
block roads in western Iraq in protest against Prime Minister Nouri al-
Maliki and discrimination against their community. Demonstrations by
Sunni, in their tens of thousands, began with the arrest of the bodyguards
of a Sunni politician on 20 December 2012, and are still continuing. For
the first time since 2003 the Sunni are showing signs of unity and intelligent leadership as they try to escape political marginalisation.

In the first days of the protests, Sunni demonstrators held up pictures
of Saddam Hussein and waved the old regime's version of the Iraqi flag.
This changed when a revered Sunni scholar, Abdul-Malik al-Saadi, taking a

leadership role, instructed that these symbols of Sunni supremacy should be dropped and substituted with slogans acceptable to the Shia. Saadi issued a fatwa condemning 'regionalism,' which is the code for a semi-independent Sunni region, a demand which, if granted, would mean the break-up of Iraq. He appealed instead for Sunni and Shia unity against the Maliki government. A Shia political observer noted that 'they are aware that without winning over the Shia south of the country they face isolation and defeat.'

The new direction of Sunni opposition has met with a positive response. Muqtada al-Sadr, once dreaded by Sunni as the inspiration for the death squads of the Mehdi Army Shia militia, supported the protests, saying: 'Iraq is not only composed of Shia, but Sunni, Kurds, Turkmen, Christians, Mandeans and Jews as well.' The cross-sectarian appeal by the Sunni makes it more difficult, but not impossible, for Maliki to play the sectarian card in upcoming local and parliamentary elections this year.

The Sunni have a lot to complain about. Anger is deep over an anti-terrorism law that allows detention without trial of a suspect on the word of an unidentified informer. Sheikh Qassim al-Kerbuli, a leader in the Sunni heartland province of Anbar, says: 'I know a Sunni teacher in Baghdad who threw a Shia student out of an examination because he caught him cheating. The student told the security forces the teacher was a terrorist and he is now in prison.'

Worse things can and do happen in prison. Torture of detainees is habitual, leading to false confessions and long prison sentences. This is not confined to Sunni, but they are most frequently targeted for abuse. 'When the security forces arrest someone they torture them with electricity,' says Nazar Abdel Hamid from Fallujah, who is helping organise the protests. 'They are hung up by their hands or forced to sit on a broken bottle.' The demonstrators are enraged over women being detained for long periods by the security forces because their male relatives are under suspicion, but cannot be found. Sheikh Kerbuli says: 'I know of one woman who has been held for six years because her husband was seen with a suspicious-looking black bag. Nobody knows what was in the bag but he escaped, so they took away his wife instead.'

Such stories are confirmed by human rights activists who have visited prisons. Pascale Warda, a former minister and one of the heads of the Hammurabi Human Rights Organisation, visited the women's prison in Baghdad last year. She says 'there were 414 inmates of whom 169 had been arrested but not sentenced. Our team saw traces of torture at the time of the investigation. Some women prisoners had been raped, usually when they were being moved from the place where they were being investigated to the prison.' The accusation of rape caused outrage when a government supporter claimed the women had been paid to make the allegation. William Warda, Pascale's husband, who also belongs to the Hammurabi Human Rights Organisation, says the authorities 'always depend on confessions from those arrested under the anti-terrorism law so they always use torture on them.' He says that when he asks why prisoners have been detained without charge for so long they say 'they are still looking for evidence against them after three or four years.'

Sunni grievances are much more extensive than false imprisonment and mistreatment. They feel they have been reduced to the status of second-class citizens, discriminated against when it comes to getting a fair share of jobs and projects to provide electricity, water and health care. They see anti-Baathist legislation, supposedly directed against leading members of the party that ruled Iraq from 1968 to 2003, as a sectarian weapon used to take away the jobs and pensions of Sunni teachers and minor civil servants. Ghassan al-Atiyyah, a political scientist and activist, says he visited a teacher in the Sunni district of Abu Ghraib in Baghdad who 'after 30 years as a school teacher is out of a job and a pension. They just sent him a message written on a scrap of paper saying "Go home." He is penniless. If he was younger he would get a gun.'

Many Shia express sympathy for cases like this, but they add that Sunni in Anbar, Salahudin, Nineveh and Sunni districts of Baghdad are frequently unemployed because they used to have plum jobs under Saddam Hussein as army, police or intelligence officers. In the 1980s it was said that 80 per cent of army officers were Sunni and 20 per cent were Shia, while the proportions were the reverse in the lower ranks. A retired Shia general says 'it is hypocritical of Sunni to demand back security jobs that they only held in the past because of sectarian bias in their favour.'

The Sunni demonstrations, now entering their third month, raise a question crucial to the future of Iraq: how far will the Sunni, once dominant, accept a lower status? Members of the government fear the real agenda of the Sunni is not reform but regime change, a counter-revolution reversing the post-Saddam Hussein political settlement. 'Shia leaders believe they have been elected, are legitimate and any change should come through an election,' says one senior official. 'If there should be any attempt to take power from them by force, they will fight.'

There is no doubt that in 2003, with the fall of Saddam Hussein, and again in the sectarian civil war of 2006–07, the Sunni of Iraq suffered historic defeats. Baghdad became a largely Shia city with few mixed districts and remains so to this day. 'More than half of all Baghdad neighbourhoods now contain a clear Shia majority,' reads a US embassy cable on the changed sectarian balance in the capital dating from the end of 2007 and published by WikiLeaks. 'Sunni have largely fled to outlying areas or have been concentrated into small enclaves surrounded by Shia neighbourhoods.' A sub-heading in the cable about these enclaves reads 'islands of stability in a sea of fear'. Shia and Sunni do not necessarily hate each other, but they do fear each other and that fear will take a long time to dissipate.

Much of Iraq has been cantonised into Sunni, Shia and Kurdish areas in a way that was not true before 2003. In places, burnt out Sunni mosques, or mosques taken over by Shia, underline the extent of Sunni defeat. Abdul-Karim Ali, a real estate broker, says Sunni may want to return, but they are frightened by rumours of action against them, even when these are not true. 'I was just with a Sunni family in Doura, who want me to sell a good house in Bayaa in another part of Baghdad, where they used to live, but they think it is now too dangerous for them to go there even to visit.'

Sunni hopes and Shia fears are being heightened by the struggle for power in Syria with the Sunni majority there likely to emerge the winners. This boosts the Sunni of Iraq who no longer feel isolated and sense that they benefit from a region-wide Sunni counter-attack against the Shia led by Saudi Arabia, Qatar and Turkey. 'Extreme Sunni and Shia both feel a sense of power,' says Dr Atiyyah, 'The Sunni say we have the whole Arab world behind us. The Shia leadership says we are the majority in Iraq.' He fears these beliefs are a recipe for mutual destruction.

Al-Qa'ida in Iraq is using the protests to issue a call for Sunni to take up arms against the government. There has been an increase in suicide bomb attacks on Shia targets and harassment of government forces, mostly in areas where al-Qa'ida has traditionally been strong north of Baghdad. There is no doubt these attacks fuel sectarian animosities, particularly as the government suspects Sunni politicians and religious leaders of giving a green light to such actions as a form of leverage against the state. 'There are those who will close their eyes to what al-Qa'ida is doing,' says a leading politician. 'Maybe al-Sahwa, the Sons of Iraq [the government-paid Sunni militia], will not be so interested in fighting al-Qa'ida.'

At the heart of the problem of creating an acceptable consensus and balance of power between Shia, Sunni and Kurd in Iraq is that they have all been traumatised by atrocities inflicted on them by other Iraqi communities in the recent past. In the case of the Shia and Sunni the memory of the sectarian slaughter of 2006–07 is still fresh and it takes little to revive past terrors. For instance, in the largely Shia Jihad district of south-west Baghdad in recent days, menacing notes have been turning up at Sunni homes. They read: 'The zero hour has come. So leave along with your families … you are the enemy.' They are signed by the Mukhtar Army, a newly formed Shia sectarian group, though their spokesman denies the flyers come from them. Even so, many Sunni residents are panicking, packing up and fleeing to Sunni enclaves in other parts of the city.

Many Sunni have seen their lives torn apart by occupation and sectarian violence over the last decade and are fearful of it happening again. A Sunni friend with a middle ranking post in a ministry says most jobs are going to members of the ruling Dawa party of Maliki. 'They run it like a tribe,' he says. 'Every appointee is one of their relatives.' He speaks fearfully of civil war but adds that 'if the Sunni could just get jobs and pensions all this fury would ebb away.'

6 March 2013

Iraq is the first Arab country to be ruled by a Shia government since Saladin overthrew the Fatimids in Egypt in 1171, claims an Iraqi friend. But Shia rule is deeply troubled, and Shia leaders have been unable to share power in a stable way that satisfies the Sunni, the Kurds and even the Shia community. This is not wholly the leaders' fault. They fear the Kurds want independence and the Sunni hope to regain their old dominance. Qusay Abdul Wahab al-Suhail, the Sadrist deputy speaker of parliament, says 'the problem is that the Sunni do not accept power in the hands of the Shia.'

Prime Minister Nouri al-Maliki's response to all this has been to grab as much control as he can, circumventing agreements that would parcel out power in a nominally fair way, that, in practice, paralyses the state machinery. The government in the Green Zone, the great fortress it inherited from the Americans, is not shy about its sectarian allegiance. Shia banners and posters of Imam Ali and Imam Hussein decorate checkpoints and blockhouses in the Green Zone and much of the rest of Baghdad, including prisons and police stations.

Maliki's efforts to monopolise power—though less effective than his critics allege—have alienated powerful Shia individuals, parties and religious institutions. Grand Ayatollah Ali al-Sistani, the pre-eminent Shia religious leader of immense influence, whom the Americans at the height of their power found they could not defy, will no longer see the prime minister's emissaries. The Marji'iyyah—the small group of men at the top of the Shia religious hierarchy—have come to see Maliki as a provoker of crises that discredit Shi'ism and may break up the country. Iran, the only other large Shia-controlled state, with strong but not overwhelming influence in Iraq, says privately that it is unhappy with Maliki, but does not want a political explosion in the country while it is facing ever-mounting pressure over Syria, its other Arab ally, and its economy is buckling under the impact of sanctions.

Iran tells Iraqi politicians it would like Maliki to stay in office until the parliamentary elections in 2014 but maybe not thereafter. Muqtada al-Sadr, whose support has been crucial for Maliki in the past, says he wants the prime minister to go, though the Sadrists remain an important part of his government. The idea of including all the opponents of the government within it may have seemed a good way of giving all interests a share of the cake, but means a leadership so fragmented that no decision can be taken.

The Sadrists' position is the most interesting and significant because they have so frequently made the running in Iraqi politics before and after Saddam Hussein's fall. They are seeking to transform themselves from a feared paramilitary organisation—the Mehdi Army—into a respected political movement. There are parallels here with the way Sinn Fein and the IRA in Northern Ireland demilitarised during the 1990s in order to gain power constitutionally and share it with their former enemies. Earlier this year Muqtada attended a Christian service in the Our Lady of Salvation Church in central Baghdad where some 50 worshippers had been slaughtered by al-Qa'ida in 2010. He later prayed in the Sunni Abdul-Qadir al-Gailani Mosque in central Baghdad. He supports the protests in Anbar and Sunni areas on the condition they do not demand regime change, saying they are 'not a crisis, but a healthy phenomenon that reflects a popular and democratic movement'.

The Sadrists have gone back and forth with Maliki over the last two years. They often denounce him but observers note that at crucial moments they appear to pull their punch. Muqtada, though often labelled by the

Western media as a 'firebrand cleric', has always been a subtle and cautious politician, underestimated by the Americans during the occupation ('they never figured out that he was anti-Iranian,' says one Iraqi observer). Critics say the Sadrists are eager to have it both ways, simultaneously supporting and opposing Maliki. In their defence, it should be said that the Kurds and other political parties behave similarly and this is the nature of Iraqi politics. Maliki plays the same game, and, although the Sadrists have several ministers in his cabinet, he holds 600–1,000 of their militants in jail for fighting Americans and government forces before Muqtada reconciled with him.

Probably the Sadrists do not want to go into outright opposition to Maliki until they know they can displace him. Diaa al-Asadi, a linguistics expert, former minister and the secretary general of the al-Ahrar bloc, as the Sadrist movement is called, says that in his personal opinion: 'We are not talking about Maliki's integrity or him being good or bad. He is a person who does not know how to plan. He is a simple-minded person. He is focused on undermining his enemies. He doesn't have a vision of rebuilding Iraq.' He ticks off as acceptable the Sunni protesters' demands, such as the release of prisoners, but adds: 'There are some slogans used by the demonstrators saying there should be a revolution against the Shia because they come from Iran.'

Iraqi politicians say the Sadrists may lose some votes in the local elections in April because of Muqtada's openly expressed sympathy for the Sunni protesters. Yet all these calculations may become obsolete if Iraq is destabilised by the reverberations from the war in Syria. The moderation of the Sunni protesters in Anbar and the sympathetic response of Sadrists is important because these were the two main protagonists in the sectarian civil war six years ago. But suspicions run deep and people fear the ingredients are there for a new sectarian war, however much the thought horrifies them.

7 March 2013

Kurdistan presents itself as the new economic tiger of the Middle East, flush with the prospect of exploiting its oil fields. The tall towers of two new luxury hotels rise high above the Kurdish capital Arbil, the oldest inhabited city in the world, whose skyline had previously been dominated by its ancient citadel for thousands of years. Nearby, a glittering new airport has replaced the old Iraqi military runway. In contrast to Baghdad and other Iraqi cities, the cars in the streets look new. Above all, and again in sharp contrast to further south, there is a continuous supply of electricity.

'I cannot find employees to go and work in the oil field,' complains a Kurdish manager in a Western oil company. 'I cannot even find rooms in the new hotels for visiting executives because they are so full.' Convoys of shiny black vehicles conveying delegations of visiting businessmen from Germany, France, the UAE and Turkey race through the city. Many of those now coming to Kurdistan could not have found it on the map a few years ago and—so Kurds who have met them caustically remark—are often still unsure of its location when they leave. But there is no doubting international business enthusiasm for the Kurdistan Regional Government (KRG), the semi-independent enclave in northern Iraq that is prospering like no other part of the country. A Kurdish businessman says: 'We are benefiting from having a boom at a time of austerity and slow growth in the rest of the world, so the boardrooms of international companies are particularly interested in us.'

At the heart of the boom are 50 or 60 foreign oil companies seeking to find and exploit Kurdistan's oil, on better terms and with greater security and official backing than they could find in the rest of Iraq. This influx started with small and obscure foreign companies in the years after the fall of Saddam in 2003. But foreign interest deepened, the size of the oil companies increased, and in 2010 ExxonMobil signed an exploration contract with the KRG. The central government in Baghdad was furious and threatened to punish Exxon, which has large interests in southern Iraq, but failed to do so as other oil majors—Chevron, Total and Gazprom—had also signed their own deals.

When the Kurds first encouraged foreign oil companies to look for oil on territory they controlled, Baghdad was sanguine. In 2007 Iraq's oil minister Hussein Shahristani, now deputy prime minister in charge of energy-related issues, said to me that, even if foreign oil companies found oil, they would not be able to export it. He asked sarcastically: 'Are they going to carry it out in buckets?' It is this calculation that has changed radically in the last year. A new pipeline is being built between the KRG and Turkey, which in theory would enable the Kurds to export crude and get paid for it without permission from Baghdad. This would give the 5 million Iraqi Kurds an economically and politically independent state for the first time in their history after decades of war, ethnic cleansing and genocide. On the other hand, Turkey may decide that it is not in its interests to defy Baghdad and break up Iraq.

It is a moment of unprecedented political change in the region. Iraq as a country is getting close to disintegration as a single state, but this is not inevitable. Old alliances are being junked and hated enemies embraced. KRG president Massoud Barzani, long demonised in Turkey, was a guest at the conference of Turkey's ruling AKP party and was given a standing ovation. The Iraqi Kurds are tipping towards Ankara and away from Baghdad. For a decade Turkish companies have poured into KRG and are doing trade worth at least $8 billion a year there. Only a few years ago the Turks would regularly close the Khabour bridge, the main crossing point between the KRG and Turkey, leading to enormous traffic jams. These days it is Baghdad that tries to emphasise the KRG's isolation, refusing even to allow the plane carrying the Turkish energy minister to cross its airspace for a conference in Arbil.

The contrast between Kurdistan as a ruined battlefield just a decade ago and its appearance today is so striking as to take one's breath away. It may also be so great as to unbalance its leaders' sense of the feasible. One critic says: 'We are making the same mistake with the Turks today as we did with the Americans and the Shah in 1975. We are once again becoming over-reliant on foreign powers.' For all the economic development in KRG it remains dependant on getting a 17 per cent share of Iraqi oil revenues proportionate to its population. The KRG likes to present itself as 'the other Iraq' so different from the rest of the country. But some things work the same. For instance, some 660,000 Kurds have official jobs though at least half do nothing at all. Much government revenue goes on paying them and without a share of Iraq's oil revenues the economy would collapse. 'Ease of doing business in Arbil compared to Baghdad is very good,' says a businessman. 'Compared to the rest of the world it is rubbish.'

Momentous decisions must be taken by the Kurds and their neighbours when the pipeline to Turkey is finished. One expert on Kurdistan asks: 'Is Turkey playing a game of bluff or will it give up on Baghdad? Do they see it as having fallen permanently into the hands of Iran?' The Kurds are gambling for high stakes in balancing between Turkey, Iran and Baghdad. They have hitherto done so with success, but they are in danger of over-playing their hand.

SIXTEEN

Iraq on the Brink

Iraq, 2013–14

23 April 2013

Iraqi security forces raided a Sunni Arab protest camp in the provincial town of Hawijah this morning, leading to clashes in which 36 people were killed and more than 70 injured. The army's assault on mostly peaceful demonstrators threatens further armed conflict between the Shia-dominated government and Iraq's Sunni minority, who are protesting at being treated as second-class citizens since the fall of Saddam Hussein 10 years ago.

The violence in Hawijah, a Sunni bastion 30 miles west of Kirkuk, started at 5 a.m. when security forces, backed by helicopters, entered the protesters' encampment. The defence ministry claims the demonstration had been infiltrated by militants, of whom it says 20 were killed along with an army officer and two soldiers. The army reported finding weapons including 34 Kalashnikovs and four PKM machine guns, and made 75 arrests. It said its target was a Sunni insurgent group, the Naqsh-bandiya Army, which is inspired by a mixture of Sufi Islam and Iraqi nationalism. Hawijah is known for its militancy and was the scene of fierce fighting between insurgents and US troops during the American occupation.

In response to the raid there were attacks on two army checkpoints near Hawijah in which 13 people died. Protesters say security forces provoked the violence. 'They invaded our sit-in, burned the tents and opened fire indiscriminately and killed and wounded dozens,' Abdulmalik al-Juburi, a leader of the Hawijah sit-in, told the AFP news agency. 'This pushed

Arab tribesmen to go to the streets and attack several checkpoints to avenge protesters. We only have four rifles to protect the sit-in, and there are no wanted people among us.'

As news of the clashes spread through Sunni Iraq, street protests erupted in solidarity with Hawijah. Some 1,000 people took to the streets in Fallujah after calls for protests broadcast from the minarets of mosques. 'War! War!' was the chant of some. In Ramadi, capital of the Sunni Anbar province, crowds threw stones at a military convoy, overturning and setting fire to a Humvee.

The violence is by far the worst since the protests began in December when bodyguards of the Sunni finance minister Rafe al-Essawi were arrested. One aim is to initiate a 'Sunni Spring', emulating the Arab Spring uprisings. Until now, the demonstrators were largely peaceful, emphasis-ing human rights and using non-sectarian slogans while demanding the resignation of Iraq's prime minister, Nouri al-Maliki. A danger for the gov-ernment is that the protest movement is uniting the Sunni, who have been divided on how to respond to their displacement from power since 2003. Security in Sunni areas is partly reliant on the 80,000 Sunni militiamen of the al-Sahwa movement that allied itself to the US Army in opposition to al-Qa'ida's extreme violence in 2006 and 2007. If these forces are alienated by the killing of peaceful protesters, the government might find itself hard put to retain control of Sunni provinces.

2 May 2013

Iraqi leaders fear that the country is sliding rapidly into a new civil war which 'will be worse than Syria'. Baghdad residents are stocking up on rice, vegetables and other foodstuffs in case they are prevented from getting to the shops by fighting or curfews. 'It is wrong to say we are getting close to a civil war,' says a senior Iraqi politician. 'The civil war has already started.' This is borne out by the sharp rise in the number of deaths from political violence in Iraq in April, with the UN claiming more than 700 people were killed, the highest monthly total for five years.

The situation has deteriorated since the killing of at least 36 Sunni Arab protesters in Hawijah. An observer in Baghdad, who does not want to be named, says 'ever since Hawijah, people are frightened of a return to the massacres of 2006.' She adds that Sunni and Shia are avoiding going into each other's areas. Signs of deteriorating security are everywhere. Al-Qa'ida showed its reach this week when five car bombs blew up in overwhelmingly

Shia southern Iraq, leaving 21 dead. The Sunni fundamentalist group is responsible for killing a majority of the almost 1,500 Iraqis who have died in political violence so far this year. Last week it seized the town of Sulaiman Bek, shot the chief of police, stormed the police station and took weapons after agreeing a truce with the Iraqi Army. Al-Qa'ida members are now able to roam freely in Anbar province where a year ago they were a secretive underground movement.

Residents in Baghdad say that soldiers, whom they claim are Shia militiamen in uniform, have massed around Sunni enclaves in the city and are setting up checkpoints. Memories of the sectarian civil war in 2006 and 2007 may be exacerbating the sense of threat, but old fears are reawakening. Bombs have usually been directed against Shia in the past, but in recent weeks Sunni mosques and cafés have been targeted. 'Before we could escape to Syria, but with the violence there where can we go?' asks one Iraqi. 'There is no way out.'

The government of Prime Minister Nouri al-Maliki is floundering in its response. In dealing with the four-month-old protest movement by Sunni Arabs, Maliki varies between denouncing them as terrorists and admitting that they have real grievances. The government has closed the main road from Iraq to Jordan, which the Sunni say is a collective punishment for their community. Overall, Maliki badly miscalculated in believing that, if he played for time, the Sunni protests would die away and he could divide the Sunni leadership with promises of money and jobs.

Sunni demonstrations, often taking the form of sit-ins in town and city squares, are now being guarded by well-armed fighters who set up their own checkpoints. At the weekend one stopped a car containing five Iraqi soldiers in civilian clothes, who were suspected of being intelligence officers, near a protest in Ramadi, the capital of Anbar. The men were all killed.

Speaking of the incipient Sunni revolt, Fuad Hussein, the Kurdistan Regional Government president's chief of staff, says 'the western part of the country is caught up in an uprising against the government. We don't want to have a second Syria here and we are heading in that direction. The fire is very bad and we don't have many firemen.' He believes the present crisis is worse than previous ones because there is nobody to mediate. The last American troops left at the end of 2011, President Jalal Talabani is ill in hospital in Germany and the Kurds are too much at odds with Baghdad to play a moderating role between Shia and Sunni. Hussein fears that if the present crisis deepens there is nothing to prevent it exploding into a bloodbath.

The crises in Iraq and Syria are now cross-infecting each other. The two-year-old uprising of the Sunni in Syria has encouraged their neighbours in Iraq. The revolts in the two countries are ever more running in parallel. Iraqi leaders in Baghdad and Arbil are convinced that the whole region is on the edge of being convulsed by a sectarian war between Sunni and Shia. In such a conflict Iran and Iraq will be very much in a minority. Mahmoud Othman, a veteran Kurdish leader and MP, believes that the government in Baghdad has an exaggerated idea of its own strength and underestimates the degree to which the international environment is hostile to it. He says: 'I remind them that of 56 Islamic states in the world, only two are fully Shia.'

Many Iraqi politicians blame Maliki for exacerbating the crisis. In consolidating his support among the Shia, Maliki has permanently alienated the Sunni who view him with distrust. 'He may have won over the Shia but he has lost Iraq,' says Ghassan al-Attiyah, a political scientist in Baghdad. He believes that the key to defusing the present crisis is for Maliki to step down and be replaced by a more neutral figure as prime minister until the parliamentary elections next year. It is not likely to happen. The Shia of Iraq suspect that they could be facing a fight for their existence. These fears may be exaggerated, and deliberately inflated by the government, but they secure Maliki's political base.

The uprisings in Syria and Iraq are merging with explosive results for Iraq, the region and the world. An Iraq only recently stabilised is becoming unstable again.

28 October 2013

A vast area of eastern Syrian and western Iraq is turning into a zone of war. Groups like the Islamic State of Iraq and the Levant (ISIS) are growing stronger by the day. Its advance in Syria has been well publicised and has done enough to frighten the US and its allies into doubting how far they want to see President Bashar al-Assad replaced by Sunni fanatics. Less well publicised is the tightening grip of ISIS over great areas of western Iraq where it has not been a power since the confrontation with the Americans and the Sunni tribes six or seven years ago.

This is not a well-reported part of the world because of the growing dangers facing foreign and local journalists. Some 16 foreign reporters have been kidnapped in northern Syria this year, so even the most intrepid are no longer going there. Syrian rebel commanders who protected journalists can no longer defend themselves against ISIS, the al-Nusra Front or Ahrar al-Sham. Iraq, which once had hotels filled with foreign journalists, has long fallen off the media map.

Unsurprisingly, important developments such as the weakening grip of the Iraqi government on Anbar—the vast Sunni province west of Baghdad centred on the towns and cities of the Euphrates—have not been properly reported. Jihadis are once again making attacks on cities like Fallujah from which they were driven by US Marines in 2004. The same is true of the city of Mosul in northern Iraq, where ISIS reportedly has a strong enough presence to levy protection money on everybody from the local greengrocer to satellite phone and construction companies—bringing in monthly revenue of $8 million. Reinvigorated by its gains in Syria, ISIS has gained popular support in Iraq and has been able to launch a wave of bombings that has been killing up to 1,000 people, mostly Shia civilians, every month.

22 December 2013

Who was the most successful leader in the Middle East in 2013? It is a hoary tradition of newspapers and magazines to produce end-of-year league tables listing the successful and the unsuccessful. The results are often anodyne or quirky, but in the Middle East over the past 12 months such an approach has the advantage of cutting through the complexities of half a dozen distinct but inter-related crises by focusing on winners and losers.

In this year of turmoil, so many leaders in the Middle East are in more trouble at the end of the year than they were at the beginning. But there is one leader who can look back on the achievements of the past year with unmitigated satisfaction. He leads an organisation that was supposedly on its way to extinction or irrelevance three years ago, but today it is an ever more powerful force in the vast triangle of territory in Iraq and Syria between Mosul, Baghdad and the Mediterranean coast.

Unfortunately, the most successful leader in the Middle East this year is surely Abu Bakr al-Baghdadi, also known as Abu D'ua, the leader of al-Qa'ida in Iraq, which has changed its name to the Islamic State of Iraq and the Levant and claims to be the sole al-Qa'ida affiliate in Syria as well as Iraq. The US says al-Baghdadi is based in Syria and is offering $10 million to anyone who can kill or capture him.

One of the most extraordinary developments in the Middle East is that 12 years after 9/11 and six years after 'the surge' in Iraq was supposed to have crushed al-Qa'ida in Iraq, it is back in business. It is taking over its old haunts in northern and central Iraq and is launching attacks on Shia civilians that have killed 9,000 people so far this year. Yesterday it killed a general commanding a division in an ambush in Anbar province. Al-Qa'ida has benefited from the Iraqi government failing to conciliate the Sunni Arab protest movement that began a year ago, with the result that it is mutating into armed resistance. In July, a carefully planned ISIS attack on Abu Ghraib prison in Baghdad freed 500 prisoners, many of them al-Qa'ida veterans.

Even more spectacular has been the rise of ISIS in Syria, where it is the most effective single military group aside from the Syrian Army. It has taken control of Raqqa, the one Syrian provincial capital held by the rebels, and has started killing off leaders of the Western-backed Free Syrian Army that do not come over to its side.

29 April 2014

Will Iraqi Prime Minister Nouri al-Maliki survive tomorrow's election? Quite likely. Will Iraq survive it as a country? Here the answer is much more doubtful. Eight years after Maliki first took office, al-Qa'ida-type fighters are at the gates of Baghdad—or about 16 miles from the city centre, to be more precise.

Over the last year, almost every week has brought news of loss of government control over Sunni majority provinces and of savage bombings the length and breadth of Iraq. Two bombs in a vegetable market in al-Saadiyah, a town 90 miles north east of Baghdad, killed 17 people today and wounded 42. One bomb was at the centre and another at the exit to kill people fleeing the first blast. A day earlier, a suicide bomber had blown himself up killing 25 people in the largely Kurdish town of Khanaqin.

Since the start of the year ISIS has taken control of Fallujah, 40 miles west of Baghdad. Though they share power with other groups, they are being more cautious than in the past in enforcing a fundamentalist Islamic lifestyle such as obligatory beards for men and a ban on cigarette smoking. The government in Baghdad has been trying to turn the tribes against them as the Americans did in 2006–07, but the alienation of the Sunni community as a whole and the military weakness of the government may be too great for this strategy to succeed today.

ISIS and its allies control much of Anbar, Mosul and Salahudin provinces as well as having a strong presence in Diyala and Kirkuk. They hold the Fallujah dam in the Euphrates and have flooded areas downstream, causing 100,000 people to leave the Abu Ghraib district just west of the capital. ISIS has also blown a main oil pipeline at Baiji, heavily polluting the Tigris River. Government forces are believed to have suffered 5,000 casualties including over 1,000 dead in the struggle for Anbar this year. Many government units are depleted by desertion, with soldiers complaining that they are short of food, ammunition and fuel because money to pay for them has been embezzled by their officers.

These waves of disastrous news would weaken many governments, but in the case of Maliki it may serve to strengthen him at the polls. He can present himself as the saviour of the Shia majority who may feel he remains their leader against an escalating Sunni counter-revolution. A member of his State of Law Alliance estimates the battles in Anbar over the last three months might increase the number of seats won by Maliki from 70 to 90 seats in a 328-member chamber.

18 May 2014

Thousands of civilians are fleeing Fallujah amid fears that the Iraqi Army might launch an all-out assault on the rebel-held city which is under heavy bombardment. Some 42,000 Iraqi security forces are reported to be taking part in operations in the Fallujah area where there has been heavy fighting over the last four months.

Fallujah has come increasingly under the control of ISIS since it took over the city in alliance with Sunni tribal fighters in early January. Since then ISIS has grown in strength as it expands its power in a swath of territory in western Iraq and eastern Syria. It has even held a military parade in Abu Ghraib on the western outskirts of Baghdad, forcing the hasty evacuation of the infamous prison.

Refugees from Fallujah expect a repeat of the assault by the US Marines in November 2004 when much of the city was destroyed by artillery and air attack. Some 60,000 families or about 300,000 people have fled on foot, mostly making for the western part of Anbar province, according to a local council member.

As government ground forces face difficulties fighting their way into Fallujah against an entrenched resistance, there are reports that they are relying increasingly on bombardment from conventional artillery and 'barrel bombs', which are large quantities of explosives packed into containers and dropped from helicopters. The use of barrel bombs, which have become notorious because of their employment by government forces in

Syria, is denied by government spokesmen in Baghdad, but residents are quoted as saying that they are causing heavy destruction in Fallujah. A mid-level security officer is quoted by Reuters as confirming that barrel bombs have been used, saying: 'It's the scorched earth policy—the destruction of a whole area. The army is less experienced in house-to-house fighting which the rebels have mastered. That's why they've resorted to this.' The army has five divisions in Anbar province which should mean 100,000 soldiers, but the real figure is lower because of casualties and desertions, according to an Iraqi source.

9 June 2014

Islamic fundamentalists have opened new fronts in their battle to establish an Islamic state across Iraq and Syria as they launch attacks in cities which were previously under the control of the Baghdad government. A multi-pronged assault across central and northern Iraq in the past four days shows that ISIS has taken over from the al-Qa'ida organisation founded by Osama bin Laden as the most powerful and effective extreme jihadi group in the world.

ISIS now controls or can operate with impunity in a great stretch of territory in western Iraq and eastern Syria, making it militarily the most successful jihadi movement ever. It has proved itself even more violent and sectarian than what US officials call the 'core' al-Qa'ida, led by Ayman al-Zawahiri, who is based in Pakistan. ISIS is highly fanatical, killing Shia Muslims and Christians whenever possible, as well as militarily efficient and under tight direction by top leaders. The creation of a sort of proto-caliphate by extreme jihadis in northern Syria and Iraq is provoking fears in surrounding countries, such as Jordan, Saudi Arabia and Turkey, that they will become targets of battle-hardened Sunni fighters.

In Iraq in the past four days ISIS has fought its way into the north-ern capital of Mosul, sent a column of its fighters into the central city of Samarra, taken over Iraq's largest university at Ramadi and launched devas-tating bombings in Baghdad. The well-coordinated attacks appear designed to keep the Iraqi security forces off balance, uncertain where the next strike will hit. They started four days ago on Thursday when ISIS fighters in trucks with heavy machine guns stormed into the city of Samarra, which is mostly Sunni but contains the golden-domed al-Askari shrine sacred to Shia. Destruction of this shrine by al-Qa'ida bombers in 2006 led to whole-sale massacres of Sunni by Shia.

The ISIS tactic is to make a surprise attack, inflict maximum casualties and spread fear before withdrawing without suffering heavy losses. On Friday, they attacked in Mosul, where their power is already strong enough to tax local businesses, from family groceries to mobile phone and construction companies. Some 200 people were killed in the fighting, according to hospitals, though the government gives a figure of 59 dead, 21 of them policemen and 38 insurgents. This assault was followed by an early morning attack on Saturday on the University of Anbar at Ramadi, which has 10,000 students. Ahmed al-Mehamdi, a student who was taken hostage, told a news agency that he was woken up by the sound of shots, looked out the window and saw armed men dressed in black running across the campus. They entered his dormitory, said they belonged to ISIS, told everybody to stay in their rooms but took others away. One leader told female students: 'We will teach you a lesson you'll never forget.' They turned the science building into their headquarters, but may later have retreated. On the same day, seven bombs exploded in an hour in Baghdad, killing at least 52 people.

SEVENTEEN

The Islamic State Expands

The Caliphate, 2014

10 June 2014

Islamic militants have captured Iraq's northern capital, Mosul, in a devastating defeat for the Iraqi government, whose forces fled the city discarding weapons and uniforms. As well as police stations, army bases and the airport, the insurgents have captured two prisons and freed 1,200 prisoners, many of whom are fighters from the Islamic State of Iraq and the Levant. An Iraqi Army colonel admitted: 'We have lost Mosul this morning. Army and police forces left their positions and ISIS terrorists are in full control. It's a total collapse of the security forces.'

Roads out of Mosul are choked with refugees heading for what they hope is safety in Kurdish-held territory. A university lecturer from a well-known family in Mosul says: 'Mosul has fallen completely into the hands of the terrorists. Everyone is fleeing.... We are also packing up to leave home, but we have no idea where to go.' Many of the refugees fleeing towards the Kurdistan Regional Government and the Kurdish capital Arbil are Sunni Arabs but they are likely to be joined by members of small sects and ethnic groups such as the Yazidis and Shabak, whom ISIS might kill.

In Baghdad the prime minister, Nouri al-Maliki, has asked parliament to declare a state of emergency and called on the international community to support Iraq in its fight against 'terrorism'. But in the streets of the capital, where the population is mostly Shia, there is growing panic and fear that ISIS forces may take the Sunni city of Tikrit, which they are approaching, and then move on to Baghdad. One woman in Baghdad, who does not want to give her name, says: 'People are buying up food and may not come to work tomorrow because they think the situation is going to get worse.' She adds that her relatives in Mosul who had been living in the western part of the city, which is bisected by the Tigris River, have moved to the eastern side that contains large Kurdish districts and is defended by well-trained and resolute Kurdish Peshmerga troops. She says: 'People in Mosul have seen government forces run away so they think the government will use aircraft to bomb Mosul indiscriminately.'

Mosul is a majority Sunni Arab city and traditionally the home of many families that joined the Iraqi Army under Saddam Hussein. His defence minister was normally somebody from the area. Ever since the US-led invasion in 2003, control of the city by Baghdad has been unstable. In 2004 it was stormed by Sunni insurgents who captured most of it and held it for three days until they retreated after the US military appealed to the Kurds to send Peshmerga units to reclaim it. Could this happen again? The Kurds lay claim to large parts of Nineveh province though not to Mosul itself. The ISIS success shows that the local Sunni political leadership has little influence since the governor, Atheel Nujaifi, only narrowly escaped from his provincial headquarters before ISIS captured it.

What will the Iraqi government do now? It could counter-attack. In theory it has 900,000 soldiers under arms. But the Iraqi Army is more of a patronage system to provide jobs rather than a trained military force. Though ISIS took Fallujah in January, the government has shelled it and dropped barrel bombs but has failed to retake it. Soldiers in Anbar province, where much of the fighting has been concentrated, complain that money for their food and fuel is embezzled by officers and many have deserted. Even so, the failure of the Iraqi armed forces to fight in Mosul is very striking. 'We can't beat them,' one officer told a news agency. 'They're trained in street fighting and we're not. We need a whole army to drive them out of Mosul. They're like ghosts; they appear to hit and disappear within seconds.'

ISIS has grown swiftly in strength over the past three years under the leadership of Abu Bakr al-Baghdadi. It has become highly organised and controlled from the centre, but without becoming less merciless and fanatical. Its propaganda films frequently show non-Sunni Muslims being executed and its reputation for savagery may have helped demoralise the Iraqi security forces in Mosul. The resurgence of ISIS is also explained by the Iraqi Sunni being emboldened by the revolt of the Sunni in Syria in 2011. The Sunni uprisings in Iraq and Syria have combined into one crisis.

11 June 2014

The capture of Mosul by ISIS is an earthquake in the politics of Iraq and Syria. Moreover, the impact of this event will soon be felt across the Middle East as governments take on board the fact that a Sunni proto-caliphate is spreading. The next few weeks will be crucial in determining the outcome of ISIS' startling success in taking over a city of 1.4 million people, garrisoned by a large Iraqi security force, with as few as 1,300 fighters.

Will victory in Mosul be followed by success in other provinces where there is a heavy concentration of Sunni, such as Salahuddin, Anbar and Diyala? Already, the insurgents have captured the important oil refinery town of Baiji, with scarcely a shot fired, by simply calling ahead by phone to tell the police and army to lay down their weapons and withdraw. These spectacular advances would not be happening unless there was tacit support and no armed resistance from the Sunni Arab community in northern and central Iraq. Many people rightly suspect and fear ISIS' bloodthirsty and sectarian fanaticism, but for the moment these suspicions and fears have been pushed to one side by even greater hatred of Iraq's Shia-dominated government.

The fall of Mosul has changed the balance of power between Iraq's three main communities: Shia, Sunni and Kurds. Shia rule in non-Shia areas has received a blow from which it will be difficult for it to recover; Kurdish dominance in mixed Kurdish–Arab areas will expand; the 5 or 6 million Sunni Arabs will never be marginalised again. It is not just in Iraq that the balance of power is changing. The Iraq–Syria border no longer exists for most practical purposes. In Syria ISIS forces will become vastly more powerful because the movement can draw on fighters, weapons and money from its newly conquered territories in Iraq. The rest of the Syrian military opposition to President Bashar al-Assad will find it difficult to compete on the battlefield with ISIS if it manages to consolidate its recent victories.

12 June 2014

ISIS is itself amazed by its spectacular victories this week. In a speech its spokesman, Abu Mohamed al-Adnani, says that 'enemies and supporters alike are flabbergasted' by its triumphs that he attributes to divine intervention. He calls on ISIS fighters, who have captured Mosul, Tikrit and a string of other towns, to not become arrogant but to behave modestly. 'Do not let your egos fall prey to your recent military gains such as the Humvees, helicopters, rifles and military equipment,' he says.

The speech is interesting and significant because Adnani gives the first insight into how ISIS views its stunning territorial gains as well as its intentions in the immediate future. Ominously, he stresses hatred for the Shia as apostates with whom no compromise is possible, saying it is 'the Lord alone who overpowers the Shia. Praise be the Lord who brings terror to their hearts.' The sectarian denunciations imply that Iraq will be plunged into a renewed war between Sunni and Shia. There is a warning against any faltering in the present advance: 'Do not concede territory gained to the Shia unless they walk over your dead bodies to retrieve it. March towards Baghdad. Do not let them breathe.'

Adnani is derisive about 'the Fool of the Shia. Nouri [al-Maliki]: Look at what you have done with your people, fool! You were always an underwear merchant! … Your people could have reigned supreme over Iraq, but you made them lose that opportunity. Even the Shia will curse you now.' This analysis, though rhetorical, is probably correct and many Shia today blame Maliki's leadership for the disasters that face them.

In contrast with ISIS' bloodthirsty threats against the Shia, Adnani recommends fighters to behave moderately against Sunni, even those who may previously have fought on the government side. He says: 'Accept repentance and recantations from those who are sincere, and do not bother those who do not bother you, and forgive your Sunni folk, and be gentle with your tribes.'

Overall, there is a strong sense that ISIS did not expect such a swift victory, recalling that only recently they had been subjected to 'imprisonment, torture, military raids.' Their houses had been occupied and they had had to take refuge 'in the mountains, in underground bunkers, in valleys, and in the expanse of the desert.' The flight of 30,000 Iraqi Army troops and police from Mosul in the face of 1,300 or so ISIS fighters seems to have caught the group's leadership by surprise, much as it did the rest of the world.

Again and again Adnani spits out sectarian hatred of the Shia. 'The Shia are a disgraced people,' he says, accusing them of being polytheists 'who worship the dead and stone'. The new war in Iraq could be even more savage than the horrors that went before.

16 June 2014

Iraq is breaking up, with Shia and ethnic minorities fleeing massacres as a general Sunni revolt, led by ISIS, sweeps through northern Iraq. The ISIS assault is still gaining victories, capturing the Shia Turkoman town of Tal Afar west of Mosul after heavy fighting against one of the Iraqi Army's more effective units.

Pictures and evidence from eyewitnesses confirm that ISIS has massacred some 1,700 Shia captives, many of them air force cadets, at the air force academy outside Tikrit, showing that it intends to cleanse its new conquests of Shia. Sunni cadets were told to go home. If the battle moves to Baghdad, then the Shia majority in the capital might see the Sunni enclaves, particularly those in west Baghdad, such as Amiriya and Khadra, as weak points in their defences, and drive out the inhabitants.

In a misguided effort to sustain the morale of people in the capital, the government has closed down the internet. It had already closed YouTube, Facebook and Twitter. The excuse is that ISIS uses them to communicate, but this is extremely unlikely since ISIS has a more professional communications system of its own. Since there is little confidence in the news on government-run television stations, or provided by official spokesmen, the internet shutdown is creating a vacuum of information filled by frightening rumours that are difficult to check. The result is an atmosphere of growing panic in Baghdad with volunteers from the Shia militias being trucked to Samarra, north of the capital, to stop the ISIS advance.

Many civilians are leaving Baghdad and the better-off have already gone abroad. The head of an Iraqi security company tells me: 'I am off to Dubai on an unscheduled holiday to see my daughters because all the foreigners I was protecting have already left.' The price of a cylinder of propane gas, used by Iraqis for cooking, has doubled to 6,000 Iraqi dinars, because it normally comes from Kirkuk, the road to which is now cut off by ISIS fighters.

Rumours swirl through Baghdad. There was a report this morning that the whole of Anbar, the giant Sunni province, which normally has a population of 1.5 million, had fallen. But a call to a friend in its capital Ramadi revealed that fighting is still going on. A former minister last night told me that ISIS, unable to take Samarra, had switched its assault to Baquba in Diyala province, one of the gateways to Baghdad, but a resident denied there was fighting.

30 June 2014

Abu Bakr al-Baghdadi, the leader of ISIS, has declared himself the caliph of a new Islamic state larger in size than Great Britain. The move by al-Baghdadi and ISIS, which wants to be known as simply the Islamic State, has the power to convulse many of the 57 countries that follow the Islamic faith. The group's spokesman, Abu Mohamed al-Adnani, said: 'The legality of all emirates, groups, states and organisations becomes null by the expansion of the caliph's authority and the arrival of its troops to their areas.' Many Sunni leaders inside and outside Iraq have criticised or derided al-Baghdadi's declaration of a new caliphate, but it will have a deep appeal for millions of young Sunni men for whom the political and economic status quo promises nothing but joblessness and poverty. 'Listen to your caliph and obey him. Support your state, which grows every day,' Adnani said.

The Islamic State has a large territory from which to draw recruits and money. In the past, the Iraqi security forces found that when al-Qa'ida in Iraq took over an area it could recruit between five and 10 times the original attack force. These new recruits might not be shock troops, and many would have joined to protect their families, but the numbers fighting for ISIS have grown rapidly.

For Iraq the declaration of a new caliphate, to replace the one abolished 90 years ago by Mustafa Kemal Ataturk in Turkey in 1924, is a declaration of war. For people in Baghdad, a city of 7 million mostly Shia Iraqis, the expansion of the newly declared Islamic State is a terrifying prospect.

There is now considered to be no chance of Nouri al-Maliki retaining the job he has held since 2006. A call last Friday from Grand Ayatollah Sistani—who makes a point of not involving himself in politics—for new leadership is regarded as decisive in ending Maliki's rule. Although his coalition of parties did well in the parliamentary election of 30 April, he has been discredited by the loss of Mosul and the collapse of the army in northern Iraq. He was acting as defence minister, interior minister and supreme commander of the army, so it is impossible for him to avoid personal responsibility for the debacle. Despite the vast expenditure on the army, said to total $41.6 billion in the past three years, units were sent to the front short of ammunition with only four magazines for each assault rifle. ISIS produced chilling videos showing the ease with which its snipers could wound and kill soldiers.

4 July 2014

In early June, Abbas Saddam, a private soldier from a Shia district in Baghdad serving in the 11th Division of the Iraqi Army, was transferred from Ramadi, the capital of Anbar province in western Iraq, to Mosul in the north. The fighting started not long after he got there. But on the morning of 10 June the commanding officer told his men to stop shooting, hand over their rifles to the insurgents, take off their uniforms and get out of the city. Before they could obey, their barracks were invaded by a crowd of civilians. 'They threw stones at us', Abbas recalls, 'and shouted: "We don't want you in our city! You are Maliki's sons! You are the sons of mutta! You are Safavids! You are the army of Iran!"'

The crowd's attack on the soldiers shows that the fall of Mosul was the result of a popular uprising as well as a military assault by ISIS. The Iraqi Army was detested as a foreign occupying force of Shia soldiers, regarded in Mosul—an overwhelmingly Sunni city—as creatures of an Iranian puppet regime led by Nouri al-Maliki. Abbas says there were ISIS fighters—always called Daesh in Iraq after the Arabic acronym of their name—mixed in with the crowd. They said to the soldiers: 'You guys are OK: just put up your rifles and go. If you don't, we'll kill you.' Abbas saw women and children with military weapons; local people offered the soldiers *dishdashas* to replace their uniforms so that they could flee. He made his way back to his family in Baghdad, but he has not told the army he is there because he is afraid of being put on trial for desertion, as happened to a friend. He feels this is deeply unjust: after all, he says, it was his officers who ordered him to give up his weapon and uniform. He asks why Generals Ali Ghaidan Majid, commander of ground forces, and Abboud Qanbar, deputy chief of staff, who fled Mosul for Kurdistan in civilian clothes at the same time, have not been 'judged and executed as traitors'.

Shock at the disintegration of the army in Mosul and other Sunni-majority districts of northern Iraq is still determining the mood in Baghdad weeks later. The debacle marks the end of a distinct period in Iraqi history: the period between 2006 and 2014 when the Iraqi Shia under Maliki sought to dominate the country much as the Sunni had done under Saddam Hussein. The Shia feeling of disempowerment after the Mosul collapse has been so unexpected that they believe almost any other disaster is possible. In theory, the capital should be secure: it has a population of 7 million, most of them Shia, and is defended by the remains of the regular army as well as tens of thousands of Shia militiamen. But then almost the same might have been said of Mosul and Tikrit, where the insurgents may have had popular support but were always outnumbered and outgunned. Before they collapsed—four or five divisions have still not been re-formed—the Iraqi security services counted 350,000 soldiers and 650,000 police. They were opposed by an estimated 6,000 ISIS fighters in total, though these were backed up by local tribes and former army officers. Even if ISIS is seen only as the shock troops of a revolt by the 6- or 7-million-strong Sunni community in Iraq, it was still an extraordinary military success on one side and an unprecedented failure on the other.

The government's first reaction to defeat was disbelief and panic. Maliki blamed the fall of Mosul on a deep conspiracy, though he never identified the conspirators. He looked both baffled and defiant, but appeared to feel no personal responsibility for defeat despite having personally appointed all 15 of the army's divisional commanders. A Baghdad newspaper reported that no fewer than seven ministers and 42 MPs had taken refuge in Jordan along with their families. Those politicians who have stayed are apprehensive: Dhia'a al-Assadi, one of the leaders of the movement of the populist cleric Muqtada al-Sadr, says: 'We expect terrible days to come. They will be crucial in deciding whether Iraq stays united.'

There is nothing paranoid or irrational about the ever-present sense of threat in Baghdad. Iraq's acting national security adviser, Safa Hussein, tells me that 'many people think' ISIS will 'synchronise attacks from inside and outside Baghdad'. He believes such an assault is possible though he thinks it would lead to defeat for ISIS and the Sunni rebels who joined them. The Sunni are in a minority but it would not take much for an attacking force coming from the Sunni heartlands in Anbar province to link up with districts in the city such as Amariya, Khadra and Dora. Much depends on how far ISIS is overextended, surprised by its own victories and lacking the resources to strike at the capital. In Baghdad, unlike Mosul, the Shia mass of the population would oppose them and the militiamen would fight to the death for their families. A fatwa by Grand Ayatollah Ali al-Sistani, the most influential leader for Iraqi Shia, called for a levee en masse of 'able-bodied Iraqis' to defend the country, and tens of thousands volunteered to join the army or establish their own militias. Even so, ISIS could create mayhem in the capital without a direct assault by sending in its suicide bombers, closing the airport or taking over the Sunni towns just south of Baghdad—the area the Americans used to call the Triangle of Death—and partly encircling the capital.

A rational calculation of the balance of forces in any prospective battle for Baghdad shows that ISIS has shot its bolt for the moment and cannot advance out of Sunni-dominated provinces. But Baghdadis are wary of assuming that they are safe because they know they have to take into account the gross incompetence of the ruling elite around Maliki, which still clings to power. Even the generals who openly abandoned their troops in Mosul, Ali Ghaidan Majid and Abboud Qanbar, still hold their old jobs, two of the three most important in the army. 'I still see them turning up to military meetings in Baghdad and they often sit in the front row as if nothing had happened,' a senior official says despairingly. 'It is beyond a joke.'

Discredited by military defeat, Maliki has few allies left in the outside world: even the Iranians, under whose influence he was supposed to be, no longer fully support him. During his eight years in power he created what one former minister calls 'an institutionalised kleptocracy, more corrupt than anything in central Africa', which will do everything to stay in power or, at least, avoid prosecution if it has to go. Though Baghdad looks tattered and impoverished, oil revenues run at $100 billion a year, and great fortunes can be made by anyone with the right connections to government. In the bird market in Baghdad, which sells all types of pets aside from birds, a shopkeeper offered to sell me a tiger cub last year and took out his phone to show me a picture of it gambolling on the ground at his farm outside the city. I asked him who had the money to buy such expensive pets and he became circumspect, saying his customers were tribal leaders and government people but he gave no names.

There is a connection between the buoyant market for tiger cubs and the fall of Mosul. I asked a recently retired four-star general why he thought the army fell apart so quickly and why its commanders fled. 'Corruption!' was his reply. Pervasive corruption had turned the army into a racket and an investment opportunity in which every officer has to pay for his post. He said the opportunity to make big money in the Iraqi Army goes back to the US advisers who set it up ten years ago. The Americans insisted that food and other supplies should be outsourced to private businesses: this meant immense opportunities for graft. A battalion might have a nominal strength of 600 men and its commanding officer would receive money from the budget to pay for their food, but in fact there were only 200 men in the barracks so he could pocket the difference. In some cases there were 'ghost battalions' that did not exist at all but were being paid for just the

BIRTH OF A CALIPHATE

same. Soldiers would kick back half their salaries to their officers in return for never going near a barracks. Checkpoints on roads acted like private customs posts, charging a fee to every truck passing through. A divisional commander might have to pay $2 million for his job; when one candidate asked where he could get that kind of money, he was told to borrow it and pay back $50,000 a month through various forms of extortion. Safa Hussein at the National Security Council confirms that prices for military posts soared in the last five years—a position that cost $20,000 in 2009 is now worth 10 times as much.

The corruption had devastating effects on every level of the Iraqi Army. Defeat in Mosul was preceded by defeat in Anbar province in the first six months of the year, with the army suffering 5,000 casualties and 12,000 desertions. Even the depleted units that did reach the front were often left without food for days. Fuel was scant and shortages of everything grew worse as ISIS and its allies swept through the Sunni provinces. Corrupt private companies had no intention of delivering supplies over roads where they risked bombs and ambushes. 'The army is still dissolving,' Dhia'a al-Assadi says. 'It is dysfunctional and so is the police force.'

The government has asked the Americans for drone and air strikes on ISIS' convoys of trucks: the vehicles are packed with fighters skilled at waging guerrilla war, suddenly attacking and withdrawing, since experienced fighters are never used to hold captured territory. ISIS describes the strategy as 'moving like a serpent through rocky ground'.

Iraq now has a political crisis and a military crisis, neither of which is likely to be resolved soon. People in the capital wonder apprehensively when the battle for Baghdad will begin. When an American military delegation came to review the capital's defences, a senior Iraqi official told them 'to look to see which ministers had put fresh sandbags around their ministries. Those that have done so like myself will stay and fight; where you see old sandbags it means the minister doesn't care because he is intending to run.'

6 July 2014

The meltdown of American and British policy in Iraq and Syria attracts surprisingly little criticism at home. Their aim for the past three years has been to get rid of Bashar al-Assad as ruler of Syria and stabilise Iraq under the leadership of Nouri al-Maliki. The exact reverse has happened, with Assad in power and likely to remain so, while Iraq is in turmoil with the government's authority extending only a few miles north and west of Baghdad.

By pretending that the Syrian opposition stood a chance of overthrowing Assad after the middle of 2012, and insisting that his departure be the justification for peace talks, Washington, London and Paris have ensured that the Syrian civil war would go on. 'I spent three years telling them again and again that the war in Syria would inevitably destabilise Iraq, but they paid no attention,' the Iraqi foreign minister Hoshyar Zebari says. I remember in the autumn of 2012 a senior British diplomat assuring me that talk of the Syrian war spreading was much exaggerated.

Now the bills are beginning to come in, with Abu Bakr al-Baghdadi calling on all Muslims to pledge allegiance to the Islamic State, effectively denying the legitimacy of Muslim rulers throughout the world. No wonder Saudi Arabia has moved 30,000 troops to guard its 500-mile-long border with Iraq. There is a certain divine justice in this, since until six months ago the Saudis were speeding jihadis in the general direction of Syria and Iraq. It is now dreading their return.

The Iranians have started acting in Iraq, though they have not committed many people. They are trying to repeat their tactics in Syria, which is to create a parallel army out of the militias to buttress or replace the regular Iraqi Army. They openly say they are doing so. But there is another aspect of their Syrian strategy which shows signs of appearing in Iraq and is bad news for Iraqis. This is to cut off electricity and water to rebel areas and pulverise any town or city held by the enemy with shellfire and bombing but without assaulting it, forcing the civilian population to flee; then to advance cautiously seeking to encircle enemy positions with checkpoints so they can be gradually strangled. This appears to be happening in Tikrit, a city of 200,000 on the Tigris river. The city centre is being systematically smashed according to eyewitnesses and any point of resistance is pounded by artillery.

13 July 2014

How far is Saudi Arabia complicit in the ISIS takeover of much of northern Iraq, and is it stoking an escalating Sunni–Shia conflict across the Islamic world? Sometime before 9/11, Prince Bandar bin Sultan, once the powerful Saudi ambassador in Washington and head of Saudi intelligence until a few months ago, had a revealing and ominous conversation with the head of the British Secret Intelligence Service, MI6, Sir Richard Dearlove. Prince

Bandar told him: 'The time is not far off in the Middle East, Richard, when it will be literally "God help the Shia." More than a billion Sunni have simply had enough of them.'

The fatal moment predicted by Prince Bandar may now have come for many Shia, with Saudi Arabia playing an important role in bringing it about by supporting the anti-Shia jihad in Iraq and Syria. Since the capture of Mosul by ISIS, Shia women and children have been killed in villages south of Kirkuk, and Shia air force cadets machine-gunned and buried in mass graves near Tikrit. In Mosul, Shia shrines and mosques have been blown up, and in the nearby Shia Turkoman city of Tal Afar, 4,000 houses have been taken over by ISIS fighters as 'spoils of war'. Simply to be identified as Shia or a related sect, such as the Alawites, in Sunni rebel–held parts of Iraq and Syria today has become as dangerous as being a Jew was in Nazi-controlled parts of Europe in 1940.

There is no doubt about the accuracy of the quote by Prince Bandar, secretary-general of the Saudi National Security Council from 2005 and head of General Intelligence between 2012 and 2014, the crucial two years when al-Qa'ida-type jihadis took over the Sunni-armed opposition in Iraq and Syria. Speaking at the Royal United Services Institute last week, Dearlove, who headed MI6 from 1999 to 2004, emphasised the significance of Prince Bandar's words, saying that they constituted 'a chilling comment that I remember very well indeed'. He does not doubt that substantial and sustained funding from private donors in Saudi Arabia and Qatar, to which the authorities may have turned a blind eye, has played a central role in the ISIS surge into Sunni areas of Iraq. He said: 'Such things simply do not happen spontaneously.' This sounds realistic since the tribal and communal leadership in Sunni majority provinces is much beholden to Saudi and Gulf paymasters, and would be unlikely to co-operate with ISIS without their consent.

The forecast by Prince Bandar that the 100 million Shia in the Middle East face disaster at the hands of the Sunni majority will convince many Shia that they are the victims of a Saudi-led campaign to crush them. Shia see the threat as not only military but stemming from the expanded influence over mainstream Sunni Islam of Wahhabism, the puritanical and intolerant version of Islam espoused by Saudi Arabia. Dearlove says that he has no inside knowledge obtained since he retired as head of MI6 10 years ago to become master of Pembroke College in Cambridge. But, drawing on past experience, he sees Saudi strategic thinking as being shaped by two deep-seated beliefs or attitudes. First, they are convinced that there 'can be no legitimate or admissible challenge to the Islamic purity of their Wahhabi credentials as guardians of Islam's holiest shrines'. But, perhaps more significantly given the deepening Sunni–Shia confrontation, the Saudi belief that they possess a monopoly of Islamic truth leads them to be 'deeply attracted towards any militancy which can effectively challenge Shia-dom'.

Western governments traditionally play down the connection between Saudi Arabia and its Wahhabist faith, on the one hand, and jihadism. There is nothing conspiratorial or secret about these links: 15 out of 19 of the 9/11 hijackers were Saudis, as was bin Laden and most of the private donors who funded the operation. The difference between al-Qa'ida and ISIS can be overstated: when bin Laden was killed by US forces in 2011, al-Baghdadi released a statement eulogising him, and ISIS pledged to launch 100 attacks in revenge for his death.

But there has always been a second theme to Saudi policy towards al-Qa'ida-type jihadis, contradicting Prince Bandar's approach and seeing jihadis as a mortal threat to the Kingdom. Dearlove illustrates this attitude by relating how, soon after 9/11, he visited the Saudi capital Riyadh with Tony Blair. He remembers the then head of Saudi General Intelligence 'literally shouting at me across his office: "9/11 is a mere pinprick on the West. In the medium term, it is nothing more than a series of personal tragedies. What these terrorists want is to destroy the House of Saud and remake the Middle East."' In the event, Saudi Arabia adopted both policies, encouraging the jihadis as a useful tool of Saudi anti-Shia influence abroad but suppressing them at home as a threat to the status quo. It is this dual policy that has fallen apart over the last year.

Saudi sympathy for anti-Shia 'militancy' is identified in leaked US official documents. The then US secretary of state Hillary Clinton wrote in December 2009 in a cable released by WikiLeaks that 'Saudi Arabia remains a critical financial support base for al-Qa'ida, the Taliban, LeT [Lashkar-e-Taiba in Pakistan] and other terrorist groups.' She said that, in so far as Saudi Arabia did act against al-Qa'ida, it was as a domestic threat and not because of its activities abroad. This policy may now be changing with the dismissal of Prince Bandar as head of intelligence this year. But the change is very recent, still ambivalent and may be too late: it was only last week that a Saudi prince said he would no longer fund a satellite television station notorious for its anti-Shia bias based in Egypt.

Saudi Arabia may come to regret its support for the Sunni revolts in Syria and Iraq as jihadi social media begins to speak of the House of Saud as the next target. It is the unnamed head of Saudi General Intelligence quoted by Dearlove after 9/11 who is turning out to have analysed the potential threat to Saudi Arabia correctly and not Prince Bandar, which may explain why the latter was sacked earlier this year. Nor is this the only point on which Prince Bandar was dangerously mistaken. The rise of ISIS is bad news for the Shia of Iraq but it is worse news for the Sunni whose leadership has been ceded to a pathologically bloodthirsty and intolerant movement, a sort of Islamic Khmer Rouge, which has no aim but war without end.

The Caliphate rules a large, impoverished and isolated area from which people are fleeing. Several million Sunni in and around Baghdad are vulnerable to attack and 255 Sunni prisoners have already been massacred. In the long term, ISIS cannot win, but its mix of fanaticism and good organisation makes it difficult to dislodge. 'God help the Shia,' said Prince Bandar, but, partly thanks to him, the shattered Sunni communities of Iraq and Syria may need divine help even more than the Shia.

31 July 2014

In the early hours of 24 July a Saudi volunteer belonging to ISIS drove a car packed with explosives towards the perimeter wall of a base manned by 300 soldiers of the 17th Division of the Syrian Army near the city of Raqqa in north-east Syria. As the Saudi raced at high speed towards the wall, he was given covering fire by a barrage of artillery shells and rockets. But he did not quite make it. His car was hit by Syrian Army fire and blew up with an explosion that shook buildings miles away in Raqqa city. The plan had been for 40 ISIS fighters to burst through a breach in the perimeter wall made by the suicide bomber. A further 600 ISIS fighters were to follow up the first assault, if it made headway.

A second Saudi suicide bomber in a truck drove towards the base, but his explosives also detonated prematurely when hit by Syrian fire. Even so, the Syrian Army detachment appears to have been too small to defend the base and 50 of them were ambushed and killed as they pulled back. A Twitter account linked to ISIS later showed horrific pictures of the heads of decapitated soldiers stuck on the spikes of what looks like a gate.

It turned out that the attack on the 17th Division was not even ISIS's main assault, which was directed against Regiment 121, a major Syrian

Army stronghold outside Hasakah City in north-east Syria. The regimental commander General Mozid Salama was reported killed and pictures posted by ISIS show captured T-55 tanks, artillery pieces and multiple rocket launchers. The fighting was among the most severe between the Syrian Army and the armed opposition for a year. It puts an end to a conspiracy theory that Bashar al-Assad's army and ISIS secretly collaborate and never fight each other.

1 August 2014

As the attention of the world focused on Ukraine and Gaza in July, ISIS captured a third of Syria in addition to the quarter of Iraq it had seized in June. The frontiers of the new Caliphate are expanding by the day and now cover an area larger than Great Britain and inhabited by at least 6 million people, a population larger than that of Denmark, Finland or Ireland. In a few weeks of fighting in Syria ISIS has established itself as the dominant force in the Syrian opposition, routing the official al-Qa'ida affiliate, Jabhat al-Nusra, in the oil-rich province of Deir Ezzor and executing its local commander as he tried to flee. In northern Syria some 5,000 ISIS fighters are using tanks and artillery captured from the Iraqi Army in Mosul to besiege half a million Kurds in their enclave at Kobani on the Turkish border. In central Syria, near Palmyra, ISIS fought the Syrian Army as it over-ran the al-Shaer gas field, one of the largest in the country, in a surprise assault that left an estimated 300 soldiers and civilians dead. Repeated government counter-attacks finally retook the gas field but ISIS still controls most of Syria's oil and gas production. The Caliphate may be poor and isolated but its oil wells and control of crucial roads provide a steady income in addition to the plunder of war.

The birth of the new state is the most radical change to the political geography of the Middle East since the Sykes–Picot Agreement was implemented in the aftermath of the First World War. Yet this explosive transformation has created surprisingly little alarm internationally or even among those in Iraq and Syria not yet under the rule of ISIS. Politicians and diplomats tend to treat ISIS as if it is a Bedouin raiding party that appears dramatically from the desert, wins spectacular victories and then retreats to its strongholds leaving the status quo little changed. Such a scenario is conceivable but is getting less and less likely as ISIS consolidates its hold on its new conquests in an area that may soon stretch from Iran to the Mediterranean.

The very speed and unexpectedness of its rise make it easy for Western and regional leaders to hope that the fall of ISIS and the implosion of the Caliphate might be equally sudden and swift. But all the evidence is that this is wishful thinking and the trend is in the other direction, with the opponents of ISIS becoming weaker and less capable of resistance: in Iraq the army shows no signs of recovering from its earlier defeats and has failed to launch a single successful counter-attack; in Syria the other opposition groups, including the battle-hardened fighters of al-Nusra and Ahrar al-Sham, are demoralised and disintegrating as they are squeezed between ISIS and the Assad government. Karen Koning Abuzayd, a member of the UN's Commission of Inquiry in Syria, says that more and more Syrian rebels are defecting to ISIS: 'They see it's better, these guys are strong, these guys are winning battles, they were taking territory, they have money, they can train us.' This is bad news for the Syrian government, which barely held off an assault in 2012 and 2013 by rebels less well trained, organised and armed than ISIS; it will have real difficulties stopping the forces of the Caliphate advancing west.

In Baghdad there was shock and terror on 10 June at the fall of Mosul and as people realised that trucks packed with ISIS gunmen were only an hour's drive away. But instead of assaulting Baghdad, ISIS took most of Anbar, the vast Sunni province that sprawls across western Iraq on either side of the Euphrates. In Baghdad people know what to expect if the murderously anti-Shia ISIS forces capture the city, but they take heart from the fact that the calamity has not happened yet. 'We were frightened by the military disaster at first but we Baghdadis have got used to crises over the last 35 years,' one woman says.

Even with ISIS at the gates, Iraqi politicians have gone on playing political games as they move ponderously towards replacing the discredited prime minister, Nouri al-Maliki. 'It is truly surreal,' a former Iraqi minister says. 'When you speak to any political leader in Baghdad they talk as if they had not just lost half the country.' The volunteers who went to the front after a fatwa from Grand Ayatollah Ali al-Sistani are now streaming back to their homes, complaining that they were half-starved and forced to use their own weapons and buy their own ammunition. The only large-scale counter-attack launched by the regular army and the newly raised Shia militia was a disastrous foray into Tikrit on 15 July that was ambushed and defeated with heavy losses. There is no sign that the dysfunctional nature of the Iraqi Army has changed. 'They were using just one helicopter in support of the troops in Tikrit,' the former minister says, 'so I wonder what on earth happened to the 140 helicopters the Iraqi state has bought in recent years?'

Probably the money for the missing 139 helicopters was simply stolen. The sole aim of many officials has long been to get the largest kickback possible and they did not much care if jihadi groups did the same. I met a Turkish businessman in Baghdad who said he had had a large construction contract in Mosul over the last few years. The local emir or leader of ISIS, then known as al-Qa'ida in Iraq, demanded $500,000 a month in protection money from the company. 'I complained again and again about this to the government in Baghdad,' the businessman said, 'but they would do nothing about it except to say that I could add the money I paid al-Qa'ida to the contract price.' The emir was soon killed and his successor demanded that the protection money be increased to $1 million a month. The businessman refused to pay and one of his Iraqi employees was killed; he withdrew his Turkish staff and his equipment to Turkey. 'Later I got a message from al-Qa'ida saying that the price was back down to $500,000 and I could come back,' he said. This was sometime before ISIS captured the city.

In the face of these failures Iraq's Shia majority is taking comfort from two beliefs that, if true, would mean the present situation is not as dangerous as it looks. They argue that Iraq's Sunni have risen in revolt and ISIS fighters are only the shock troops or vanguard of an uprising provoked by the anti-Sunni policies and actions of Maliki. Once he is replaced, as is almost certain, Baghdad will offer the Sunni a new power-sharing agreement with regional autonomy similar to that enjoyed by the Kurds. Then the Sunni tribes, former military officers and Baathists who have allowed ISIS to take the lead in the Sunni revolt will turn on their ferocious allies. Despite all signs to the contrary, Shia at all levels are putting faith in this myth, that ISIS is weak and can be easily discarded by Sunni moderates once they have achieved their goals. One Shia said to me: 'I wonder if ISIS really exists.'

Unfortunately, ISIS not only exists but is an efficient and ruthless organisation that has no intention of waiting for its Sunni allies to betray it. In late June and early July ISIS detained between 15 and 20 former officers from Saddam Hussein's time, including two generals. Groups that had put up pictures of Saddam were told to take them down or face the consequences. 'It doesn't seem likely', Aymenn al-Tamimi, an expert on jihadis, says, 'that the rest of the Sunni military opposition will be able to turn against ISIS successfully. If they do, they will have to act as quickly as possible before ISIS gets too strong.' He points out that the supposedly more moderate wing of the Sunni opposition has done nothing to stop the remnants of the ancient Christian community in Mosul from being forced to flee after ISIS told them they had to convert to Islam, pay a special tax or be killed. Members of other sects and ethnic groups denounced as Shia or polytheists are being persecuted, imprisoned and murdered. The moment is passing when the non-ISIS opposition could successfully mount a challenge.

The Iraqi Shia offer another explanation for the way their army disintegrated: it was stabbed in the back by the Kurds. Seeking to shift the blame from himself, Maliki claims that Arbil, the Kurdish capital, 'is a headquarters for ISIS, Baathists, al-Qa'ida and terrorists'. Many Shia believe this: it makes them feel that their security forces failed because they were betrayed, and not because they would not fight. One Iraqi tells me he was at an *iftar* meal during Ramadan 'with a hundred Shia professional people, mostly doctors and engineers, and they all took the stab-in-the-back theory for granted as an explanation for what went wrong'.

The confrontation with the Kurds is important because it makes it impossible to create a united front against ISIS. The Kurdish leader, Massoud Barzani, took advantage of the Iraqi Army's flight to seize all the territories which have been in dispute between Kurds and Arabs since 2003, including the city of Kirkuk. By trying to scapegoat the Kurds, Maliki is ensuring that the Shia will have no allies in their confrontation with ISIS if it resumes its attack in the direction of Baghdad. ISIS and their Sunni allies have been surprised by the military weakness of the Baghdad government. They are unlikely to be satisfied with regional autonomy for Sunni provinces and a larger share of jobs and oil revenues. Their uprising has turned into a full counter-revolution that aims to take back power over all of Iraq.

Many in Baghdad hope the excesses of ISIS—for example, blowing up mosques it deems shrines, like that of Younis (Jonah) in Mosul—will alienate the Sunni. In the long term they may do just that, but opposing ISIS is very dangerous and, for all its brutality, it has brought victory to a defeated and persecuted Sunni community. So far Baghdad's response to its defeat has been to bomb Mosul and Tikrit randomly, leaving local people in no doubt about its indifference to their welfare or survival. The fear will not change even if Maliki is replaced by a more conciliatory prime minister. A Sunni in Mosul, writing just after a missile fired by government forces had exploded in the city, told me: 'Maliki's forces have already demolished the University of Tikrit. It has become havoc and rubble like all the city. If Maliki reaches us in Mosul he will kill its people or turn them into refugees. Pray for us.' Such views are common, and make it less likely that Sunni will rise up in opposition to ISIS and its caliphate. A new and terrifying state has been born.

8 August 2014

The US has sent aircraft to bomb ISIS fighters in a desperate attempt to stop their advance on the Kurdish capital, Arbil. The US intervention comes after the surprise defeat of Kurdish Peshmerga forces by ISIS. The strikes were authorised by President Barack Obama to protect Christians and to avert 'a potential act of genocide' against tens of thousands of Yazidis, an ancient sect denounced by ISIS as 'polytheists'. Many Yazidis have taken refuge on a mountain in Sinjar to escape massacre and are receiving relief supplies dropped by US aircraft. The Iraqi government says hundreds of Yazidi women have been taken captive by the Islamic militants.

The sudden ISIS offensive has shown the Peshmerga, the fighting forces of the Kurdistan Regional Government (KRG), to be weaker than expected. They offered little effective resistance in Sinjar and failed to protect Christian towns in Nineveh province. In a humiliating series of reverses, they retreated back to Kalak, a town on the Greater Zaab river, which is the last defensible position on the road to Arbil. The Kurds have lost the Mosul dam on the Tigris river, enabling ISIS to control the flow of water and electricity from a hydroelectric power station. ISIS could blow the dam, sending a 65 feet-high wall of water down the Tigris Valley, but is unlikely to do so because territory it already holds would be worst affected.

The Kurds did not expect to be targeted by ISIS at this time, believing that it was fully engaged in Syria and further south against the Iraqi Army. The Peshmerga were over-extended after the KRG had expanded its territory by 40 per cent in an opportunistic land-grab following the fall of Mosul, when it took districts long disputed with the Arabs. This left the KRG with a 600-mile-long frontier to defend against ISIS. 'The Peshmerga didn't have the military equipment to face ISIS,' says Professor Gareth Stansfield, an expert on Kurdish and Iraqi affairs at the Institute of Arab and Islamic Studies at Exeter University. 'They basically use Kalashnikovs and rocket-propelled-grenade launchers.' Over the past two months ISIS has captured weapons including tanks, artillery, heavy machine guns and hundreds of US Humvees. Professor Stansfield says the Arab population of the disputed territories has become more anti-Kurdish since the KRG took over. Powerful Sunni tribes sympathise with ISIS in a bid to drive the Kurds out, even putting the oil city of Kirkuk at risk.

15 August 2014

After eight years as prime minister of Iraq, Nouri al-Maliki, deserted by his allies, has finally stood down and will be replaced by Haider al-Abadi. Applause for the new Iraqi leader, not always a front runner for the succession, has come from individuals, parties and countries which normally detest each other, such as Iran, the US, Kurds, Sunni politicians and Shia militia leaders. As a commentator on Iraq caustically remarks: 'Somebody is going to be disappointed.'

Maliki's stubbornness in clinging to power was finally overcome when Iran decided that there must be a new leader in Baghdad who is not detested by the Sunni and the Kurds. Maliki's Dawa Party put forward Abadi as a candidate and this was accepted by Tehran. The former prime minister's late-night speech ceding power may have been motivated by fear that, if he did not withdraw, he would be denounced at Friday prayers by Grand Ayatollah Ali Sistani.

The chorus of cheers inside and outside Iraq that has greeted Maliki's departure is not unanimous. The most significant of those who say the change will make no difference is ISIS and Sunni armed groups. They see Abadi as just one more representative of a Shia religious party that will seek to maintain Shia dominance over Iraq.

11 September 2014

A friend emailed the letter below soon after her neighbourhood in Mosul was hit by Iraqi Air Force bombers. This was some hours before President Barack Obama announced a plan to weaken and ultimately destroy ISIS by a series of measures including air attacks. The letter illustrates graphically one of the most important reasons why American air power may be less effective than many imagine.

The bombardment was carried out by the government. The air strikes focused on wholly civilian neighbourhoods. Maybe they wanted to target two ISIS bases. But neither round of bombardment found its target. One target is a house connected to a church where ISIS men live. It is next to the neighbourhood generator and about 200–300 metres from our home.

The bombing hurt civilians only and demolished the generator. Now we don't have any electricity since yesterday night. Now I am writing from a device in my sister's house, which is empty.

The government bombardment did not hit any of the ISIS men. Now I have just heard from a relative who visited us to check on us after that terrible night. He says that because of this bombardment, youngsters are joining ISIS in tens if not in hundreds because this increases hatred towards the government, which doesn't care about us as Sunni being killed and targeted.

Government forces went to Amerli, a Shia village surrounded by tens of Sunni villages, though Amerli was never taken by ISIS. The government militias attacked the surrounding Sunni villages, killing hundreds, with help from the American air strikes.

The 5 or 6 million Sunni Arabs who live in areas controlled by ISIS in Iraq and Syria may not be happy with the brutality, bigotry and violence of their new rulers. But they are even more frightened of the prospect of the soldiers and militiamen of the Baghdad or Damascus governments recapturing and wreaking vengeance in Sunni cities, towns and villages. The Sunni communities in both countries have little choice but to stick with ISIS as their defenders.

For all its bellicose rhetoric, Obama's plan is more of a strategy to contain ISIS rather than eradicate it—and he may find that even this is difficult to do. His problem is that the US does not have reliable local partners in either Iraq or Syria. US air power should be enough to prevent ISIS capturing the Kurdish capital Arbil or launching a successful assault on Baghdad. It might also be employed to save Aleppo or Hama from ISIS. But without American forward air observers embedded in Iraqi units, as happened in Afghanistan in 2001 and Iraqi Kurdistan in 2003, the Iraqi Army is unlikely to make real progress on the ground. Given that the Sunni community would probably fight the Shia-dominated army to the last man or flee in front of it, this may be no bad thing.

The missing element in the Obama plan is the creation of the framework for new peace negotiations between Assad's government and the moderate Syrian opposition such as it is. The Geneva II talks got nowhere because in practice US and British policy was a recipe for an endless war. So long as the civil war in Syria goes on, ISIS cannot be beaten.

Despite Obama's caution, the US is being dragged into new conflicts in Iraq and Syria. By beheading two American journalists in retaliation for US air strikes ISIS has shown that it will strike back against any US or British attack. Concern is expressed about the possibility of ISIS bombers blowing themselves up 'in the streets of London' but they could more easily target the 2.5 million British tourists who visit Turkey every year.

EIGHTEEN

The Islamic State Remains

The Caliphate, 2014–15

24 October 2014

Over the summer Islamic State defeated the Iraqi Army, the Syrian Army, the Syrian rebels and the Iraqi Kurdish Peshmerga; it established a state stretching from Baghdad to Aleppo and from Syria's northern border to the deserts of Iraq in the south. Ethnic and religious groups of which the world had barely heard—including the Yazidis of Sinjar and the Chaldean Christians of Mosul—became victims of ISIS cruelty and sectarian bigotry. In September, ISIS turned its attention to the 2.5 million Syrian Kurds who had gained de facto autonomy in three cantons just south of the Turkish border. One of these cantons, centred on the town of Kobani, became the target of a determined assault. By 6 October, ISIS fighters had fought their way into the centre of the town. Turkish President Recep Tayyip Erdoğan predicted that its fall was imminent; John Kerry spoke of the 'tragedy' of Kobani, but claimed—implausibly—that its capture would not be of great significance. A well-known Kurdish fighter, Arin Mirkan, blew herself up as the ISIS fighters advanced: it looked like a sign of despair and impending defeat.

In attacking Kobani, the ISIS leadership wanted to prove that it could still defeat its enemies despite the US air strikes against it, which began in Iraq on 8 August and were extended to Syria on 23 September. As they poured into Kobani, ISIS fighters chanted: 'The Islamic State remains, the

Islamic State expands.' In the past, ISIS has chosen—a tactical decision—
to abandon battles it does not think it is going to win. But the five-week
battle for Kobani had gone on too long and been too well publicised for
its militants to withdraw without loss of prestige. The appeal of the Islamic
State to Sunni in Syria, Iraq and across the world derives from a sense that
its victories are God-given and inevitable, so any failure damages its claim
to divine support.

But the inevitable ISIS victory at Kobani did not happen. On 19 October,
in a reversal of previous policy, US aircraft dropped arms, ammunition
and medicine to the town's defenders. Under American pressure, Turkey
announced on the same day that it would allow Iraqi Kurdish Peshmerga
safe passage from northern Iraq to Kobani; Kurdish fighters have now
recaptured part of the town. Washington had realised that, given Obama's
rhetoric about his plan 'to degrade and destroy' IS, and with congressional
elections only a month away, it could not afford to allow the militants yet
another victory. And this particular victory would in all likelihood have
been followed by a massacre of surviving Kurds in front of the TV cameras
assembled on the Turkish side of the border.

When the siege began, US air support for the defenders of Kobani
had been desultory; for fear of offending Turkey the US Air Force had
avoided liaising with Kurdish fighters on the ground. By the middle of
October the policy had changed and the Kurds started giving detailed
targeting information to the Americans, enabling them to destroy ISIS
tanks and artillery. Previously, ISIS commanders had been skilful in
hiding their equipment and dispersing their men. In the air campaign so
far, only 632 out of 6,600 missions have resulted in actual attacks. But as
they sought to storm Kobani, ISIS leaders had to concentrate their forces
in identifiable positions and became vulnerable. In one 48-hour period
there were nearly 40 US air strikes, some only 50 yards from the Kurdish
front line.

It was not US air support alone that made the difference. In Kobani,
for the first time, ISIS is fighting an enemy—the People's Defence Units
(YPG) and its political wing, the Democratic Union Party (PYD)—that
in important respects resembles itself. Syria and Iraq are full of armies and
militias that do not fight anybody who can shoot back, but the PYD and
YPG are different. The PYD is the Syrian branch of the Kurdistan Workers'
Party (PKK), which since 1984 has been fighting for self-rule for the 15
million Turkish Kurds. Like IS, the PKK combines fanatical ideological

commitment with military expertise and experience gained in long years of guerrilla war.

Marxist-Leninist in its original ideology, the PKK is run from the top and seeks to monopolise power within the Kurdish community, whether in Turkey or Syria. The party's imprisoned leader, Abdullah Ocalan, the object of a powerful personality cult, issues instructions from his Turkish prison on an island in the Sea of Marmara. The PKK's military leadership operates from a stronghold in the Kandil mountains in northern Iraq. Most of its fighters, estimated to number 7,000, withdrew from Turkey under the terms of a ceasefire in 2013, and today move from camp to camp in the deep gorges and valleys of the Kandil. They are highly disciplined and intensely dedicated to the cause of Kurdish nationalism: this has enabled them to wage a war for three decades against the enormous Turkish Army, always undeterred despite the devastating losses they have suffered. The PKK, like IS, emphasises martyrdom: fallen fighters are buried in carefully tended cemeteries full of rose bushes high in the mountains, with elaborate tombstones over the graves. Pictures of Ocalan are everywhere: six or seven years ago, I visited a hamlet in Kandil occupied by the PKK; overlooking it was an enormous picture of Ocalan picked out in coloured stones on the side of a nearby mountain. It is one of the few guerrilla bases that can be seen from space.

The Islamic State's successes have been helped not just by its enemies' incompetence but also by the divisions evident between them. John Kerry boasts of having put together a coalition of 60 countries all pledged to oppose IS, but from the beginning it was clear that many important members were not too concerned about the ISIS threat. When the bombing of Syria began in September, Obama announced with pride that Saudi Arabia, Jordan, the United Arab Emirates, Qatar, Bahrain and Turkey were all joining the US as military partners against IS. But, as the Americans knew, these were all Sunni states which had played a central role in fostering the jihadis in Syria and Iraq.

This is a political problem for the US, as Vice President Joe Biden revealed to the embarrassment of the administration in a talk at Harvard on 2 October. He said that Turkey, Saudi Arabia and the UAE had promoted 'a proxy Sunni–Shia war' in Syria and 'poured hundreds of millions of dollars and tens of thousands of tons of weapons into anyone who would fight against Assad—except that the people who were being supplied were al-Nusra and al-Qa'ida and the extremist element of jihadis coming from other parts of the world'. He admitted that the moderate Syrian rebels, supposedly central to US policy in Syria, were a negligible military force. Biden later apologised for his words, but what he had said was demonstrably true and reflects what the administration in Washington really believes. Though they expressed outrage at Biden's frankness, America's Sunni allies swiftly confirmed the limits of their co-operation. Prince al-Waleed bin Talal al-Saud, a business magnate and member of the Saudi royal family, said: 'Saudi Arabia will not be involved directly in fighting ISIS in Iraq or Syria, because this does not really affect our country explicitly.' In Turkey, Erdoğan said that so far as he was concerned the PKK was just as bad as IS.

Excluded from this bizarre coalition are almost all those actually fighting IS, including Iran, the Syrian Army, the Syrian Kurds and the Shia militias in Iraq. This mess has been much to the advantage of the Islamic State, as illustrated by an incident in northern Iraq in early August when Obama sent US special forces to Mount Sinjar to monitor the danger to the thousands of Yazidis trapped there. Ethnically Kurdish but with their own non-Islamic religion, the Yazidis had fled their towns and cities to escape massacre and enslavement by IS. The US soldiers arrived by helicopter and were efficiently guarded and shown around by uniformed Kurdish militiamen. But soon afterwards the Yazidis—who had been hoping to be rescued or at least helped by the Americans—were horrified to see the US soldiers hurriedly climb back into their helicopter and fly away. The reason for their swift departure, it was revealed later in Washington, was that the officer in charge of the US detachment had spoken to his Kurdish guards and discovered that they were not the US-friendly Peshmerga of the Kurdistan Regional Government but PKK fighters—still listed as 'terrorists' by the US, despite the central role they have played in helping the Yazidis and driving back IS. It was only when Kobani was on the verge of falling that Washington accepted it had no choice but to co-operate with the PYD: it was, after all, practically the only effective force still fighting ISIS on the ground.

And then there is the Turkish problem. US planes attacking ISIS forces in Kobani have to fly 1,200 miles from their bases in the Gulf because Turkey will not allow the use of its airbase at İncirlik, just a hundred miles from Kobani. By not preventing reinforcements, weapons and ammunition from reaching ISIS in Kobani, Ankara showed that it would prefer ISIS to hold the town: anything was better than the PYD. Turkey's position has been clear since July 2012, when the Syrian Army, under pressure from rebels elsewhere, pulled out of the main Kurdish areas. The Syrian Kurds, long persecuted by Damascus and politically marginal, suddenly won de facto autonomy under increasing PKK authority. Living mostly along the border with Turkey, a strategically important area to IS, the Kurds unexpectedly became players in the struggle for power in a disintegrating Syria.

This was an unwelcome development for the Turks. The Syrian branch of the PKK, which fought for so long for some form of self-rule in Turkey, now ruled a quasi-state in Syria centred on the cities of Qamishli, Kobani and Afrin. Much of the Syrian border region was likely to remain in Kurdish hands, since the Syrian government and its opponents were both too weak to do anything about it. Ankara may not be the master chess player collaborating with ISIS to break Kurdish power, as conspiracy theorists believe, but it saw the advantage to itself of allowing ISIS to weaken the Syrian Kurds. It was never a very far-sighted policy: if ISIS succeeded in taking Kobani, and thus humiliating the US, the Americans' supposed ally Turkey would be seen as partly responsible, after sealing off the town. In the event, the Turkish change of course was embarrassingly speedy. Within hours of Erdoğan saying that Turkey would not help the PYD, permission was being given for Iraqi Kurds to reinforce the PYD fighters at Kobani.

Turkey's volte face was the latest in a series of miscalculations it has made about developments in Syria since the first uprising against Assad in 2011. Erdoğan's government could have held the balance of power between Assad and his opponents, but instead convinced itself that Assad—like Gaddafi in Libya—would inevitably be overthrown. When this failed to happen Ankara gave its support to jihadi groups financed by the Gulf monarchies, which included al-Nusra and IS. Turkey played much the same role in supporting the jihadis in Syria as Pakistan had done supporting the Taliban in Afghanistan. The estimated 12,000 foreign jihadis fighting in Syria, over which there is so much apprehension in Europe and the US, almost all entered via what became known as 'the jihadis' highway', using Turkish border crossing points while the guards looked the other way. In the second half of 2013, as the US put pressure on Turkey, these routes became harder to access but ISIS militants still cross the frontier without too much difficulty.

The exact nature of the relationship between the Turkish intelligence services and ISIS and al-Nusra remains cloudy but there is strong evidence for a degree of collaboration. When Syrian rebels led by al-Nusra captured the Armenian town of Kassab in Syrian government–held territory early this year, it seemed that the Turks had allowed them to operate from inside Turkish territory. Also mysterious was the case of the 49 members of the Turkish Consulate in Mosul who stayed in the city as it was taken by ISIS in June; they were held hostage in Raqqa then were unexpectedly released after four months in exchange for ISIS prisoners held in Turkey.

Had Erdoğan chosen to help the Kurds trapped in Kobani rather than sealing them off, he might have strengthened the peace process between his government and the Turkish Kurds. Instead, his actions provoked protests and rioting by Kurds across Turkey; in towns and villages where there have been no Kurdish demonstrations in recent history tyres were burned and 44 people were killed. For the first time in two years, Turkish military aircraft struck at PKK positions in the south-east of the country.

It appears that Erdoğan has thrown away one of the main achievements of his years in power: the beginnings of a negotiated end to the Kurdish armed insurgency. Ethnic hostility and abuse between Turks and Kurds have now increased. Police suppress anti-ISIS demonstrations but leave pro-ISIS demonstrations alone. Some 72 refugees who fled to Turkey from Kobani were sent back into the town. When five PYD members were arrested by the Turkish Army they were described by the military as 'separatist terrorists'. There have been hysterical outbursts from Erdoğan's supporters: the mayor of Ankara, Melih Gökçek, tweeted that 'there are people in the east who pass themselves off as Kurdish but are actually atheist Armenians by origin.' The Turkish media, increasingly subservient to or intimidated by the government, has played down the seriousness of the demonstrations. CNN Turk, famous for showing a documentary on penguins at the height of the Gezi Park demonstrations that rocked Turkey last year, chose to broadcast a documentary on honeybees during the Kurdish protests.

9 November 2014

'It is like a terrible dream,' says a man who has just fled Mosul for Arbil, describing conditions in the city five months after Islamic State captured it. He adds that 'from the day they started to blow up the mosques people hated them,' referring to the destruction mosques denounced by ISIS 'as places for apostasy not prayer'. The small businessman, who was an army officer under Saddam Hussein and is now on a pension, is very nervous that anybody should learn his name. Some of his family have stayed on in Mosul to prevent their house being confiscated by IS. Its officials check house-to-house demanding to see documents proving that the occupant is the owner. If they discover that the real owner has left the city, he is given 10 days to return or his house is confiscated.

Life in Mosul for a Sunni Arab—Christians and Yazidis have been forced to flee—is a mixture of normality, inconvenience and fear. Surprisingly, pensions are still being paid by the central government in Baghdad and the man who fled is still receiving his. But there is the burden of complying with new rules and regulations as ISIS imposes its fundamentalist Islamic ideology. Some of these are inconvenient, such as the ban on smoking in public, or trivial, such as the removal of all pictures of Tom and Jerry from the walls of schools. The imposition of the niqab, fully covering a woman's face, is deeply resented. One woman in Mosul, whose name must also be concealed, writes: 'Just this evening, with my old mum, I went out to shop and buy medicines in my car with a thin cloth showing my eyes only. What can I do? Last week, a woman was standing beside a kiosk, and uncovered her face to drink a bottle of water. One of them [IS] approached her and hit her on the head with a thick stick. He didn't notice that her husband was close to her. Her husband beat him up and he ran away, shooting randomly in the sky as the people, in sympathy, chased him so they could share in beating him. This is just one story of the brutality we are living.'

Such examples of open opposition to ISIS are limited because people are terrified of savage retaliation at its hands. The retired businessman says this sense of dread never left him, 'though generally if you don't interfere with them, they don't interfere with you'. But he recalls public executions in the middle of a roundabout, such as that of the lawyer Sameera Salih Ali al-Nuaimy, who had written on Facebook that the blowing up of mosques and shrines by ISIS was 'barbaric'. He says he stays mostly in his house, 'going out 10 times in the past two months'. 'I was one of the people who hated [Nouri al-Maliki's] army, but now I would like the Iraqi Army to come back,' he says. 'People in Mosul would welcome them. Anybody would be better than IS, even the Israelis. We are dying.' Such words may be joy to the government in Baghdad and its supporters in Washington or Tehran. But while detestation of ISIS is common in the Sunni community in Iraq, so too is fear of the Iraqi Army and the Shia militias that are the main fighting force of the Baghdad government.

17 November 2014

Aziz, a young Yazidi man, holds up his phone and shows a video of what looks and sounds like a fireworks display on a dark night. 'These are the gun flashes from the weapons of Daesh fighters when they entered our village of Gire Ezer on the night of 3 August and killed between 200 and 300 people,' he explains.

The surviving Yazidis from the village, mostly poor farmers and labourers, fled in panic from their homes in the Sinjar mountains to safety in the territory of the Kurdistan Regional Government where they joined 300,000 or more other Yazidis escaping massacre, rape and enslavement by IS. They were first housed in a school in Zakho and are being moved to a camp called Bercive in a valley filling up with large tents. It is getting cold in northern Kurdistan and Aziz's father, Mahmoud Matto Abbas, complains that so far there is no heat, water or electricity.

At the time of their initial flight in August, the Yazidis achieved notoriety for the first time in their history as thousands of them were trapped on Mount Sinjar, their holy mountain. Television showed biblical scenes of terrified Yazidis trying to escape slaughter. President Barack Obama sent US Special Forces to report on their condition and started bombing ISIS's motorised columns. But in September and October the television cameras departed and international attention switched to the siege of the Kurdish town of Kobani. The Yazidis of Mount Sinjar were largely forgotten, though 6,000 or more, many of them fighters and their families, remain there, surrounded by ISIS and with one road intermittently open into Syria. They receive supplies from two Iraqi Army helicopters and a C-130 transport plane as they defend their temples from being destroyed by IS.

Most of the 576,000 displaced people in Duhok province are Yazidis. Their religion is a blend of traditions including veneration for fire from the Zoroastrians, baptism from the Christians and circumcision from Islam. But at the centre of it is the Peacock Angel, leading to their persecution as devil worshippers.

Mahmoud Matto Abbas says that long before the arrival of IS, Yazidis lived in poverty. He says 'everything in our region was miserable: we didn't even have enough petrol or cement to build houses. Until we got here, nobody helped us. We asked the Peshmerga and the Iraqi government for weapons to defend ourselves against ISIS but they ignored us.' He says that the only people who helped them escape were the PKK Turkish Kurd guerrillas, many of whom were killed by ISIS while doing so. He wonders why the US and Turkey call the PKK 'terrorists' when he and the other Yazidis have nothing but praise for them.

There is a numbed and despairing resignation about many of the Yazidis who have lost everything. Haji Ayyo Eabo says: 'I have spent my life saving money to build a house, but I had lived in it for only a month when I had to run for my life.' He points to an elderly man with a white walrus moustache, saying 'he used to be one of the wealthiest men in our village with 60 or 70 sheep and goats.' Many speak of relatives who did not make it to safety and express anger at the speed with which the Peshmerga, who were supposed to be defending Sinjar, fled, often without firing a shot. Yusuf Amar from Tel Qasar village says 'the commanders of the Peshmerga fled and their men told us "get out, our commanders have disappeared and we are going to go."'

There is a feature of the flight of the Yazidis that is likely to produce further violence in future. The Yazidis complain that the Sunni Arabs who lived near them sided with ISIS and aided in the massacres, sometimes even beginning the killings before ISIS death squads arrived. It is difficult to know how true this is, but it will make it next to impossible for Yazidis and Sunni Arabs to live together when the Yazidis return to their villages as they fully expect to do.

23 November 2014

Two years ago Jalal Yako, a Syriac Catholic priest, returned to his home town of Qaraqosh to persuade members of his community to stay in Iraq and not to emigrate because of the violence directed against them. 'I was in Italy for 18 years, and when I came back here my mission was to get Christians to stay here,' he says. 'The Pope in Lebanon two years ago had established a mission to get Christians in the East to stay.' Father Yako laboured among the Syriac Catholics, one of the oldest Christian communities in the world, who have seen the number of Christians in Iraq decline from over 1 million at the time of the American invasion in 2003 to about 250,000 today.

But in the past six months Father Yako has changed his mind, and he now believes that, after 2,000 years of history, Christians must leave Iraq. Speaking at the entrance of a half-built mall in the Kurdish capital Arbil, where 1,650 people from Qaraqosh have taken refuge, he says that 'everything has changed since the coming of Daesh. We should flee. There is nothing for us here.' When Islamic State fighters captured Qaraqosh on 7 August, all the town's 50,000 or so Syriac Catholics had to run for their lives and lost all their possessions. Many now huddle in dark little prefabricated rooms provided by the UN High Commission for Refugees amid the raw concrete of the mall, crammed together without heat or electricity. They sound as if what happened to them is a nightmare from which they might awaken at any moment and speak about how, only three-and-a-half months ago, they owned houses, farms and shops, had well-paying jobs, and drove their own cars and tractors. They hope against hope to go back, but they have heard reports that everything in Qaraqosh has been destroyed or stolen by IS.

Some have suffered worse losses. On the third floor of the shopping mall down a dark corridor sits Aida Hanna Noeh, 43, and her blind husband Khader Azou Abada, who was too ill to be taken out of Qaraqosh by Aida, with their three children, in the final hours before it was captured by ISIS fighters. The family stayed in their house for many days, and then ISIS told them to assemble with others who had failed to escape to be taken by mini-buses to Arbil. As they entered the buses, the jihadis stripped them of any remaining money, jewellery or documents. Aida was holding her three-and-a-half-month-old baby daughter, Christina, when the little girl was seized by a burly ISIS fighter who took her away. When Aida ran after him he told the mother to get back on the bus or he would kill her. She has not seen her daughter since.

Before ISIS arrived in Qaraqosh, Kurdish Peshmerga had moved into the towns and villages of the Nineveh Plain. They swore to defend their inhabitants, many of whom stayed because they were reassured by these pledges. Father Yako recalls that 'before Qaraqosh was taken by Daesh there were many slogans by the KRG saying they would fight as hard for Qaraqosh as they would for Arbil. But when the town was attacked, there was nobody to support us.' He says that Christian society in Iraq is still shocked by the way in which the Iraqi and Kurdish governments failed to defend them. Johanna Towaya, formerly a large farmer and community leader in Qaraqosh, says that up to midnight on 6 August the Peshmerga commanders were assuring the Syriac Catholic bishop in charge of the town that they would defend it, but hours later they fled. Previously, they had refused to let the Christians arm themselves on the grounds that it was unnecessary. Ibrahim Shaaba, another resident of the town, said that he saw the ISIS force that entered Qaraqosh early in the morning of 7 August and it was modest in size, consisting of only 10 vehicles filled with fighters.

At first, ISIS behaved with some moderation towards the 150 Christian families who, for one reason or another, could not escape. But this restraint did not last; looting and destruction became pervasive. Towaya says that the ISIS authorities in Mosul started 'giving documents to anybody getting married in Mosul to enable them to go to Qaraqosh to take furniture [from abandoned Christian homes].'

As so many had fled, there are few who can give an account of how ISIS behaved in their newly captured Christian town. But one woman, Fida Boutros Matti, got to know all too well what ISIS was like when she and her husband had to pretend to convert to Islam in order to save their lives and those of their children, before finally escaping. Speaking in a house in Arbil, where she is now living, she explains how she and her husband Adel and their young daughter Nevin and two younger sons, Ninos and Iwan, twice tried to flee but were stopped by ISIS fighters. 'They took our money, documents and mobile phones and sent us home,' she says. 'After 13 days they knocked on our door and the men were separated from the women. Thirty women were taken with their children to one house and told they must convert to Islam, pay a tax or be killed. We told them that since they had taken all our money, we could not pay them.' Four days later, some fighters burst into the house saying they would kill the women and the children if they did not convert.

Soon afterwards, Matti was taken to Mosul in a car with three other women and a guard who, she recalls, threw a grenade into a house on the way to frighten them. In the Habba district of Mosul she and the three other Christian women were put in one room, next to another in which there were 30 Yazidi girls between 10 and 18 who were being repeatedly raped by the guards. Matti says that 'the Yazidi girls were so young that I worried about Nevin and told the guards that she was eight years old though she is really 10.' They told her that her husband, Adel, had converted to Islam. She asked to speak to him on the phone, saying she would do whatever he did. They spoke, and agreed that they had no choice but to convert if they wanted to survive.

When they appeared before an Islamic court in Mosul to register their conversion their three children were given new, Islamic names: Aisha, Abdel-Rahman and Mohammed. They went to live in a house in a Sunni Muslim district and from there—here the husband and wife are circumspect about what exactly happened—they secured a phone and contacted relatives in Arbil. They said that they needed to take one of their children for medical treatment in Mosul city centre, and, once there, they had a pre-arranged meeting with a driver who took them by a roundabout route through Kirkuk to the protection of the KRG.

18 December 2014

The Islamic State is becoming even more repressive and violent as it comes under increased military pressure from its many enemies. It shows no mercy to those who resist its rule—such as the Albu Nimr tribe in western Iraq, 581 members of which ISIS recently executed. This is not random slaughter: ISIS has a well-organised security service that strikes pre-emptively at potential critics and opponents. Last month in Mosul two women who had stood as candidates in the Iraqi parliamentary election were shot dead, though they had publicly repented their actions. ISIS is convinced that spies are everywhere working against it. Shortly after the former candidates were executed, Mosul's 2 million inhabitants suddenly found that their mobile phones were no longer working: ISIS had closed the whole network down, apparently because informers were tipping off the US Air Force about the location of its leaders—one of them, the governor of Mosul, had been killed in his car by an air strike. In a sign of the Islamic State's nervousness about the situation in Mosul, it has ordered that at least one man from every family must join its military forces or pay a fine equivalent to $1,250.

But there is more to ISIS than cruelty, violence and religious fanaticism: since it wants the state to endure, it has to satisfy the basic needs of the population. In Mosul it terrifies people but it also controls the price of food and accommodation, so that fruit and vegetables are cheaper than in the nearby Kurdish cities of Arbil and Duhok. Bread makes up about half the diet of poor Syrians and Iraqis, so IS, which took a million tonnes of grain from government silos in Iraq, has made sure that bakeries have kept on working and the price of bread stays low. These efforts may seem paltry: there are severe shortages of mains electricity, fresh tap water and petrol of usable quality. But for many Sunni in Mosul, ISIS's actions compare favourably with the sectarianism and criminality displayed by the Iraqi Army and federal police during the 10 years they held the city.

After a series of easy victories on the battlefield, things for ISIS have become more difficult. It has not succeeded in taking Kobani in northern Syria, though it is still trying, despite suffering heavy casualties during the long siege. American air strikes make it hard for ISIS to pursue the tactics that worked so well over the summer: flying columns of fighters in captured US-made Humvees and trucks would launch blitzkrieg attacks and catch their enemies by surprise. Its strategy of demoralising the opposing forces before the first shot was fired was also successful: jihadi propagandists would publicise ISIS atrocities in professionally made videos and release them on the internet. And its military tactics can be extremely effective: ISIS specialises in the use of suicide bombers, either moving on foot and wearing suicide vests or driving vehicles packed with up to 15 tonnes of explosives. It also makes use of more traditional methods: highly trained snipers, mortar teams, mines and booby traps. Small but useful items apparently left behind when a unit withdraws, such as torches, turn out to be packed with explosives that detonate when the torch is switched on. A Kurdish tribal leader told me that 92 members of his tribe in the Peshmerga had been killed, many by such devices. He had just come from the funeral of three of his men who believed they had captured a car abandoned by IS: it blew up when they switched on the ignition.

The balance of power in Iraq has changed, but it is not clear by how much. 'In August they were threatening Arbil and now we are threatening Mosul,' says Fuad Hussein, the Kurdistan regional president's chief of staff. 'They held the initiative then and now we do.' It is true that in recent weeks ISIS has lost some important towns, including Zumar, near the Syrian border, and Jalawla and Sa'adiyah near the border with Iran. At the end of October Shia militias captured an ISIS stronghold at Jurf al-Sakhar, 30 miles south-west of Baghdad, possession of which had enabled the jihadis to threaten the capital from the south. Further north on the Tigris River, the Iraqi Army has retaken the town of Baiji where Iraq's largest oil refinery is situated. These five successes have one factor in common: in all cases, Sunni civilians fled before the towns were recaptured, showing that Iraq's 5- or 6-million-strong Sunni Arab population is more frightened of ISIS's opponents than it is of IS. They have every reason to be fearful of the Shia militias, Kurdish Peshmerga and Shia-dominated Iraqi Army. But—unfortunately for them, and for the future of Iraq—the Sunni have nowhere to run to except ISIS-held territory.

There are, however, many Sunni in Mosul who say they would accept any ruler other than IS. Sameer, a Kurd with a shop in Mosul, says that in the first days of what he calls the ISIS occupation, the shopkeepers in the city were horrified to find that ISIS was totally serious about implementing a regulation according to which if a shop is open at the time of prayer 'the shopkeeper will receive 40 lashes and pay a fine.' Sameer has no love for ISIS and lists the miseries it has inflicted on his city, but he says that more Sunni Arabs are joining it every day: 'Although they admit that ISIS is not a great option, at least it is some kind of reaction to the corruption of the Iraqi government.' He was shocked to find that there are even some Sunni

Kurds joining IS. He recently ran into an old friend, a Kurd from Halabja who had worked in Mosul for 10 years. 'I saw him with ISIS forces wearing their uniform,' Sameer says. 'I asked him if he was happy and he said: "I know they are doing many bad things, but the Kurdistan leaders just care about their jobs and big business deals. ISIS is better for me, because at least it gives me a job and pays a good salary."' The ISIS basic salary is $400 a month, though those with military experience earn more. Fuad Hussein believes that ISIS now has many more fighters than the 31,500 the CIA estimated in September. 'I am talking about hundreds of thousands of fighters,' he says, 'because they are able to mobilise Arab young men in the territory they have taken.'

Sameer stayed in Mosul after it fell because he did not want to lose his shop. As a Kurd, he knew he was vulnerable and considered leaving for Arbil, just 50 miles away. But a week after their victory armed ISIS men came to his door and told him that if he left permanently his shop and house would be confiscated. This sort of threat is one of the ways ISIS ensures that its new state does not become depopulated. There are plenty of reasons why anybody might want to leave Mosul, if only they could. Sunni Arabs in the city have always been conservative, but they never believed in the compulsory wearing of the niqab and hijab, which is now enforced. When ISIS militants found one woman without a veil waiting for her son to come back from school they told her to call her husband; as soon as he arrived he was given 40 lashes. Someone in Mosul told me that he had seen an ISIS man run up to a woman at a bus stop; he grabbed her arm, put his other hand on her head and shouted: 'Allahu Akbar'. Then he told his men to take her to his house because 'she had become his wife'. There is a fear that ISIS will demand that unmarried women marry jihadi fighters. One Mosul resident tells me that ISIS checked the identity cards of his family, but he was alarmed when the only cards they photocopied were of his two unmarried daughters, one a university student and the other a 13-year-old.

Whatever the hostility people in Mosul feel towards IS, there is not much they can do about it. Unlike Sunni Arab tribesmen in the countryside, very few people in Mosul have weapons, since under the Iraqi government having a Kalashnikov without explanation was enough to get the owner arrested, jailed and tortured. 'They can't do anything,' a local observer says. 'They don't have arms and they know there are informers. They'd like to leave but ISIS won't let them go.'

Trying against these odds to turn the Sunni Arab community against ISIS is at the heart of the policy of both the Baghdad government and the White House. But it is not proving easy, partly because of the distrust and even hatred that divides the Islamic State's many opponents. The leader of the Albu Nimr tribe, Sheikh Naim al-Gaood, describes how 3,000 of his men went to Ain al-Asad, one of the few government bases still holding out in Anbar province, expecting the Iraqi Army to give them weapons to fight IS. The soldiers inside the base, fearful of Sunni tribesmen and uncertain of their allegiance, would only let a small number approach. Sheikh Naim tried to arbitrate and suggested that 500 tribesmen be armed. But the soldiers would not agree and eventually a hundred men were given weapons—but no ammunition. It was soon after this that the 581 Albu Nimr were slaughtered by IS, their bodies thrown down wells or taken to the desert to be burned.

19 March 2015

Mahmoud Omar (not his real name), a young Sunni photographer, is angered though not entirely surprised by the way in which the Baghdad government continues to mistreat his fellow Sunni. Political leaders inside and outside Iraq all agree that the best, and possibly the only, way to defeat ISIS is to repeat the success in 2006–07 when the US supported the Sunni 'Awakening Movement' which weakened, though it never destroyed, al-Qa'ida in Iraq. Now, as then, many Sunni hate the extremists for their merciless violence and enforcement of outlandish and arbitrary rules on personal behaviour that have no connection to even the strictest interpretation of sharia.

The fact that many Sunni are alienated from or terrified by ISIS should present an opportunity for Baghdad, since Prime Minister Haider al-Abadi's government is meant to be more inclusive than that of his predecessor, Nouri al-Maliki. With the new government lauded internationally for its non-sectarian stance, the Sunni hoped they would face less day-to-day repression. 'IS has shocked many Sunni by its actions,' says Mahmoud. 'But instead of the government treating us better to win us over, they are treating us even worse.' As an example he cites the behaviour of police in Ramadi, the capital of the vast and overwhelmingly Sunni province of Anbar. His family comes from the city, which used to have a population of 600,000. Now 80 per cent have fled the fighting as ISIS and government forces battle for control. ISIS launched seven almost simultaneous suicide bomb attacks last week and was already holding 80 per cent of Ramadi.

The situation inside the government-held enclave is desperate. Trucks bringing in supplies have to run the gauntlet of ISIS checkpoints and ambushes. Food prices have risen sharply and in outlying cities, like al-Qaim and al-Baghdadi, Mahmoud says that 'the people are reduced to eating fodder.' Schools are closed to pupils because they are full of refugees. But in the midst of this crisis, Mahmoud says the local police are as predatory and corrupt as ever when dealing with the Sunni. He says that in one police station in the government-held part of Ramadi 'the police go on arresting Sunni, torturing them and refusing to release them until their families come up with a bribe. I know one man who was in there for a week before his family paid the police $5,000 to get him released.' All the old methods of surveillance remain in place with shopkeepers forced to spy on their customers and hand in daily reports to the police. Predictably, Mahmoud dismisses as 'promises and words' the pledges of the Abadi government to be more even-handed—intentions the Americans and Europeans apparently take at face value.

As a photographer and educated member of a politically moderate, well-off family, Mahmoud would be seen by ISIS as a natural enemy. His family has lost much because of the jihadi group's takeover of Anbar. His father only stayed in Ramadi until recently because he wanted to safeguard two houses he owned. A third house in Fallujah has been taken over by ISIS and the family does not know what has happened to it. But for all his dislike of IS, Mahmoud would have great difficulty trusting the Baghdad government. This is because a relative, Muad Mohammed Abed, who was a teacher and has a wife and daughter, has been in prison since 2012, under sentence of death for murder. It is a crime he and his family vehemently deny he committed, saying that the only evidence against him is a confession obtained after torture. They have photographs of Muad taken after his interrogation, showing him covered in bruises and burns. His sentence was ultimately quashed, but he remains in jail. A promised retrial may be a long time coming because there are 1,500 similar cases to be heard by a court before his turn comes. His wife, who visits him in prison, says that he is kept in a cell four metres square with seven other prisoners. They are forbidden to have a radio or television.

Most of Mahmoud's family have now fled to Kurdistan. He sees their misfortunes as mirroring the suffering of the Sunni community as a whole.

He fears that the Iraqi Sunni will be ground to pieces in the struggle between ISIS and the government and that, as ISIS is pushed back, the Sunni community will share in its defeat so 'we will end up like the Christians who are being forced out of the country.'

For all Mahmoud's passionate sense of injustice, his belief that the government is irredeemably anti-Sunni is only part of the story. Sunni and Shia have both used mass violence against one another's communities in the past 50 years, but the Sunni have most often been the perpetrators. The explosive growth of sectarian killings in 2012 to 2014, when 31,414 civilians were killed according to Iraqi Body Count, very much reflects the growth of IS.

But Mahmoud may well be right that in the long run the Sunni will be forced to take flight or become a vulnerable minority like the Christians. If ISIS is beaten back, the Sunni may hold on to their strongholds where they are the great majority, but where populations are mixed they are likely to be losers. A final ethnic and sectarian shake-out in Iraq seems to be under way. Even if the government in Baghdad wanted to share power with the Sunni, ISIS has, quite deliberately, ensured through its atrocities that this will be near impossible. The so-called Islamic State will not go down without fierce resistance and, if it does fall, the Sunni community will be caught up in its destruction.

1 April 2015

Iraq's prime minister, Haider al-Abadi, has joined in a triumphal parade through the centre of Tikrit as his government claimed victory over ISIS after a month-long battle for the city. Abadi's defence minister, Khalid al-Obeidi, said: 'We have the pleasure, with all our pride, to announce the good news of a magnificent victory.' Naming two Iraqi provinces still under ISIS control, he added: 'Here we come to you, Anbar! Here we come to you, Nineveh!' It is the first real success for the Iraqi Army since it lost northern and western Iraq to ISIS in the summer of 2014.

But for all the official euphoria, the slow pace of the assault on Tikrit, a small Sunni Arab city that once had a population of 200,000, is not a good omen for further advances. The attack began on 2 March with some 20,000 Shia militiamen encircling the city with only 3,000 government soldiers, some special forces and 1,000 Sunni tribal fighters. The operation appears to have been under the control of Iranian officers and the Iraqi government was only told about it at the last moment. The US, suspicious of an Iranian-led militia assault, was not at first asked for air support and did not give it until the last week, following a request by Abadi. ISIS appears to have decided that it would not fight to the end in Tikrit, where its forces would have to engage in a slogging match against greatly superior numbers backed by artillery. The jihadist group is at its most effective when its forces act as guerrillas rather than as a regular army defending or attacking fixed positions.

At the very moment of jubilation over Tikrit in Iraq, ISIS has made a significant advance in neighbouring Syria. The British-based Syrian Observatory for Human Rights says that ISIS fighters have taken over a large part of the Yarmouk Palestinian refugee camp, not far from the heart of Damascus. ISIS is said to control some main streets in the camp after clashing with a Palestinian group. ISIS may well think it has greater military opportunities in Syria than Iraq. The Syrian Army has suffered a series of setbacks in recent weeks north of Aleppo and has lost the provincial capital of Idlib to Jabhat al-Nusra. It is short of recruits after four years of war and shows signs of being fought out.

19 May 2015

IS fighters have defeated elite units of the Iraqi armed forces and captured the city of Ramadi, the provincial capital of Anbar province 70 miles west of Baghdad. The fall of Ramadi is the worst military disaster suffered by the Iraqi government since it lost the north of Iraq to an ISIS offensive almost a year ago. One local councillor in Ramadi described the situation as 'total collapse'.

Burnt bodies litter the streets and there are reports of massacres of policemen and tribesmen opposed to the self-proclaimed Islamic State. Armoured vehicles belonging to the Iraqi Army's so-called Golden Division were seen streaming out of Ramadi in a retreat that looked, at times, as if it had turned into a rout. Heavy equipment, including armoured Humvees and artillery, was abandoned. Some 500 soldiers and civilians have been killed in fighting over the past few days. Suicide bombers destroyed fortifications by ramming them with vehicles packed with explosives.

In some respects, the fall of Ramadi is a worse defeat for the Iraqi government than the capture of Mosul on 10 June 2014. ISIS has been pressuring Ramadi since April and a further assault was fully expected. The garrison of the city consisted of some of the best troops in the Iraqi Army, supported by US air power. American generals have been downplaying the extent of the calamity, but the US policy of rebuilding the Iraqi Army and aiding it with air strikes is in ruins. The Baghdad government now has little choice but to deploy the Hashd al-Shaabi, the Shia paramilitaries which the US views as being under Iranian influence and which it has not wanted to see in front line fighting in Sunni areas. ISIS had been portrayed inside and outside Iraq as having lost momentum, symbolised by the loss of Tikrit in April, but the capture of Ramadi will strengthen its appeal to Sunni people as a winner.

23 May 2015

In a room in a house on the slopes of Mount Abdulaziz, five ISIS fighters are under siege by Syrian Kurdish fighters. 'They can't get out,' says a voice cutting through the crackle on the field radio. 'But one of those bastards just shot and wounded one of our men.'

This is a mopping-up operation, a day after a major battle for Mount Abdulaziz ended with the defeat of some 1,000 ISIS fighters who had been besieged. The mountain was one of the jihadis' strongholds in this corner of north-east Syria, from which they could fire artillery into the nearby Kurdish city of al-Hasakah and menace a fertile Kurdish enclave with a population of 1 million.

IS fighters did not leave much behind in their retreat. There remain a few freshly painted slogans in praise of ISIS and some burned-out hulks of cars that had been used as bombs. Crisp new cards lie discarded on the floor of one building, saying 'Office of Zakat [obligatory tax for the benefit of the poor] and Insurance', which appear to be ration cards requiring the listing of names, numbers and other details. The cards underline the extent to which ISIS is well organised.

The defeat of ISIS in the battle which started on 6 May is in sharp contrast to the jihadi group's victories over the Iraqi Army at Ramadi and the Syrian Army at Palmyra over the last week. An explanation for the difference in the outcome of the three battles is that the Syrian Kurdish forces are highly motivated, disciplined and come from the area in which they are fighting. The Kurdish commander General Garzan Gerer, speaking beside a pine forest just below the mountain, says: 'We fight better than the Syrian Army at Palmyra because we have strong beliefs and we are defending our own land.' There is another more material reason why the Kurds won and ISIS lost. Young Kurdish fighters resting in a captured ISIS command post are open about how much they benefit from US air strikes. Botan Damhat, a smooth-faced squad commander aged only 18, says: 'Without the

American planes, it would have been much harder to take the mountain. We would have won in the end, but we would have lost a lot more men.'

Kurdish commanders are unclear about casualties, saying they have buried 300 bodies of ISIS fighters but many more have been carried away. They put their own fatalities at between 25 and 30, the disparity perhaps being explained by the effectiveness of American air strikes. General Gerer says the two main problems in capturing the mountain were the terrain and the fact that 'many of the local villages are Arab and they often supported Daesh.' He says that there are also 25 Assyrian Christian villages where the jihadis prevented people from leaving so they could be used as hostages in the event of a Kurdish attack. He does not think more than a few of the Arabs who supported ISIS will come back. As we leave, we see a party of Arabs with their belongings returning to their house in a village. They wave rather frantically as we drive past in a military vehicle, as if uncertain about how they will be treated by the victorious Kurds.

Who were the ISIS fighters holding Mount Abdulaziz? The Kurds insist their opponents were Muslims from all over the world, one of three of those captured turning out to be Chinese. In one building, they found neat little notebooks with translations of different words into a variety of languages, and drawings of a desk and chair with their names in tiny handwriting. Yalmaz Shahid, 25, another squad leader, says that ISIS fought well. 'We were particularly afraid of their suicide bombers and booby traps.' Another fighter, who gives his name as Ernesto, says 'they are very professional snipers.'

The victory at Mount Abdulaziz is the biggest Kurdish success since the four-and-a-half-month siege of the town of Kobani on the Turkish border which ended earlier this year. In the town of Amuda, where I am staying, there was the rattle of festive gunfire well into the night and parties of children patrolled the streets singing patriotic songs in celebration.

But not all the news this week is good for the Kurds. With the fall of Palmyra, ISIS now holds half of Syria and part of the rest is held by Jabhat al-Nusra. Overall, ISIS is much stronger than it was pre-Ramadi and Palmyra in terms of morale and prestige, not to mention captured equipment. The problem for the Syrian Kurds is that, although their discipline, backed by US air power, has been effective, they number only about 2.2 million or 10 per cent of the Syrian population. They will have difficulty holding off an Islamic State able to draw on resources in Syria and Iraq and having recently defeated the regular armies of both countries.

The outcome of the battle for Mount Abdulaziz shows the Syrian Kurds are militarily strong and can hold their own against ISIS in a way that Syrian and Iraqi soldiers cannot. But in the long term, their de facto independent enclaves, ruling themselves for the first time in history, are very vulnerable to whoever turns out to be the winner in the Syrian civil war.

26 May 2015

The Kurdish soldiers relax half a mile behind the front line where they have been battling ISIS forces west of the Syrian town of Ras al-Ayn. The women are in no doubt about why they are fighting. Nujaan, who is 27 and has been a soldier for four years, says that Islamic State's 'target is women'. She says: 'Look at Shingal [in Iraq] where they raped the women and massacred the men. It is a matter of honour to defend ourselves first, and then our families and lands.' Sitting beside her is Zenya, 22, who adds that she also 'is fighting for myself and my family'.

The Kurds in this north-east corner of Syria know, somewhat to their own surprise, that, encircled by enemies though they may be, they are living in the safest part of the country. The territory behind the front line where Nujaan and Zenya are fighting is full of farmers bringing in the wheat harvest and is without the undercurrent of terror you find in the rest of Syria. Of course, the greater safety in Jazira, the triangular-shaped Kurdish canton, only stands out because of the contrast with everywhere else on the borders of the Caliphate. But, for the moment, there are no car bombs, kidnappings, bandit gangs at checkpoints or fear of massacre. The PYD and its armed wing, the YPG, have an effective monopoly of power here, as they do in the two other cantons on the Turkish frontier. Together, these three cantons make up what the Kurds call Rojava, their de facto autonomous state-let in Syria. Though the militarised rule of the PYD is not popular with all Kurds, its militiamen and -women do provide genuine protection—unlike the Syrian or Iraqi armies.

Overhead, the drone of US aircraft is clearly audible and Nujaan reports that there have been numerous air strikes that morning, as well as ground fighting. She says that several Kurdish soldiers have been killed and wounded, though she does not know the details. She adds that the YPJ Kurdish women's militia, to which she belongs, is gradually driving ISIS towards the west. She and the other women appear remote and detached from what they are saying, possibly because they are exhausted from days on the front line. In fact, the push westwards is of great military and possibly political significance because the Syrian Kurdish armed forces are closing in on a crucial ISIS-controlled border crossing point from Syria into Turkey at Tal Abyad. The Syrian Kurds note bitterly that Turkey has closed the crossing points into Kurdish-held territory, but has kept open those used by IS. But now Tal Abyad, the northern end of the road that leads straight to the Islamic State's Syrian capital Raqqa, is threatened by a pincer movement by Kurds advancing from both the east and from Kobani in the west.

Sehanok Dibo, an adviser to the leaders of the PYD, says that Tal Abyad is the Kurds' next military target. 'We are 18 kilometres from Tal Abyad in the east and 20 kilometres in the west. We hope to liberate it soon.' This will not only be a serious blow to IS, but also to Turkey, which will see even more of the Syrian side of its southern frontier controlled by Kurds. Turkey has demanded a 'buffer zone' in Syria that would conveniently allow it to occupy the Kurdish enclaves along the border. Dibo takes it as a matter of proven fact that 'Turkey supports Daesh'. He says that it is difficult to predict what will happen next as 'the balance of power in the war in Syria can be changed abruptly at any moment by the actions of one of the outside powers.'

25 July 2015

Turkey has made a significant foreign policy shift by saying it will allow US planes to use its air base at İncirlik to attack ISIS positions in Iraq and Syria. And, for the first time, Turkish aircraft have been in action against ISIS across the border in northern Syria. The growing engagement by Ankara against ISIS comes after an ISIS suicide bombing killed 32 young Turkish socialists and wounded 104 in the Turkish border town of Suruç on 20 July. They were on their way to build a kindergarten and children's care centre in the ruined Syrian Kurdish town of Kobani.

2 August 2015

The deal between the US and Turkey, which will allow American bombers to use İncirlik airbase while Turkey takes action against IS, looks stranger and stranger. When first announced over a week ago, US officials spoke triumphantly of the agreement being 'a game-changer' in the war against IS. In fact, the war waged by Turkey in the days since this great American diplomatic success has been almost entirely against the Kurds, at home and abroad.

Turkish jets are pounding sites occupied by PKK guerrillas in the Kandil Mountains and other parts of northern Iraq. Inside Turkey, the majority of those detained by the security forces turn out to be Kurdish or left-wing activists and not suspected ISIS sympathisers. Prosecutions are threatened against MPs of the largely Kurdish Peoples' Democratic Party (HDP) which has tirelessly advocated peace between the PKK and the Turkish government. Evidently, the HDP's offence was to win 13 per cent of the votes in Turkey's general election on 7 June, thereby depriving President Recep Tayyip Erdoğan's ruling AKP of its parliamentary majority for the first time since 2002.

It is now becoming clear that two crucial parts of the accord were not agreed at the time of the historic announcement. The US Air Force was desperate to get the use of İncirlik, 60 miles from the Syrian border, in order to intensify its bombardment of IS. American planes currently have to fly long distances from Bahrain, Jordan and an aircraft carrier in the Gulf. The failure of the US air campaign to prevent ISIS fighters capturing Ramadi and Palmyra in May intensified the sense of urgency. But at the time of writing, US aircraft have not started using İncirlik because Turkey does not want air strikes in support of the Syrian Kurds to be launched from its base. The PYD, through its determined and well-disciplined militia, the YPG, has hitherto been America's most effective military ally against ISIS in Syria, but it is the Syrian branch of the PKK which Turkey is now busy trying to destroy with its own air campaign.

Even if this dispute is ultimately resolved, it highlights the contradiction at the heart of US policy: Washington is teaming up with a Turkish government whose prime objective in Syria is to prevent the further expansion of PYD/YPG territory. This now extends along 250 miles of the 550-mile-long Syrian–Turkish border after the Kurds captured the important crossing point of Tal Abyad from ISIS on 16 June. In brief, Ankara's objective is the precise opposite of Washington's and little different from that of IS, which has been battling on the ground to hold back the PYD/YPG advance.

A second point of difference between the US and Turkey is over a plan to establish an ISIS-free zone in an area between the Turkish border and Aleppo. This would close off ISIS from Turkey, but who is to do it? Turkey says it is not going to commit ground troops. Public opinion in the US would likewise veto American involvement on the ground so its military pressure on ISIS must entirely depend on its air power. The Turks and their allies in Saudi Arabia and Qatar would like to rebrand Jabhat al-Nusra and

Ahrar al-Sham, whose beliefs and actions differ little from IS, as born-again moderates.

The US has been training carefully vetted fighters to form a 'third force' on the ground which would be different from both pro-Assad forces and al-Qa'ida-type rebels. But al-Nusra has decided that attempts to start such a moderate military movement, in competition with itself, are best strangled at birth—or even before birth, as was shown last week when it abducted Nadeem Hassan, the leader of a small faction trained by the US. Last year, al-Nusra wiped out two groups, the Syrian Revolutionary Front and Harakat Hazm, who were being trained and supplied by the CIA.

So far, ISIS has not done too badly out of Turkey's 'game-changing' turn against it. If and when the US starts using İncirlik, ISIS will have had more than a week to change the disposition of its forces in preparation for a heavier air assault. If US aircraft based at İncirlik are forbidden to attack ISIS fighters when they are battling either the Syrian Kurds or the Syrian Army, the militants' two main opponents on the ground, then they will be no worse off militarily than they were before. This may explain why ISIS has responded so little to the US–Turkish agreement that is supposed to deal it a crippling blow. Close observers say that it welcomes the Turkish attack on the PKK.

Were world leaders just a bit simple-minded or ill-informed when they congratulated Turkey on finally turning against IS? Probably there is as much cynicism as naivety at work here since their intelligence services will have told them that Turkey has long been giving covert support to ISIS and al-Nusra, the most important element of which was not closing the border. The most pressing concern of European countries is the actions of their citizens who have joined ISIS or al-Nusra and may return home to commit atrocities. Given this preoccupation, governments may calculate that whatever Turkey does or does not do, the Turkish–Syrian border will be more closely guarded in future.

But in terms of the stability of the region President Barack Obama may turn out to have made a poor deal with Turkey. It will not be a killer blow to ISIS and may not even weaken it, but it will hit its most resolute opponents, the Kurds. It will spread the violence stemming from the civil wars in Iraq and Syria into Turkey. And it will rekindle a Kurdish–Turkish civil war that had long been on the wane. The game may have changed but peace is even further away.

NINETEEN

Life in the Caliphate

The Caliphate, 2015

16 March 2015

It is one of the strangest states ever created. The Islamic State wants to force all humanity to believe in its vision of a religious and social utopia existing in the first days of Islam. Women are to be treated as chattels, forbidden to leave the house unless they are accompanied by a male relative. People deemed to be pagans, like the Yazidis, can be bought and sold as slaves. Punishments such as beheadings, amputations and flogging become the norm. All those not pledging allegiance to the Caliphate declared by its leader, Abu Bakr al-Baghdadi, on 29 June 2014 are considered enemies.

IS may be regarded with appalled fascination by most people, but conditions inside its territory remain a frightening mystery to the outside world. This is scarcely surprising, because it imprisons and frequently murders local and foreign journalists who report on its activities. Despite these difficulties, it is possible to build up a picture of what life is like inside the Islamic State by interviewing people who have recently lived in Sunni Arab cities like Mosul and Fallujah that are held by IS. The interviewees are necessarily Sunni Arabs living in Iraq, with the exception of some Kurds still living in Mosul, as most Christians, Yazidis, Shabak and Shia have already fled or been killed.

A great range of questions need to be answered. Do people support, oppose or have mixed feelings about ISIS rule and, if so, why? What is it like to live in a place where a wife appearing on the street without the niqab, a cloth covering the head and face, will be told to fetch her husband, who will then be given 40 lashes? How do foreign fighters behave? What is the reaction of local people to demands by ISIS that unmarried women should wed its fighters? More prosaically, what do people eat, drink and cook, and how do they obtain electricity? The answers to these and many other questions show instances of savage brutality, but also a picture of the Islamic State battling to provide some basic services and food at low prices.

A crucial early success for the Islamic State came when ISIS-led forces seized the city of Fallujah, 40 miles west of Baghdad, on 3 January 2014, and the Iraqi Army failed to win it back. This was the first time that ISIS had ruled a large population centre and it is important to understand how it behaved and how and why this behaviour became more extreme as ISIS consolidated its authority. The stories of two men, Abbas (generally known as Abu Mohammed) and Omar Abu Ali, who come from the militant Sunni strongholds of Fallujah and the nearby town of al-Karmah, explain graphically what happened during those first crucial months when ISIS was in power.

Abbas is a 53-year-old Sunni farmer from Fallujah. He recalls the joyous day when ISIS first entered the city: 'At the beginning we were so happy and called it "the Islamic Conquest". Most of the people were offering them feasts and warmly welcoming their chief fighters.' ISIS told people that it had come to set up an Islamic state, and at first this was not too onerous. A Sharia Board of Authority was established to resolve local problems. Abbas says that 'everything was going well until ISIS also took Mosul. Then restrictions on our people increased. At the mosques, local imams started to be replaced by people from other Arab states or Afghanistan. During the first six months of ISIS rule, the movement had encouraged people to go to the mosque, but after the capture of Mosul it became obligatory and anybody who violated the rule received 40 lashes.' A committee of community leaders protested to ISIS and received an interesting reply: 'The answer was that, even at the time of the Prophet Mohammed, laws were not strict at the beginning and alcoholic drinks were allowed in the first three years of Islamic rule.' Only after Islamic rule had become strongly entrenched were stricter rules enforced. So it had been in the 7th century and so it would be 1,400 years later in Fallujah.

Abbas, a conservative-minded community leader with two sons and three daughters in Fallujah, says he had no desire to leave the city because all his extended family are there, though daily life is tough and getting tougher. As of February 2015, 'people suffer from lack of water and electricity which they get from generators because the public supply only operates three to five hours every two days.' The price of cooking gas has soared to the equivalent of £50 a cylinder, so people have started to use wood for cooking. Communications are difficult because ISIS blew up the mast for mobile phones six months ago, but 'some civilians have managed to get satellite internet lines.'

However, it was not the harsh living conditions but two issues affecting his children that led Abbas to leave Fallujah hurriedly on 2 January 2015. The first reason for flight was a new conscription law under which every family had to send one of their sons to be an ISIS fighter. Abbas did not want his son Mohamed to be called up. Previously, families could avoid conscription by paying a heavy fine but at the start of this year military service in ISIS-held areas became obligatory. The second issue concerned one of Abbas's daughters. He says that one day 'a foreign fighter on the bazaar checkpoint followed my daughter, who was shopping with her mother, until they reached home. He knocked on the door and asked to meet the head of the house. I welcomed him and asked, "How I can help you?" He said he wanted to ask for my daughter's hand. I refused his request because it is the custom of our tribe that we cannot give our daughters in marriage to strangers. He was shocked by my answer and later attempted to harass my girls many times. I saw it was better to leave.'

Abbas is now in the Kurdistan Regional Government (KRG) area with his family. He regrets that ISIS did not stick with its original moderate and popular policy before the capture of Mosul, after which it started to impose rules not mentioned in sharia. Abbas says that 'we need ISIS to save us from the government but that doesn't mean that we completely support them.' He recalls how ISIS prohibited cigarettes and hubble-bubble pipes because they might distract people from prayer, in addition to banning Western-style haircuts, T-shirts with English writing on them or images of women. Women are not allowed to leave home unaccompanied by a male relative. Abbas says that 'all this shocked us and made us leave the city.'

A more cynical view is held by Omar Abu Ali, a 45-year-old Sunni Arab farmer from al-Karmah (also called Garma) 10 miles north-east of Fallujah. He has two sons and three daughters and he says that, when ISIS took over their town last year, 'my sons welcomed the rebels, but I wasn't that optimistic.' The arrival of ISIS did not improve the dire living conditions in al-Kharmah and he did not take too seriously the propaganda about how 'the soldiers of Allah would defeat Maliki's devils.' Still, he agrees that many people in his town were convinced, though his experience is that Saddam Hussein, Nouri al-Maliki or ISIS were equally bad for the people of al-Kharmah: 'They turn our town into a battlefield and we are the only losers.'

Al-Kharmah is close to the front line with Baghdad and endures conditions of semi-siege in which few supplies can get through. A litre of petrol costs £2.70 and a bag of flour more than £65. Omar tried to buy as much bread as he could store to last his family a week or more 'because even the bakeries were suffering from lack of flour.' There was constant bombardment and in February 2015 the last water purification plant in town was hit, though he is not clear if this was done by artillery or US air strikes: 'The town is now in a horrible situation because of lack of water.'

Omar spent five months working for IS, though it is not clear in what capacity, his main purpose being to prevent the conscription of his two sons aged 14 and 16. Rockets and artillery shells rained down on al-Karmah, though Omar says they seldom hit ISIS fighters because they hid in civilian houses or in schools. 'The day I left, a school was hit and many children were killed,' he recalls. He says US air strikes and Iraqi Army artillery 'kill us along with ISIS fighters. There is no difference between what they do and the mass killings by IS.' Omar had been trying to flee for two months but did not have the money until he managed to sell his furniture. He is now staying outside Arbil, the Kurdish capital, where his sons and daughters work on local farms which 'is at least better than staying in al-Kharmah'.

He says the Americans, Iraqi government and ISIS have all brought disaster and lists the wars that have engulfed his home town in the past 10 years. 'All of them are killing us,' he says. 'We have no friends.'

17 March 2015

Hamza is a 33-year-old from Fallujah who became an ISIS fighter last year after being attracted by its appeal to his religious feelings. Two months ago, however, he defected, after being asked to help in execution-style murders of people he knew and being appalled by invitations to join in what amounted to rape of captured Yazidi women. Speaking from the safety of another country he gives a vivid account of why he joined IS, what it was like to be a member of the jihadi group, and why he left. He reveals extraordinary details about how the army of ISIS operates, the elaborate training that its fighters receive in Iraq and Syria and the way in which taking part in executions is an initiation rite, proof of the commitment and loyalty of fighters.

An intelligent, idealistic, well-educated and religious man, Hamza defected from ISIS after six months as a trainee. He became conscious that if he stayed in ISIS he would soon have to carry out an execution himself. 'I don't like Shia but when it comes to killing them I was shocked,' he says. He refused to execute some Sunni accused of working with Iraq's mostly Shia government 'or what they [IS] call "the pagan government"'. Surprisingly, he was not punished for this, but was told by his commander that he would be asked to carry out an execution later and, in the meantime, foreign jihadis would do the job.

Hamza gives a fascinating insight into the lives led by ISIS fighters. 'I was paid 400,000 Iraqi dinars [£231] a month in addition to many privileges, including food, fuel and more recently, access to the internet,' he says. His disillusionment stemmed not only from his future role as an executioner but the offer of sex with captured Yazidi women, something he considered the equivalent of rape. 'It was in the first week of December 2014 when they brought about 13 Yazidi girls,' he says. 'The commander tried to tempt us by saying that this is Halal [lawful] for you, a gift from Allah that we are allowed to satisfy ourselves without even marrying them because they are pagans.

'On the other hand, there were some Tunisian Muslim girls who came from Syria. Those Muslim girls were sleeping with some commanders under a marriage contract for a week only and then they were divorced and married to another one. I asked one of them how she had come to be in Syria and she answered that she had travelled first to Turkey and then across the Turkish–Syrian border.'

Hamza does not want his real name or location disclosed, though he believes that for the moment he is safe. He asks for certain details about his escape in January to be concealed, but otherwise is open about how he came to join ISIS forces and what he did. In many cases what he says can be confirmed by other witnesses from Fallujah I have interviewed, though none of these were fighters.

'It's a complicated story,' he says, when asked how he came to join IS. Last year, the group captured Fallujah, where Hamza and his family were living. 'They were kind to people in general and did not force them to join their military service,' he recalls. 'They had many ways of gaining people's goodwill and support: for example, they would go house to house, asking those living there if they needed anything and offering services such as education, saying "We will enlighten your children, so don't send them to the government's schools." In addition, they were giving small lectures and sermons after prayers. Most of the lecture topics were about how to reform and improve society, using the Koran and Hadith [traditional Islamic teachings] to support their arguments. This was like some kind of brain-washing but it happened slowly over six months. I was attending many of those lectures and, after a time, I was preparing in advance the Koranic verses and Hadith texts relevant to the topics. There were weekly competi-tions between groups of youths. I won two competitions on these religious topics and each time I received 300,000 Iraqi dinars.'

In July 2014, his family left Fallujah for Baghdad, but he remained behind. 'After winning two prizes, I felt I liked their system,' he says. 'When my family left, my father asked me not to stay and told me not to be too influenced by the prizes I had won. He said the situation would get worse. He was not very opposed to IS, but he is so old and cannot cope with the hard life in Fallujah after conditions deteriorated—in terms of work, elec-tricity, water, food and the militarisation of life.'

Hamza told his family that he would follow them to Baghdad within a few days, but had decided at this moment, July 2014, to join IS. His motive was primarily religious and idealistic. He says that he 'decided to join them willingly because I was convinced that the Islamic State is the ideal state to serve and to work for Allah and the afterlife, which is the surest part of life'. He was accepted immediately by IS, his preacher rec-ommending him to a military commander, though he was not at first sent to a military unit. The details Hamza gives of his induction and training by ISIS are significant because they help explain how it has created such a formidable military machine.

First, he was told to do exercises to get him into good physical shape. 'The exercises I did in July and August 2014 were physical activity exercises, fitness training, and abdominal exercises,' he says. 'After that, I was trans-ferred to a military unit outside Fallujah for a month and then I was sent for a month-and-a-half to Raqqa [in Syria] where I was taught military skills through intensive training courses. In Fallujah, I had learned to shoot using Kalashnikov rifles and how to throw grenades. It was a more advanced level of training in Raqqa where I, together with a group of volunteers, learned to use RPG [rocket-propelled grenade] launchers and different kinds of machine guns.'

Asked why ISIS had taken him and other volunteers to Raqqa for mili-tary training, Hamza has an interesting response. 'The reason wasn't because training is not available in Iraq. All kinds of training, equipment and facilities are available in Fallujah, but we were taken to Raqqa to increase our sense of what is called "patriotism towards the Caliphate lands" and to introduce us to a new experience and a new revolution. When they took us to Raqqa, all the fighters became convinced that the boundary between Syria and Iraq is fake and we are all united under the rule of the Caliphate. Psychologically speaking, I was so relaxed and happy to go there because it was a nice feeling to destroy the borders between two governments and pass through them. This was really a great achievement.'

Executions play an important role in the life of IS, not only as a means of intimidating enemies but as an initiation rite and proof of faith by new fighters. Hamza says that in Raqqa trainees like him were sent to watch public executions: 'I attended three executions in Raqqa and others in Fallujah. One was of a man believed to be working with the Syrian regime; he was just shot.' In Fallujah, captured Shia soldiers of the Iraqi Army were executed. 'This was the first time that I witnessed a beheading,' he says. 'I had been shown some videos made with impressive visual and audio skill. After watching many of these, we were being taken to attend public executions.'

Asked if he carried out any executions himself, Hamza says that he did not and explains why. 'I was not ordered to do so because according to ISIS rules, the trainee needs more than six months to be ready to carry out an execution. But this is not the only criterion. The trainee should also show additional skills in his religious education and military tactics as well as many other tests. However, the problem was that I was a little bit shaken after attending those executions. I don't like Shia but when it came to killing them, I was shocked. Although they were showing us videos of Shia militias killing Sunni people, we were troubled when we attended real executions.

'In November 2014, a large number of Sunni men were taken prisoner on the grounds that they were working with the government. In the fourth week of November there were some executions to be carried out. One of our commanders asked me and my fellow fighters to bring our guns to be used in an execution the following day. But the victims were Sunni, some of whom I knew. I couldn't endure what we were going to do. I tried to explain that if they were Shia I would do it immediately. The commander said: "I will give you another chance later. For now we have mujahedin to carry out the killing."' It may also have been that Hamza had not served the full six months normally required in ISIS before becoming a fully fledged executioner.

It was shortly after he had refused to execute Sunni prisoners that Hamza and other ISIS volunteers were offered the 13 Yazidi girls for sex. He says that the two events together shattered his idealistic enthusiasm for ISIS and created doubts in his mind. He gives a compelling description of his mental turmoil at this time, thinking of 'the executions, or more horribly the beheadings, as well as the raping of the non-Muslim girls. These scenes terrified me. I imagined myself being caught up in these shootings, executions, beheadings and raping if I stayed where I was.'

Now he started to plan his escape, but he knew that this would be difficult and dangerous. He says one ISIS fighter had tried to run away but was caught and executed for treason. 'The problem is that no one was trustworthy, not even close friends,' he says. Nevertheless, he managed to make arrangements with a friend outside the Caliphate to help him using the instant messaging service Viber, taking advantage of the satellite internet connection that was available to fighters in Fallujah for three hours at a time, three days a week.

Mobile phones evidently worked in at least part of Fallujah (though ISIS has blown up mobile masts elsewhere as a security measure), but only some particularly trusted fighters were allowed to have them. 'I told my commander that I needed a mobile to talk to my family and he agreed, saying that I will be given more privileges as I prove my loyalty and courage,' Hamza says. This enabled him to arrange his escape, through friends and smugglers whom he paid to help him. He made his move one night in early January when he was put on guard duty on the outskirts of Fallujah, enabling him to slip away easily. It took him five days to reach a place of safety. He is not sure if ISIS will pursue him actively and says that he has held back some information about the group because he fears their reaction.

He admits that there are also limits to what he does know: 'For example, we, the fighters, were not able to enter what they call the operation rooms, which have many computers and foreign experts, though sometimes my comrades would use the internet nearby and get the wi-fi passwords through giving money to the technicians.' As a recently recruited fighter, he did not meet any senior members of ISIS or lieutenants of its leader, Abu Bakr al-Baghdadi. 'No, they were always moving from one place to another,' he says. 'And they keep talking about al-Baghdadi, saying that he is still living.

I am sure and have been told that they [the ISIS leadership] are Iraqis only.' Asked if he thinks ISIS will be defeated, he says that this will not be easy, even though coalition air strikes mean 'they cannot advance now.'

Hamza says he is entirely disillusioned with IS. 'At the beginning I thought they were fighting for Allah, but later I discovered they are far from the principles of Islam. I know that some fighters were taking hallucinatory drugs; others were obsessed with sex. As for the raping, and the way different men marry by turn the same woman over a period of time, this is not humane. I left them because I was afraid and deeply troubled by this horrible situation. The justice they were calling for when they first arrived in Fallujah turned out to be only words.'

18 March 2015

It was on 4 October, 2014 that ISIS captured the small city of Hit, seizing complete control in the space of just a few hours. For the city's 100,000 mostly Sunni residents the takeover by the self-proclaimed Islamic State has brought changes that some support, but others deeply resent.

Among those living in Hit when ISIS rolled in was Faisal, a 35-year-old government employee who is married with two children, and a keen observer of all that has befallen the agricultural centre and former transport hub over the past five months. He recently fled to the Kurdish capital, Arbil, where he describes the rule of ISIS and its impact on Hit, starting with the day the city was captured. 'First let me tell you how ISIS entered the city,' he says. 'At 4 a.m. we heard an explosion; ISIS had exploded a bomb at the main checkpoint. Then they started fighting inside and outside the city. This was because some of their fighters were attacking from outside but others were locals, who belonged to sleeper cells and attacked the Iraqi security forces from behind. They captured all the police stations, aside from two that resisted until 5 p.m., after which ISIS had total control.'

Faisal (not his real name), says he had no problems with ISIS checkpoints even during the first days after the jihadist group captured Hit, because they were often manned by his neighbours who knew who he was. They had lists of wanted people and they sometimes checked ID cards.

One of the first things that happened was that the electricity went off. This was because 90 per cent of power in Anbar province comes from a hydroelectric power station, the largest in Iraq, at Haditha, 50 miles up the Euphrates river from Hit. ISIS had seized most of the province but not

Haditha. Faisal explains: 'When ISIS took Hit, they stopped food being sold to people in Haditha because it was still held by the government. In response, Haditha cut off the supply of electricity to Hit and many other cities which had come under ISIS control.' This stopped all projects in Hit dependent on electricity, including the water-treatment stations, so there was a water shortage. People had to obtain their water from the heavily polluted Euphrates.

Because Hit is at the centre of an agricultural area there continues to be plentiful food available at cheap prices. The problem is that, although food is inexpensive, many cannot afford to buy it because all paid work has stopped and nobody is earning any money. Paradoxically, the only people still paid are Iraqi government employees, because even though it has lost control of the city, Baghdad wants to retain their loyalty, and ISIS does not want to prevent earnings that it can tax. ISIS provides some services itself by taking domestic gas cylinders, almost invariably used in Iraq for cooking, to be refilled in the group's Syrian capital Raqqa.

Faisal particularly resents ISIS's vigorous intervention in every aspect of daily life in Hit. 'They poke their noses into education, mosques, women's clothes, taxes on shops [Zakat], and many other aspects of life,' he says. 'My parents and brothers told me yesterday via satellite internet call that there are about 2,000 men appointed to check the shops in the city and collect the taxes under the name of Zakat, not just from the shops, but from employees' salaries.

'In education they changed the courses taught before and brought in new ones that are being taught now in Raqqa and Fallujah. Some courses are modified or cancelled, like philosophy and chemistry. They cancelled classes in art, music, geography, philosophy, sociology, psychology and Christian religion, and asked mathematics teachers to remove any questions that refer to democracy and elections. Biology teachers can't refer to evolution. Arabic classes are not allowed to teach any "pagan" poems.' (IS refers to anything outside the boundaries of its self-declared caliphate as the Pagan World.)

IS is paranoid about mobile phones and the internet being used to communicate information about it, giving away the location of its leaders and military units which could then be destroyed by US air strikes. Until February 2015, mobile phones were working in Hit, but then there was heavy fighting in the nearby town of al-Baghdadi and IS, fearing spies, blew up the mobile telephone masts. The internet has not worked in Anbar

Province for the past eight months, compelling people to use satellite internet connections that are monitored by IS. More recently the group offered a limited internet service, though this is only available in internet offices and other locations monitored by the jihadist group. There is no internet access from private homes, while in the public locations, Faisal says, 'ISIS can spy on computers so they can see what you are surfing and to whom you are talking.'

Predictably, ISIS focuses on religion and spreading its variant of Islam. Faisal says: 'Many preachers (imams) were replaced by foreign preachers from the Arab world, mostly Saudis, Tunisians and Libyans, as well as Afghans. Some new imams are appointed temporarily just for Friday speech and prayer, while others are permanent appointments. ISIS removed some of the old preachers who have left for Baghdad or KRG. These are often Sufis, whose beliefs are rejected by IS.'

There are many other signs of ISIS imposing its cultural agenda in Hit. Faisal says that 'at the entrance to every main street and bazaar, there are ISIS groups holding black dresses that cover the whole body including the face and head. If a woman does not have one, she must buy one [for about £8] and the money goes to the ISIS treasury.'

Are people joining ISIS in Hit? Faisal says they are, often for economic reasons. 'I know many people in my neighbourhood in Hit who joined IS,' he says. 'They are paid little money, about 175,000 dinars [£80], but they say that the salary is enough because they also enjoy many privileges, including free fuel, cooking gas, sugar, tea, bread and many other foodstuffs and services.

'ISIS still has a strong financial basis. It confiscates the houses of the people who were previously employed in the police, courts and security forces. These houses, and any furniture in them, are confiscated by the sharia [legal or religious] court, where the judges are Libyan and Tunisian, though the other staff are locals. The ruling authority in Hit is headed by the military governor, the religious [legal] governor, the security governor and finally the administrative governor.'

When discussing the origins and motivations of ISIS as a movement, Faisal, hitherto factual and down-to-earth, falls back on conspiracy theories. Because he believes that the actions of ISIS will be very damaging to the Sunni in the long term, he is convinced that it must be under the control of the Sunni's traditional enemies. 'To me, ISIS is an Iranian–American project and, when its mission ends, ISIS may leave the region,' he says.

'Most of the Sunni people who experience the rule of ISIS do not believe it is establishing a state, but intends to destroy Sunni areas.'

More realistically, Faisal detects a lack of seriousness in Baghdad's efforts to drive out IS, saying that 'so long as corruption prevails, any solution to the problems of the country, including the recapture of cities taken by IS, will not work.' As for the impact of US air strikes, 'they are limiting the movement of ISIS a little bit and weakening it, but not more.'

How does ISIS compare with its predecessor, al-Qa'ida in Iraq? Faisal has strong opinions on this: 'I remember when we were dealing with al-Qa'ida in 2005 and 2006. Al-Qa'ida men are angels compared to the demons of IS. In Hit 10 years ago, there were many military operations by al-Qa'ida, but nobody thought of leaving the city as many do today. The old al-Qa'ida was much better than IS. We hate the government, but ISIS is not the appropriate substitute. We hate IS, but imagine if the Shia militia were the substitute for it! The situation would be more horrible. Every substitute is worse than the previous one.'

16 May 2015

It was when ISIS issued a fatwa saying a wife should obey her husband in all matters, including becoming a suicide bomber, that Aysha, a 32-year-old mother of two children, decided to flee her home in Mosul. She recalls that her husband did not ask her directly to be a suicide bomber, but gradually started talking about it. 'He was coming home once a week,' she says, 'but recently he came home every day, and finally asked me to attend a new course showing how a Muslim woman could support Muslim society with her soul and body.'

Aysha, which is not her real name, attended the course for two days along with many other women. She was appalled by what she heard. She says 'the course was a sort of brainwashing, teaching women to sacrifice cheap worldly things—blood, flesh, soul—for the victory of more precious things—religion, Allah, the Prophet, and, most importantly, the eternal afterlife.' But instead of being persuaded by these teachings, Aysha was thinking about her children and how to rescue them from the situation she found herself in. On the third day of the course she pretended to be ill and claimed that her son had flu so she had to stay at home. She says that on 3 April 2015, 'at the time of the Friday prayers I took my children and told them that we were going to visit their aunt in the same district, al-Rifa'ey, that we lived in, but in fact I had already arranged what to do through my cousin. He lives in Zakho [in north-west KRG] and he has helped many people to escape Mosul.' She adds that the cousin knows many smugglers in Mosul and KRG. 'It cost me about $1,200 to flee with my son and daughter,' she says.

Aysha was forced to pledge total obedience to her husband, even when it came to suicide bombing. What happened to her illustrates the complete subjection of women under the rule of the self-proclaimed Islamic State. Their status has been reduced to that of chattels without rights or independence. A woman is not allowed to leave her house without being accompanied by a male relative. If she does so and is stopped by ISIS fighters or officials, they take her back to her home and her husband is given between 40 and 80 lashes for allowing her out alone. All women going outside must wear the niqab, a cloth covering the head and face. In no other society on earth are women treated like this, not even in Saudi Arabia, where they are forbidden to drive, or in Afghanistan, where girls' schools have been attacked and burnt.

Aysha's story gives an insight into marriage and daily life within the Caliphate. She gives a fascinating account of the last months of her marriage and her relations with her husband, whom she does not want to name because this might compromise the safety of her children. Prior to ISIS forces unexpectedly capturing Mosul last year her husband had been an officer in the Iraqi Army. ISIS kills many of its opponents who are Shia or Yazidi and has driven Christians out of Mosul and surrounding towns, but it offers forgiveness to Sunni Muslims who publicly repent working for the Iraqi Army or government. Aysha says that her husband announced his repentance and offered his services to ISIS as a soldier, though it was five months before they trusted him enough to accept him into their ranks where he became a unit commander. Aysha was never sure exactly what he did. 'He never told me anything,' she says, 'and I didn't dare ask him because when I once did so his answer was: "Don't poke your nose into things."' She found drops of blood on his uniform and suspected he took part in killings. He was earning a lot of money and had his share of spoils, property and valuables confiscated by ISIS from those it deems to be its enemies. Aysha stole part of her husband's savings, recalling that 'when I left home, I had about $6,000 in addition to my jewellery, but I paid a lot to get out of the city and I paid in advance to get to Turkey.'

After her husband was accepted into ISIS as a military officer, Aysha found that his behaviour began to change and he became more aggressive.

She says that recently he had started to ask her for obedience 'even when it comes to the sacrifice of the soul and body, otherwise I will not win paradise in the afterlife and hell will be my place. In this life I may be punished or be taken to jail.' She responded to these threats by pretending to be wholly obedient to him and to sharia. Aside from pressure on her to become a suicide bomber, she feared that if her husband were killed she would be compelled to marry another ISIS commander. It was when her husband was absent on some military operation that Aysha fled to Arbil, the capital of the KRG. She has had no contact with him since her escape.

Becoming a martyr in the cause of defeating the enemies of religion is at the heart of the ISIS ideology, as Aysha was taught during the course her husband insisted she attend. Suicide bombing is an effective military tactic, turning fanatical but untrained volunteers into lethal weapons. Families across the Caliphate, which has a population of 6 million, are fearful that their children will be brainwashed into this self-sacrifice.

This was why Noura, a 36-year-old married woman, fled Mosul with her husband and six children. ISIS had established camps where young teenagers were trained for suicide bombing. Noura, who wants her real name kept secret, reached Arbil on 22 March 2015. She says that the main reason she and her family left is that 'my children were under threat because ISIS decided to establish camps for adolescents between 12 and 16 to educate and train them for suicide bombing.' She says the preachers did not speak of 'suicide bombing' but of 'martyrdom honour'. When these camps were first established it was possible for families to pay a fine instead of sending their children to them, but later attendance became compulsory.

Unlike Aysha, Noura had little money and her husband was jobless. This was a further reason for the family to leave Mosul. She explains that 'people don't find jobs, so they offer their services to ISIS for food. The problem is that many jobless people start to be attracted to the idea of working with IS, not because they are happy with it, but because it is the only option available even if it is undesirable.'

Aside from the threat of her children being trained as suicide bombers, Noura found day-to-day living difficult in Mosul. She says there was no public supply of electricity 'and we didn't have the money to pay for the [electric] generators so it was terrible'. Cooking-gas cylinders were expensive, costing 80,000 Iraqi dinars (£44), and tomatoes and potatoes each cost 15,000 dinars (£8) a kilo. There was a lack of clean water. More recently, she has heard by phone from her parents, who are still in Mosul, that things have improved a little and there are two hours' electricity per day and the price of gas has halved. ISIS must have received more money, says Noura. Her father told her that wheat farmers around Mosul will sell their harvest this year to ISIS because it is the only buyer and has promised to pay a high price.

Aysha and Noura's accounts of life under ISIS corroborate each other, but on one point they disagree. Aysha does not think that ISIS will be defeated 'because, although they are in financial crisis, they have solutions to their crises.' They impose fines on people and on those leaving Mosul: some leave with permission after paying a lot of money, though others are not allowed out for security reasons.

Noura, on the contrary, believes that ISIS will be defeated because it is running out of money and becoming more corrupt. She says bribery has become rampant but she does not think that US air strikes will defeat IS. 'The devastating factor internally is corruption—bribery, nepotism, favouritism—that will be the final blow.' Significantly, neither woman speaks of any armed resistance to ISIS despite its moves to recruit women and children as suicide bombers.

17 May 2015

Many administrative documents issued by ISIS and collected and translated by Aymenn al-Tamimi now form part of an online archive which gives an invaluable insight into ISIS workings and beliefs. An early regulation about restrictions on women's clothing in Tal Abyad in northern Syria, issued in December 2013, spells out what is required. It says that 'there will be a complete ban on unveiling, as well as the wearing of tight trousers and cloaks, and the adorning of oneself and imitation of kafir [disbelieving] women. And any woman who contravenes this will expose herself to the severest consequences.' On the question of whether both eyes and part of the cheek of a woman should be concealed, a fatwa orders that 'it is necessary for her to cover her two eyes with something delicate.'

At times ISIS prurience regarding anything to do with sex beggars belief. For instance, in February 2015, an announcement banned the keeping of pigeons above the roofs of houses, with those who continue to do so threatened with fines, imprisonment and flogging. The reason for this is that pigeons 'are harming one's ... Muslim women neighbours, revealing the genitals [of the pigeons]'.

The world of IS, going by the regulations collected by al-Tamimi, often varies markedly from other human societies because every aspect of religious, social and economic life is determined by its intolerant variant of Islam. There is a fatwa on whether an 'apostate' prisoner can be ransomed for money or as part of a prisoner exchange (answer: on the whole, not). Numerous theologians, jurists and figures from Islamic history are quoted to support the ruling.

Many orders are mundane and are to do with the orderly running of the new state, including, for example, instructions on setting up kindergartens and the proper regulation of the Cub Scouts. Prices are set for everything from the sale of vegetables in the markets to Caesarean operations in hospitals. Certain games such as billiards and table football are allowed, but under strict conditions. Car owners are told that they must carry tool kits including a spare tyre or face punishment. Overall, the impression comes across that ISIS and the society it wants to create is based on a conviction that its leaders know what is right and wrong in all circumstances.

19 June 2015

Many Iraqi and Syrian men in their twenties have done nothing all their lives but fight. One such man is Faraj (not his real name), a 29-year-old ISIS fighter who comes from a Sunni Arab village between the cities of Hasakah and Qamishli in north-east Syria. He was in Tal Abyad, a major crossing point on the Syrian–Turkish border, waiting for the final assault as Kurdish YPG militiamen closed in. A Kurdish colleague from the area contacted Faraj via WhatsApp before Kurdish forces captured the town on 16 June 2015. He transcribed the conversation for me.

Faraj's replies to questions were sometimes confused and disjointed, but when he spoke of the town's impending loss he was calm—possibly because, though a graduate of the Faculty of Education at Hasakah University, fighting is all he has known over the last four years. 'So what if we lose the Turkish border?' he said. 'I think Islamic State still has open borders with Iraq. It will remain strong and, according to our commanders' reports, it may lose some battles, but it has its own strategies for winning the war.' He was philosophical about American air strikes, saying that they cannot achieve much without ground forces: 'I think that Islamic State is winning not losing.'

Faraj did not say whether he expected to survive the fight for Tal Abyad. On other occasions, experienced ISIS veterans have slipped away at the last minute. But Faraj's account of why he joined ISIS and is loyal to its cause must be true for others: a great many reasonable Syrians and Iraqis have joined this fanatical movement, despite its barbaric and very public cruelty, outlandish ideology and cult of death, and they stay with it despite the likelihood of temporary defeat. 'Even if this happens,' Faraj said, 'I still believe that we are right because most of us are not fighting for women or money; we are fighting because both the regime and the opposition failed us, so we need an armed organisation to fight for our rights.'

Until last year, Jabhat al-Nusra was strong in Kurdish areas, but was squeezed out in heavy fighting by the YPG on one side and ISIS on the other. Faraj and his extended family joined al-Nusra in the year after the Syrian uprising began in 2011. 'At first we dreamed of having a revolution and gaining our liberty,' he said, 'but unfortunately the popular movement was not well organised and was manipulated by neighbouring countries such as the Gulf states, so revolution turned into jihad.' He says that to fight back against the regime the rebels had no choice but to turn to a religious movement that appealed to the conservative people of eastern Syria. Another motive was revenge: for 'the oppression and injustice of the regime over the last 40 years that weighed down our souls'.

In July 2012 the Syrian Army almost entirely withdrew from the three Kurdish cantons to reinforce regime strongholds elsewhere. It held on to a couple of small symbolic enclaves in Qamishli and Hasakah so that the regime in Damascus could claim still to have a presence everywhere in the country, even though it was no longer in control. 'When the Kurdish forces took over we felt we had gained nothing by our revolution,' Faraj said. 'They were just as oppressive as the regime.' He fought back as a member of al-Nusra until it was defeated by the YPG. ISIS then came to his home village, where he says that 'members of al-Nusra were given a choice of joining Islamic State or leaving the village.' He was one of five who decided to join, two locals and three Tunisians. In February 2015, Kurdish forces entered the village and he was sent on a mission to Raqqa while the others stayed to fight: 'They resisted for five hours, but were only four men against 30 so the three Tunisians were killed and only the local fighter escaped.' Faraj returned to the area from Raqqa and spent a month contacting villagers he knew.

At this point, Faraj says he met many foreign fighters from Britain, Turkey and France, some of whom had learned Arabic well. He was not impressed by them: 'I know many fighters from the Gulf states, Europe and Australia who are fighting for arms, fame, women and money.' When he asked volunteers from Europe why they were in Syria some told him that their lives were miserable at home or that they had simply been bored. Many had found 'spiritual happiness in Islam', but Faraj said that they were often recent converts who did not seem to know much about Islam or local customs. The foreign fighters, he said, were mostly used for suicide attacks and propaganda, 'while the locals are used for fighting'.

This is the pattern across the territory controlled by IS. It is often difficult to know how many foreign fighters are present in a battle: Kurdish and Iraqi army commanders like to claim that almost all the fighters facing them are heavily armed foreigners from the Muslim world or Western Europe. This was the official line when the Iraqi Kurdish Peshmerga was defeated by ISIS in August 2014. But when I talked to Christian and Yazidi villagers who had seen their attackers before they fled, they said the fighters were all Iraqis, few in number and driving unarmoured vehicles.

What makes Faraj's account of his life and views so interesting is that he is not a defector or a propagandist. He is somebody with a deep hatred of the Assad regime who joined the organisation that was most able to fight against it. He told the story of his former leader or emir, an Iraqi Kurd with the nom de guerre Abu Abbas al-Kurdistani, who had recently been killed in battle. Faraj asked him why he had joined ISIS and Abu Abbas replied that he had been imprisoned by the KRG for four years without a fair trial. 'Corruption and torture', Faraj said, 'had pushed him to find any organisation that gives him the opportunity for taking revenge. Our emir's pain was similar to ours. We all fight as a reaction to the tyranny and injustice we had known before. Islamic State is the best option for oppressed people in the Middle East.'

27 June 2015

Even in a city as dangerous as Fallujah, Salem had a peculiarly dangerous occupation which meant that he was at risk of corporal punishment and financial ruin every day he lived there. A 35-year-old man, who, like everybody else quoted, does not want his real name published, he is the sole breadwinner of his family and also cares for his sick and elderly father. At the time ISIS took over Fallujah in January 2014, he was earning his living as a barber.

During the first six months of ISIS occupation, the militants were generally moderate in their enforcement of Islamic fundamentalist regulations.

ISIS did not have a complete monopoly of power in the city and did not want to alienate its people. But on important issues of principle, such as the correct Islamic haircut, the militants were adamant from the beginning. Beards were obligatory: no man could be clean shaven and Western haircuts were forbidden.

'Shaving was prohibited and the punishment for shaving someone was severe,' says Salem. ISIS closed most of the barber salons in Fallujah, but not Salem's, 'because mine was a simple poor salon without posters so they didn't close it.' Even though his salon remained open, there were strict limits on what Salem could do for his customers, so he did not make enough money to feed his family. He tried supplementing his income by selling vegetables in the market and only worked as a barber when he got a call from old customers, friends and relatives.

He had no trouble until the day of his cousin's wedding when disaster struck. He says: 'My cousin came to my salon and asked me not only to dress his hair, but to shave his beard.' Salem was horrified by such a dangerous proposal because he was conscious of the punishment ISIS was likely to inflict on any barber ignoring the shaving ban. He turned his cousin down flat, but the man then asked for his hair to be cut short in a modern way rather than left to grow long as ISIS demanded. The cousin argued that 'nobody would notice because it was the afternoon and the street was empty.' Unwillingly, Salem complied with his cousin's request and 'dressed his hair, adding gel to make it look good'.

Salem and his cousin soon found out that they had badly underestimated how closely ISIS monitored illicit haircuts. Four days after the wedding, Salem learned that his action had been reported by an ISIS informant to the local religious authority. He was arrested and then sentenced to 80 lashes to be administered in public and, in addition, his salon was to be closed. In the event, he had received only 50 lashes when 'I fainted and was taken to hospital.'

Deprived of his ability to make a living in Fallujah, Salem went first to Ramadi, the capital of Anbar province, which was mostly under ISIS control. ISIS monitors and restricts movement within its boundaries but he was able to pass through ISIS checkpoints, explaining that he was going to visit his brother in Ramadi. He stayed there only four days because of continuing air strikes and shelling shortly before ISIS captured the last government-held enclaves on 17 May 2015. He left for Baghdad and finally Arbil, the capital of Iraqi Kurdistan, where he hopes to find a job.

Salem says that many families were leaving Ramadi, but adds reveal-ingly that 'many preferred to stay, among whom was my brother. He says that, although they are living under bombs, ISIS is far better than the Shia militia and the Iraqi Army.' For all its failings, Sunni Arabs in Iraq con-trast ISIS with an arbitrary and dysfunctional Shia-dominated government in Baghdad. Asked to compare the situation in Ramadi before and after the ISIS takeover, Salem says that under government rule, Ramadi had no electricity, no fuel, no internet and no clean water. The local hospital and medical centre were not working despite vain pleas to the government from local people. 'Under the rule of IS,' says Salem, who has no reason to like the group which beat him savagely and closed his business, 'many big generators have been brought to Ramadi from Fallujah and Raqqa. In addition, they are repairing the power station at Khesab. As for the hospital, ISIS brought in doctors, surgeons and nurses from Syria, so it is working again.'

The 5 or 6 million people living in ISIS-controlled territory exist in a world full of prohibitions and regulations. Breach of these divinely inspired rules is savagely punished. Salem says that nobody in Fallujah is ignorant of ISIS rules because they were previously read out in public every day, though this has now been reduced to three times a week. Speaking from memory, he gives a number of examples:

- Girls are not allowed to wear jeans and must wear Islamic dress (abaya and veil). Make-up is prohibited.
- No smoking of cigarettes or hubble-bubble. The punishment is 80 lashes, but may include execution if there are repeated violations.
- Using the word 'Daesh' is forbidden and the punishment is 70 lashes.
- Women's sewing shops are closed in case a man enters.
- Women's hairdressers are closed for the same reason.
- Gynaecologists must be female.
- Women shall not sit on chairs either in the market or in a shop.
- Shops must close at the time of prayers.
- Taxi drivers who take customers to a distant destination they have not asked for and then demand money to bring them back are consid-ered to have acted 'to disrupt the interests of the people' (apparently a common crime in Fallujah). The punishment is amputation or beheading.

There are many other crimes and prohibitions that Salem might have mentioned.

When ISIS declared on 29 June 2014 that it was re-establishing the Caliphate, its opponents in the outside world hoped that its eccentric laws and their brutal application would provoke resistance. After all, what was being enforced went far beyond sharia or Saudi Wahhabism, so many of whose tenets are similar to those of IS. But there is as yet no sign of counter-revolution or even effective armed resistance against a movement that has mercilessly crushed all opponents. Those living within ISIS territory who hate and fear it have reacted by fleeing rather than resisting. The self-declared Caliphate is too well rooted to disappear. Its slogan, 'The Islamic State remains, the Islamic State expands,' is still true.

TWENTY

The Islamic State at Bay

21 September 2015

The Syrian Kurds are confident they can defeat ISIS, which dominates the rest of eastern Syria, after they withstood a four-and-a-half-month siege of Kobani by ISIS that ended in January. The success of the YPG came because its fighters fought ferociously against the Islamic militants and, since October last year, its commanders have been able to call in US air strikes. It was the support of some 700 US air strikes that helped the YPG win the battle for Kobani, though it reduced this small city to a seascape of shattered concrete where buildings have been pounded into rubble by the force of the bomb blasts. In between the ruins there are individual shops and houses that survive intact, but 70 per cent of the city is destroyed and construction workers are only slowly making an impact.

Victory at Kobani boosted the self-confidence of the YPG, which is the only ground force in Syria or Iraq that has regularly defeated ISIS. After the end of the siege, the YPG won back the rest of Kobani canton, including 380 villages. And in June it captured the border town of Tal Abyad which ISIS had held for more than two years. This linked up the two main Kurdish cantons. Its capture was also important because it is only 62 miles north of Raqqa, the de facto ISIS capital in Syria.

Important though Tal Abyad was to ISIS, it did not commit many fighters to holding the town, having apparently decided that it was indefensible. YPG forces were advancing from west and east towards the road linking it to Raqqa. A 21-year-old YPG fighter called Misro Munzer, hit in the knee by a machine gun bullet in a later battle and interviewed in a military hospital in Kobani, says that he had fought at Tal Abyad where 'Daesh [ISIS] did not fight hard'. He explains that the more battle-hardened ISIS men had retreated leaving only a remnant of 25 men without much combat experience who were demoralised and confused by US air strikes. There is no doubt that YPG light infantry backed by US air power are highly effective and ISIS cannot hold fixed positions against a combination of the two. ISIS suffers heavy casualties when it tries to do so.

But this does not mean that it cannot hit back, as became evident on the drive east from Kobani on what was meant to be an entirely safe road going to al-Qomishli, the capital of the largest Syrian Kurdish enclave. There are some early signs that the road is not quite as secure as we had been told. As we enter an Arab village called Qayyil, 9 miles west of Tal Abyad, we are stopped by a large detachment of YPG troops who say they are conducting a search. One of them tells us that 'we have information that four or five Daesh [ISIS] fighters have penetrated the village and we are looking for them'. Other YPG fighters are guarding crossroads and entry points into Qayyil. We drive on to Tal Abyad, a town which locals say once had a population that was half Arab and half Kurdish, Turkoman and Armenian. Three months ago it had been in the hands of ISIS. We want to look at the closed border crossing with Turkey and the police agree to take us there. But, as we follow a police vehicle down the street, a Kurdish woman in a black robe rushes out of a house shouting that she needs the police and our escort stopped to help her. She says that she and her daughters had been sitting in the courtyard of her house when 'a man dressed in black with a beard who looked like Daesh had climbed over a wall and run past us'. The police say that there are still ISIS fighters hiding in the many abandoned houses in Tal Abyad.

These two incidents are not too surprising since Tal Abyad and nearby villages have only recently been captured by the Kurds. But soon after we enter Ras al-Ayn, the next town on our route which has been held by the YPG for two years, there are two bangs. They sound like gunshots close together, but then we see a cloud of dense smoke rising from a checkpoint just ahead. Kurdish security men block the road in front of us within a couple minutes, turning back vehicles, and news soon spreads that there has been a suicide car bomb that killed at least five people. It also emerges that there has been a suicide bombing just behind us at a checkpoint at the entrance to Ras al-Ayn that we had just driven through. A man on a motorbike had blown himself up but failed to kill or injure anybody. These incidents are all probably attempts by ISIS to show that it is still to be feared despite its recent defeats. In June it sent a detachment into Kobani, disguised in Kurdish and Free Syrian Army uniforms, that killed over 200 men, women and children.

23 October 2015

The military balance of power in Syria and Iraq is changing. The Russian air strikes that have been taking place since the end of September are strengthening and raising the morale of the Syrian Army, which earlier in the year looked fought out and was on the retreat. With the support of Russian airpower, the army is now on the offensive in and around Aleppo, Syria's second largest city, and is seeking to regain lost territory in Idlib province. Syrian commanders on the ground are reportedly relaying the coordinates of between 400 and 800 targets to the Russian Air Force every day, though only a small proportion of them come under immediate attack. The chances of Bashar al-Assad's government falling—though always more remote than many suggested—are disappearing. Not that this means he is going to win.

The drama of Russian military action, while provoking a wave of Cold War rhetoric from Western leaders and the media, has taken attention away from an equally significant development in the war in Syria and Iraq. This has been the failure over the last year of the US air campaign—which began in Iraq in August 2014 before being extended to Syria—to weaken Islamic State and other al-Qa'ida-type groups. By October the US-led coalition had carried out 7,323 air strikes, the great majority of them by the US Air Force, which made 3,231 strikes in Iraq and 2,487 in Syria. But the campaign has demonstrably failed to contain ISIS, which in May captured Ramadi in Iraq and Palmyra in Syria. There have been far fewer attacks against the Syrian branch of al-Qa'ida, Jabhat al-Nusra, and the extreme Islamist group Ahrar al-Sham, which between them dominate the insurgency in northern Syria. The US failure is political as much as it is military: it needs partners on the ground who are fighting ISIS, but its choice is limited because those actually engaged in combat with the Sunni jihadis are largely Shia—Iran itself, the Syrian army, Hezbollah, the Shia militias in Iraq—and the US cannot offer them full military co-operation because that would alienate the Sunni states, the bedrock of America's power in the region. As a result, the US can only use its air force in support of the Kurds.

Washington tried to mitigate the failure of its air campaign, officially called Operation Inherent Resolve, by making exaggerated claims of success. Maps were issued to the press showing that ISIS had a weakening grip on between 25 and 30 per cent of its territory, but they conveniently left out the parts of Syria where ISIS was advancing. Such was the suppression and manipulation of intelligence by the administration that in July fifty analysts working for US Central Command signed a protest against the official distortion of what was happening on the battlefield. Russia has now taken advantage of the US failure to suppress the jihadis.

———

Over the last three years I have found that the best way of learning what is really happening in the war is to visit military hospitals. Most wounded soldiers, eyewitnesses to the fighting, are bored by their convalescence and eager to talk about their experiences. In July, I was in the Hussein Teaching Hospital in the Shia holy city of Karbala, where one ward was reserved for injured fighters from the Shia militia known as the Hashid Shaabi. Many had answered a call to arms by the Grand Ayatollah Ali Sistani after ISIS captured Mosul last year. Colonel Salah Rajab, the deputy commander of the Habib battalion of the Ali Akbar brigade, who was lying in bed after having his lower right leg amputated, had been fighting in Baiji City, a town on the Tigris close to Iraq's largest oil refinery, for 16 days when a mortar round landed near him, leaving two of his men dead and four wounded. When I asked him what the weaknesses of the Hashid were, he said that they were enthusiastic but poorly trained. He could speak with some authority: he was a professional soldier who resigned from the Iraqi Army in 1999. He complained that his men got a maximum of three months of training when they needed six months, with the result that they made costly mistakes such as talking too much on their mobile phones and field radios. ISIS monitored these communications, and used intercepted information to inflict heavy losses. The biggest problem for the Hashid, which probably numbers about fifty thousand men, is the lack of experienced commanders able to organise an attack and keep casualties low.

Omar Abdullah, an 18-year-old militia volunteer, was in another bed in the same ward. He had been trained for just 25 days before going to fight in Baiji, where his arm and leg were broken in a bomb blast. His story confirmed Colonel Rajab's account of enthusiastic but inexperienced militiamen suffering heavy losses as they fell into traps set by ISIS. On arriving in Baiji, Abdullah said, 'we were shot at by snipers and we ran into a house to seek cover. There were 13 of us and we didn't realise that the house was full of explosives.' These were detonated by an ISIS fighter keeping a watch on the house; the blast killed nine of the militiamen and wounded the remaining four. Experienced soldiers, too, have been falling victim to traps like this. A bomb disposal expert in the ward told me he had been examining a suspicious-looking wooden bridge over a canal when one of his men stepped onto it and detonated a bomb that killed four and wounded three of the bomb disposal team.

The types of injury reflect the kind of combat that predominates. Most of it takes place in cities or built-up areas and involves house-to-house fighting in which losses are high. Syrian, Kurdish and Iraqi soldiers described being hit by snipers as they manned checkpoints, or being injured by mines or booby traps. In May, I talked to an 18-year-old Kurdish YPG fighter called Javad Judy in the Shahid Khavat hospital in the city of Qamishli in northeast Syria. He had been shot through the spine as his squad was clearing a Christian village near Hasaka of ISIS fighters. 'We had divided into three groups that were trying to attack the village', he said, 'when we were hit by intense fire from behind and from the trees on each side of us'. He was still traumatised by finding out that his lower body was permanently paralysed.

For some soldiers, injuries aren't the only threat to their survival. In 2012, in the Mezze military hospital in Damascus, I met Mohammed Diab, a 21-year-old Syrian Army soldier who a year earlier in Aleppo had been hit by a bullet that shattered his lower left leg. After making an initial recovery he had gone back to his home village of Rahiya in Idlib province, which was a dangerous move since it was under the control of the opposition. Hearing that there was a wounded government soldier in the village, they took Diab hostage and held him for five months; they even sold his metal splint and gave him a piece of wood to strap to his leg instead. Finally, his family ransomed him for the equivalent of $1,000, but his leg had become infected and so he was back in hospital.

19 November 2015

The massacre in Paris has exposed the bankruptcy of Western policy towards the so-called Islamic State and the war in Syria and Iraq. This has long had an Alice in Wonderland feel to it, with Western leaders claiming they 'believed six impossible things before breakfast'. These impossible things included the belief that they could contain and even destroy ISIS, while at the same time getting rid of President Bashar al-Assad and his regime in Damascus. The US, Britain, France and their allies have refused to admit that the fall of Assad would create a power vacuum that would inevitably be filled by Islamic fundamentalists from ISIS or al-Qa'ida clones such as Jabhat al-Nusra and Ahrar al-Sham.

What this strategy has meant on the ground is that when ISIS attacked the Syrian army in Palmyra in May, the US Air Force did not bomb its fighters because Washington did not want to be accused by Saudi Arabia, Turkey and the Gulf monarchies of helping Assad. The result was a victory for ISIS as it seized Palmyra, beheaded captured Syrian soldiers and advanced westwards close to the crucial north–south highway linking Damascus to the northern cities. Western leaders have said they do not have to choose between ISIS and Assad, because there is a moderate opposition prepared to fight both.

The mythical nature of this claim was revealed earlier this year when a US general admitted that the US had just four such 'moderate' fighters in Syria after it spent $500 million on training them. Others had either defected to Jabhat al-Nusra or been murdered by it. Saudi Arabia, Qatar and Turkey have since tried to re-brand these al-Qa'ida-type groups as preferable enemies to ISIS, though this may be difficult to argue in the future given al-Nusra's enthusiastic endorsement of the slaughter in Paris. The only way to defeat ISIS is to create a coalition of those who are demonstrably fighting it. There is a myth that Russia and the Syrian Army are not doing so, but Syrian soldiers supported by Russian air strikes won a significant victory over ISIS by breaking its siege of Kweiris military air base east of Aleppo, where 2,000 Syrian soldiers had been under attack by ISIS for months.

If the Russians had really only been launching air strikes against Syrian moderates and not against ISIS, it is unlikely that ISIS would have gone to such trouble as to place a bomb on a Russian plane leaving Sharm el-Sheikh, killing 224 passengers. To be effective, air strikes require a partner on the ground to identify targets. The US air campaign over the past year has only had real success when conducted in close co-ordination with Kurdish forces in Syria and Iraq. Western 'boots on the ground', in the words of that terrible cliché, are not necessary or desirable, but local military partners are a necessity. Such a partnership should include Russia, Iran, the Syrian Army, the Syrian and Iraqi Kurds, Hezbollah, the Iraqi Army and the Shia militias in Iraq. A military coalition rather than a diplomatic one is required if we are to end the butchery we have just seen in Paris, Beirut, Sinai, Ankara and Baghdad.

4 February 2016

Hundreds of family members dressed in black gathered this week at the Hamasur mosque in Sulaimaniyah, in eastern Kurdistan, to mourn 10 relatives who drowned when their boat capsized between Turkey and the Greek island of Samos as they tried to reach Europe. All the dead came from Halabja, the city where up to 5,000 people were killed in a poison gas attack carried out by Saddam Hussein's forces against the civilian population in 1988. 'We only decided to go a week before we flew to Istanbul and paid a smuggler $2,500 per person to get us to Greece,' says Sardar Hama Rashid, a waiter in a restaurant whose wife and daughter were drowned on the crossing. He is tearful and looks stunned by what had happened. A relative, a retired truck driver called Omar Hama Amin, says the reason so many Iraqi Kurds were trying to get to Europe was 'not because of the war but the economic disaster here'.

Though the outside world is well informed about the savage war being fought between ISIS and the Kurds, there is much less awareness of the economic calamity that has devastated the Kurdistan Regional Government (KRG) and the disputed territories it has taken from ISIS and the Iraqi government. The disaster stems from three main causes: the Kurdish leadership's quarrel, since 2014, with Baghdad over oil exports, which led to the Kurds no longer getting a share of Iraq's oil revenue; the rise of ISIS and its capture of Mosul; and the fall in the price of oil sold independently by the KRG, which is today only $21 a barrel. Some 1.4 million Kurds out of a total population of six million work for the KRG or receive benefits from it, but over the past two years they have been paid only part of their salary or no money at all. Government expenditure is estimated to be $1.1 billion a month and revenue only about $400 million. The skylines of Kurdish cities are dotted with half-completed hotels and apartment buildings, their concrete shells sometimes housing displaced people and refugees.

The slogan of only a few years ago about KRG becoming 'the new Dubai of the Middle East' sounds today like an absurd fantasy amid the general economic ruin. 'Nobody has been paid for five or six months', says Amin, explaining why his relatives had made their disastrous effort to get to Europe. 'I rent a house but there is no way I can pay for it.' Anger runs deep at what is seen as the incompetence and greed of the Kurdish leaders.

Asos Hardi, editor of the independent newspaper *Awene*, says, 'You can feel the anger in the streets over government corruption.' When he investigated and exposed the theft of $18 million three years ago, he was badly beaten by thugs sent by the government official he had accused of taking the money. He says that many people blame the government for trying and failing to turn Kurdistan into an oil state independent of Baghdad. Agreeing with this, a Western oil expert said that 'the KRG made a gigantic bet on a high price for oil and they have lost.'

The high expectations among Kurds in the decade after the overthrow of Saddam Hussein shattered as their standard of living collapsed even more precipitously than that of the Greeks after 2008, and from a much lower level. But it is primarily an economic rather than a security disaster because, paradoxically, the Iraqi Kurds are politically and militarily stronger today than they have ever been in their history—though this may not last. This is the view of a renowned Peshmerga commander, Muhammad Haji Mahmud, a large landowner in the fertile valley between Sulaimaniyah and Halabja. He is also the general secretary of the Socialist Party, and reckons that he has been in 700 fights or battles over the past 40 years of warfare in Kurdistan and has been seriously wounded six times. After ISIS captured Mosul and before they attacked the Kurds, Haji Mahmud led 1,000 Peshmerga from his party to defend Kirkuk. His son Atta was killed in the fighting.

In an interview at his house, he says that, overall, the Kurds have gained more than they have lost in their struggle against the self-declared 'Islamic State'. He lists the benefits: 'We have become a regular army, rather than a guerrilla force; are supported by US and European air power; can buy weapons openly; and are praised internationally for fighting terrorism. The Syrian Kurds won the battle for Kobani and we sent 150 Peshmerga to help them, while in Iraq we became a safe haven for Arabs and Christians.' The KRG took advantage of the collapse of the Iraqi Army in 2014 to expand its size by 40 per cent through seizure of areas, often with mixed Arab–Kurdish populations, control over which had long been disputed with Baghdad.

The danger is that these big political and territorial gains depend on the Iraqi government being weak and ISIS being strong, so the Kurds are courted by all as the best defence against ISIS. World leaders treat the KRG as if it were a world power rather than an isolated quasi-independent 'statelet'. 'My big fear is that, once Mosul is liberated and ISIS defeated, the Kurds won't have the same value internationally', says Mahmud. He believes that with international support the Kurds 'may keep the disputed territories, but not otherwise'. Bitter experience has made the Kurds suspicious that, once again, they will be used as convenient cannon fodder by outside powers and then discarded when no longer needed. There is also a popular suspicion among Kurds, again rooted in harsh experience, that their leaders can justify and prolong their authoritarian misrule by presenting themselves as the patriotic defenders of their people, diverting attention from their corruption and their failure to create a self-sufficient state in Kurdistan.

A striking example of just how much resentment bubbles beneath the surface, obscured by patriotic flag-waving, is the Halabja Memorial Museum. It is a peculiarly ugly building, like a concrete circus tent, but inside there is an affecting display of photographs, household goods and children's toys, evoking the terrible events of 16 March 1988 when a poison gas cloud enveloped the unsuspecting town. It is not obvious to the first-time visitor, but the museum in Halabja today is in fact the second to stand on this spot. The first, more garish, folkloric and less effective than its successor, was burned out, though the concrete walls survived, during a demonstration by locals in 2006. The remarkable destruction of what was supposedly a memorial to the mass murder of their own relatives was an expression of local outrage that Kurdish officials had repeatedly taken American and other foreign dignitaries to the museum, but had completely ignored the grim living conditions of those in Halabja who were still alive.

Ten years after the burning of the museum, the same rage is building up, not just in Halabja but across Kurdistan, against a government that provides security but is otherwise self-serving and dysfunctional.

19 February 2016

The Kurdistan Regional Government promoted itself as a 'different Iraq', and so, in some respects, it is: it is much safer to live in the KRG area than in Baghdad or Basra. Though Mosul is not far away, there have been few bomb attacks or kidnappings in Iraqi Kurdistan compared to elsewhere in the country. But the KRG is an oil state that depends wholly on oil revenues. The region produces almost nothing else: even the vegetables in the markets are imported from Turkey and Iran, and prices are high. Nazdar Ibrahim, a local economist, says that clothes she could buy in Turkey cost three times as much at home; Iraqi Kurdistan, she suggested, is as expensive to live in as Norway or Switzerland. The KRG's president, Massoud

Barzani, has declared he will hold a referendum on Kurdish independence, but this is not an attractive option at a time of general economic ruin. Asos Hardi, editor of the newspaper *Awene* in Sulaymaniyah, says protests are spreading and in any case, 'even at the height of the boom there was popular anger at the clientism and corruption.' The Iraqi Kurdish state— far from becoming more independent—is being forced to look to outside powers, including Baghdad, to save it from further economic collapse.

Similar things are happening elsewhere in the region: people who have been smuggled out of Mosul say that the Caliphate is buckling under military and economic pressure. Its enemies have captured Sinjar, Ramadi and Tikrit in Iraq, and the YPG and the Syrian Army are driving it back in Syria and are closing in on Raqqa. The ground forces attacking ISIS—the YPG, the Syrian Army, Iraqi armed forces and Peshmerga—are all short on manpower (in the struggle for Ramadi the Iraqi military assault force numbered only 500 men), but they can call in devastating air strikes on any ISIS position. Since it was defeated at Kobani, ISIS has avoided set-piece battles and has not fought to the last man to defend any of its cities, though it has considered doing so in Raqqa and Mosul. The Pentagon, the Iraqi government and the Kurds exaggerate the extent of their victories over ISIS, but it is taking heavy losses. The administrative and economic infrastructure of the Caliphate is beginning to break under the strain of bombing and blockade. This is the impression given by people who left Mosul in early February and took refuge in Rojava.

Their journey wasn't easy, since ISIS prohibits people from leaving the Caliphate—it doesn't want a mass exodus. Those who have got out report that ISIS is becoming more violent in enforcing fatwas and religious regulations. Ahmad, a 35-year-old trader from the al-Zuhour district of Mosul, where he owns a small shop, reports that 'if somebody is caught who has shaved off his beard, he is given 30 lashes, while last year they would just arrest him for a few hours.'

Ahmad also says that living conditions have deteriorated sharply and the actions of ISIS officials become more arbitrary: 'They take food without paying and confiscated much of my stock under the pretence of supporting the Islamic State militiamen. Everything is expensive and the stores are half-empty. The markets were crowded a year ago, but not for the last ten months because so many people have fled and those that have stayed are unemployed.' There has been no mains electricity for seven months and everybody depends on private generators that run on locally refined fuel.

This is available everywhere, but is expensive and of such poor quality that it works only for generators and not for cars—and the generators often break down. There is a shortage of drinking water. 'Every ten days, we have water for two hours,' Ahmad says. 'The water we get from the tap is not clean, but we have to drink it.' There is no mobile phone network and the internet is available only in internet cafés that are closely monitored by the authorities for sedition.

There are signs of growing criminality and corruption, though this may mainly be evidence that ISIS is in desperate need of money. When Ahmad decided to flee he contacted one of many smugglers operating in the area between Mosul and the Syrian frontier. He said the cost for each individual smuggled into Rojava is between $400 and $500. 'Many of the smugglers are ISIS men,' he said, but he didn't know whether the organisation's leaders knew what was happening. They certainly know that there are increasing complaints about living conditions because they have cited a *hadith*, a saying of the Prophet, against such complaints. Those who violate the hadith are arrested and sent for re-education. Ahmad's conclusion: 'Dictators become very violent when they sense that their end is close.'

24 February 2016

People in Mosul call it 'the Biter' or 'the Clipper'—a metal instrument newly introduced by ISIS officials to punish women whose clothes they claim do not completely conceal their body. A former school director, who fled from the city earlier this month, describes the tool as causing agonising pain by clipping off pieces of flesh. Fatima, a 22-year-old housewife who does not want to give her full name, said she had finally escaped from Mosul after several failed attempts because her children were starving and ISIS had become more violent and sadistic compared with a year ago, especially towards women. 'The Biter has become a nightmare for us,' Fatima says after reaching safety in Mabrouka Camp for displaced people near Ras al-Ayn in Kurdish-controlled north-east Syria. 'My sister was punished so harshly last month because she had forgotten her gloves and left them at home.'

ISIS insists that women be fully veiled, wear loose or baggy trousers, socks and gloves, and be accompanied by a male relative whenever they step outside their homes. Fatima says that a month after the use of this metal tool to punish her sister 'the bruises and scars are still visible on her arm'. She quotes her sister as saying that 'the biting punishment is more painful than labour pains'. Other witnesses describe the Biter as operating like an animal trap, or a metal jaw with teeth that cut into the flesh. It is difficult and dangerous to escape from Mosul, which ISIS has held since capturing it from the Iraqi Army in June 2014. But people from the city, who have had themselves smuggled across the border to Syria and then to Kurdish-controlled territory known as Rojava in the past two months, all confirm that living conditions in Mosul have deteriorated sharply. There are serious shortages of almost everything including food, fuel, water and electricity.

ISIS was violent from the start of its rule 20 months ago, but public whippings and executions have become far more common in recent months. Mosul residents say that Saudi and Libyan volunteers, who have joined ISIS, are the most likely to impose penalties for minor infringements of regulations in the self-declared Caliphate. It is as if ISIS fighters and officials are compensating for setbacks in the war by showing that they still have power over the population under their control.

Ibraham, a 26-year-old pharmacist who left Mosul on 16 January, says that there is little food and only a limited supply of medicine left in the city. 'My pharmacy became half empty,' he said. Pharmaceutical factories around Mosul have stopped production and there are fewer medicines being imported from Syria. Simple painkillers like Panadol that cost $1 for a bottle last year now cost $8, according to Ibrahim. There is a shortage of food and what is available is very costly. The Caliphate is increasingly cut off from supplies from Turkey and the rest of Syria. It also has less money to spend because of air attacks on its exports of crude oil, combined with the fall in the price of oil.

The Baghdad government continued to pay the salaries of public servants in Mosul even after ISIS took over, but Ibrahim says that money stopped coming through nine months ago. 'I have spent almost all my savings,' he says. 'Last year, $500 a month was enough for a family to live on, but now even $1,000 is not enough because prices are twice or even five times what they used to be.' Refugees speak of starvation spreading throughout the city because of this economic siege. 'For me, I could stand the bad treatment and lack of food, but when my toddler of 11 months began to starve it became impossible to stay,' says Fatima. Baby milk has not been available for six months and other foodstuffs are prohibitively expensive. Rice costs $10 a kilo. Nor are these problems confined to Mosul. Farmers are leaving their fields because 'there is no electricity to pump water so they cannot irrigate their crops', according to Ghanem, 25, an unemployed plumber who is now in north-east Syria.

He insists that the main reason he fled Mosul was not the bad living conditions, but ISIS 'poking their noses into the details of people's daily lives with their arbitrary fines and punishments'. He speaks of the increasingly harsh treatment of women, with the Biter being used as a punishment 'on women deemed to have shown too much skin'.

ISIS was always a paranoid organisation, seeing traitors and spies everywhere, and this is growing worse. Anything can be grounds for suspicion: one woman, who eventually reached safety in Erbil, mentioned casually that her brother-in-law had been arrested and executed because he had once been a member of a police unit that specialised in protecting the oilfields. Wisam, a 19-year-old student, had worked in a minor capacity as a photo editor in the local TV station and for news agencies, an activity he thought might put him at risk. 'I spent more than a year working in the bazaar selling vegetables,' he said. 'I could not work online because the internet is heavily monitored by ISIS.'

Mosul is returning to a pre-modern era without electricity or drinking water, say its former inhabitants. During the first year of its Caliphate, ISIS made great efforts to ensure that public services worked as well as, or better than, under the Iraqi government, but it appears to have abandoned the attempt.

'We only get drinking water once a week,' said Wisam. 'Pipes are broken and need repair, but the administration in Mosul has become careless and confused over the past five months.' For electricity, people mostly rely on private generators, their own or those of local businessmen who sell the power. This can be too expensive for many families. Fatima said that 'most areas of the city are dark and Mosul has become like a ghost town.' Ghanem said, 'we feel we are living in the Stone Age: no mobiles, no TV, no cars, even no lighting.'

28 February 2016

When Mohammed al-Ghabban became interior minister of Iraq in 2014, he found that he was employing 230 brigadier generals and 660,000 police officers. The bloated size of the Iraqi security forces, most of whose members hold their jobs through political patronage, goes a long way to explaining why they cannot stop ISIS bombers from murdering people in the streets and markets of Baghdad. Seventy-three people died in a single incident in the Sadr City district of the capital last Sunday and another 40 died when a suicide bomber blew himself up at a funeral at Muqdadiya in

Diyala province. 'I have reduced the number of brigadier generals to 110 and I am not recruiting new policemen or replacing those who retire,' says Ghabban in an interview in his office in Baghdad. He admits that the Iraqi public do not trust the police because of their failure to stop the bombers and the high level of corruption, which is pervasive in the system.

He cites the infamous case of 1,500 fake bomb detectors, which were bought for £52m by the interior ministry in 2008 and 2009, even though they were a patent fraud—consisting only of a metal aerial that supposedly detected explosives, attached to an empty plastic casing. Although the British businessmen who sold the useless devices were given lengthy prison sentences last year, the detectors known as the ADE-651 are still used extensively in Iraq. Reliance on them, rather than a physical search of vehicles, makes it easier for bombers to pass through checkpoints and slaughter large numbers of civilians. Ghabban uses the example of the fake bomb detectors to underline the saturation levels of corruption among Iraqi government officials, which damages security, and to explain why nothing is done about it. 'The equipment cost the Iraqi government about $50,000 for each item, but the real cost to the manufacturers was only between $40 and $50.' He assumes that much of the difference was pocketed by officials in Baghdad who were bribed to sign off on the deal, so today they have every reason to prevent an investigation of the scam.

The Iraqi bureaucracy is like a beached whale that does little except employ seven million people whose salaries cost $4 billion a month. With Iraqi oil revenues running at half that figure because of the fall in the oil price, there is deep apprehension in Baghdad about what will happen when the money begins to run out in April. One woman said that 'even when things were at their worst in Baghdad in 2006–07, when there were the mass sectarian killings, people were still being paid their salaries.' Another senior government official, who did not want his name published, said, 'We have nearly one million fighters [army and police], but we would be much more effective if we had only 200,000.' The Iraqi National Intelligence Service employs 12,000, although it needs only half that number. 'We don't have money for food,' said the second senior official. He adds: 'The corruption is a huge support for Daesh [ISIS].' He said that bombers frequently travel through the checkpoints that supposedly protect Baghdad because they have bribed the police, soldiers or paramilitaries in charge.

1 May 2016

Iraqis bursting into the Green Zone in Baghdad are able to see for the first time the palatial homes and offices of the corrupt and dysfunctional Iraqi leadership that has misgoverned the country for the last 13 years. As the security forces stand aside, protesters topple a section of the 15-foot-high blast walls and pour through the gap into this well-fortified and exclusive enclave on the banks of the Tigris, in the centre of the Iraqi capital. After taking over the parliament building, the crowd chants the name of the Shia populist nationalist cleric Muqtada al-Sadr, whose movement many of the protesters belong to, and denounced the failures of the present government of Prime Minister Haider al-Abadi. The Green Zone, with its fountains and well-watered lawns, has long been a hated symbol of the isolation of the rulers of Iraq, who never experience the harsh living conditions and shortages endured by ordinary Iraqis. By breaching its walls, the demonstrators who splash in the fountains and take pictures of themselves on the lawns show that the Iraqi elite is more vulnerable than in the past to expressions of popular anger.

Sadr's stated aims are reform rather than revolution: he does not want Abadi to resign, but he does want him to appoint a cabinet of technocrats, and to end the quota system by which the sectarian or ethnically based parties appoint loyalists regardless of their abilities. This is opposed by existing parties, which operate extensive client and patronage systems. At least 8,000 of Iraq's bureaucrats—some put the figure as high as 25,000—are political appointees who are notorious for their corruption and incompetence. Sadr's purpose may be to strengthen the Iraqi state and make it more effective and honest. But the very ease with which the Sadrists and their supporters penetrated the Green Zone and took over parliament without resistance from the security forces makes the state look even weaker and more ineffectual.

Though the Sadrists say that many of the protesters do not belong to their movement, they appeared to have the eruption into the Green Zone very much under control from the beginning. Sadrist stewards prevented equipment in parliament being smashed and say they cleaned up the parliamentary chamber on leaving. The well-disciplined exodus of protesters from the zone on Sunday without any looting shows the degree to which the action was organised by the Sadrist movement. 'The people are saying that if the government does not appoint a government they will be back [to take over the Green Zone again],' a Sadrist leader, who did not want

his name published, tells me. He believes that the other political parties
had been hoping that the protests would get out of hand and lead to the
ransacking and looting of the Green Zone, which would have provided an
excuse for the Iraqi security forces to use force against the demonstrators.
'The parties hoped for chaos so the army would clear away the protesters,'
he says.

5 May 2016

In northern Syria carnage alternates with ceasefires as the Syrian Air
Force pounds the rebel-held eastern side of Aleppo in a bid to drive out
the remaining civilians. Rebel artillery replies in kind against government
areas in the west of the city, but cannot match the firepower used against
their enclave. Air strikes kill at least 28 people in a refugee camp close
to the Turkish border. The purpose of the Syrian government's air and
artillery attacks has remained the same over the last five years and is to
separate opposition fighters from the civilian population. 'This is the same
classic counter-insurgency strategy that was used by the French in Algeria
and the US in Vietnam,' says Fabrice Balanche, an expert on Syria at the
Washington Institute for Near East Policy. Syrian government forces target
rebel-held zones and essential infrastructure such as hospitals and markets,
so whole districts of cities like Damascus and Homs are reduced to rubble.

In Iraq, the US-led coalition is more careful to avoid civilian casualties, but even so 70 per cent of Ramadi, the capital of Anbar province,
has been destroyed and surviving houses are perilous with booby traps
and IEDs planted by ISIS. In both Syria and Iraq, inadequate numbers
of ground troops—Syrian Army, Syrian Kurds, Iraqi Kurds, Iraqi Army
—claim great victories but in reality act as mopping-up forces that can
only advance after a devastating aerial bombardment. The Syrian, Russian
and US-led air campaigns have all had their successes, but they have their
limitations. Dr Balanche says that the population of opposition-held east
Aleppo may be down to as low as 100,000 because of air strikes, while
the much safer government-controlled west of the city still has a population of two million. The US and the coalition have carried out 8,067
air strikes in Iraq and 3,809 in Syria which have inflicted heavy casualties on ISIS and interrupted their communications. But ISIS and al-Nusra
fighters can stay safe by taking over one floor in a five storey building and
leaving the other four floors occupied by ordinary families. While the term
'human shield' is much abused, the armed opposition in places like Mosul,

Raqqa and Eastern Ghouta forbid civilians from leaving, so terrified people must balance the possibility of being killed by air strikes with that of being murdered or detained by salafi-jihadi checkpoints.

Bombs and drones weaken the Islamic State, but probably not as much as is hoped in Washington and European capitals. ISIS fighters have generally not been fighting to the last man for cities like Ramadi and Palmyra, but pulling back and resorting to guerrilla warfare. They claim to have captured the important Shaer gas field in the desert not far from Palmyra. ISIS and al-Nusra's many enemies are divided and pursue different goals. The US and its allies want to defeat ISIS, but do not want the Syrian Army or the Iraqi Shia militias to be the instruments which inflict that defeat. Syrian and Iraqi Kurdish leaders detest each other, but they are together in fearing that their value to the West will lapse once ISIS is defeated, and that they will be left to the mercy of Turkey and resurgent regimes in Baghdad and Damascus.

ISIS is battered and on the retreat, but is unlikely to be defeated this year. It is losing territory but it is important to keep in mind that much of this is desert or semi-desert. More important is its progressive loss of access to the Turkish border, which has been largely sealed off by the advance of the Syrian Kurdish YPG militia assisted by a US air umbrella. The increasingly narrow corridor between Aleppo and the Euphrates that links the self-declared Caliphate to Turkey is under threat from the YPG and their Arab proxies in the east and the Syrian Army in the west. If this gap is closed then ISIS will have great difficulty receiving foreign volunteers or dispatching terrorists to carry out attacks abroad. Alternatively, direct intervention by the Turkish army can never be ruled out.

If ISIS and al-Nusra are defeated, what will be the impact on the political geography of this part of the Middle East? Sunni Arabs make up 20 per cent of the population in Iraq and 60 per cent in Syria, but there is really only one battlefield, so if the Salafi-jihadis lose, so too will the Sunni Arabs as a whole in the band of territory between the Iranian border and the Mediterranean. 'In Iraq the war is destroying the Sunni population,' says Professor Joshua Landis who heads the Center for Middle East Studies at the University of Oklahoma, pointing out that most of those displaced in the fighting in Iraq over the last two years are Sunni Arabs and the Sunni had already been driven out of much of Baghdad in the sectarian slaughter of 2006–07. A prolonged struggle for Mosul would reduce the last great Sunni stronghold in the country to ruins. 'We Sunni in Iraq are going to end up like the Palestinians,' predicted a Sunni Arab from Ramadi last year before the city was partly destroyed.

It may not come to this. Not all the news is bad. The most hopeful sign in Syria is that Russia and the US are occasionally acting in unison and have been able to prod their allies into agreeing to ceasefires, however shaky and short term, for the first time in five years. The lesson of the last five years in Syria and the last 13 years in Iraq is that it is very difficult for any single army, government, militia, party, sect or ethnic group to fight successfully for a long period without the support of a foreign power or powers. They may not want to compromise but they may be forced to do so if the alternative is the loss of this essential outside backing. Given that the Assad and anti-Assad forces hate each other, want to kill each other and have no intention of sharing power in future, such compromises are likely to be grudging and short term.

The real test will be the extent to which the US and Russia have the desire and capability to enforce a ceasefire or at least a de-escalation of the fighting. Many Syrians who do not like Assad feel that the only alternative to his regime, as the French Algerians used to say, is 'the suitcase or the coffin'. Anti-Assad Syrians are likewise faced with a black-or-white choice between a murderous government and murderous Islamists. Only a de-militarisation of Syrian politics might open the way to other alternatives and a distant prospect of permanent peace.

Eight Wars

There are now eight wars being fought in Muslim countries in the Middle East and North Africa. The latest addition to the list is the renewed Turkish–Kurd armed conflict, which joins civil wars in Afghanistan, Iraq, Syria, Yemen, Libya, Somalia and north-east Nigeria. In all these countries the central government is fighting a guerrilla war, controls only part of its territory or has disintegrated. The conflict with the longest history is in Somalia where it began with the overthrow in 1991 of the President Siad Barre, the last Somali leader to rule the whole country. As Somalia was engulfed by violence, the US intervened militarily in 1992–94 with disastrous results, a failure now largely remembered for horrific pictures of a dead American soldier being dragged through the streets of Mogadishu.

Dangerous though Somalia evidently was, it could be dismissed as a 'failed state', a lair of Islamic militants and pirates but otherwise of marginal importance. But when a state fails it leaves a vacuum that can be filled by fanatical and violent movements. Such a place seldom festers for long without affecting its neighbours. In the event, Somalia was not an exception, but the ominous first sign of a trend whereby 'Somalianisation'—a permanent state of chaos and warfare—was to become common two decades later. From 2001 on, countries from the mountains of the Hindu Kush to the deserts of the Sahara were being torn apart by rebellions too powerful to crush, though not strong enough to win a decisive victory.

Somalia is an early and instructive example of the implosion of a nation state, though the speed of its collapse owes much to its pre-existing fragmentation. Elsewhere, the combination of lethal ingredients necessary to produce such devastating political explosions had not yet fully come together. This happened after the millennium, and more specifically after 9/11, beginning with the overthrow of the Taliban in Afghanistan in 2001 and continuing up to the re-emergence of the Turkish–Kurd conflict in 2015. A purpose of this book is to explain why we have entered an era of civil wars in a large part of the Islamic world. It is a story of deepening chaos which has provided fertile soil for the growth of fanatical Sunni Muslim movements espousing an extreme version of the Wahhabi variant of Islam. Their rise culminated in the establishment of the Islamic State and the Caliphate in 2014. At first derided as an act of fantasy and hubris, the Islamic State was still there over a year later and was still winning victories in Iraq and Syria. Meanwhile, Yemen, Turkey and 25 million Kurds living in four different countries have been drawn into the maelstrom.

There is much argument about who is responsible for these calamities, with blame being placed on corrupt dictatorships, self-serving foreign interventions or savagely sectarian opposition movements. Convincing analysis is frequently undermined by over-emphasis on a single cause or set of causes, or is tainted by propaganda and wishful thinking. Demonisation of Saddam Hussein in Iraq in 2003—demonic though in many ways he was—or of Bashar al-Assad in Syria and Muammar Gaddafi in Libya in 2011, led to their portrayal as the root of all evil, people and regimes so bad that no alternative policies needed to be devised different from the ones they pursued. Within a few years, successful opposition leaders who had replaced these dictators, such as Prime Minister Nouri al-Maliki in Iraq, were getting the same dismissive treatment. At best these explanations of what was going wrong are over-simple and at worst they promote conspiracy theories, such as a widely held belief that ISIS is Saddam's Baath Party or security services under a new guise. Alternatively, there are those who are convinced that ISIS is a proxy of Assad's Mukhabarat (security services), secretly fostered to displace and discredit more moderate opposition to the government in Damascus.

These crude explanations sometimes take hold even among sophisticated observers of the Syrian crisis because they make a complex situation seem simple, requiring no serious rethinking about what is going on. Such theories are all the more alluring because they often contain an element of truth: Assad knew that he would benefit politically, though not militarily, if opposition to his rule was dominated by extreme Sunni jihadis, who terrified many Syrians as well as the US and the Western powers. The Iraqi armed opposition is rooted in the Sunni community from which Saddam Hussein drew most of his military and security officers: all the rebel groups, and not just ISIS, have contained a proportion of these people. The battlefields of Syria and Iraq are filled with players whose motives and intentions are diverse and contradictory. This complicated reality is strikingly summarised by Anthony Cordesman, a military expert at the Centre for Strategic and International Studies in Washington, who is quoted as saying 'one of the problems is that we keep trying to describe this [situation] as if it were black and white, and what we are really watching again is three-dimensional chess with nine players and no rules.'

The new game may have no rules but it has trends, even if these are not immediately apparent. I was correspondent in Moscow between 1999 and 2001 and, soon after I arrived, I flew to Grozny, the capital of Chechnya, to report the second Chechen war that was just beginning. I was housed with other journalists in an old army barracks while we waited to see Chechen President Aslan Maskhadov, who was desperately but vainly trying to fend off the Russian invasion that had just begun. I was a little worried that Russian bombers might choose our barracks as a suitable target, but the presidential guard that was protecting us turned out to more fearful that we would be abducted. This was understandable as Chechnya was at this time the world capital of kidnapping with villagers earning extra money by renting out their basements where captives could be kept until a ransom was paid. I imagined at the time that this was a consequence of the leading role played by the Chechen gangsters in the crime wave in post-Communist Russia. But in the coming years it became clear that criminalisation of elites with a stake in protecting the status quo, and also of the insurgents trying to overthrow them, was a common feature of all the conflicts I was writing about. Almost every officer in the Iraqi Army, at the time of its defeat in 2014, had bought his job so he could make money by pocketing the salaries of 'ghost' soldiers who did not exist—the Iraqi government later admitted to 50,000 of these—or by levying a toll on vehicles passing through military checkpoints. For all its murderous ferocity, Islamic State provided relatively honest, effective if brutal administration.

BIRTH OF A CALIPHATE

There was a further feature of the war in Chechnya, the significance of which I did not quite grasp at the time, which I was to see replicated in future upheavals in the Islamic world. If nationalism was not entirely dead, it no longer provided the ideological glue necessary to hold together and motivate people who were fighting a war. Unlike the Islamic faith, it was no longer a belief or a badge of identity for which people would fight very hard. Chechen opposition to Russia swiftly became dominated by 'Wahhabis', as Islamic fundamentalist fighters were nicknamed. They formed the core of the armed resistance, but they alienated more moderate and secular Chechens. The same pattern was to be repeated in Iraq where loyalty to the nation could seldom compete successfully with the loyalty of Shia and Sunni to their own communities. After the Iraqi Army was twice humiliatingly defeated by inferior ISIS forces at Mosul in 2014 and Ramadi the following year, I asked an Iraqi politician why it had not been possible to rebuild the army into an effective force. 'There just aren't enough soldiers who see themselves as part of an Iraqi nation,' he replied. 'Very few are prepared to die for it and they are facing enemies willing to give up their lives in suicide attacks.'

As ISIS columns advanced inexorably towards Baghdad in the summer of 2014, the government-controlled television blared out nationalist rhetoric along with news of imaginary victories, though few viewers took either very seriously. There was no sign of Iraq's nominally vast and expensively equipped army making a stand. Contrast this with the overwhelming response to a fatwa from the Shia Grand Ayatollah Ali Sistani issued on 13 June 2014, calling for people to join the armed forces in order to stop ISIS. A commander of the largely Shia militia later told me that it was difficult to persuade the tens of thousands of religiously inspired recruits to accept more than 25 days' basic training because they demanded to be sent immediately to the front line. I wondered if nationalism might have retained its old potency among the Iraqi Kurds, but when ISIS attacked the Peshmerga in August 2014 the Kurdish soldiers broke and ran even faster than the Iraqi Army at Mosul a few months earlier.

The Chechen war provided pointers to the future and had interesting similarities with the eight wars that are today being waged between Pakistan and Nigeria. But one aspect of the war in Chechnya differed crucially from those that followed: it ended with a Russian victory over the Chechen resistance and not in a bloody stalemate. This was hardly unexpected given the disparity in strength between the two sides (there are 144 million Russians and 1.4 million Chechens). But even this might not have been enough to produce a decisive outcome if it had not been accompanied by another factor: Chechnya was geographically isolated and the Chechen resistance had no foreign patron which it could use as a safe haven or from whom it could obtain money and weapons.

This lack of sponsorship by a foreign state made the war in Chechnya very different from those in Afghanistan, Iraq, Syria, Libya and Yemen, where opponents of the central government have all been sustained and probably rendered undefeatable by aid from outside powers. The identity of these foreign allies might change, but their intervention prevented wars ending in compromise through mutual exhaustion or by the victory of one side or another. Only in Libya was the opposition to the old regime completely successful because Gaddafi was self-isolated and his enemies had military support from NATO airpower and political and financial backing from the Arab oil states. The Gulf monarchies believed that the same formula that had worked in Libya would work against Assad in Syria in 2012 and 2013. They were wrong because, in the Syrian case, the enmity of the Western powers, Turkey and the Sunni monarchs of the Gulf was balanced by Syria's alliance with Russia, Iran and Hezbollah in Lebanon.

Alliances between domestic protagonists and foreign powers make these civil conflicts doubly difficult to resolve, or even to de-escalate, as the ability to take decisions for war or peace falls into foreign hands. A cat's cradle of conflicting interests stymies compromise. In Syria, for example, the crisis is the outcome of at least four inter-related confrontations: the struggle between the ruling Alawite minority, in power since the 1960s, and part of the Sunni Arab community; a popular uprising against a Baathist dictatorship; Kurds against Arabs; and secular Syrians against extreme Salafi-jihadi movements such as ISIS and the al-Qa'ida-affiliate Jabhat al-Nusra. This domestically generated chaos and violence becomes even more unstoppable when it is connected to and fuelled by regional and global conflicts: there is the epic struggle between Shia and Sunni; intertwined with this is the rivalry between Iran and its Shia allies on one side and Saudi Arabia and the Sunni powers on the other; in addition, the revival of competition between the US and Russia.

Some features of the political landscape in the Middle East and North Africa go back a long time, but have become more significant in recent years. Iraqis and many others sincerely believe that sectarian animosities between Sunni and Shia are largely a new development, fomented by

Saddam, Saudi Arabia or Iran, and that once the two communities lived in relative harmony. It is true that sectarian relations have seldom been as bad as at present, but Sunni and Shia in Baghdad were burning each other's mosques and villages a thousand years ago. Sectarian hatred became much fiercer after the Iranian Revolution overthrew the Shah and established a Shia theocracy in 1979, events which were immediately followed by the Iran–Iraq War in 1980–88. People in Baghdad have never escaped the legacy of terror left by the Sunni and Shia death squads who slaughtered thousands at the height of the battle for the capital in 2006–07. Baghdad became a predominantly Shia city with few mixed areas and with the Sunni confined to some enclaves—called 'islands of fear' by one American diplomat—mostly in the west of the city. The degree to which sectarian hostility ebbed after the Sunni defeat was always exaggerated. The Sunni faced discrimination and persecution, but they did not think there was a lot they could do about it until the Sunni in Syria revolted in 2011. Maliki and his government may have exacerbated Sunni alienation, but the Shia leadership was not convinced that the Sunni had ever really accepted that they no longer ruled Iraq. A fact often neglected when seeking causes for sectarianism in that country is that year after year al-Qa'ida in Iraq and later ISIS kept up a constant drum-beat of sectarian massacres—so frequent that they are now barely reported—by exploding bombs in Shia marketplaces, bus queues and pilgrimages, wherever they would cause most casualties.

The mechanics of sectarianism are not always obvious. It is fuelled as much by job discrimination as fear of sudden death. Control of the government is so important because Iraq is an oil state whose oil revenues finance a vast patronage system. An Iraqi's livelihood, and that of his family, depends on his access to such patronage, which will in turn be determined by what sect he belongs to. Distributing jobs in this way helps explain why Iraq has a dysfunctional government and army, since those employed by the state may be wholly unqualified or never turn up to work except to collect their salary. The Baghdad government is vilified for such practices, but the Kurdish-held part of Iraq—the Kurdistan Regional Government (KRG) area—works in the same way: people get work through political or family connections, often holding jobs which they cannot perform. In the days after ISIS almost captured the Kurdish capital Arbil, it was common to find Peshmerga fighters in the front line who had not been paid for three months or longer, while others were earning a pittance by driving taxis. The KRG had advertised itself as a new Dubai or 'the other Iraq', but governments in both Shia and Kurdish controlled parts of the country turned out to be equally fragile when ISIS attacked them.

The crises and wars described in this book have tended to cross-infect each other. Iraq in particular was the crucible in which so many of the troubles now visiting other Islamic countries first took shape. Unlike Yemen, Libya or even Afghanistan, Iraq and Syria are countries at the heart of the Middle East where it is impossible to move one piece on the political chessboard without impacting the others. Iraq borders six other states and Syria borders five. By way of contrast, the US-backed overthrow of the Taliban in Afghanistan in 2001 angered Pakistan, but it did not destabilise the region. Iraq was very different because what happened there was going to transform the politics of all its neighbours. Essentially, the US faced the same dilemma in 2003 that it had wrestled with when Saddam Hussein was in power: it could have got rid of him after he was defeated in Kuwait in 1991 if the US Air Force had supported the Shia and Kurdish uprisings. It refused to do so because Washington thought that a Shia takeover of Baghdad would enable Iran to become the dominant influence in Iraq. Between 2003 and 2015, the US could not decide what role Iran should play in Iraq with which America could live comfortably. In 2015, both the US and Iran wanted to defeat ISIS, but did not want the other to benefit from that defeat. As a result, they ended up fighting two different wars against the same opponent, much to the militants' advantage. The US–Iran deal on Iran's nuclear programme might enable them to co-operate more closely against ISIS, but so far it has not happened and may never do so.

Another example of cross-infection is Yemen, where the political struggle was essentially local until in March 2015, when Saudi Arabia started bombing the Houthi rebels who had seized much of the country. The Houthis were frequently described as 'Iranian-backed Shia'. In fact they belong—as do one third of Yemenis—to the Zaidi sect that is very different from other variants of Shi'ism, while Iranian influence was always limited. Once the war and Saudi intervention had started, the Houthis were branded as being on the Shia and Iranian side of the fence, an accusation that was self-fulfilling. Sunni–Shia hostility had never previously been important in Yemen, but now it was taking root. Soon ISIS was setting up cells and executing captured soldiers. Developments in Yemen began to resemble what was happening in Iraq and Syria.

At the end of December 2011, early on in the Syrian crisis and before Iraq had begun to disintegrate, I wrote that the Arab world and the wider Middle East 'are facing a period of prolonged struggle for power that has not been witnessed since the 1960s'. That was the period half a century ago when nationalist leaders, often with a military or security background, had taken over by coups d'état. Men like Muammar Gaddafi, Saddam Hussein and Hafez al-Assad monopolised power in what were ultimately to become corrupt family fiefdoms reliant on total control by the secret police. But at first, they could justify their rule as the only way that weak and backward states, not long free of European imperial rule, could achieve national self-determination and gain control of their economies and natural resources, notably oil and gas. In this they had a fair measure of success in the 1960s and 1970s. Externally, these states all depended either on an alliance with the Soviet Union or at least sufficient rivalry between the superpowers in Washington and Moscow to give them space to pursue independent policies. When the Soviet Union collapsed in 1991, they became vulnerable to US or West European intervention, often under the guise of humanitarian concern over their brutal rule. The pendulum only began to swing away from American unilateral dominance of the Middle East after its failure to win wars in Iraq and Afghanistan, despite sending large land armies. In addition, Russia began to re-emerge as a great power, though never as strong as it had been in Soviet times. A senior Iraqi minister, who asked not be named, told me how he had questioned an American general in 2013 about the crisis in Syria and why its course was so different from that in Libya. The general replied: 'I can explain the difference between the two situations in one word: Russia. Russia is back as a power you have to take into account.'

The nationalist regimes that had seized power in the late 1960s and early 1970s had turned into decrepit family dynasties by 2011. Their base of support was limited, as they discovered when popular demonstrations engulfed their world in the first months of the Arab Spring. But their decline over the previous two decades had not been the only change in the regional balance of power. Saudi Arabia, Qatar, UAE and Kuwait had taken over leadership of the Arab world because of their vast oil wealth. It was one of the peculiarities of the Arab Spring that movements lauded in the West as progressive, secular and democratic very swiftly became dependent for money and later arms on the last theocratic absolute monarchies left on earth. Opposition to the old regimes was in any case led by Islamic movements which showed their regressive nature the closer they got to power. In Libya, one of the first measures advocated by leaders replacing Gaddafi was a law ending the ban on polygamy.

In an important sense I was wrong in 2011 to suggest that we were seeing a return to the turmoil of the 1960s. It was going to get a lot worse than that. In reality, we have gone back further to the period during and after the First World War when the remains of the Ottoman Empire was carved up by Britain and France with a few scraps thrown to their allies. There has been much talk of 'the end of Sykes-Picot' which is a rather confusing short hand for the boundaries of states agreed by Mark Sykes and Francois Georges-Picot in 1916—in fact one of several such agreements ignoring the wishes or even the existence of local inhabitants. It is true that the Caliphate has very publicly abolished the Iraqi–Syrian frontier posts and reunited the Sunni Arabs living between Mosul and Aleppo, and along the Euphrates Valley between Fallujah and the Turkish border. The Syrian–Turkish frontier may have proved porous for ISIS and Jabhat al-Nusra, probably thanks to a deliberate decision by Ankara, but other boundaries are not disappearing, however artificial their origin.

Instead, we are revisiting one of the most catastrophic features of the end of Ottoman rule, namely the murder and migration of whole groups of people. Some 4.3 million Syrians are refugees and a further 7.6 million are displaced, according to the UN High Commission for Refugees. There are another 3.1 million displaced in Iraq. What does not come across from these bald statistics is that many of these people will never go back to their homes because it will be too dangerous or they will be physically prevented from doing do so. The Palestinians call their expulsion and flight from Palestine in 1948 'al-Nakba', the Catastrophe, but many such catastrophes are now happening in Iraq and Syria where Sunni, Shia, Alawites, Christians, Yazidis and smaller communities are running for their lives.

Many thought the same in the 10 years after 1914, if they survived at all. At the time of the outbreak of the First World War some 20 per cent of those living in what is now modern Turkey were Christian, but a decade later the figure had dropped to less than 1 per cent because of the extermination of the Armenians and the forced migration of the surviving Greeks and other Christian communities. This same process is now happening in Iraq and Syria. Such is the level of violence that no community wants to find out what will happen to it once it is at the mercy of another. ISIS, with its bombing campaign against non-Sunni civilians, has raised the level of hatred and fear to the point that Shia, Yazidis, Christians, Alawites and Druze will always flee its approach. By the same token, they will take revenge, if they do return, on any Sunni whom they see as complicit in ISIS's crimes. In recaptured villages south of Kirkuk, flight by Sunni is seen as an admission of guilt, while those who stay may be accused of belonging to ISIS sleeper cells. At one time people spoke of the partition of Iraq as a solution to ethnic and sectarian friction. But Mowaffaq al-Rubaie, the former Iraqi National Security Adviser, says that those who made this proposal did not realise how bloody such a separation of communities was likely to be. 'It will be like the Partition of India in 1947 with massacres everywhere,' he said. Another parallel might be Eastern Europe in the decade after 1939 with its terrible history of mass killings and expulsions. 'Existential threat' is a phrase so overused as to lose its value, but for many in Iraq and Syria it is a very real prospect. The demons released by this age of chaos and war in the Middle East have become an unstoppable force.

Acknowledgements

This book is in the form of a contemporary diary drawing on my notes, diaries and writings produced between 2001 and 2015. It starts with the Afghan war and concludes with much of the Middle East and North Africa engulfed by violence. I have tried to combine the vividness of eyewitness testimony with chapters seeking broader explanations for these wars and conflicts.

I developed many of these ideas and covered many of these topics in articles for *The Independent* and the *London Review of Books* and am truly grateful for the encouragement and support of their editors over the years. Thanks also to the many people who helped me to travel in the region and to try to understand it. I only wish the outcome had been better for them, their families and their countries.

I am extremely grateful to Alex Nunns of OR Books who selected and arranged the material with great intelligence and sensitivity. It is impossible to overstate his contribution. Thanks are also due to my agent, Anna Stein of Aitken Alexander Associates in New York, for her wise advice. I have also been assisted by Simon Blundell, the librarian of the Reform Club in London, who has frequently helped me find urgently needed information at great speed.

Index